Cases on Professional Distance Education Degree Programs and Practices:

Successes, Challenges, and Issues

Kirk P.H. Sullivan
Umeå University, Sweden

Peter E. Czigler
Örebro University, Sweden

Jenny M. Sullivan Hellgren
Umeå University, Sweden

A volume in the Advances in Mobile and Distance Learning (AMDL) Book Series

Information Science REFERENCE

An Imprint of IGI Global

Managing Director:	Lindsay Johnston
Editorial Director:	Joel Gamon
Production Manager:	Jennifer Yoder
Publishing Systems Analyst:	Adrienne Freeland
Development Editor:	Joel Gamon
Assistant Acquisitions Editor:	Kayla Wolfe
Typesetter:	Lisandro Gonzalez
Cover Design:	Jason Mull

Published in the United States of America by
Information Science Reference (an imprint of IGI Global)
701 E. Chocolate Avenue
Hershey PA 17033
Tel: 717-533-8845
Fax: 717-533-8661
E-mail: cust@igi-global.com
Web site: http://www.igi-global.com

Library of Congress Cataloging-in-Publication Data

Cases on professional distance education degree programs and practices : successes, challenges and issues / Kirk P.H. Sullivan, Peter E. Czigler, Jenny M. Sullivan Hellgren, editors.
     pages cm
 Includes bibliographical references and index.
 Summary: "This book examines the best practices for executing technology applications and the utilization of distance education techniques, serving as a reference for academics and instructors running distance education programs, initiating distance education courses, and implementing such programs for those earning professional degrees"-- Provided by publisher.
  ISBN 978-1-4666-4486-1 (hardcover) -- ISBN 978-1-4666-4487-8 (ebook) -- ISBN 978-1-4666-4488-5 (print & perpetual access) 1. Distance education--Case studies. I. Sullivan, Kirk P. H.
  LC5800.C38 2013
  371.35'8--dc23
                                      2013014343

This book is published in the IGI Global book series Advances in Mobile and Distance Learning (AMDL) (ISSN: 2327-1892; eISSN: 2327-1906)

British Cataloguing in Publication Data
A Cataloguing in Publication record for this book is available from the British Library.

Advances in Mobile and Distance Learning (AMDL) Book Series

ISSN: 2327-1892
EISSN: 2327-1906

MISSION

Private and public institutions have made great strides in the fields of mobile and distance learning in recent years, providing greater learning opportunities outside of a traditional classroom setting. While the online learning revolution has allowed for greater learning opportunities, it has also presented numerous challenges for students and educators alike. As research advances, online educational settings can continue to develop and advance the technologies available for learners of all ages.

The **Advances in Mobile and Distance Learning** (AMDL) Book Series publishes research encompassing a variety of topics related to all facets of mobile and distance learning. This series aims to be an essential resource for the timeliest research to help advance the development of new educational technologies and pedagogy for use in online classrooms.

COVERAGE

- Cloud Computing in Schools
- Economics of Distance and M-Learning
- Educational Apps
- Ethical Considerations
- Lifelong Learning
- Managing Sustainable Learning
- Pedagogy & Design Methodology
- Tablets & Education
- Technology Platforms & System Development
- Ubiquitous & Pervasive Learning

IGI Global is currently accepting manuscripts for publication within this series. To submit a proposal for a volume in this series, please contact our Acquisition Editors at Acquisitions@igi-global.com or visit: http://www.igi-global.com/publish/.

Titles in this Series

For a list of additional titles in this series, please visit: www.igi-global.com

Cases on Professional Distance Education Degree Programs and Practices Successes, Challenges, and Issues
Kirk P.H. Sullivan (Umeå University, Sweden) Peter E. Czigler (Örebro University, Sweden) and Jenny M. Sullivan Hellgren (Umeå University, Sweden)
Information Science Reference • copyright 2014 • 315pp • H/C (ISBN: 9781466644861)
• US $175.00 (our price)

Mobile Pedagogy and Perspectives on Teaching and Learning
Christian Penny (West Chester University of Pennsylvania, USA) Douglas McConatha (West Chester University, USA) Jordan Shugar (West Chester University, USA) and David Bolton (West Chester University, USA)
Information Science Reference • copyright 2014 • 338pp • H/C (ISBN: 9781466643338)
• US $175.00 (our price)

Outlooks and Opportunities in Blended and Distance Learning
J. Willems (Monash University, Australia) B. Tynan (University of Southern Queensland, Australia) and R. James (University of New England, Australia)
Information Science Reference • copyright 2013 • 358pp • H/C (ISBN: 9781466642058)
• US $175.00 (our price)

Cases on Formal and Informal E-Learning Environments Opportunities and Practices
Harrison Hao Yang (State University of New York at Oswego, USA) and Shuyan Wang (The University of Southern Mississippi, USA)
Information Science Reference • copyright 2013 • 454pp • H/C (ISBN: 9781466619302)
• US $175.00 (our price)

Refining Current Practices in Mobile and Blended Learning New Applications
David Parsons (Massey University - Auckland, New Zealand)
Information Science Reference • copyright 2012 • 334pp • H/C (ISBN: 9781466600539)
• US $175.00 (our price)

IGI GLOBAL
DISSEMINATOR OF KNOWLEDGE
www.igi-global.com

701 E. Chocolate Ave., Hershey, PA 17033
Order online at www.igi-global.com or call 717-533-8845 x100
To place a standing order for titles released in this series,
contact: cust@igi-global.com
Mon-Fri 8:00 am - 5:00 pm (est) or fax 24 hours a day 717-533-8661

Editorial Advisory Board

Table of Contents

Chapter 12

Detailed Table of Contents

Chapter 1
Studying Professional Degrees via the Internet: Challenges, Issues, and
Relevance from the Student's Perspective 1
    Kirk P. H. Sullivan, Umeå University, Sweden

This case places the student in focus and considers through a reflective case study four distance professional degree programs. The author of this case followed these programs as life-long learning professional activities. The case considers the nudge, the study, and degree completion. The reflection is structured around the themes of initial contact, communication, support, deadlines, work, and keeping going. These themes reveal challenges, issues, and questions of relevance for the student and university. Key skills to assist the student towards completion are suggested along with what the potential student should consider prior to enrolling in a professional degree program that is delivered via the Internet. The growth in distance professional degrees, including professional doctorates, demonstrates the importance of the challenges, issues, and questions of relevance considered in this case from the student's perspective.

Chapter 2

Despina Varnava-Marouchou, European University Cyprus, Cyprus
Mark A. Minott, University College of the Cayman Islands, Cayman Islands

This chapter outlines the benefits and challenges experienced by two students who had completed an online doctoral programme at a popular United Kingdom university. Benefits include accessing courses from anywhere in the world, engaging in synchronous and asynchronous communication, and the development of creative thinking and reflective skills. The most important benefit was the fact that the online programme allowed the students to fulfill the dream of achieving a doctoral degree in teacher education while maintain family and work commitments. Some challenges of online learning include feelings of isolation, balancing family commitment with study, managing time, and coping with additional workload brought on by course requirements. The conclusion was made that the online environment is an excellent way of placing students at the centre of the learning experience, allowing them to have total control of their time and the process of learning. This, however, required an alteration in their thinking and a willingness to change certain attitudes about learning.

Chapter 3

Hakim Usoof, Unviersity of Colombo, Sri Lanka
Brian Hudson, Sussex Unviersity, UK
Eva Lindgren, Umeå University, Sweden

Plagiarism has gained much public attention with media, corporations, and researchers leading the way. The general public's perception is that plagiarism is a "plague" spreading without control within our educational institutes. Furthermore, a social perception has been created that the Internet is the "catalyst" of modern-day plagiarism. This chapter explores the domain of plagiarism, taking into consideration some definitions of plagiarism, the recent history, the cultural context, the view of students and teachers, and the situation in Distance Education. The chapter goes on to discuss the actual catalysts of plagiarism and methods used to detect plagiarism. Finally, the chapter forwards some good practices that may help prevent and act as deterrents of plagiarism and addresses challenges faced in tackling the problem of plagiarism.

The challenges in creating a collaborative environment for online learning are great. This chapter describes some practical examples of community building in online learning contexts and discusses the effects of such activities. It draws its data from six years of online courses in English at Mid Sweden University, where the author was employed from 2003-2009 and worked with development and implementation of their Internet course program.

Chapter 5

This chapter proposes a model of introducing networked peer assessment to an online course. In the organisation background, the benchmark model of peer assessment is introduced in terms of its theoretical and empirical bases. The discussions about Dadaelous Integrated Writing Environment (DIWE) and empirical studies on its use in language classes set the stage of the model of networked peer assessment. The model is then described in detail in terms of its structure and its use within DIWE. Challenges for using networked peer assessment are then discussed in the light of learners' technological skills, online collaboration skills, and shifted teachers' and students' role in online learning. This chapter ends with solutions and recommendations in dealing with the three challenges mainly in terms of training students in technological use and in developing online collaboration skills and training teachers in using networked peer assessment.

Chapter 6

The following case reports on the involvement of children in online discussion with student teachers within initial teacher education in New Zealand. The focus is on listening to children, with wider implications for listening as a professional capability extending beyond the teaching profession. In this case, student teachers and pupils communicated online, exchanging ideas, debating, and engaging in co-construction of understandings around the place of Information and Communication Technologies in teaching and learning. The case explores the interaction and social dynamics observed and mutual learning experienced, with links to theoretical perspectives including constructivist and democratic pedagogies. Implications for improved practice are considered. It is argued that there is a need to explicitly teach listening skills and to encourage professionals in training to listen to clients. It is argued that the online environment is an excellent training ground for developing effective listening skills as it lends itself to reflective practice and to meta-listening awareness.

This chapter examines the socio-cultural contexts of Asian/Pacific islanders in a Western Pacific island to identify key components for culturally responsive online course development. A model for constructing an online learning environment is proposed using McLoughlin and Oliver's (2000) principles as design frameworks for designing a culturally inclusive instructional design that will support Asian/ Pacific islanders' learning in blended courses.

This chapter presents a case study that examines the perceptions of online students and instructors regarding their their experiences in a reputable online MBA program. The findings indicate that both the instructors and students exhibited a high level of satisfaction with their online experiences in the program and positive attitude toward online learning in general. This study also explores the in-depth views of the online participants on several key components of online business education, including online learning facilitation and interaction, virtual teamwork, and Case-Based Learning (CBL). The issues and challenges identified in the study indicate a need for the instructors and students to receive more guidance and support, technologically and pedagogically, in order to create a more engaging and fruitful online learning environment.

The English Department at Högskolan Dalarna, Sweden, participates in a distance-learning program with the Faculty of Education at Vietnam National University. Students who enroll in this program are teachers of English at secondary or tertiary institutions, and will study half time for two years to complete a Master's degree in English Linguistics. The distance program, adapted specifically to accommodate the Vietnamese students in terms of cultural differences as well as inexperience with distance methodology, is characterized by three design features: testing, technical training, and fostering a community of learners. The design of the courses also reflects a learner-centered approach that addresses common problem areas in distance education by promoting interactivity. Central to the overall program is the maintenance of different channels of communication, reflecting an effort to support the students academically and socially, both as individuals and members of a learning community. In this way, the effects of physical and cultural distances are minimized.

Chapter 10

Klara Bolander Laksov, Karolinska Institutet, Sweden
Charlotte Silén, Karolinska Institutet, Sweden
Lena Engqvist Boman, Karolinska Institutet, Sweden

In this case, the introductory course in an international masters program in medical education (MMedEd) called "Scholarship of Medical Education" is described. Some of the background to why the MMedEd was started and the underlying ideas and principles of the program are provided. The individual course, which consists of 10 weeks part time study on-line with an introductory face to face meeting, is described in terms of the intentions and pedagogical principles underlying the design, the teaching and learning activities, and how the students were supported to achieve the intended learning activities, as well as the challenges and concerns that arose throughout and after the course. Finally, some solutions to these problems are discussed.

Chapter 11

Gordon Joyes, University of Nottingham, UK
Tony Fisher, University of Nottingham, UK
Roger Firth, University of Nottingham, UK
Do Coyle, University of Nottingham, UK

This chapter provides a case study of a wholly online professional doctorate in Teacher Education that has been running successfully since 2003 within the School of Education at the University of Nottingham, UK. It begins with both the background and context in which the development took place—this covers the team involved and identifies the drivers that led to this innovative course. The main body of the chapter focuses on the course itself, which was constructed collaboratively through written reflections of the team. This illuminates the reasons for its success as measured by healthy recruitment, high student evaluation scores, and high retention and completion rates. The pedagogic rationale for the design of one module involving collaborative knowledge creation is presented with some student reactions to this. Six student voices are then presented, which provide an insight into the value of the course. This leads to a consideration of the current context and the new challenges facing the course.

Chapter 12

Wasim A. Al-Hamdani, Kentucky State University, USA

This chapter investigates the problem of secure e-learning and the use cryptography algorithms as tools to ensure integrity, confidentiality, non-reputations, authentication, and access control to provide secure knowledge delivery, secure student feedback, and secure assessments. Providing privacy in e-learning focuses on the protection of personal information of a learner in an e-learning system, while secure e-learning focuses on complete, secure environments to provide integrity, confidentiality, authentication, authorization, and proof of origin. The secure e-learning system and the use of cryptography is the main theme of this chapter. In addition, the authors present a new cryptograph e-learning model based on PKI and cryptography access control. The model is based on creating secure shell system based on PKI, and each adding block has to certified itself to be assessable.

Foreword

by Virginia Langum

In a famous cinematic moment of the end of the past century, the futuristic character Neo has years of martial arts training uploaded to his brain in mere seconds. His simple statement "I know kung fu" serves as a shorthand for a vision of future educational capabilities driven by technology.

Frequent in science fiction narratives is the idea that future students no longer learn, but rather, upload knowledge. They are thus freed from the temporal and physical constraints of traditional campus-based education.

Some science fiction writers have couched their conceptualizations of the future university and technologically enhanced education in political terms. The hopes of the "computer revolution" said as much about equality as about technology. In their 1993 speech to the National Academy of Sciences Convocation on Technology and Education, the science fiction writers William Gibson and Bruce Sterling urged that all education be put online.

A recurring theme in Gibson's novels is the possibility of the mind freed from the limitations of the body or "meatspace." A significant means by which the mind is liberated is through the development of knowledge transfer. Since the prophetic view of uploading information directly to the mind described in Gibson's *Neuromancer* and *Johnny Mnemonic* and a host of other futuristic narratives such as the earlier mentioned film *The Matrix*, online education has been at the center of debate concerning the future of education.

Although it has lost its revolutionary rhetoric, the idealistic potential of online education is still championed by some. Yet to others online education, particularly in its MOOC (Massive Open Online Course) manifestation, is part of the "McDonaldization" of higher education. According to this line of argument, online education widens the gap between homogenized, pre-packaged degree programs and the ivory-towered elite. Others point to the financial motives behind online education and inflation of degrees.

This collection of essays offers experiential and specialized voices in the current conversation about online education. Professional distance education degrees constitute an important part of the market as evidenced by the categories chosen by *US News and World Report*'s first ever guide to online degree programs. These categories are education, nursing, business, engineering, and computer information technology. However, while acknowledging online degree programs as "an essential part of the higher education landscape," the editor of the report admits the need to develop new and different standards of evaluation to traditional models.

The variety of programs and analyses represented in this collection testifies to the unique challenges of evaluating online degree courses, as well as other concerns central to ongoing discussions. These issues concern the student experience, peer review, and other possibilities for collaborative learning in an online environment. Perhaps most significantly, the authors present an international perspective to online professional degree courses. Online education has been suggested to be both a product and producer of globalization. As they continue to attract international students outside of the host institution's physical base, online degree programs pose diverse opportunities and problems for instruction. Furthermore, certain countries are developing programs more rapidly than others. An educational columnist recently adapted William Gibson's line to describe the lagging progress in online education in some countries: "the future of education is here, it's just not evenly distributed." However, the fear is that with an uneven market of online degree programs, knowledge is becoming even more centralized and controlled. With case studies from Sweden, New Zealand, the Asian Pacific, Vietnam, the United States, and the United Kingdom, this collection offers an increasingly urgent perspective on the international phenomenon of online education. However, the cases go beyond merely representing global online communities, interrogating specific concerns of cultural responsiveness and adaptation. In addition, the case studies speak to practical concerns that are shared by all online educational programs, such as the detection of plagiarism and the use of specific tools.

Virginia Langum
Umeå University, Sweden

Virginia Langum *is a postdoctoral research fellow in the Department of Languages and the Umeå Group for Premodern Studies at Umeå University. Her current project investigates the physiology of the seven deadly sins in the later Middle Ages. Before moving to Sweden, she completed her doctorate at Cambridge University in English. She also has Master's degrees in medieval literature and journalism. She has published on confessional and religious literature, as well as intersections of medical knowledge and religious and literary discourse in medieval culture. In addition to research, she has worked as a print and radio journalist. She has also taught distance and traditional classroom courses in literature and writing for several years.*

Foreword

by Dean Sutherland

The development and proliferation of higher education programmes available via online and digital technologies is the most significant change in tertiary education over the past 20 years. This rise in online modes of delivery is due to factors such as technological advances (e.g., high speed Internet and availability of digital content) and financial pressures on tertiary institutions (e.g., reduced public funding). My own student experience late last century included regular face-to-face lectures, browsing collections in the library, and plenty of time standing by a photocopier and socializing on and off campus. Contact with lecturers was face-to-face and generally by appointment only. During the late 1990s, the use of email and availability of online journal articles, publications, and Web resources increased. These and subsequent changes have now resulted in a very different educational experience for most students.

Online teaching and learning is challenging and rewarding for students and teachers alike. A wide range of professional studies can now be undertaken from the comfort of home, while working fulltime and participating in family life. Many people who may never have considered traditional on-site higher education can now access programs offered by many national and international university programs. These benefits can be countered by students' perceptions of isolation, lack of support, and poor digital literacy skills. Many teachers have also struggled to grasp the idiosyncrasies of the development and delivery of online programs.

As the coordinator of a professional university program delivered online via a *blended* model (i.e., online content and activity together with some face-to-face sessions), much of my teaching time is spent "online." This includes moderating forum discussions, marking online assignment submissions, recording and uploading video clips, video conference calls with student groups, linking students to external Web-based resources, and dealing with a multitude of student emails that arrive all hours of the day, every day of the week. The development of new media and technologies also presents challenges. For example, how can we be sure that content and student contributions are secure? Can effective Masters and Doctoral programmes be delivered online? What is the most effective approach to developing a learning community when face-to-face contact between students and teachers is minimal or non-existent? The breadth and depth of many of these issues as well as the benefits of online learning are well captured in the following pages.

The book you are holding (or viewing online) is essential reading for anyone with an interest in developing and delivering educational programs via online technologies, in particular programs designed for students undertaking professional programs. From the first chapter, investigating student perspectives of online learning, to the final chapter, considering the security and protection of online programs and content, the book provides in-depth consideration and reflection on cases that illustrate the challenges, benefits, and issues surrounding online teaching and learning. Topics, such as developing a sense of community among students (chapter 4) and designing culturally responsive programs (chapter 7), are central to providing students from distant lands and diverse backgrounds with effective educational experiences.

Contextual features of effective teaching and learning programs include: appropriate and organized (and secure) information; student motivation; student engagement in activities on their own and with others; and opportunity for self-monitoring (Biggs, 2003). The development of online learning programs should address each of these features. The information in the following chapters will help you make more informed decisions about the design and functionality of your online program.

Although future changes to online learning are difficult to predict, I suspect new technologies will play a central part. What will not change is the need for engaging, knowledgeable, and supportive tertiary teachers who possess an understanding of the learning process, students' needs, and a willingness to learn new ways of doing things.

Dean Sutherland
University of Canterbury, New Zealand
March 2013

Dean Sutherland *is a Senior Lecturer in the School of Health Sciences Centre and College of Education at the University of Canterbury, Christchurch, New Zealand. He coordinates the University's Specialist Teaching programme which provides an online teaching and learning program for practising teachers to become specialized in supporting students with a range of learning needs (e.g., deaf and hearing impairment, learning and behaviour difficulties). His research interests include Deaf Education, Autism Spectrum Disorder, Communication between adults and children, and the use of Augmentative and Alternative Communication by children and adults with significant communication difficulties.*

REFERENCES

Biggs, J. (2003). *Teaching for quality learning at university* (2nd ed.). Maidenhead, UK: Open University Press.

Preface

This book was inspired by the growth of the professional degree and its delivery via the Internet, as well as by the editors' personal experiences of studying and teaching via the Internet. The Internet has afforded many individuals, who may never have been able to achieve their ambitions if the only study option was on-campus study, the opportunity to study for a professional degree. This opportunity has proven popular, and is one that the academy has been quick to offer. However, challenges, issues, and questions of relevance and quality of delivery have increasingly been raised in relation to these professional degree programs.

This volume presents a set of 12 cases that interrogate the presentation of the professional degree via the Internet, and present a balanced picture of the state of the art for such degrees during the second decade of the 21st century. Twelve cases by different authors collected together in one volume can turn out to be disappointing. We, however, are confident that the current volume will not disappoint. The individual cases have their particular styles and approaches to the professional degree delivered via the Internet. In some cases, this is explicit and in others, implicit. Yet, even when implicit, the relevance to the professional degree delivered via the Internet is apparent to the reader with experience of such degrees as a student, as a member of a teaching team, or as a program designer. The relevance of all the chapters is heightened and made dynamic in the supporting materials that accompany each case. These materials offer the reader, student, or lecturer the opportunity for directed reflection about the case they have just read. These materials also provide suggested further readings that provide the reader with a route into the body of literature surrounding each case. The tensions within and between the cases also become more apparent when the cases are worked with using the supporting materials. The reader ought not view these as minor appendixes to each case, but as integrated elements that will develop her personal understanding of each case and assist in placing the messages into her teaching and learning context.

This volume will speak to academics currently involved in presenting professional degrees via the Internet and provide them with tools to reflect upon their program design, develop and improve their programs, and find support for how their program is currently designed and presented. This volume will also speak to academics who have yet to be involved in presented professional degrees via the Internet, or are in the process of developing such a degree program for their academy, and the volume will speak to past, current, and potential students of professional degrees via the Internet.

To set the scene, the first chapter, "Studying Professional Degrees via the Internet: Challenges, Issues, and Relevance from the Student's Perspective," presents a personal reflective case based on studying four professional degrees via the Internet over the first 12 years of the 21st century. The case raises many of the questions that form the core of later chapters. Specifically, the chapter points to the cases by Joyes, Fischer, Firth and Coyle, Bolander Laksov, Silén, and Engqvist Boman, and Deutschmann. The case considers aspects that reoccur in more detail in later cases and as such provides a personalized entrance into the issues, challenges, and questions of relevance for the reader to juxtapose with the more formal cases that follow. This first chapter discusses the key themes of initial contact, communication, support, deadlines, work, and keeping going. Of most use to the potential student is the list of key skills that should be considered by the potential student prior to enrolling in a professional degree program that is delivered via the Internet. These key skills also resonate in the later chapters of the volume.

Chapter Two, "Experiences of an Online Doctoral Course in Teacher Education," continues the student perspective theme, but this time at doctoral level. Although the first case discusses the diversity of the professional doctorate and its rapid rise in popularity, the first case only considers studying graduate taught degrees. This case focuses on the doctoral level and is an excellent complement to the first case. The case is a personal reflective case study by Despina Varnava-Marouchou and Mark A. Minott. They look back on the nudge, motivators, and experiences of studying for a Doctorate in Education delivered from a second country that is far from home. Despina was based on Cyprus and Mark even further away on the Cayman Islands while they studied the Doctor of Education program presented by The University of Nottingham, England (see the case in this volume by Joyes, Fisher, Firth, and Coyle for more details of this Doctor of Education program from the lecturers', course designers', and other students' perspectives). Many of the elements of first case can be found in the case, suggesting that the shift from graduate to doctoral level does not majorly impact the distance professional degree and the students' experiences. Varnava-Marouchou and Minott conclude that placing students at the centre of the learning experience allows them to have control of their time and the process of learning, but for this to result in successful study requires the student to change how she thinks about planning, teaching, and learning.

Chapter Three, "Plagiarism: Catalysts and Not so Simple Solutions," considers one of the growing concerns of distance (and non-distance) education—plagiarism. The use of technology to check for plagiarism has recently resulted in the fall of a number of German politicians who took their doctorates many years ago, and may even have used a typewriter to produce them. Immediate detection was unknown 15 years ago. Today there are many plagiarism detection tools that can be used to assist the lecturer. Usoof, Hudson, and Lindgren present a balanced case discussion of plagiarism that does not fall into the common traps of, for example, claiming plagiarism is new, that it is easily defined, or that is can easily be detected. This aligns with the work of Eriksson and Sullivan (2008) that examined lecturers' understandings and attitudes. Usoof, Hudson, and Lindgren problematize plagiarism before turning to plagiarism in distance education, catalysts of plagiarism, and methods used to detect plagiarism before presenting good practices that may help prevent and act as deterrents of plagiarism. Here they stress the need for innovative teaching and assessment design.

Part of creating innovative teaching and assessments is the creation of online communities that afford such innovations. In Chapter Four, Mats Deutschmann presents the case, "Creating Online Community: Challenges and Solutions." His case reports on a study based at Mid Sweden University, which is a small multi-campus university in Northern Sweden. Forty-five percent of this university's students are distance-based students who undertake much of their study via the Internet. Mats's case reports on building collaborative learning into online professional degree programs. Perhaps not surprisingly, we again see elements of the first two cases reflected in the program design—the importance of supporting prospective students, fostering community building and collaborative learning, and creating contexts beyond the virtual classroom. Mats effectively illustrates his case with student examples, and he wisely ends his case by pointing out "what may be a good model today, might be less so tomorrow." The technology associated with providing distance professional degree programs via the Internet is evolving rapidly. Future devices supporting the ubiquity of teaching and learning will impact on best practice.

In Chapter Five, Huahui Zhao discusses how to introduce peer collaboration in a networked English writing class. This case links with the previous case by Mats Deutschmann. Peer collaboration in writing both requires and creates online community. Huahui introduces the Dadaelous Integrated Writing Environment (DIWE) before discussing challenges to creating networked peer collaboration and assessment. These challenges again resonate with the other cases in this volume—students' technological skills, students' online discussion skills, and shifted teachers' and students' roles in online learning. Huahui concludes her case with elements that are often oddly missing, those of training in technological use (cf. making sure the students and staff have this prior to starting the program), training in online collaboration skills (cf. hoping they will develop naturally), and teacher training in using networked peer assessment (cf. assuming the campus teacher can easily shift to the online mode of delivery).

The next case, "Listening and Learning through ICT with Digital Kids: Dynamics of Interaction, Power, and Mutual Learning between Student Teachers and Children in Online Discussion," by Dianne Forbes of the University of Waikato, New Zealand focuses on students undertaking their Bachelor of Teaching degree as a distance education degree at the University of Waikato, New Zealand. The case is excitingly different from the others in this volume as it reports on the experiences of, as Forbes writes, "involving children in online discussion with student teachers." Rather than focusing on the student body and peer interaction, this case shows how distance-based teaching can use ICT to include clients, in this case children. The case explores the interaction and social dynamics observed, and mutual learning experienced, with links to theoretical perspectives including constructivist and democratic pedagogies. Forbes' case not only shows that it has implications for practice, but also that the distance professional degree can turn the online environment to its advantage.

In Chapter Seven, Catherine E. Stoicovy of the University of Guam, presents a case that focuses on creating "Culturally Responsive Online Learning for Asian/Pacific Islanders in a Pacific Island University." Catherine's case draws on the Cahmorro and Filipino core cultural values, and constructs a model for constructing an online learning environment based on a culturally inclusive instructional design that will support Asian/Pacific islanders' learning in blended courses. Catherine paints a detailed picture of Guam and its indigenous population, and discusses culturally responsive education as the base for her case. Many of the case's recommendations find resonance in this volume's other cases.

In Chapter Eight, Rich Magjuka and Xiaojing Liu present "A Case Study of Online MBA Courses: Online Facilitation, Case-Based Learning, and Virtual Team." The case focuses on an online MBA program in business school at a large Mid-Western university and uses interviews with instructors and students to find out how satisfied the students are, what strategies the instructors use in teaching, how the students perceived the effectiveness of their teaching and learning experience, and what challenges and issues the students and instructors perceive for professional online courses. Rich and Xiaojing identify the need for the instructors and students to receive more guidance and support, technologically and pedagogically, in order to create a more engaging and fruitful online learning environment.

The minimization of the effects of physical and cultural distances is a core element of the case, "A Case Study of a Distance Degree Program in Vietnam: Examples from a Learner-Centered Approach to Distance Education," presented in Chapter Nine by Kristy Beers Fägersten. Kristy reports on the distance-learning program for English teachers at secondary and tertiary institutions in Vietnam. The English Department at Högskolan Dalarna, Sweden, participates in a distance-learning program with the Faculty of Education at Vietnam National University, and the Vietnamese students study half time for two years to complete a Master's degree in English Linguistics. This degree strengthens the students' professional standing as teachers of English. Kristy's case echoes Catherine Stoicovy's case on culturally responsive online learning. The learner-centered design of the Kristy's case prioritizes a culture of groups and a learning community that is designed to foster a learning community composed of students who are academically equal and trained to participate actively in the Web-based environment. Kristy concludes, "The distance format can be effectively exploited to overcome such challenges and ultimately enable successful intercultural education." Fostering a community of learners again resonates as a core element of this case.

Chapter Ten, "Implementation of Scholarship of Teaching and Learning through an On-Line Masters Program," by Klara Bolander Laksov, Charlotte Silén, and Lena Engqvist Boman of Karolinska Institutet, Stockholm, Sweden links back to the first case of this volume. The international masters program in medical education is one of the professional distance degrees that form part of the personal reflective case presented in Chapter One, and is the first of two student-instructor case pairs. This case focuses on the first course of the master's program, "Scholarship of Medical Education," and follows its development and first presentation. The case presents the underlying ideas and principles for what the authors wanted to accomplish in the program. One point made in this case is that over half of the participants did not feel their employers supported their study. This is of interest to professional degree providers, and resonates with the first case study where the importance of grounding the intention to study with family, friends, and work is viewed as an important action. This finding is important for assessment, and Klara, Charlotte, and Lena write in relation to revision of the course "Scholarship of Medical Education," "The examination task needs to be somewhat reduced so that students are not put into a situation with work overload and steered into a reproductive approach to learning." This case also provides the students' evaluation comments about the course. These provide a picture of how the teaching and learning was experienced.

The second of the two student-instructor case pairs, "The Nature of a Successful Online Professional Doctorate," presents and discusses the professional doctorate in Teacher Education offered by the University of Nottingham, England, that Despina Varnava-Marouchou and Mark A. Minott discussed from the students' perspective in Chapter Two. Gordon Joyes, Tony Fisher, Roger Firth, and Do Coyle provide a case that gives voice to both those teaching and supervising the students and the students. These authentic student voices reveal the breadth of competencies and skills the professional doctorate in education provides. These voices juxtapose the description of the course and its development. This, together with Chapter Two, allows for a multi-layered understanding of how course design, mode of delivery, teaching, learning, and teacher and student bodies interact.

The final case, "Secure E-Learning and Cryptography," presents a very different perspective on distance professional degrees. Wasim A. Al-Hamdani introduces the readers of this volume to the world of cryptography. Wasim investigates the problem of secure e-learning and how cryptography algorithms can be used as tools to ensure integrity, confidentiality, non-reputations, authentication, and access control to provide secure knowledge delivery, secure student feedback, and secure assessments. These are issues that educationalists and students rarely consider, but are required if the validity of distance professional degrees is not to be compromised. Wasim presents a new cryptograph e-learning model based on PKI and cryptography access control. The mathematical details of this case may challenge some readers, but the message of the case can be accessed without understanding the mathematical detail.

Each of the twelve cases contained in this volume contribute to our understanding of the complexities of creating, delivering and studying a distance professional degree. The cases illuminate these complexities from different angles, and the unique collection that this volume represents shows that students are generally happy. Yet things can be better, and most importantly, that they will get better! This volume will contribute to the improvement of distance professional degrees.

Kirk P.H. Sullivan
Umeå Univeristy, Sweden

Peter E. Czigler
Örebro University, Sweden

Jenny M. Sullivan Hellgren
Umeå University, Sweden

REFERENCES

Eriksson, E. J., & Sullivan, K. P. H. (2008). Controlling plagiarism: A study of lecturer attitudes. In Roberts, T. S. (Ed.), *Student plagiarism in an online world: Problems and solutions* (pp. 23–36). Hershey, PA: IGI Global.

Acknowledgment

This collection of cases is the work of the authors, the reviewers, and support staff at IGI Global. Without them, this book never would have been published. We are also thankful for the students who study via professional degree programs via the Internet. Without them, this book would never have been conceptualized or brought to fruition.

Kirk P.H. Sullivan
Umeå Univeristy, Sweden

Peter E. Czigler
Örebro University, Sweden

Jenny M. Sullivan Hellgren
Umeå University, Sweden

Chapter 1

Studying Professional Degrees via the Internet:
Challenges, Issues, and Relevance from the Student's Perspective

Kirk P. H. Sullivan
Umeå University, Sweden

EXECUTIVE SUMMARY

This case places the student in focus and through a reflective case study considers four distance professional degree programs. The author of this case followed these programs as life-long learning professional activities. The case considers the nudge, the study, and degree completion. The reflection is structured around the themes of initial contact, communication, support, deadlines, work, and keeping going. These themes reveal challenges, issues, and questions of relevance for the student and university. Key skills to assist the student towards completion are suggested along with what the potential student should consider prior to enrolling in a professional degree program that is delivered via the Internet. The growth in distance professional degrees, including professional doctorates, demonstrates the importance of the challenges, issues, and questions of relevance considered in this case from the student's perspective.

BACKGROUND

Today, universities and colleges provide a wide-range of professional degrees and degrees that support the professional. The development of these degrees is particularly noticeable in the proliferation of professional doctorates. Today the professional looking to gain a doctoral degree can, for example, study for a Doctorate in Education

DOI: 10.4018/978-1-4666-4486-1.ch001

(EdD), Ministry (DMin), Tourism (DTourism) Clincial Psychology (DClinPsy), Business Administration (DBA), Medical Ethics (DMedEth), or Audiology (AuD). Many of these doctoral degree programs are designed so that the student can continue in full-time employment during their period of registration, and designed so that study can occur flexibly. Two cases in this volume (Joyes, Fisher, Firth & Coyle, and Varnava-Marouchou & Minott) consider the Doctor of Education program in Higher Education at the University of Nottingham, UK. Joyes et al.'s case examines the design and running of the EdD program, Varnava-Marouchou & Minott's case examines case examines how the program meets the students' needs and expectations.

The range of professional degrees offered via distance teaching is not limited to doctoral training; one example is the Masters in Medical Education discussed in Bolander Lakov, Silén and Engqvist Boman (this volume). Many other examples are readily found with a simple Google search; this type of degree is common and the market competitive. This case examines and reflects upon my own experience of distance degrees. Challenges, issues and relevance from the student's perspective frame this examination and reflection. This case begins by setting the stage and asks why people want to become distance students and read a professional degree (or a degree with professional application), before proceeding to my own reflections and finally suggesting ways forward for the potential professional degree student in the hunt for the ideal distance professional degree or course.

SETTING THE STAGE

Lindgren, Sullivan, Zhao, Deutschmann, and Steinvall (2011) wrote:

Lifelong learning and the importance of generic skills have gained a clearer position in higher education in Europe thanks to the Bologna Declaration (1999) in general and the Bergen Communiqué (2005) in particular as it "explicitly mentions the chance to further implement lifelong learning in higher education through qualification frameworks" (Jakobi & Rusconi, 2009: 52), and policy development in the European Union (see Dehmel, 2006 for a good overview of this policy development). What is worth mentioning here are the subtle changes in the definition of lifelong learning between 2000 and 2001 from "all purposeful learning activity, undertaken on an ongoing basis with the aim of improving knowledge, skills, and competence" (CEC, 2000, p. 3) to "all learning activity undertaken throughout life, with the aim of improving knowledge, skills and competences within a personal, civic and/or employment-related perspective" (CEC, 2001, p. 9). Dehmel highlights the removal of purposeful as informal learning with no specific purpose is a core element of lifelong learning, and the change from on an ongoing basis to throughout life that stresses continuous learning from the cradle to the end of life. Dehmel also points out a shift in the understanding of life-long learning from the 1970s to today; a shift from humanistic ideals of Bildung to "primarily utilitarian, economic objectives" (p. 52), even if these have been nuanced recently to combine the social and cultural with the economic (p. 188).

The distance professional degree is a life-long learning event. At various stages of a professional's life the need for a more structured and formal learning context can arise. It is here that the distance professional degree comes in; it aims to offer the working professional a life-long learning experience that leads to an academic award that can also assist the professional in their professional, or career, development. The impetus for venturing into part-time distance formal degree awarding education can be to improve career prospects, perhaps with a view to finding a new job, can be a career requirement from the employer who in which case may fund part or all of the costs of the degree program, or simply personal interest. Personal interest is a key lifelong learning motivator that initial degrees aim to teach students. For example, Bachelor's degrees in Sweden have the expected learning outcome that the student: "visa förmåga att identifiera sitt behov av ytterligare kunskap och att utveckla sin kompetens" *demonstrates an ability to identify the need for further knowledge and to develop their skills* (Högskoleförordning, 1993:100). If this is to mean more than learning by doing as directed by the manager or boss, the distance professional degree has to inspire students out of personal interest. That is the degree award, per se, ought not be the sole motivator. Naturally, with the development of spaces such as the Open University's Learning Space (http://openlearn.open.ac.uk/) that provides over 600 free online courses from The Open University, UK, and public iTunes U (http://www.apple.com/education/itunes-u/what-is.html), sites run by universities such as Yale, Stanford, UC Berkeley, Oxford, Cambridge and MIT via Coursera (http://www.coursera.org) and edX (http://www.edx.org) providing access to numerous courses, the opportunities for interest-based non-award studies are multitudinous. An award can, however, nudge (see Thaler & Sunstein, 2008 for a theoretical perspective on how the concept of nudging can operate) the learner into actualising her or his desire to learn and to provide the discipline required to complete a course of study in a way that free online courses may not.

The combination of professional and personal interest, and company-directed study pose not only a complexity for the academy in designing and implementing distance professional degree programs, but also a plethora of options for potential students negotiating the options available to them. Individuals have their personal learning contexts, and it is the nexus of the individual's possibilities and demands, and the academy and its professional degrees that provides a frame to the success or otherwise, and the perception of high quality, or otherwise, by the learner.

CASE DESCRIPTION

This case aims to inform the discourse surrounding the challenges, and perceived quality of distance professional degrees through reflection from one student's perspective, the author. Higgens (2011) sees the reflection as suggesting: *a method of inquiry which is characterised by engagement, pondering alternatives, drawing inferences and taking diverse perspectives, especially in situations which are complex and novel, calling for situational awareness and understanding* (p. 583). Schön (1988) saw two types of reflection: one, that done while engaged in an action, situation or event, and two, that done afterwards. Kottkamp (1990) talked about online and offline reflection. The reflection for this case is offline, that is after the learning situation. At times there are online notes written during study that inform the offline reflection.

The discussion that follows does not examine the courses from a quality assurance perspective and does not question the academic standards of the degree courses. Rather it presents a student's reflections upon their experiences as a way to inform debate about the online provision of professional degrees and courses. Johnson (2001) summarized Knowle's (1990) work on adult learning and wrote:

In his [Knowle's] view, the adult learner, in whatever guise, has to need to know. All learning engaged in by adults— not just the blue ribbon of the PhD—will be assessed in terms of its 'benefits, consequences, and risks'. This assessment will undertaken [sic] before 'involvement in the learning situation'. Knowles stressed that it was the 'self-concept and intellectual responsibility' of adults as learners that supported and was entirely appropriate for 'self-directed learning situations'. However, Knowles goes on to emphasise that experiential learning based on 'the adult learner's past experiences is essential' (Johnson: 55).

The elements of Knowle's theory that Johnson lifted in her summary, *benefits, consequences and risks*, are elements that will find voice in my reflection as will *'need to know'*. The case continues with an autobiographical statement, and an overview of the professional degrees that underpin this case. Thereafter reflection, combined with elements of the archived literature, and the development of themes that inform the student's view of the challenges, issues and relevance when studying professional degrees via the Internet will be developed and discussed.

Autobiographical Statement

I work as an academic and am professor of linguistics at Umeå University in Sweden. I moved to Sweden in 1994 to take up a post at Umeå University. I grew up in the United Kingdom and studied Applied Linguistics at what today is Bangor University, Information Technology at Loughborough University, and took my PhD in the Department of Electronics and Computer Science, Southampton University. As may be guessed, my academic interests are eclectic and I find most things worth learning. Once I started lecturing, I rapidly saw the need to broaden my knowledge of education and develop my teaching skills. This has nudged me into reading a range of (professional) distance degree courses. Interesting, I have not always completed the entire degree program; this is something I will return to later. The only awards I have completed and been awarded are the Postgraduate Certificate in Teaching and Learning in Higher Education awarded by the Open University, UK, and the MA in Research Ethics awarded by Keele University, UK. All study has been conducted outside of work even when supported by my department. It is worth considering how my behavior of not completing the degree programs that I engaged in as an adult learner can be assessed in terms of benefit, consequence and risk, and what this suggests about the challenges, issues and relevance of Internet based professional degree programs.

The Degrees

The degree programs have all been taught in English. The programs studied are:

- Postgraduate Certificate in Teaching and Learning in Higher Education awarded by the Open University, UK. For this award I took the course Teaching and Course Design in Higher Education
- Master of Arts in Pedagogical Work in national, trans-national and global contexts awarded by the Stockholm Institute of Education, Stockholm, Sweden. The institute has now merged with Stockholm University, Sweden.
- Master of Medical Science in Medical Education awarded by Karolinska Institutet, Stockholm, Sweden. This degree is presented in the case in this volume by Bolander Kaksov, Silén and Engqvist Boman.
- Master of Arts in Research Ethics awarded by the University of Keele, UK.

Before reflecting upon each degree program in turn, the nudge for starting the program will be discussed and the program briefly overviewed. Links between the nudge, study, and completion will be considered under current challenges facing professional degrees via the Internet.

Postgraduate Certificate in Teaching and Learning in Higher Education

The nudge for me entering this program was to sharpen my competitiveness if I was to return to the UK or apply for another position in Sweden. My own university provides professional develop courses via the University Centre for Teaching and Learning, but these courses are not examined, nor do they lead to a professional certificate that would have validity outside of my own institution. The Open University course was also accredited by the Higher Education Academy (http://www.heacademy.ac.uk/), and the Staff and Educational Development Association (http://www.seda.ac.uk/); this increased its attractiveness as a program that could enhance my career prospects and would fit in my professional portfolio. Another aspect of the nudge was the perceived increasing importance of tertiary level teaching qualifications and their potential impact on success in the academic job market. Hence, the nudge for me taking the course was the desire to improve my teaching skills, and perceived need of a qualification rather than attendance at courses not leading to an accredited qualification.

The course ran for one academic year, was part-time and distance taught with no campus meetings. In the course's 2002 guide (Tait, 2002) the assessed work is described as follows:

The assessed work for this course cycles you through various aspects of teaching and learning:

- *Making online connections with colleagues and tutors – building a community for learning (TMA 00).*
- *Thinking about your professional context and identifying your development needs (TMA 01).*
- *Understanding how people learn – monitoring and reviewing your teaching from a student perspective (TMA 02).*
- *Designing assessment and giving feedback (TMA 03).*
- *Planning a course and producing an outline (TMA 04).*
- *Choosing and using teaching methods and evaluating their effectiveness in your context (TMA 05).*
- *Producing a course review that focuses on one question from your learning with this H850 programme. (examinable component) (p. 4).*

The course was taught using FirstClass. This course was my first encounter with a distance course taught via the Internet. Accompanying the course was a course reader that had been specifically written for the course. Reading beyond this reader was only necessary to develop arguments in the TMAs and in the examinable component.

Master of Arts in Pedagogical Work in National, Trans-National, and Global Contexts

The nudge of this degree program was less focused than for the Postgraduate Certificate. I felt that I needed to understand education and in particular what I was doing in the classroom in more detail. Further, and as someone living and working in a country other than the one in which I was educated, the contexts provided by this program appealed. The nudge for studying this program was not to improve my professional portfolio, but to satisfy personal intellectual inquiry. A secondary nudge was to provide me with an understanding of what is required of students at Master level by another university and discipline in Sweden. This program was initially run by the Institute of Education, Stockholm, and then by Stockholm University after the Institute of Education had merged into Stockholm University.

The program ran for two years, was part-time and distance taught with no campus meetings. The courses that made up the program were:

- Theories and Models of Teaching and learning, 7.5 hp.
- Assessment and Evaluations, 7.5 hp.
- Methods of Inquiry, 7.5 hp.
- Human Rights, Children and Youth Rights, 7.5 hp.
- Becoming a European/Cosmopolitan Educationalist, 7.5 hp.
- Educational Leadership and Management, 7.5 hp.
- Thesis, 15 hp.

The course was taught in Moodle. A reader did not accompany the program. Each of the courses had separate reading lists that included books and articles, and each course had a separate course Website I Moodle. Some of the set texts were made available via the course Websites.

Master of Medical Science in Medical Education

The nudge of the degree program was two-fold: a desire to understand what is special about medical education and a desire to learn how to increase the praxis-based relevance of the theoretical courses taught by my department to students based in the Faculty of Medicine. The nudge for studying this program was again not to sharpen my competitiveness, but rather to support course development in my department. The same secondary nudge was as for the Master's program in Pedagogical Work in National, Trans-national and Global Contexts, a desire to gain an interdisciplinary and interfaculty understanding of the level regarded for the master's degree along with an understanding of how much study is viewed as being appropriate for 7.5 hp or 7.5 ECTS credits. This degree program was based in Medicine rather than the Arts and Social Sciences, and hence permitted comparison between expectations, and teaching and learning styles with, for example, the MA in Pedagogical Work in National, Trans-national and Global Contexts at Stockholm University. Further the Medical Education program was taught by one of the world's leading Medical Universities, Karolinska Institutet, Stockholm, and it is The Nobel Assembly at Karoinska Institutet that awards The Nobel Prize in Physiology or Medicine.

The program ran for four years, was part-time and distance taught with campus meetings once a semester. The courses that made up the program were:

- Scholarship of Medical Education, 7.5hp.
- Learning Processes, 7.5hp.
- Integration of Theory and Practice, 7.5hp.
- Design for and Assessment of Learning, 7.5 hp.
- Interprofessional Education, 7.5hp.
- Leading Change and Learning, 7.5hp.
- Degree Project in Medical Education, 1 15hp.
- Elective courses, 15hp.
- Research in Medical Education, 15hp.
- Degree Project in Medical Education, 2 30hp.

The course was taught in the Web-platform PingPong. There was no course reader, but each course Website contained detailed online readings, links to further readings, interviews, podcasts and the assignments.

Master of Arts in Research Ethics

The nudge for me beginning this degree was purely professional. The importance of ethical approval for the research I conduct and the research than many doctoral students in my department conduct made me realize that I needed a better and more academically grounded understanding of research ethics.

The program ran for two years, was part-time and distance taught with campus meetings at the beginning of each academic year. The focus of the first campus meeting was the technical aspects of learning at a distance, the course structure and how to approach the assignments. The focus of the second campus meeting was on delimiting and structuring the dissertation. The courses that made up the program were:

- Introduction to Ethical Theory and Research Ethics, 30 credits.
- Autonomy, Consent and Research, 30 credits.
- Ethics in Research Trials, 30 credits.
- Ethics and Different Research Methodologies, 30 credits.
- Dissertation, 60 credits.

The course was taught in Blackboard. There was no course reader, although a course handbook and a writing guide were provided. Further each module contained online material/a textbook chapter on the topic of the module together with links to articles, Webpages and other useful materials. Reading lists for the set essays were also provided. The final taught module, Ethics and Different Research Methodologies, provided less information that the previous three modules. The course leaders felt that by this stage of the degree program the student had sufficient skills to study more independently and creatively than at the onset of the degree program. The dissertation element was supported by tutor contact rather than within the peer group. The course was based in Keele University's Centre for Professional Ethics (also known as PEAK – Professional Ethics at Keele). PEAK is *amongst the largest and most successful providers of postgraduate ethics courses in Europe, with over 200 postgraduate students, eight permanent academic staff, and a portfolio of distinctive MA/PgDip program as well as the UK's first Professional Doctorate in Medical Ethics* (http://www.keele.ac.uk/ethics/).

Summary of the Programs Studied

All of the programs were taught in English, were at postgraduate level and lead to either an MA or a postgraduate certificate to which more credits could be added at a later date to allow the student to be awarded an MA. Two programs were taught by English universities, one of which runs all its taught degree programs using distance teaching modes, and the other two programs were taught by Swedish universities. The difference in funding structure between England and Sweden meant that the English degree programs attracted fees, while the Swedish degree programs attracted no fee and were free. In Sweden there are no fees for European Union, European Economic Area and Swiss citizens or for those resident in the European Union, the European Economic Area or Switzerland.

Two of the programs had campus meetings; one had two two-day meetings per year, and one had one one-day meeting per year. The other two programs had no face-to-face meetings. One of the programs had a course-reader written specifically for the program, the other programs combined in various ways Web-based information with set reading, generally a combination of books and articles.

REFLECTION

This case examines professional degree programs and considers the challenges, issues and relevance from the student's perspective. The reflection is thematically organized with each theme taking illustrations and reflections across the degree programs before returning to the meta-themes of challenge, issue and relevance after the benefits, consequences and risks of these degree programs have been considered.

The reflection is structured around the themes of *Initial Contact*, *Communication*, *Support*, *Deadlines*, *Work*, and *Keeping Going*.

Initial Contact

As a distance student initial contact with the program and university administration is important. It helps to set concerns at rest and set the tone for the course of study ahead. Initial contact covers both the immediate general information about the program and the course start-up phrase. The Research Ethics program at Keele University provided a folder about the University, the library, the Web platform and other generic information, and the program leader emailed copies of the Course Handbook and the Writing Guide prior to the start of the program. Contact between application and registration gave a positive impression, and encouraged me to feel part of the Keele community before starting the program. Of particular note was the way the program leader contacted me to ask if my application for full-time study was a system error (this had happened previously) as the advised mode of study for the degree was part-time. I had applied for part-time study and the problem was rapidly solved.

The availability of pre-program support from the Karolinska Institute was a determining factor to begin the program. I had applied via the Swedish Central Application System, the Website studera.nu, and my application had been rejected on the basis that I was did not meet the entrance requirements. When I applied I was not committed to the program as I was not sure I would have the time to meet the study demands. However, when I was rejected, I contacted the program coordinator and asked why I had been rejected. She was unsure and suggested that I reapply and that they would override the central decision. This friendly and productive conversation, convinced me to apply and commit to the program, or at least commit to attempting to fit the program in around my professional and family life.

This type of pre-program support was provided in-program by the Postgraduate Certificate in Teaching and Learning in Higher Education program. The first compulsory activity "Making online connections with colleagues and tutors – building a community for learning (TMA 00)." Part of this task was to introduce yourself online to your tutorial group and the other part was to submit a detailed overview of the year and yourself as the TMA (Tutor Marked Assignment) to your tutor. The first part of this assignment occurred in one way or another in all four programs: The MA in Pedagogical Work in National, Trans-national and Global Contexts asked up to present ourselves in a Moodle forum at the start of the first module, the Master of Medical Science in Medical Education asked us to present ourselves in a discussion forum and to take part in a synchronous chat at a pre-determined time by the course team, and the MA in Research Ethics asked us to present ourselves in a Moodle forum.

Initial contact was supported in two cases by campus day(s). Program registration was conducted during a campus day onsite at Keele University Campus that included, for those able to attend, and introduction to the Moodle, the requirements for the modules and time to socialize with other students taking the MA and teaching staff. For the Master of Medical Science in Medical Education, the support was not coupled with registration but was a few weeks into the semester. The campus days at KI (see Bolander Laksov, Silén & Engqvist Boman, this volume, for more details) fulfilled both a social function—a rather nice dinner was arranged by the program—and an academic function with work already undertaken by the students discussed and developed, and the semester's modules presented, overviewed and initiated. They offered an opportunity to focus on academic study in a way that offered the chance to get immersed in studying away from the usual routine and other pressures, and that allowed learning from other course members in social as well as academic contexts.

Communication

As a distance student feeling part of a community of learners can be motivating and feeling separated from others can be demotivating (see Deutschmann, this volume). A lack of community is not, per se, demotivating and feeling forced to be social can be demotivating. This section reflects upon the various forms of communication and community building used by the four degree programs, but begins by considering how I functioned as a campus student.

Turning back the clock to the 1980s when I was an undergraduate student and then a master's level student, I see two very different communities of practice (Lave and Wenger, 1991) that supported my studying and my learning. As an undergraduate my learning community was one or two friends from the classes I was taking as my social life was linked to a few university social societies. I tended to attend class and then study on my own. Even labs I undertook required individual reports so there was no requirement to work with someone else outside of the classroom. I remember one exception was a class in syntax in which we were placed in pairs to solve problems for the next class. An impacting factor for the creation of a learning community was our ability to choose courses that ran in parallel as this reduced possible overlap of peers. The student body of each group was very different. During my master's degree, my learning community heavily overlapped with my social life. The result of this was a higher degree of studying together and solving assignments and writing essays in discussion. The primary motivator for this overlap was that my master's class took all their classes together during the first semester of the program and then during the second semester groups of students took predetermined sets of courses together. Little of the study required communication between us, but we helped each other by discussing assignments and supporting each other when preparing for the written examinations. However, both as an undergraduate and as a graduate student, communication relating to study was weak.

My experience of communication and peer learning support during my campus student days left me with no expectations for communication and peer learning support when I started my first professional distance learning degree. However, as my first experience included forums for student discussion including what I will call a virtual coffee room, my expectations of communication with my fellow student grew. This was reinforced by the request that we present ourselves to the others in the group. This differed from my on-campus experience of turning up to lectures, seminars and labs and being expected to take the social initiative of making contact with fellow students. Naturally, online there is no one standing next to someone waiting for a classroom to be opened, or sitting next to someone in a lecture or seminar, or working with someone in a lab. Neither is there a natural gyration to form mini-groups in the class that happens in the campus classroom nor a visual or physical link between students.

The expectations for communication with my peers, and in particular the tutorial group I had been assigned to, grew once I saw how the course team had set up communication areas and asked us to introduce ourselves to each other. However, at least in my case, my newfound expectations were not met. Communication and peer learning did not occur during the Postgraduate Certificate in Teaching and Learning in Higher Education program. The course team had set up communication possibilities, yet as students we failed to use them. I remember initially trying very hard, but after a few weeks of firing messages off into empty space, I gave up trying to communicate or undertake peer learning with my tutorial group. A knock on effect of this was that I logged into the course learner space increasingly infrequently, and ultimately missed important messages from my course tutor.

A few years later when I started the MA in Pedagogical Work in National, Trans-national and Global Contexts, my expectations for communication with my peers and peer learning were lower. I recognized the set-up with the students being asked by the course leader to present themselves, the virtual coffee room and the assignment associated discussion forums. Once again the discussion was notable by its absence. However, I had learnt from my previous course experience to be more disciplined with logging into the learning platform so that I did not miss any important messages from the course leader. Things were, however, different with both the MA in Research Ethics and the MMSc in Medical Education.

The MA in Research Ethics followed the pattern of introduction, even if for most of the students this had already occurred in person on campus, and the virtual coffee room. However, for each of the taught modules the course team had designed assessed discussion and case exercises. What was noticeable about these exercises was how during the first couple of modules, people left their contributions to the discussion until the last minute, but for the final two modules, people had begun to realize that the exercises supported the main assignment, and that a high level of participation and thought was needed to achieve a high mark in the exercises. People also began to talk about what they did not understand and questioned aspects of the case exercises that did not happen in the first two modules. As students, I felt that we learnt to trust each other and as our trust grew, we felt able to show vulnerabilities and move beyond agreeing with the literature and each other. These exercises also supported the development of philosophical discussion as well as our knowledge and abilities in research ethics. Hence, communication among peers was achieved, and driven by assessed peer learning.

In the MMSc program in Medical Education, a synchronous group discussion that included the course team was how we introduced ourselves to each other and tried out the chat function in the learning platform. We also introduced ourselves in a forum discussion list. However, the active synchronous introduction provided an element of intimacy and familiarity that the static presentations in the discussion area failed to provide. Once the course started, before and after the campus meeting, the activity in the learning platform was greater than in the Postgraduate Certificate in Teaching and Learning in Higher Education program and the MA in Pedagogical Work in National, Trans-national and Global Contexts program. In comparison with the MA in Research Ethics, the MMSc included group tasks, c.f. discussion exercises.

The group tasks in the MMSc program required regular communication within tutorial groups, giving and reading peer-reviews and peer-feedback, and collaborative writing assignments using googledocs, an Internet-based writing tool provided by Google. A third semester task involved creating a radio program. All of these tasks were interaction and communication heavy. Regular, if not daily, commitment to the group was required to complete the tasks on time. As for the MA in Research Ethics communication among peers was achieved, and driven by assessed peer learning. However, the MMSc program created a commitment and support frame between the students that was not achieved by any other of the other programs. This program set high demands on communication for learning and this resulted in the creation of a community of practice focused on learning. These demands recognized that collaborative technology, e.g. a course Web-platform, does not automatically lead to collaborative learning as has been pointed out by many researchers (e.g. Biesenbach-Lucas, 2004; Bonk & King, 1998; Garrison, Anderson, & Archer, 2000; Herring, 2004; 1996; Johnson, Johnson, Stanne, & Garibaldi, 1990) and that collaboratively demanding tasks can assist in creating a collaborative learning process that makes maximal use of the synchronous and asynchronous communication possibilities afforded by the learning platform.

Support

As a distance student studying for a professional degree, you come to the program you are studying with professional experience and knowledge that fits and interacts with the program's goals and the expected learning outcomes. This section reflects upon the various forms of support the programs provided (that I recollect making use of or that I noticed).

Support in the Postgraduate Certificate in Teaching and Learning in Higher Education was always available via our tutor group's tutor. The tutor wrote to each of us and introduced herself, and as part of the first tutor marked assignment (TMA 00: Making online connections with colleagues and tutors – building a community for learning) we were to introduce ourselves, reflect upon our intention with studying the for the postgraduate certificate, how we learn and what our year looked like. The latter was to make both the tutor and the student aware of particular points in the year when study could be difficult and to develop a plan to still meet deadlines and find time to study. The tutor always responded to questions rapidly and informed the group if she was going to be away from her computer for more than a couple of days. Thus, support was always available. The most important act of support from my tutor came when I was allowed to resubmit a TMA. I had hastily completed it on time, but its forms and contents did not achieve the learning goals. I received feedback informing me in a very positive way what was lacking and how I should proceed to complete the TMA within the new timeframe. My tutor has picked upon the time issues I had mentioned at the onset of the course in my first tutor marked assignment (TMA00) and seen how this had affected my work with the TMA. I was thus allowed time to compete the TMA successfully, and my tutor supported me in doing this. Tutor support was always available via email and the telephone. Apart from the (unrequested) support my tutor provided that allowed me to revise a TMA, I made no explicit use of the support system provided from the postgraduate certificate, however I was always aware that academic support was readily available.

When I started the MA in Pedagogical Work in National, Trans-national and Global Contexts it was clear that there was no overarching support for the program other than the support the department leading the program offered to their other students. That is there was neither specific support for the program, nor for students studying at a distance. Much education is modular in Sweden and these modules may then be linked into degree programs. Although this MA was advertised as program, this designation meant that students on the program did not have to apply for the modules and that the University was required to teach the courses even if only one student remained on the program. Support was offered at the course level, and the same lecturer taught half of the courses. This created a program level of support by accident rather than by design. However, as little happened in the online forums, the modules in this program became a series of individual study units. I read the literature and undertook the course assignment(s) and then submitted them. Feedback given was appropriate and helpful, and the course tutors did make attempts to engage my peers and me in discussion, but this did not happen so support for learning was absent beyond the occasional direct email between the student and the tutor. I cannot comment on what support may have been given if I have missed a deadline or failed a module. Under Swedish Law, the student is permitted to retake modules, however, whether the retake would have included teaching and learning support I can only speculate upon.

The MA in Research Ethics was refreshing after the MA in Pedagogical Work in terms of information about and actual support. The course handbook and essay writing manual overviewed many things and outlined all contact procedures. Further each student was assigned a tutor; two lecturers ran the course and the class was divided between them. These lecturers were our first point of contact for support. During the teaching of the modules teaching support was sometimes led by one of the tutors and at other time by the other of the course tutors. Support was given to the online discussion forums and the conversation was often supported and led forward by the tutors. The tutors responded rapidly to email questions and returned work with useful summary grades and more detailed comments on the submitted work. Tutors were also ready to comment on a draft form of the assignments early on in each module to make sure that we were answering the question posed. This element was structured into the first module of the program to demonstrate the value of submitting the argument for comment prior to completion of the full essay. The tutors were also the first point of support for requesting an extension to an assignment deadline. The tutors were fully aware of the issues of studying online and taking a distance degree while working. Support here was balanced and appropriate. Suggestions as how best to continue and meet the deadline were combined with support on how the extension process was to be undertaken and which forms were to be sent to whom. The level of support and the information as to where to find support was excellent in this program. Of particular note is that support during the dissertation phrase of the program was also outlined in the handbook and pointed to a number of milestones for contact and support with the thesis supervisor(s). This support recognized the issue of writing a longer piece of work at a distance while working part or full-time.

Support in the MMSc program in Medical Education teaching and learning platform was immediately clear from the information about the program, the program teaching and administrative staff presented on the program's teaching and learning platform. The information created an immediate sense of security; I immediately knew who was responsible for the program, who were members of the teaching teach and what they looked like, and who to contact when in need of support. The design of the learning experience in the program also created peer support. The frequent use of peer-feedback, collaborative tasks, and discussion forums meant that community support among the learners grew rapidly and the community of practice and support involved both students peers, the teaching and administrative staff. The course tutors made regular supportive comments in the discussions and collaborative groups. They also pointed people in the right direction when confused about where to do things on the teaching and learning platform, and confirmed that things were in the correct place. These simple actions had large impact. The tutors were aware of the issues of learning online and the complexities of studying a professional degree while working full-time: Fixing study around work, meeting deadlines and most importantly keeping going. The MMSc tutors also used the telephone to talk to, to support and to help students resolve study crises when the going got tough and juggling study and work became difficult. The support recognized that studying part-time off-campus while working full-time is a complex situation, and that it is one that does not always result in teaching and learning time alignment.

Working around Work and Home Life to Meet Course Deadlines

A core challenge for the student studying for a professional degree via the Internet is aligning study time with work and home life. The ability to be flexible varies with professional assignments and the family situation. Unexpected events happen in both professional and personal life that affect the amount of time that can be committed to study. Sometimes it is necessary to adapt the desire to produce the best quality assessment as possible to one that achieves a pass grade. To consider how professional and personal life impact upon how high one can aim with an assignment I will again discuss my four experiences in turn and place them in the context of my professional and personal life of the time I was studying each of the professional degrees.

When beginning to study for the Postgraduate Certificate in Teaching and Learning in Higher Education I had just started to look for a house to buy. I then moved into the house along with my partner between the second and third Tutor Marked Assignments (TMAs) and my partner completed and defended her PhD. Hence, there were many changes in my personal life during the time I was studying for this award. At work, my situation changed little over the year of study; naturally some periods involved more intense work than others. However, I do not remember anything or any period at work as being unusually demanding. At this point in time I had no children, small or large, to compete for my time. This allowed for me to plan my periods of study—not that I always followed my planning.

Twice during the course my planning fell apart. Once during the period building up to my partner's PhD examination, and once at the end of the course as the work increased. During the first period I cut corners and attempted to pass the TMA, when as better option would have been to discuss things with my tutor and discuss an extension (something I got by default when she asked for a revision of my submitted TMA). The second time was when putting together my portfolio and examinable component. I thought long without starting the examinable component. This resulted in working lots over a short period. On top of this I had to produce folders containing my portfolio. I remember spending a long night in the office printed and organizing the files of my work so that I could get them in the post to reach the Open University on time. Over-estimating my capacity and time-management skills impacted negatively on the quality of my work, both for the course and within my job. The final deadline was meet and the adrenaline kick felt good, but this euphoria was short-lived, and did not make up for not completing the task as well as I could have if I had planned more effectively or if the support from the University had been greater to assist in the structuring of the final stages of the postgraduate certificate.

I enrolled in the MA program in Pedagogical Work in National, Trans-national and Global Contexts a year after the birth of my first child. I failed to find the time to complete a single module and re-registered the year after when I was working part-time and part-time at home on parental leave. I thought that parental leave would result in time I could use to study. This was not the case; pre-school children require, and demand, attention. I fitted my studies for this module into the time when my child slept for an hour during the day and at night. Perhaps, luckily, there was no requirement to take part in the on-line forums discussions, and given that my peers were also very busy, the discussion here was sporadic from the onset and fizzled as the program progressed. With time at a premium, I focused on writing the course papers and getting them finished on time rather than on learning and making maximum use of the teaching support available. My planning for completing assignments was better than for the post-graduate certificate in teaching and learning, yet by doing this my learning become instrumental and my reading directed towards the assignments alone.

I started to read the MA in Research Ethics because the importance of research ethics was increasing in my work context. As this degree was directly linked to work, I felt able to use work time to read and complete the assignments. However, as my workload was not reduced and the expectations on performance remained unadjusted, I had to study and complete the assignments out of work and at home as well. When I was studying for this MA my family had grown to include two pre-school children, with all the associated activities such as dropping and picking up the children from pre-school, entertaining and playing with them after pre-school and at the weekends, and getting up to comfort them when they wake up at night.

Getting up at night coupled with the children waking up early had an impact upon my ability to concentrate and to have the energy to study in the evenings—it was always easier to relax on the sofa and watch television before going to sleep. Underestimating the energy required to be a parent of pre-school children and the gradual onset of general fatigue due to sleep loss over a longer period of time, restricted my ability study and think. This fatigue also meant that office work took longer, and therefore studying in the office often meant bringing work home.

The result of the factors impacting upon fixing study around work and home life, resulted once again is less active participation of group exercises and discussion online. For the MA, these exercises and discussion were constructively aligned to support the summative assignments of each module, and also formed a minor element of each module's final grade. Participating at the minimum level, impacted upon my learning, my reflection, and my ability to produce high quality assignments. In two modules I requested submission extensions as I found it was impossible to juggle work, home and study. The inability to complete the assignments on time was also due to a knock-on effect of minimal participation in the online learning activities. Fitting around work and home life was complicated by fatigue resulted in planning that supported instrumental participation in online activities, but due to the immediate relevance of the degree instrumental assignment writing was not always possible, and planning failed. The time to finish assignments was longer than permitted without an approved extension. Once behind, I never caught up—work and home life did not afford this. After one submission was late, all the following ones were submitted late. The relevance of the degree to my professional situation inspired me to try and find time to study, learn and not be totally instrumental. However, the home and work context restricted my ability to be as committed to my intentions as I would have liked.

I enrolled on the MMSc in Medical Education program during the time I was on part-time parental leave with my second child. I failed to remember how little time parental leave left for study. Once I started study on this professional degree and realized what I had forgotten (repressed), I believed, incorrectly, that the demands of parenting reduce once the pre-school child starts pre-school. In fact, the demands of work are added to those of parenting. The MMSc demanded peer learning. This required micro-level planning each week, rather than macro-level planning for the course. This both increased and decreased completion on time, and level of stress. The idea that someone was relying on me to complete something, comment on something, discuss something etc. created a motivation to complete as I do not like letting other students suffer due to my inability to complete. When I failed to complete on time, it was difficult to accept this in same way I could accept it for the other professional degree courses when no one else was reliant upon my work. This feeling was guilt did not motivate me, but rather made me wary of continuing. This wariness ultimately resulted in my withdrawing from the program at the start of the second year when it was required that the students produce a radio program in their learning groups. I was wary of committing to something that I was not sure I had the time to commit to, and which would be difficult to fix around work and home life to contribute appropriately to this group assignment. I was wary of becoming the student who slid through the assignment by doing less than necessary.

In sum, it is clear that placing family first, work second, and study third makes juggling time to permit the fitting of study around family and work a difficult task. Aligning these three demands is difficult and impossible to do perfectly. Adaption at home and at work is a prerequisite for successful completion of the professional degree via the Internet. Adaption requires support if is to allow the student to complete a professional degree via the Internet over many years.

Keeping Going

Keeping going requires more than adaption at home and at work. In this section, rather than considering how I kept going professional degree by professional degree as I have in previous sections, I will provide, based on my experience, 10 tips to help the student reading the professional degree via the Internet to keep going, and three tips of things to consider before enrolling. These tips also point to aspects that the lecturer designing the professional degree delivered via the Internet needs to consider.

1. **Computer Skills:** It is important that the students can use word processing programs, can navigate the course learning platform, can remotely use the library to access journals and e-books, and can install computer programs, such as Skype. It is also important the course introduces computer skills that are specific to the course to allow all to take part in the learning. Some students are overwhelmed by the computer skills demanded and that they drop out at an early stage. It is very easy to forget that the speed of the university network is not the one most students will be using. Similarly it is important for the student to consider installing a high-speed Internet connection at home before enrolling to study a professional degree via the Internet.

2. **Literacy Skills:** It is important that the students have the literacy skills necessary to understand written messages and instructions, are able to/develop the ability to critically respond to information and tasks, and are able to express their thoughts, ideas, feelings around assignments using discussion forums. If these skills are not present, the designer of the professional degree needs to have designed in support for their development.

3. **Peer Skills:** It is likely that within the student body, each student has different skills and knowledge. As a student it is important to be supporting of others, and not be afraid to ask others when help is needed to complete a task. For example, how to install a computer program, or access the library.

4. **Create a Social Network with your Peers:** A student's peers are those who best understand what is happening in the course, what the current learning is about, what the current assignments are asking, and what is expected. Further, peers reading professional degrees via the Internet are also fixing their study around home and work, and recognize the issues and problems and often experience the same or similar stresses and demotivators. Being able to discuss the things blocking study can help alleviate stress, help the student focus on the core aspects of the program, discuss strategies for negotiating course content and strategies for catching up.

5. **Time Management Skills:** It is important that the student realizes the amount of study time required for the professional degree, how it is distributed over the semester, the degree of flexibility, or otherwise, the degree program permits, and can make use of time management apps and computer tools to support the planning of their studies.

6. **Be Prepared for Feedback:** Make the most of all feedback. Your peers and your tutors want to help even if their feedback questions your work. Feedback, however, has no purpose if you can neither interpret it nor develop your understanding, skills, and assignment based on feedback. Be prepared for feedback, understand its role in learning, and do not solely aim for instrumental assignments and expect feedback that is neither positive nor negative. Be prepared for feedback and use it constructively for the future.

7.   **Leadership Skills:** Group assignments form elements of many professional degrees. To successfully complete these assignments requires at least one member of the group who has leadership skills and who can lead the group in the discussion that is necessary to set up time-lines, divide the task up between the group members and align contributions into the whole.

8.   **Support from Employer:** A professional degree has relevance for the working situation. Study requires time and support from an employer can result, for example, in study time at work, and greater flexibility in working conditions to assist in alignment of study and work. Further an employer can provide emotional support by asking how things are progressing, whether what has been learnt has application in the working context, and checking whether combining study with work is functioning or not.

9.   **Support from Family:** All students need distraction from study, and all students need family to understand that extra space and disjuncture from the family is needed during the time the student is studying the professional degree. Family support is also important when study is not going well and when feedback is received that is difficult to deal with, and when study is going well and highly positive feedback is received.

10.   **Support from Friends:** Friends who you can talk to about your studies, your successes, your failures, and the difficulties of fixing study around work and home life are of central important. Friends can form a social network that provides not only support, but also a distraction that can provide energy to continue. Friends who are studying, or who have studied, the same or other degree programs are able to understand the complex social issues that come with studying professional degrees via the Internet, and this support can assist the completion of the degree. Someone to talk to can turn thoughts of dropping out into thoughts that the degree may still be possible to complete.

Three things to consider prior to enrolling in a professional degree via the Internet are:

1.   **Benefits:** What is the benefit for me? Is it professional, personal or a combination? Is it the immediate reward that motivates or it is a long-term goal that motivates? Is it the act of studying that motivates? Before applying to study it is important to understand what motivates you and whether it is the perceived benefits that motivates you and to consider whether you would continue to study if these evaporated during your time studying for the professional degree.

2.   **Consequences:** What are the consequences of committing the required amount of study time to the professional degree? Where will this time come from and what will you need to stop doing to find the time? What will the consequences

of your study be on work, family and friends? How will your social network be affected? These need to be fully and correctly considered before embarking upon a professional degree via the Internet. It is very easy to underestimate the time required, and the consequences of shifting time from something to study.

3. **Risks:** Studying involves risks may seem a odd perspective, but there is risk that the professional degree has no impact upon career development, that study can have negative consequences for family life and your social network, and the possibility of non-completion of the professional degree. Study includes risks and it is paramount that these are considered prior to starting to study. Loss of face due to non-completion or failure can be difficult. These risks and how you will react to them need to be considered prior to starting the professional degree.

CURRENT CHALLENGES, ISSUES, AND QUESTIONS OF RELEVANCE FACING PROFESSIONAL DEGREES VIA THE INTERNET

Without students there can be no professional degrees via the Internet. This chapter has from a personal narrative perspective considered studying four professional degree programs via the Internet. The personal narrative covers a 10-year period ending in 2011. The current challenges, issues, and relevance from the student's perspective can be found in the narrative of *Initial Contact, Communication, Support, Deadlines, Work*, and *Keeping Going*; that is they cut through the narratives and create a matrix. In this section I will briefly tease out the challenges, issues and questions of relevance from the student perspective.

Many, if not all, of the challenges, issues and questions of relevance are the same on-campus professional degree students encounter and experience. The student community of practice is stronger on-campus, and for the full-time student the option of giving up and returning to work is far more dramatic than for the part-time distance student who is working full-time. Rather than a loss of face to those around them, the on-line distance student can give up often without losing any face at all. People tend to be sympathetic and talk in terms of how difficult it must be to combine work with study in the evenings and at weekends. The reasons for giving up are rarely seen as failure in the same way that someone who was studying full-time. The impact of the challenges, issues and questions of relevance are, I would argue greater, for the part-time distance professional degree student that for the full-time campus student.

Challenges

The challenges the distance professional degree student faces are in most ways no different to those a full-time on campus student faces. The student is challenged to understand the material and topics they are studying. That is they are challenged to learn, reflect, develop and apply their learning in the professional context. The distance professional degree student is challenged to place their study in their practice. This impacts upon perception of the relevance of the degree for which the student is studying. From the student's perspective challenges framed in this way can support or destroy the part-time distance professional degree student.

Issues

The issues the distance professional degree student faces are in some ways different to those of the full-time campus student. One difference is that sometimes the part-time distance professional degree student experiences the impact of the issue as greater. The community of practice to support the online student is frequently weaker. Central issues for these students are time for study and aligning study around daily-unexpected demands on time. These demands can be the ill child, extra overtime demands at work, relationship problems, and work travel. Some of these do not occur for the full-time student; for example, work overtime demands and work travel. Others do occur, for example, the ill child and relationship problems. However, all issues impact upon work for the part-time distance student as well as study and the impact of any issue can therefore be far greater than for the full-time on-campus student. The complexity of the distance professional degree student's life situation is one reason why these issues can affect study more profoundly than they might the full-time campus student.

Another issue affecting all students is the fear that they are not up to the level of study demanded. Students on campus can align their perception of their performance with other students, discuss their fears and gain an impression of their peers. For online students this is a more difficult thing to do. Perceptions from two days on campus, in online discussion forums etc. can be misleading. Further, the distance student does not have not ongoing chances to align that exist for campus students. Perceived ability and chance of passing can impact upon student commitment, and interact with questions of relevance.

Relevance

The student always comes to a degree course with questions relating to the relevance of their degree program. These questions may be ameliorated by intrinsic interest and motivation for the topic of the degree. The student of the online distance professional degree is likely to have at least some degree of professional motivation for studying that is in addition to any intrinsic interest. This professional motivation is vulnerable to questions of relevance. Both challenges and issues encourage students to question why they are studying for an online professional degree. A student's professional context and interests may have been nudged her into starting to study, but to study and complete a program requires that the nudge is reinforced within the program. When issues and challenges arise, students begin to question whether what they are currently studying has relevance for their professional praxis or otherwise. In my case, my non-completion of the MA in Pedagogical Work in national, trans-national and global contexts occurred because the relevance of completing a short research paper in the area was not central to my career as a professor. The timing of the research paper was poor; I was very busy at work and at home and the effort to find time to do the research paper was insurmountable. The nudge to study the program had been met by the course element of the degree, and as there was no financial aspect the feeling of having paid for something and getting value of money was not a possible motivator. Hence, relevance vanished for me once the nudge had been fulfilled. Completion of the MA was not necessary.

The other degree program I have not completed is the Master of Medical Science in Medical Education awarded by Karolinska Institutet, Stockholm, Sweden. At the beginning of the second year of the program the time demands increased and given my work and home context, I decided not to continue my studies that year, as I would most probably let down my fellow students. The course was still relevant and interesting, but the nudge to start, study and complete the program could not overcome a reality check of time available on a regular weekly basis. Relevance is balanced by reality; a nudge and relevance cannot always keep students studying and completing a distance online professional degree program. But, lack of perceived relevance can decrease the power of the nudge and lead to non-completion. The following section will suggest ways forward for the potential professional degree student in the hunt of their idea distance professional degree program.

SOLUTIONS AND RECOMMENDATIONS

This reflective case based on my personal experiences cannot produce a generalizable solution, or solutions, to the issues, challenges and questions of relevance for the student studying professional degree program via the Internet. The case study can, however, generate set of recommendations to the person considering studying a professional degree program via the Internet. This set of recommendations aims to support the potential student assess how well the professional degree program via the Internet matches her situation.

- Review your week, and ask if can you set aside the time for study? Try it, and then consider what would make your ability to see this time aside vulnerable. What would make it impossible to set aside the required time? How likely is this to happen?
- Examine the course structure and the regularity of the commitment requires. Is this determined by the course's weekly content or can it be determined within a longer period by you? Does the course include activities in groups? How does this structure align with the time you can commit?
- Examine the assignment structure. Is the assessment based on individual assignments or does it include peer assignments? How frequently are there assignments to hand in? How does this fit in with the time you have available?
- Identify your nudge, and consider how important it is for you.
- Talk to those around you about your plans. Those around you will have an impression of whether you actually have the time to study you image you have.
- Ground your idea to begin to study a professional degree via the Internet with those it will affect.
- Work through the ten tips to help the student reading the professional degree via the Internet to keep going presented in the section Keeping going.
- Consider the benefits, consequences and risks of things to consider before enrolling presented in the section Keeping going.

This set of recommendations of things to consider prior to enrolling on a professional degree via the Internet cannot guarantee completion or perception of relevance, but it might assist a potential student select a more appropriate degree course or none at all.

REFERENCES

Bergen Communiqué. (2005). *The European higher education area – Achieving the goals.* Bergen: Bergen Communiqué.

Biesenbach-Lucas, S. (2004). Asynchronous web discussions in teacher training courses: Promoting collaboration learning - or not? *AACE Journal, 12*(2), 155–170.

Bolander Lakov, K., Silén, C., & Engqvist Boman, C. (2013). Implementation of scholarship of teaching and learning through and on-line masters program. In *Cases on Professional Distance Education Degree Programs and Practices: Successes, Challenges and Issues.* Hershey, PA: IGI Global.

Bologna Declaration. (1999). *Joint declaration of the European ministers of higher education.* Bologna: Bologna Declaration.

Bonk, C. J., & King, K. S. (1998). *Electronic collaborators: Learner-centred technologies for literacy, apprenticeship, and discourse.* Mahwah, NJ: Erlbaum Associates.

Commission of the European Communities (CEC). (2001). *Communication from the commission: Making a European area of lifelong learning a reality (COM 678, final of 21.11.01).* Luxembourg: Office for Official Publications of the European Communities.

Dehmel, A. (2006). Making a European area of lifelong learning a reality? Some reflections on the European Union's lifelong learning policies. *Comparative Education, 42*(1), 49–62. doi:10.1080/03050060500515744.

Deutschmann, M. (2013). Creating online community — Challenges and solutions. In *Cases on Professional Distance Education Degree Programs and Practices: Successes, Challenges and Issues.* Hershey, PA: IGI Global.

Garrison, D. R., Anderson, T., & Archer, W. (2000). Critical inquiry in a text-based environment: Computer conferencing in higher education. *The Internet and Higher Education, 2*(2-3), 87–105. doi:10.1016/S1096-7516(00)00016-6.

Herring, S. C. (Ed.). (1996). *Computer-mediated communication: Linguistic, social and cross-cultural perspective.* Amsterdam: John Bejamins Publishing Company.

Herring, S. C. (2004). Computer-mediated discourse analysis: An approach to researching online behavior. In Barab, S. A., Kling, R., & Gray, J. H. (Eds.), *Designing for virtual communities in the service of learning* (pp. 338–376). New York: Cambridge University Press. doi:10.1017/CBO9780511805080.016.

Higgens, D. (2011). Why reflect? Recognising the link between learning and reflection. *Reflective Practice, 12*(5), 583–584. doi:10.1080/14623943.2011.606693.

Högskoleförordning. (1993). Retrieved from http://www.notisum.se/rnp/SLS/LAG/19930100.HTM

Jakobi, A. P., & Rusconi, A. (2009). Lifelong learning in the Bologna process: European developments in higher education. *Compare: A Journal of Comparative and International Education, 39*(1), 51-65.

Johnson, D. W., Johnson, R. T., Stanne, M. B., & Garibaldi, A. (1990). Impact of group processing on achievement in cooperative groups. *The Journal of Social Psychology.* doi:10.1080/00224545.1990.9924613.

Johnson, H. (2001). The PhD student as an adult learner: Using reflective practice to find and speak in her own voice. *Reflective Practice, 2*(1), 53–63. doi:10.1080/14623940120035523.

Joyes, G., Fisher, T., Firth, R. & Coyle, D. (2013). The nature of a successful online professional doctorate. In *Cases on Professional Distance Education Degree Programs and Practices: Successes, Challenges and Issues.* Hershey, PA: IGI Global.

Knowles, M. (1990). *The adult learner: A neglected species* (4th ed.). Houston, TX: Gulf.

Kottkamp, R. (1990). Means for reflection. *Education and Urban Society, 22*(2), 82–203. doi:10.1177/0013124590022002005.

Lave, J., & Wenger, E. (1991). *Situated learning: Legitimate peripheral participation.* Cambridge, UK: Cambridge University Press. doi:10.1017/CBO9780511815355.

Lindgren, E., Sullivan, K. P. H., Zhao, H., Deutschmann, M., & Steinvall, A. (2011). Developing peer-to-peer supported reflection as a life-long learning skill: An example from the translation classroom. In Chang, M. (Ed.), *Human Development and Global Advancements through Information Communciation Technologies: New Initiatives* (pp. 188–210). Hershey, PA: IGI Global. doi:10.4018/978-1-60960-497-4.ch011.

Schön, N. D. (1988). *Educating the reflective practitioner: Toward a new design for teaching and learning in the professions.* San Francisco, CA: Jossey-Bass.

Tait, J. (2002). *H850 postgraduate certificate in teaching and learning in higher education.* Milton Keynes, UK: The Open University.

Thaler, R., & Sunstein, C. (2008). *Nudge: Improving decisions about health, wealth, and happiness.* New Haven, CT: Yale University Press.

Varnava-Marouchou, D., & Minott, M. (2013). Experiences of an online doctoral course in teacher education. In Cases on Professional Distance Education Degree Programs and Practices: Successes, Challenges and Issues. Hershey, PA: IGI Global.

Chapter 2

Experiences of an Online Doctoral Course in Teacher Education

Despina Varnava-Marouchou
European University Cyprus, Cyprus

Mark A. Minott
University College of the Cayman Islands, Cayman Islands

EXECUTIVE SUMMARY

This chapter outlines the benefits and challenges experienced by two students who had completed an online doctoral programme at a popular United Kingdom university. Benefits include accessing courses from anywhere in the world, engaging in synchronous and asynchronous communication, and the development of creative thinking and reflective skills. The most important benefit was the fact that the online programme allowed the students to fulfill the dream of achieving a doctoral degree in teacher education while maintain family and work commitments. Some challenges of online learning include feelings of isolation, balancing family commitment with study, managing time, and coping with additional workload brought on by course requirements. The conclusion was made that the online environment is an excellent way of placing students at the centre of the learning experience, allowing them to have total control of their time and the process of learning. This, however, required an alteration in their thinking and a willingness to change certain attitudes about learning.

DOI: 10.4018/978-1-4666-4486-1.ch002

INTRODUCTION AND PURPOSE

There are benefits and challenges to undertaking a distance or online university programme. These programmes allow students to conveniently complete post and undergraduate studies that meet the challenges of the new century. They help students to develop the ability to work and learn with others who are in different geographical locations, time zones and, more importantly, those with differing life and academic experiences. Riel and Fulton (2001) support this point when they state that online learning communities support and expand socio-cultural links which helps participants to grow intellectually and in understanding cultural differences. Students in online programmes sometimes find it easier to share their experiences with others than they would, in the traditional learning environment of the university classroom. Challenges of online learning include feelings of isolation, balancing family commitment with study, managing time and coping with additional workload brought on by course requirements.

The aim of this chapter is to identify and discuss these and other benefits and challenges of online learning. This is achieved via a discussion of the shared reflective experiences of two persons who successfully completed doctor of education degrees via a combination of face-to-face and online methods. The degrees were awarded by a very popular United Kingdom University. The experiences shared, illuminate areas of online learning in need of improvement and offer practical insights to those who are currently enrolled, or are thinking of enrolling in an online doctoral education course.

WHY WE CHOOSE THAT PARTICULAR UNIVERSITY AND PROGRAMME

There are four reasons why we choose a United Kingdom University and a doctoral degree programme in teacher education. Firstly, seeming inefficiencies displayed by some international universities to which Despina had applied. For example, not getting a prompt reply to emails, not being given clear ideas regarding the content of the courses they offered and a general sense of disorganization in the type of promotional material sent to perspective students. Also, having completed master's degrees from United Kingdom universities we came to trust the system of higher education there, and were confident of the fact that a UK degree was recognised and accepted in most parts of the world.

Secondly, our university of choice offered overseas students what seemed to be very reasonable fee structures, when compared with other international universities offering similar programmes. The average fee for a doctoral programme in a USA

University was approximately $20,000 per annum when converted was approximately £12,000 per annum, while the average fee for a UK doctoral degree was £2,000-£3,000 per annum. What was of particular interest was the 'new deal' for overseas students offered by our chosen university. This allowed students' annual fee to remain the same throughout the duration of their studies. This meant that the fee was not subject to inflation. This was of particular interest to Mark, who at the time was a non-European resident and therefore paid a much higher fee. He paid £3,650 per annum while a local UK or European student paid approximately £1,200 per annum.

Thirdly, and most importantly, we both wanted to become teacher educators therefore a doctoral degree in teacher education was not just ideal, but a way to fulfill a dream. We realized that a doctoral degree was the accepted prerequisite for lecturing at most University and colleges worldwide. For those already lecturing it offered some prestige and recognition, in that, your peers now see you as in command of your field of study and can make a worthwhile contribution to it. In some cases, for example the USA, a doctoral degree is necessary for being tenured and for further promotion. For us, however, the traditional face-to-face method of achieving this degree was inappropriate for two reasons: family and employment commitments. Firstly, both of us had a young family to care for. Despina had two young boys who needed special attention with their studies including attending to problems associated with young growing teenagers. Mark had a young daughter with a 'special need' and who needed his full attention. Taking time away for three to five years of face-to-face studying was not a viable option for us, given these and other family demands and the undue stress that being away would have caused our spouses and children. Secondly, we were both full time employees and needed to keep our jobs so as to contribute to the financial up keep of our families. Being fully employed meant that we had signed contractual agreements and were bound to these agreements for two to three years. Contractual violation would have disastrous financial consequences for our families as well as our future career aspiration. Thankfully the online degree prevented these negative occurrences and reduced the tension that we both felt which was brought on by our dream and desire to become qualified teacher educators and our commitment to family. There were also other aspects of our lives that a face-to-face programme of study for three to five year would have disrupted. For example, social organisations in our local communities to which we were also committed.

The fourth reason why we choose the University and the programme on offer there was that an examination of the Internet (prior to and during our period of study) revealed a limited number of universities offering a doctoral degree programme in teacher education in a purely online format or hybrid, which combined online and face-to-face teaching methods. A strictly online programme of study or a hybrid, which combines online and face-to-face methods of delivery, was important to us given the reasons we outlined in the foregoing discussion. However, we found the hybrid method attractive because we attribute the life-long friendships we have developed between us and other students to the brief face-to face encounters we had on the university campus. The face-to- face encounters also made the online dialogues more meaningful, in that, we really knew who we were dialoguing with. More is said about this later in this chapter (see Figure 1).

Figure 1. Flow chart of the structure of the online degree programme

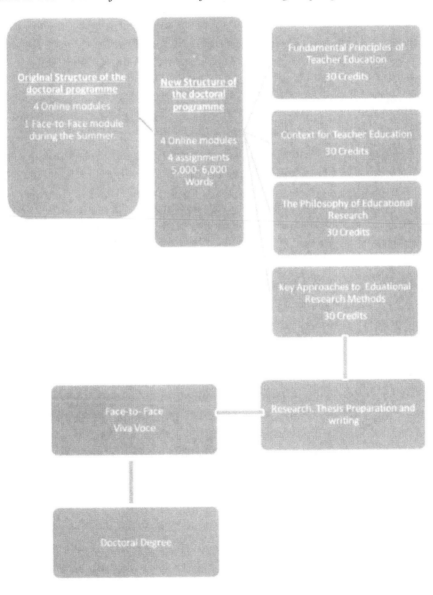

THE STRUCTURE OF THE ONLINE DOCTORAL PROGRAMME

The doctoral degree programme at our chosen university initially included face-to-face summer school components coupled with Web-based modules i.e. a hybrid approach. Later, the face-to-face summer school component was removed. The programme had also undergone another major change which was a reduction of the taught modules from five to four. The taught courses required the completion of 120 credits and were each assessed by a written assignments of 5,000- 6,000 words or equivalent. Most if not all assignment provided the opportunity for students to focus on their local context and issues that maybe occurring there, and personal or professional interests. For example, the assignment in the subject context for teacher education required the development of a teacher education framework which represents what participants consider an ideal teacher education programme. This process relied heavily on each participants reflecting on their local teacher education programme and arriving at several attributes that would contribute to creating an ideal teacher education programme. The final paper produced by each participants, also focused on issues that were of personal interest or concerns. For example, we were allowed to test the final teacher education framework produced by the cohort, in our own context. Based on the implementation of the framework we then identify and review research areas which were of concern to us and within our own local teacher education programme. Another example was the course "key approaches to educational research". The final assignment and the topic chosen for the assignment was our own choosing and based on personal or professional interest. For Mark, his assignment focussed on identifying the relationship between the ethos of schools and the part it played in students in schools choosing certain careers. Despina's assignment focussed on learning styles of students and how this affects their studies and learning outcomes.

Table 1 displays a list of the taught courses and areas covered.

Students' support during the taught stage of the degree involved academic tutorials. We were entitled to a minimum of one tutorial of approximately 30 minutes outside of the stated taught hours of the course for each module assignment. Tutors were to provide appropriate support and guidance in the preparation, process and writing-up stage of each assignment, but were not required to approve detailed drafts of assignments. After the marking of the assignment, we were provided the opportunity to contact the tutor concerned to obtain fuller feedback on the merits of the work we produced. Students whose work puts them at risk of failing were asked to discuss their work with the course leader (Advance Studies Handbook, 2002).

Upon successful completion of the taught stage we were required to submit a thesis on an original application of knowledge on some aspect of teacher education. We were also required to be available for a face-to-face viva voce examination on

Table 1. EdD courses and areas of focus

Fundamental principles of teacher education   • Theory: critical analysis of different models of teacher education   • Research: teacher thinking; teacher knowledge; teacher competences; professionalism and teacher development   • Reflection: on the interface of policy and practice; school-based and institution-based training; teacher training and teacher education; development and competence; policy and change agents
Context for teacher education   • National setting: to reflect participants' home system(s) of teacher education; contrasting national systems   • Curricular specialism: to reflect participants' own particular curriculum interest/s   Research: models of teacher education; subject pedagogy; learning to teach; pre-service and ins-service programmes
Philosophy of educational research   • Positivism in educational research - the role and scope of experience, the debate between explanation and understanding   • Hermeneutic/Interpretive approaches in educational research - the development of individual and social forms of meaning   • Foundationalism and anti-foundationalism in educational research - pragmatism, rationalism and research as a social practice   • Critical forms of educational research - the critiques posited by feminist and critical ethnographies of the possibilities and problems of insider-outsider research.
Key approaches to educational research   • This module will be based on a series of case studies of recent research carried out within the School of Education, and where appropriate from other Schools and Departments within the University. These case studies will be illustrative of the research strategies covered in the module Philosophy of educational research: positivism, interpretivism, and criticalist.   • These case studies will give students the opportunity to consider how to define a research focus, create a series of research question, design an appropriate methodology, and to apply research methods critically and appropriately.   • The case studies will also provide the opportunity to examine different forms of analysis including statistical modeling, thematic analysis and case study. The different ethical issues presented by each research strategy, including issues of consent, confidentiality and reporting will also be explored.

the thesis. The thesis supervision process and communication with our supervisors occurred mainly via email and telephone. We normally get written feedback from our supervisors within two weeks of submitting a daft thesis chapter for their evaluation. Before the viva voce examination, we met with our supervisors for a bit of coaching which involve us answering questioning about the content of our thesis. Overall, supervisors at the university were very supportive and pastoral. The following quotations taken from our thesis and that of another participant who had also completed the course of study reflect this fact.

Sincere gratitude and thanks to my supervisors, Dr. Roger Firth and Mr. Tony Fisher, also known to me as Dr. 'R' and Mr. 'T'. Gentlemen, I appreciate your regular and forthright comments about the study and your encouragement and support during my personal difficulties (Minott, 2006).

Starting with my supervisors I would like to thank Roger Firth and Tony Fisher for their valuable advice and continuous support and encouragement. I have learned much from our lengthy telephone conversations. You have shown me what it really means to carry out research and I feel lucky to have had you as supervisors (Marouchou, 2007).

I am deeply grateful to my supervisor, Dr. Daley who has made my writing of the doctoral thesis a most intellectually rewarding and emotionally pleasant experience. Dr Daley has continuously helped me to strive for excellence with her stimulating and thought-provoking questions on my work. She was always there when I needed concrete advice, and at the same time she offered me space so I could explore my own ideas. Her attention to my progress ensured that I stayed disciplined, while her generous encouragement provided me with the sustained enthusiasm which I needed (Sze, 2006).

The programme was offered on a part-time basis over four years. Each module was convened by a small core of providers with an extensive range of experience in teacher education. Sessions within each module were made up of a variety of styles including seminars, discussions and workshops activities using 'virtual' strategies. Preparatory reading and study were also required. Dates for the submission of assignments were communicated to us at the start of each module and we were expected to spend much of our time planning and carrying out systemic inquiries and preparing for our assignments and theses. Personal tutors, who offer both intellectual and moral support, were also assigned to us. Feedback on assignments took the form of written comments.

BENEFITS OF THE ONLINE DOCTORAL PROGRAMME

While doing the EdD course we experienced and learned a great deal. Learning online opened new opportunities for us and provided new and exciting skills and experiences. In this section we discuss how we benefitted from online learning.

Programme Flexibility and Immigration Issues

The flexibility of our online programme, facilitated by the university's online learning management system, made it feasible for us to pursue a doctoral degree. The use of the learning management system allowed us to register for courses and study literally from any place in the world. In other words, we attended courses without being physically present at the university and away from our families and work commitments. This is indeed an example of the university accommodating students' varied needs (McInnis, James and Hartley, 2000a). The flexibility of the programme (in terms of being able to access the course content and assignments at any time and from any part of the world) was especially beneficial to us in matters of family commitments. The following is an example of a typical day illustrated by Despina. It reveals the fact that online programmes making use of learning management systems facilitate the fulfillment of both family commitments and course requirements.

For me, as a university lecturer, my usual working day started at 8:00 am and finished around 2:00pm. I then go home to take care of my family of two boys and a husband. I found, for me, that the best time to sit at my computer was after 7:00 pm when all the household chores were completed. Luckily for me, I can concentrate through the usual noise of the television, radio and other household clutters. I usually work until 1 or 2 o'clock in the morning.

I found that I work at my computer a few hours every night of the week. I learned early, how to set limits and set my own time table. Taken that I have completed a number of hours per month I was happy. After a time, I had managed to get rid of the feeling that I had to complete everything by a certain date, and did it when I had the time. I however made sure, I made the time (Despina).

The ability to fit study in with busy work and family demands also gave us a sense of control because, we were able to choose the period of the day to work in which we functioned best. For some people, morning times are best for working and others work best during the evenings. In essence, this method fits all types of learners.

University brochures promoting online educational programmes also use the idea of 'flexibility' to attract potential students. While this was not a point pushed exhaustively by promoters of our doctoral programme, a reading of accompanying brochures and online advertisements led us to recognize that this concept was imbedded. This was so, for, while timelines were set for the completion and submission of work online and for the opening and closing of discussion forum, the fact that assigned tasks were online and could be accessed at any time and from any part of the world, offered us a degree of flexibility in terms of choices of where, when and what time of day or night we could access and complete assigned tasks.

Another benefit of doing an online programme of study is the fact that this method made it possible for overseas students to attend courses without having to apply for a visa and without having to deal with issues associated with physical re-location (Irving, 1999). This is significant for a check of our programme's students list, showed countries of origin as Barbados, Saint Lucia, Cayman Islands, Jamaica, Cyprus, Greece, Ireland, Hong Kong and China. Students from most Caribbean countries would require a United Kingdom visa to enter and study there.

As a non-European resident at the time of the course, this was truly a benefit. For it meant that I did not have to stand in front of an immigration officer at the port of entry and answer what seems to be embarrassing, bordering on inappropriate questions such as, how much money do you have? Let me see the money? How long are you planning to stay in this country? Why are you here? And over all, the feelings of being treated like a common criminal (Mark)

Interactivity

The use of online learning management systems such as ANGEL or WebCT has moved online interaction between lecturers and students away from merely sending and receiving emails. These systems now allow synchronous and asynchronous communication and exchange of ideas to occur orally, visually and in written forms. 'Chat rooms' built in these systems for example, is one feature which facilitates these happenings. As doctoral students on the online programme we found another benefit of using WebCT was its ability to facilitate interaction.

All doctoral programmes (online or face-to-face) require students to take an active part in the learning process by sharing ideas and responding to comments of other students, lecturers and the literature studied. Our course required that we also took an active part in the learning process by regularly posting our ideas and responding to submissions made by fellow students and tutors and reflecting on discussion threads which had developed. Here is an example of this from a WebCT online discussion which took place between Saturday November 15, 2003 and Friday November 28, 2003. The excerpt shown in Box 1 is a section of this discussion. Where necessary, pseudonyms are used to assure anonymity.

Intellectually, these kinds of discussions involve formulating ideas, considering responses and reflecting on ideas presented. These are necessary skills and activities for doctoral students who are required to generate and assess the responses of oth-

Box 1.

Message no. 413
Posted by Greg Jelly (l) (XXD912) on Saturday, November 15, 2003 16:31
Subject: Welcome: Please post questions here by Nov 20th

Please post questions you wish to ask Tommy Finish and Greg Jelly after you have discussed the eLectures in your Portal groups. Tommy and Greg will have started a thread in which you can do this. Tommy will be live on Monday 24th and Tuesday 25th. Greg will be live Wednesday 26th and Thursday 27th. There is another discussion thread here in which you can raise questions/issues about the Andrea Haskin eLecture.

Message no. 414
Posted by Tommy Finish (XXD912) on Saturday, November 15, 2003 19:13
Subject: Questions for Tommy Finish
Hello everyone

After you have had a look at the eLecture clips and had a chance to think about them and discuss them, please post the questions you want to ask. Post them as part of the thread begun by this message. I won't answer them straight away, but will wait for them to accumulate and answer them on Monday 24th and Tuesday 25th November, *as* notified in Greg's introductory message. I'm looking forward to reading your questions, and doing my best to answer them!

Kind regards to you all
Tommy

Message no. 431
Posted by: Despina Varnava-Marouchou (texdv) Monday, November 24, 2003 08:19

1 Can one use evaluations instead of research for a PhD thesis?

2 What kind of research methods did you actually apply for the 'evaluations' and are they different from methods?

Despina

Message no. 440[Branch from no. 432]
Posted by Mark Anthony Minott (texmaml) Wednesday, November 26, 2003 17:16
Subject: Response to question 4 & 5

Mr. Finish, here are my thoughts on your philosophical stance

Question 4
From the data at my disposal, I gather that you value fairness, in the sense that your philosophical stance is to record the findings of research data as accurately as is possible, saying clearly what you think the data mean even in the face of external pressures whether real or imagined. You are amicable to the use of both quantitative and qualitative data.
Question 5
Your teaching and life experiences would be major factors contributing to you assuming the philosophical stance outlined in question 4.

Looking forward to hearing from you
Cheers Mark

Message no. 450[Branch from no. 440]
Posted by Tommy Finish (teztf) on Thursday, November 27, 2003 17:22
Subject: Re: Response to question 4 & 5

Mark I could not have put it better - you know me better than I know myself!

Cheers, Tommy

---

ers but more importantly, these skills are required to facilitate a successful academic career (Phillips and Pugh 2000). The online learning management system enabled us to develop these skills.

The university's online learning management system also facilitated interaction by archiving online discussions. These discussions could then be accessed at any time and from anywhere in the world and used to aid our reflection and thoughts, especially if we were asked to comment on the overall discussion occurring in a session.

Accessing the thoughts of others via their writings as well as recapturing the hidden essence by reading between the lines was made easier via the online learning management system. This occurrence facilitated rich thoughtful submissions and interaction. Further, to benefit from learning opportunities available via online interactions we had to develop the ability to engage in dialogues that were questioning and do so in a manner that would not offend others. Thankfully, these skills were developed and mastered whilst on the course. Most specifically creative and critical thinking as well as reflection skills were essential tools in the process of learning.

Developing Creative Thinking and Reflection Skills

The online setting supported a student-centred approach to learning placing the student as an active participant in the process of learning. This meant that students learned according to their individual learning styles and preferred methods of working. As such, the students on the course were required to develop and exercise their thinking and reflection skills. Creative thinking involves students in analysing and exploring ideas and communicating results. It also requires students to research their particular topic thoroughly, formulate their thoughts and present their findings for peer comment and review. They must also have the skills to articulate their findings and solutions clearly and accept that they are open to challenge (Stansfield et al, 2004). In this way students go through a cognitive process whereby thoughts and ideas are reflected upon, refined, and adapted to take account of other views and perspectives of the original idea of the discussion (Stansfield et al, 2004). Thus, students on the EdD course had to adapt and make changes in the way they communicated ideas in an academic environment.

The Development and Transferability of Technical and Other Skills

The age of students on the online programme meant that many had left formal university education ten or fifteen years ago and, unlike today's university students, entered the online programme with either little or no previous computer experiences or entered as 'self-taught' computer users. One benefit we enjoyed was that through our continued engagement with the university's online learning management system and the computer, we mastered certain features of the programme and learnt new skills that we would not have learnt otherwise. Some skills and information 'caught' while engaging with the online learning management system and were transferable to other setting included: password setting and resetting, accessing online material manipulating various sections of the programme, uploading and downloading files and creating links from the online learning management system to Internet files and vice-versa.

The transferability of these skills to other settings is particularly true for one of us, who, with the technical skills 'caught' was able to transfer those skills knowledge to a similar programme which was installed at his place of employment. Mark wrote the following on his application for a fellowship with a noted Australian academic organisation. The excerpt was written as a response to the question of how he supports students' learning at his current place of employment. This quotation reflects the fact that he was able to transfer the skills learnt via the programme of study.

I was introduced to virtual learning environment during my doctoral studies at my University, particularly 'WebCT'. My present place of employment makes use of the learning management system "ANGEL". I use this system as an integral aspect of my teaching. For example, I set up various student discussion groups relevant to the subject I am teaching, set 'drop-boxes for the receipt of assignments, and set up online dimensions to my courses. This system supports student learning in that it is flexible and convenient, especially for busy adults. Students can logon at convenient times, engaged with lessons and submit assignments. This convenience and flexibility works well for adults, especially those with family and other job-related responsibilities (Mark).

We also developed the skill of interacting with others exclusively through text on the computer screen and to utilize vast amounts of information in various electronic formats; emails, e-forum, Internet resources, chat rooms, blogs etc. At the beginning of the programme we often printed material such as emails, texts, blogs and Web pages in order to read them. This took time and money. However, through time and effort we learnt to read, take notes and respond to others using only electronic formats on the computer. Nevertheless, some students still prefer and continue to use paper as a medium of obtaining and reading information, making notes, and highlighting important information.

Content Layout

The physical layout of the course content aided learning and in this sense it was beneficial. The course content was set up around a menu system where the course modules were uploaded. Each module was divided into sections in accordance with its hierarchical position and further subdivided into subsections. Via this layout, the course materials were extremely accessible. This meant that all the materials had the same browsing structure which allowed us to confidently browse through the course materials without getting lost or confused. There were also clearly written instructions regarding what activities were to be done at what time, where, how, and for what length of time. The following is an example of the format for a typical online lesson outline.

Introduction to Critical Thinking: Task Resources Process Evaluation Conclusion

Research degree study requires you to engage in critical thinking. This needs to be evidenced in the ways you engage with all the tasks and the ways you learn from them. This section of the induction tutorials provides you with an insight into what it means to be a critical thinker and at the same time describe the rationale behind the skills framework you will be using throughout the course to support you in developing this approach to thinking. Critical thinking will be contextualised in this section in a consideration of the literature review process, but it applies to all tasks within this research degree course.

The Task

The intention here is for you to begin to engage with the ways a consideration of critical thinking skills will enhance your approach to study at this level and prepare you for your period of research. You will be introduced to the key concepts in critical thinking as well as a critical skills framework, which you will use throughout the course and you will carry out a critical thinking exercise based around the literature review process.

Resources

You will need to refer to the pre-module reading materials and some Web-based resources (see Table 2 for the process).

Evaluation

As an outcome of this task should be that you have an understanding of the generic skills associated with work at this level and the rationale behind the generic skills grid used on the course. It is hoped that you will now recognise how you can systematically use the grid to support you in the process of critical reflection.

Table 2. The process

Task	What to do
	Read 'What is critical thinking' and 'Generic skills frameworks 'in this section.
	• Consider what it means to carry out a literature review from a critical thinking perspective. You might try to ensure you understand fully what carrying out a literature review might mean. *When you find a useful resource relating to this task then share this with everyone on the bulletin board.* • Look at the generic skills grid and list ones that are involved in this process, in particular which ones involve critical thinking. If you email your list to Kwame, then you will receive our list and thoughts on this task. • Reflect upon the approach you have taken in developing a full understanding of what it is to carry out a literature review and perhaps a more complete review of the literature you may have done as part of your studies. Identify from the generic skills grid the ones that you would have achieved and the ones you might target for future achievement in relation to any reading you do related to the module.

Conclusion

It is hoped that you will have found this exercise useful in terms of identifying the 'behaviours' associated with work at this level. Your studies are an opportunity to develop and refine your critical thinking, which is a key characteristic of work at advanced level.

Each lesson had the following headings: introduction, tasks, resources, the process, evaluation and conclusion. The introduction section outlines the aim and generally reasons for the lesson. The task section broadly outlines what is to be done the section entitled resource may refer to the reading list, the use of various Internet-based resources, message board, follow-up reading etc. The section entitled process is a step by step account of that is to be done. The evaluation section list what should have been accomplished by participants e.g. the development of an extended understanding of the issues undertaken in the lesson and being about to critically think about various articles and comment on their usefulness. The conclusion consolidates information and sometime act as an introduction to the next lesson.

The kinds of activities on the site and the use of the computer were also beneficial in that they facilitated different learning styles (Tomlinson, 1999). Participants who were kinetic, visual or auditory learners were accommodated. This was so, because video and audio clips and the need to practically manipulate the various features were required and encouraged via the programme.

CHALLENGES OF THE ONLINE DOCTORAL PROGRAMME

While in the foregoing discussion we highlighted some general challenges which forced us to do an online degree such as family and employment commitments and issues with immigration, in this section, we discuss challenges we encountered that are specific to the actual doctoral programme.

Coping with Additional Workload

While we did highlight the fact that one benefit of pursing an online course is that we could study and attend to family and other commitments simultaneously, this was also a major challenge not only for us, but for most members of our group who also had families to support thus had to remain in full-time employment for the duration of the course. Pursuing the course meant that we had to cope with additional workload which includes assignment preparations, various online presentations and readings and collaborative exercises. We conclude that our maturation, perseverance and commitment to completing the course contributed to us overcoming the challenge of additional workload. Long, Tricker, Rangecroft, and Gilroy (1999), support this idea, for they point out that the target population for many online programmes is older students who are highly motivated to work alone and persist in meeting their goals by combining education, work and family commitments.

Being Sensitive to Cultural Background, Characteristics, and Attitudes

Online students have varied cultural backgrounds, characteristics, and attitudes. In our programme there were students from many countries as indicated in the foregoing discussion. It is plausible, therefore, to conclude that students on the doctoral course differed significantly from the regular student population of a traditional face-to-face programme. DiBiase (2000) argues that in fact, this is the key distinction between distance learning and traditional on-campus programmes.

Working with students from different cultural backgrounds was challenging, especially in collaborative exercises where there was the need to be sensitive to cultural differences, characteristics and attitudes. Working with diversity also required the need to address issues in culturally sensitive ways and to be aware of the tone in which ones ideas are written.

I recall the time that Israel bombarded a neighbouring country and we had a student on the course from the country experiencing bombardment. While I was personally and secretively sympathetic to Israel's cause, I had to be sensitive to my fellow student's predicament. Therefore, I focussed written and oral communications with him on his family's well being and how they were doing, while avoiding the political/religious aspect of the events (Mark).

Additionally, not all participants spoke English as a first language, so care had to be taken in the process and tone of 'correcting' English. Indeed, online learning is chastised for its inability to clearly make known the characteristics of students in distance education courses (Wang & Newlin, 2000).

Changes to Longstanding Ways of Operating

A common concern amongst students on the online programmes was that, in order to participate meaningfully they had to first feel comfortable with the technology in use. One of the prerequisites therefore of working online was the fact that we had to be at ease with the learning management system and the software/hardware in use. While we did indicate in the foregoing discussion that we and others developed technologically, this was not without its challenges. For many, pursuing the online programme brought tremendous and sometimes difficult changes. For example, there was the need to shift from the traditional methods of studying; based mainly on writing or making paper copies, to communicating directly online using a variety of methods such as word processing, emails, chat rooms, discussion boards and sending various types of attachments. While we both agree that the use of emails, Internet and the online learning management system had opened up a new arena of network connectivity (of which some students had been unaware until they started the course) at times their use was difficult, frustrating and required effort, perseverance, commitment and trial and error.

Difficulty of Writing for Understanding and Dealing with Large Quantities of Information

To participate effectively in the online programme required that we engaged in certain intellectual activities such as; being able to formulate written constructive views, contribute to the discussion and message board, post ideas, respond to other students and generally keep up with the numerous and constant online conversations (Hara et al., 2000). However, a common concern for most of us was how to have online contributions understood in the way they were intended. Being new to this type of learning, the underlined uncertainty therefore, of what to say, how to say it, and how to communicate with peers and tutors was a common concern. In the absence of facial cue and signals it was important for us to be able to illustrate 'thinking in writing' and be understood online. We often needed to explain our comments by providing supporting evidence of how we arrived as certain conclusions. It was therefore important for us to articulate our opinions clearly and accept the fact that our views were open to challenge (Stansfield, McLellan, & Connolly, 2004).

Another challenge was the necessity to keep track of all the ongoing discussions. This very often left us with a feeling of having to make sense of an enormous amount of information (Klemm, 1998). Kenny (2002) found that students expressed difficulty following threads in online discussions, and this often decreased their overall involvement in this aspect of online learning.

Managing Time and Other Commitments

The motivation to complete an online course must be intrinsic and strong. This is so because the course demands a high degree of student control and involvement. It demands that students take full responsibility for completing and, be self-accountable for their own learning. Therefore, we believe that being able to manage our time was essential to our successful completion of the course. This was however a challenge, for we needed to be online so as to keep up with what was happening in the programme. To achieve this required that all other commitments had to fit around the programme which was difficult to do at first, for it required that we managed our already restricted time. However, over time, and as we got to know the programme's software and how it worked, managing time became less of an issue. Nevertheless, to aid time management, some practical skills in organising our daily schedule to allow sufficient study time and time for family and work were developed. The development of practical skills in time management is commonly perceived as the major determinants of student success when pursuing an online programme of study. For us, this included thinking about, and planning our days or even weeks. This planning included time to read postings on the e-forum board, which took a long time and, having to respond to each thread took even longer. We also had to plan time to read, access, and download the course information and to keep abreast of the course requirements.

The Challenge of Working Alone

Interaction between students and students and tutors and students is an important component in the educational experience of any university learning. This is normally facilitated either through direct face-to-face contact or electronic means (Phipps, 2000). Traditionally, university learning and teaching have been considered campus-bound, taking place in lecture classrooms where tutors and students have many opportunities to be in close proximity, whether in the classroom or outside the classroom. Students' experiences in the traditional classroom greatly value face-to-face conversations with their tutors or other students. In such a setting, they learn to rely on and interpret the visual and verbal signals of each other. In online courses, students do not see each other or their tutors unless they use a video-link. Video-links do not always make interpreting facial expressions and visual cues effortless. While cameras have helped in fulfilling the need to see another's face, technology is yet to fulfill that very human instinct which is the need for proximity. Besser (1996) found that students pursing online courses with no video support and the absence of physical cues seem to be prone to confusion and anxiety which resulted in increase stress and isolation. One reason for this involves the fact that people often can effectively resolve ambiguities in face-to-face conversations by providing immediate feedback. Nevertheless, when the primary way of communication is limited to written text then resolving ambiguities or misunderstandings may be more difficult.

We are aware that there are arguments for and against the need for face-to-face meeting for learning to take place and even the need for proximity in an online programme. Feenberg (1998) and Harisim et al. (1995) arguing strongly in favour of online courses, specify that the lack of face-to-face interactions makes no difference to achieving successful learning. They also state that it is possible for the distance education environments to provide approaches whereby students' learning preference can be accommodated. For example, students who are introverts; the written discussions offers them time to think and reflect before posting their thoughts, for extroverts; viewing different perspectives otherwise unavailable, improves their learning experiences. Judging from our experience, we agree with Feenberg (1998) and Harisim et al. (1995), for we found that our online course accommodated our particular way of learning.

Technical Problems and Other Challenges

The overall reliance on the computer to complete the course and often with little or no technical support when things go wrong, have often left many students frustrated. This was a serious problem particularly for those with little or no computer experience or training. Additionally, the fact that the tutors, students and support staff are separated by both space and time make synchronous interactions very challenging. There is also the challenge of ensuring that one has access to a computer at home or at work along with sufficient support from a local Internet provider. The absence of technical staff familiar with the university's online learning management system in one's country can also be a challenge. Other technical challenges include periodic computer problems; such as network breakdowns, inability to gain access to the Internet and accessing the course material from the university. There was also trouble with downloads, absence of course guidelines for online interactions and ambiguous instructions from the learning management system.

CONCLUSION

Overall, our experiences of taking courses online have been less difficult than we thought they would be and were mostly positive although there were also negative aspects. On the positive side, we have been able to pursuit our doctoral studies which, without this medium would be near impossible. On the negative side, we missed the nonverbal cues of face-to-face encounters with tutors and other students. In fact, people we have made long-term contacts and relationships with were the ones we met on the university campus during our various face-to-face meetings. This proves that it is not possible to replace actual face-to-face meeting and communications as an important medium for facilitating life-long friendships.

Having successfully pursued and completed the doctoral degree course, we can say without a doubt, that the online environment is an excellent way of placing students at the centre of the learning experience allowing them to have total control of their time and the process of learning. From the student perspective, the online course required an alteration in thinking and a willingness to change certain attitudes about learning. We personally found online learning beneficial and challenging.

REFERENCES

Besser, H., & Bonn, M. (1996). Impact of distance independent education. *Journal of the American Society for Information Science American Society for Information Science, 47*(11), 880–883. doi:10.1002/(SICI)1097-4571(199611)47:11<880::AID-ASI14>3.0.CO;2-Z.

DiBiase, D. (2000). Is distance education a Faustian bargain? *Journal of Geography in Higher Education, 1*, 130–136. doi:10.1080/03098260085216.

Feenberg, A. (1998). *Distance learning: Promise or threat?* Retrieved December 2008 from http://wwwrohan.sdsu.edu/faculty/feenberg/TELE3.HTM

Hara, N., & Kling, R. (2000). Student distress in a web-based distance education course. *Information Communication and Society, 3*(4), 557–579. doi:10.1080/13691180010002297.

Harasim, L., Hiltz, S., Teles, L., & Turroff, M. (1995). *Learning networks: A field guide to teaching and learning online*. Cambridge, MA: MIT Press.

Irving, L. (1999). Falling through the net: Defining the digital divide. *US Department of Commerce, National Telecommunications Information Administration*. Retrieved December, 2008, from http://www.ntia.doc.gov/reports.html

Kenny, A. (2002). Online learning: Enhancing nurse education? *Journal of Advanced Nursing, 38*(2), 127–135. doi:10.1046/j.1365-2648.2002.02156.x PMID:11940125.

Klemm, W. R. (1998). *Eight ways to get students more engaged in online conferences*. Retrieved December, 2009 http://168.144.129.112/Articles/Eight%20Ways%20to%20Get%20Students%20More%20Engaged%20in%20Online%20Conferences.rtf

Long, P., Tricker, T., Rangecroft, M., & Gilroy, P. (1999). Measuring the satisfaction gap: Education in the market-place. *Total Quality Management, 10*(4/5), 772–779. doi:10.1080/0954412997794.

McInnis, C., James, R., & Hartley, R. (2000a). *Trends in the first year experience in Australian Universities*. Canberra, Australia: AGPS..

Phillips, E. M., & Pugh, D. S. (2000). *How to get a PhD A handbook for students and their supervisors* (3rd ed.). London: Open University Press.

Phipps, R., & Merisotis, J. (2000). *Quality on the line: Benchmarks for success in Internet-based distance education*. Washington, DC: The Institute for Higher Education Policy. Retrieved January 16, 2010, from http://www.ihep.org/assets/files/publications/mr/QualityOnTheLine.pdf

Riel, M., & Fulton, K. (2001). The role of technology in supporting learning communities. *Phi Delta Kappan, 82*(7), 518–523.

Sherry, L. (2000). The nature and purpose of online discourse: A brief synthesis of current research a related to the web project. *International Journal of Educational Telecommunications, 6*(1), 19–36.

Stansfield, M. H., McLellan, E., & Connolly, T. M. (2004). Enhancing student performance in online learning and traditional face-to-face class delivery. *Journal of Information Technology Education, 3*.

Tomlinson, C. A. (1999). *The differentiated classroom: Responding to the needs of all learners by association for supervision and curriculum development*. Alexandria, VA: US Government.

University of Nottingham. (2002). Advance studies handbook, B.Ed, MA/Diploma/ MRes, MPhil, PhD, EdD: Doctor of education EdD in teacher education. Nottingham, UK: University of Nottingham School of Education United Kingdom.

Wang, A., & Newlin, M. (2000). Characteristics of students who enroll and succeed in psychology web-based classes. *Journal of Educational Psychology*, *92*(1), 137–143. doi:10.1037/0022-0663.92.1.137.

Chapter 3

Plagiarism:
Catalysts and Not So Simple Solutions

Hakim Usoof
University of Colombo, Sri Lanka

Brian Hudson
Sussex University, UK

Eva Lindgren
Umeå University, Sweden

EXECUTIVE SUMMARY

Plagiarism has gained much public attention with media, corporations, and researchers leading the way. The general public's perception is that plagiarism is a "plague" spreading without control within our educational institutes. Furthermore, a social perception has been created that the Internet is the "catalyst" of modern-day plagiarism. This chapter explores the domain of plagiarism, taking into consideration some definitions of plagiarism, the recent history, the cultural context, the view of students and teachers, and the situation in Distance Education. The chapter goes on to discuss the actual catalysts of plagiarism and methods used to detect plagiarism. Finally, the chapter forwards some good practices that may help prevent and act as deterrents of plagiarism and addresses challenges faced in tackling the problem of plagiarism.

DOI: 10.4018/978-1-4666-4486-1.ch003

INTRODUCTION

Plagiarism is not a new phenomenon. Copying from other writers is probably as old as writing itself, but until the advent of mass-produced writing, it remained hidden from the public gaze (Park, 2003, pp. 473).

Integrity in general has come to become a highly prioritized issue in today's society. Scandals, unethical actions, incidents of dishonesty and cheating in world are being highly scrutinized by all sections of society as well as by the media. Institutes of Education that are considered the mould of the future leader of society are not immune from this and researchers (Hayes & Introna, 2005) as well as media (Maruca, 2004) have paid much attention to the issue of academic integrity in higher education.

With the growing focus on academic integrity, surveys have been carried out in an attempt to gauge the extent of the problem of plagiarism in academic institutions. Results have shown that academic dishonesty is abundant in our education systems. McCabe, Butterfield and Trevino (2006) report that 53 percent of Graduate Business students (GBS) and 43 percent of their Non-business peers admitted to at least one count of cheating over the past year. They further report that 23 and 33 percent of GBS admitted to test-cheating and "cut and paste" plagiarism respectively. Schab (1991) in his survey of college students in 1969, 1979 and 1989 reports that the respective percentages of students using crib sheets at a test grew from 34 to 60 to 68 percent and letting others copy their work grew from 59 to 93 to 98 percent. In this same survey the more moral questions of "sometimes it is necessary to be dishonest" increased from 34, 64 and 67 percent respectively for the years 1969, 1979 and 1989. One important observation from this study is that while there has been considerable increase in the number of students who cheat, there has also been a noticeable shift in their moral value system.

In this chapter we explore the domain of plagiarism with two main aims: 1) to create a comprehensive understanding of the phenomenon and 2) to put forward best practise guidelines that can be applied in an educational context.

Plagiarism and Digital Technology

The 'Internet Culture' has created a notion among many students that anything in the public domain is common or public knowledge (McCabe, 2001; Marshall & Garry, 2005). Increasing access to technology and the Internet has opened up an entire new sea of resources that students can use for learning. At the same time, there is much worry about how students (mis)use these resources. The main concern comes from the fact that technology and the Internet has made plagiarising as simple as "copy n paste" (McCabe, 2001). Voices of concern have, for example, been raised in relation to distance education, as this form of higher education has become more popular and depends on the Internet for distribution (Carnevale, 1999).

Furthermore, businesses such as 'paper-mills' and 'ghostwriters' have added to the negative perception of the Internet's affect on plagiarism in academic institutions. However, it is important to note that the same concepts existed prior to the popularisation of the Internet. Renard (1999) states that papers for sale used to be advertised in campus publications even during her days at university and she entitled a section in her article "No New Ideas, Just New Methods" (p. 38).

With concerns about technology aiding plagiarism, there is focus on using this very technology to find a solution to the problem of plagiarism. The most recent hype in the domain of plagiarism is "Plagiarism Detection Software". These are being advertised as the solution to the 'plague' of plagiarism. While some see this as "The Solution" (Stevenson, 2010) others see it as more of a deterrent (Savage, 2004; Carroll & Appleton, 2001; Maruca, 2004). There have been legal and ethical issues regarding these systems due to fact that they sometimes violate students' privacy and copyright (Thomas, 2008).

There are misconceptions and "unknowns" about plagiarism. In her article titled "Poll finds elite top cheats list" Shepherd (2006) quoted Jude Carroll who stated that, "This is an interesting finding because the majority of students we discipline for plagiarism are bad writers, stupid or international students. This poll shows we may not be detecting a large tranche of the culprits." Furthermore, Howard (2002) warns about hurried and short-sighted approaches to solve the issue of plagiarism in our education system. She states, "In our stampede to fight what some call a 'plague' of plagiarism, we risk becoming the enemy rather than the mentor of our students" (p. 47). With such varied and complex views about plagiarism we will now move on to definitions of plagiarism in order to understand the true heart of the phenomenon.

UNDERSTANDING THE DOMAIN OF PLAGIARISM

Attempt to Define Plagiarism

The Oxford English Dictionary (Plagiarism, n.d.) defines the noun plagiarism as:

1. The action or practice of taking someone else's work, idea, etc., and passing it off as one's own; literary theft.
2. A particular idea, piece of writing, design, etc., which has been plagiarized; an act or product of plagiary.

Literarily, these definitions seem clear, but in real life, administrators, teachers and students alike fail to understand and define what exactly plagiarism is (Price, 2002). The problem arises not from the meaning of plagiarism, but from what exactly constitutes plagiarism: a process or an occurrence.

Processes of Plagiarising

One method of defining plagiarism is by the actual process of plagiarising. Howard (1995) attempts to define plagiarism by identifying three types; cheating, non-attribution and patchwriting.

1. **Cheating:** Borrowing, purchasing, or otherwise obtaining work composed by someone else and submitting it under one's own name.
2. **Non-Attribution:** Writing one's own paper but including passages copied exactly from the work of another ... without providing (a) footnotes, endnotes, or parenthetical notes that cite the source and (b) quotation marks or block indentation ... non-attribution is sometimes the result of a student's inexperience with conventions of academic writing.
3. **Patchwriting:** Writing passages that are not copied exactly but that have nevertheless been borrowed from another source, with some changes-a practice which The Bedford Handbook for Writers calls "paraphrasing the source's language too closely" (477). However, patchwriting is not always a form of academic dishonesty. (p. 799)

Out of the three, the first two seem obvious acts of plagiarism. Whilst there is no excuse for cheating, non-attribution could be a result of intended plagiarism or the lack of knowledge of academic writing conventions. Hence, instances of plagiarism that involves non-attribution need to be investigated for intentional plagiarism or unintentional plagiarism before an appropriate action is taken.

Patchwriting is also referred to as paraphrasing. Patchwriting is a gray area and it is not always possible, nor right to accuse anyone of plagiarism in the case of patchwriting. Furthermore, patchwriting is harder to detect than the other two processes of plagiarism. In addition to the obvious cases of dishonesty, another occurrence of patchwriting could occur. Howard (1995) points out "... a form of writing that learners employ when they are unfamiliar with the words and ideas about which they are writing. In this situation, patchwriting can actually help the learner begin to understand the unfamiliar material" (p. 799). Hence, patchwritten work may be an intermediate product (a learning phase tool/product) but not the final version.

Occurrences of Plagiarism

Another attempt to define plagiarism is by categorising plagiarism into ways in which plagiarism occurs. These ways are, auto-plagiarism; when authors fail to cite themselves when presenting their previous work, self-plagiarism; when authors submit the same work for two or more assignment, substantial-plagiarism; plagiarising substantial content, incidental-plagiarism; plagiarising "bits and pieces" and unconscious-plagiarism or cryptomnesia; when a person believes himself to have had an original idea, when in fact, the idea came from the memory of an experience that he has forgotten (Carroll, 1998, as cited in Evens, 2000).

In addition to the process and occurrences of plagiarism, additional dimensions too affect the definition of plagiarism. Price (2002) states "What we think of as plagiarism shifts across historical time periods, across cultures, across workplaces, even across academic disciplines" (pp. 89-90). Therefore plagiarism is attached to a context that encompasses a historical, cultural, occupational and academic disciplinary component, thereby making it more complex and harder to pin down. Thus, the new definition of plagiarism will need to include a literary meaning, a constituent formula and an attached context.

Our attempt to define plagiarism illustrates that plagiarism is a complex issue that includes a contextual component. The perception of plagiarism depends on social value systems and relates to ways in which plagiarism is perceived by society in general and by the media.

Into the Limelight

Plagiarism has always been an issue not only in the academic world but also in media industry (e.g., Pratt, 2005), the publishing enterprise (e.g., "Harry Potter Publisher Denies Plagiarism", 2009), the corporate world (e.g., Gamet, 2006) and even politics (e.g., Zeleny, 2008; Dionne, 1987). With plagiarism being a global issue there is a trend where plagiarism is becoming a household word. There have been many cases of academic plagiarism in the media not only by students but also by teachers (e.g., Butterfield, 1991; "Plagiarism Investigation Ends at Virginia", 2002).

Further, the intense media spotlighting of plagiarism as well as the intense marketing campaign of Plagiarism Detection systems have caused, what Maruca (2004) calls, "Moral Panic". Articles like "Nip double trouble in the bud" (Swain, 2005), "The plagiarism plague" ("The Plagiarism Plague", 2003), "Student plagiarism 'on the rise'" ("Student Plagiarism", 2005) and "Plagiarism – a scourge" Rao (2008) are examples of how media and researchers contribute to this moral panic. In this context it is important that we examine the trend of how plagiarism has been a frequent topic in the news media.

Figure 1 depicts a Google News search, illustrating news frequency patters for the key words 'war' and 'plagiarism' from the year 1900 till 2010. The illustration of the keywords war shows a clear pattern with high frequencies from mid 1914 – 1920 coinciding with World War I, once again a higher frequency is observed in 1939 – 1946 coinciding with World War II, there is a small peak in the mid 1960s with the Cuban missile crisis, and in 1991, a sudden frequency peak coincides with the first Gulf war. A rapid rise in frequency is observed soon after September 11, 2001 and then the frequency peaks sharply in 2003 with the beginning of the Iraq war. When considering these patterns, there is a clear indication of how incidents at certain times get prominence in the media. Similar to the above patterns, we can observe a sudden but pronounced entry of plagiarism into the mainstream media in 1987/88 that could be attributed to the time when a US presidential candidate withdrew from the race because he had been accused of plagiarising a political speech. The frequency of plagiarism in the mainstream news marginally dips until the mid 90s, but remains in the mainstream media with incidents such as the Dr. Martin Luther King Jr. incident and the Boston University dean's incident. It is quite clear that plagiarism continued to be a prominent discussion point in the mainstream media. In 2001 and 2002, plagiarism becomes prominently featured in the media with incidents such as students being expelled and degrees of some being revoked at the University of Virginia, allegations of plagiarism against the author of Harry Potter, resignation of academic staff of universities, resignation of editors' of media organisations, plagiarism charges being levelled against prominent historians and also new found technological innovations to battle plagiarism.

Figure 1. Frequency graphs of searches on Google News from 1900 - 2010 for keywords "war" and "plagiarism"

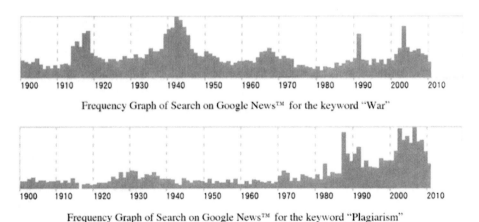

Frequency Graph of Search on Google News™ for the keyword "War"

Frequency Graph of Search on Google News™ for the keyword "Plagiarism"

Graphs generated by Google News™ Website

Previously, plagiarism required as much work as the original assignment, spending hours doing research, paraphrasing and retyping or rewriting (Evans, 2000). Today, the Internet and other technological resources have reduced plagiarism to merely a search, highlight, copy and paste, or some paraphrasing. Similarly, technology is now assisting the detection of plagiarism. More instances of detection, not only of students, but also of academics, public figures, authors and politicians, together with flashing news headlines, feed the moral panic concerning changes in our value system.

Thus, society, including the media, has strong views on plagiarism in, for example higher education. The prime actors involved in such plagiarism are the students and the teachers.

Students' Perspective

The main cause or deterrent for a student cheating or not cheating is the student's moral value system (Ashworth, Bannister & Thorne, 1997; Park, 2003; Newstead, Franklyn-Strokes & Armstead, 1996; Cummings, Maddux, Harlow & Dyas, 2002; Malinowski & Smith, 1985). Although students perceive cheating as a moral issues (Ashworth et al., 1997), they do not classify the act of plagiarising into strictly right or strictly wrong. Some cheating, even though wrong, does not harm or is unfair by others, whereas other types of cheating is unacceptable and equalled to fraud and theft (Ashworth et al., 1997; Sheard, 2002). For example, a student cheating in coursework, which does not have a major impact on his or her grades, is viewed as acceptable, while cheating in an exam with greater contribution to their grade is unacceptable. Ashworth et al. (1997) attribute this to "peer loyalty" where cheating is unfair to those who work hard to earn their grades. Ashworth et al.'s (1997) and Newstead et al.'s (1996) work contains evidence that the very "peer loyalty" that students feel, both encourages and discourages plagiarism.

Another perspective is that students see it as acceptable to cheat when they see others getting away with it (Weeks, 2001; Newstead et al., 1996; Grijalva, Nowell & Kerkvliet, 2006). Additionally, students justify cheating when courses are taught badly, deemed as unimportant (Ashworth et al., 1997; Carroll & Appleton, 2001), when there is lack of interest in topics (Rovai, 2000), when the assignments do not seem to have a meaning (Howard, 2002) or when "students believe their professor doesn't bother to read their papers or closely review their work" (Park, 2003, p. 479). Even thought the above issues do not justify cheating, it is important to note that some students use the methods of blaming others to justify or deny that they are cheating (Park, 2003; Ashworth et al., 1997)

Furthermore the lack of understanding institutional policy on academic dishonesty (Ashworth et al., 1997; Carroll & Appleton, 2001; JICS, 2005; Stefani & Carroll, 2001, Anyanwu, 2004) is also viewed as a situation when students might justify cheating. The problem is further complicated when students are encouraged to collaborate and exchange ideas in a certain task, but considered cheating when collaborating in another task. Students find the inability to recognise the point at which collaboration ends and collusion begins a major problem (Ashworth et al., 1997; Weeks, 2001; Carroll & Appleton, 2001).

In addition to the above, students may see plagiarism as a way to deal with social pressure or as a way to cope with their workload and peer pressure (Asworth et al., 1997; Park, 2003; Carroll & Appleton, 2001; Newstead et al., 1996) or as a way to simply avoid hard work (Rovai, 2000). A student's fear of failure and the social humiliation a failure may cause might push them to indulge in acts of cheating. In some cases bad time management (Rovai, 2000) from the students part and in some cases bad planning by the teacher or by the institution creates time pressure and workload that students find hard to deal with. In such situation students might be tempted to plagiarise. Peer pressure can affect students' involvement in plagiarism, either in situation where they are compelled due to peer loyalty to collude in cheating or when students engage in vast social activities due to peer pressure causing time pressure and thereby cheating.

Students from different cultures may perceive cheating differently (Anyanwu, 2004; Grijalva et al., 2006; MacKinnon & Manathunga, 2002). Grijalva et al. (2006) reports on a study done by Lupton, Chapman, and Weiss in 2000 where they observed a considerable difference in the way US and polish students perceived cheating. The section on Internationalisation of Education & the cultural context explains this situation in depth.

Teachers' Perspective

There have been studies on plagiarism where teachers have expressed their views on the issue of plagiarism in the academic arena (Anyanwu, 2004; Worthen, 2004; McCabe, 1993; Savage, 2004). An important observation coming out of these studies is that like students, teachers' understanding of, opinion about, and reactions to plagiarism differ. Hence it is natural that two teachers' responses to the same incident of plagiarism will also vary.

A majority of teachers see it as their duty to detect and deal with plagiarism. How teachers deal with plagiarism, though, differs from individual to individual as well as in level of subjectivity. While some members are sympathetic others are tougher (Anyanwu, 2004). Another example is discussed by Worthen (2004), where, upon detection of an incident of plagiarism, one teacher demanded the immediate expelling of the student from the institution, whilst other teachers pleaded for the student's claiming that the student was incapable of such an act of deceit. The Dean to whom the reporting of plagiarism took place, considered acting upon discovering the facts behind the issue, a suitable course of action and implications of any punishment. The analysis of this shows that while both sets of teachers were acting subjectively, the Dean was being more objective in his response.

In addition to these varied approaches on how to deal with plagiarism, not all teachers consider teaching students about plagiarism a part of their job. They assume that directing students to the institutions, academic dishonesty policy is sufficient and no real education is required for students to understand academic conventions (Anyanwu, 2004). Furthermore teachers make assumption about students' prior knowledge about academic conventions (MacKinnon & Manathunga, 2002), which can be problematic, in particular in relation to non-native students who come from different academic cultures.

Teachers tend to prioritise according to workload and time constraints. Some teachers ignore minor violations or deal with plagiarism on an individual basis (Anyanwu, 2004), others see that policing any plagiarism especially with large numbers of submissions is impractical and takes too much effort (Anyanwu, 2004). Further, searching for suspected plagiarised material on the Internet has added to teachers' workload. Teachers' competencies in detecting plagiarism vary (Anyanwu, 2004).

With regard to reporting students who are suspected of plagiarism, McGowan (2005) reports that teachers did not prefer to send students to the relevant authority, as they were not satisfied with the procedures involved in dealing with the case. McCabe (1993) reported that 30 percent of teachers in institutions with an *Honour Code* and 20 percent of teachers in institutions with *no Honour Code* "were either dissatisfied or very dissatisfied with the way in which suspected cases of cheating they had reported were handled" (p. 654). While many research studies point to the fact that teachers tend to deal with cases of plagiarism personally and not refer them to the academic board (McCabe, 1993), Anyanwu (2004) reports that some teachers prefer to pass all incidents to the head of the department so that no mishandling will take place and lead to a "university scandal". McGowan (2005) reports a similar observation where teachers did not want to report students to the relevant authority due to the repercussions of reporting such incidents. Teachers also have varied opinions on electronic detection systems. While some prefer them and see them as a deterrent (Savage, 2004), others see them as a negative procedure where the teacher becomes the enemy (McGowan, 2005).

Thus, students' as well as teachers' perspectives are vital for our attempt to understand plagiarism. In a situation where internationalisation has lead to students and teachers originate from varied cultures it is likely to assume that their perceptions regarding, for example, plagiarism may vary.

Internationalisation of Education and the Cultural Context

Similarly to all major spheres, education too has been affected by globalisation. One of the ways in which a country responds to globalisation is by internationalisation of education (Knight, 1999; Altbach & Knight, 2006). Internationalisation of education can be viewed from different perspectives. One of them is to provide an international dimension to study, which focuses on instruction in "non-traditional" languages, expansion of study-abroad programmes and strengthening of international studies in curriculum (Altbach & Peterson, 1998). Another much broader perspective on internationalisation is taken by Knight (1999) who encompasses both an international and an intercultural dimension to teaching, research and services of an institution.

In addition to these perspectives, Mazzarol, Soutar and Seng (2003) define three "waves" of internationalisation of education. The first is foreign students travelling to host nations; the second is foreign universities teaming up private institution abroad to create an "outlet" for students to follow degrees of foreign universities in their home countries and the third is the use of distance education to provide education to foreign students in their home countries. In addition to the above three, we identify a forth wave created due to the expansion of immigrant communities. An example for such a wave is the internationalisation of Malmö University in Sweden. From the start, the university has aimed to be an international university in order to account for the fact that the population of the city of Malmö include 35 percent of citizens with immigrants or of immigrant parents' heritage, from as many as 170 countries (Nilsson, 2003).

The internationalisation of education has been given a high degree of importance in many countries and regions. In the US much attention has been given to attracting students from other countries, teaching internationalised curricular, interaction with universities abroad, expansion of study abroad programmes and sponsorship of foreign students (Knight & de Wit, 1995; Kenny, 1998; Altbach & Knight, 2006). Europe too has given prominence to such schemes through programmes such as ERASMUS and SOCRATES, and the Bologna process aimed at harmonising the EU academic system (Callan, 2000; Altbach & Knight, 2006). Asia and the Pacific region, Africa, the Middle East and Latin America too have given a high degree of importance to internationalisation of education (Altbach & Knight, 2006).

In addition to the importance given to internationalisation of education there is a growing global demand for international higher education. The Number of foreign students in the US receiving their Bachelors, Masters and Doctorate degrees increased from 1.7, 5.5 and 11.3 percent in 1976/77 to 3.0, 11.0 and 28.0 percent in 2006/2007 respectively (National Center for Education Statistics, 2009). This trend is prominent also in countries like Sweden (Buscall, 2009), the UK ("Rise In Foreign Students In UK", 2008) and Australia (McMurtrie, 2009). It is forecasted that the number of international students will increase from 2 million in 2006 to 15 million international students by 2025 (Altbach & Knight, 2006) with Asia representing 70 percent of the international market (Böhm, Davis, Meares & Pearce, 2002).

The market of international education holds immense potential and it contributes to national economies. For example, in 2002 it contributed 11 billion US dollars and 4.2 billion Australian dollars to the US and Australian economies respectively (Böhm, Davis, Meares and Pearce, 2002). Education was also the 3rd largest export of Australia in 2008/09 (IDP Education Pty Ltd, n.d.). This potential in demand for international higher education has created economic opportunities for many institutions looking at for-profit education (Altbach & Knight, 2006). Hence, it is clear that today's educational institutes no longer cater only for native students but also for students from different countries and thereby from different cultures. Teachers in these institutions too originate from different cultures. It is natural that these teachers and students bring with them the different academic cultures they were taught in.

Cortazzi and Jin (1997) refer to Galtung's description of four academic cultures; Saxonic, Gallic, Teutonic and Nipponic. They go on to point out that Saxonic and Gallic are horizontal in relationships, but diverse in their approaches. While Saxonic favours an empirical approach, Gallic favours a non-deductive approach. Teutonic culture is what Galtung's refers to as a 'master-disciple' relationship with a deductive approach. Finally, the Nipponic culture is based on a hierarchical relationship in which debate is primarily social rather than intellectual. Cortazzi and Jin add Sinic to this list of academic cultures. They go on to explain how the Sinic culture is strictly hierarchical, and requires the learner to understand and master what those in authority say.

In the Chinese culture, students hesitate to question their teachers due to the respect they have for them. Furthermore, what a respected person says is considered as fact. Reproducing this word-for-word is expectable practise if not encouraged (Sowden, 2005). Many studies show that Chinese students find it hard to understand why attribution is a must and also why using the words as they were written by someone else, is considered wrong.

There are clear indications of the difference in the cultural value system and academic culture of foreign students when compared to Anglo-Saxon cultures.

An example is the needs of South African students who are

Immersed in highly religious cultures where oral history and a literature tradition requires and values the accuracy of memorisation". She goes on to add, "The student who is plagiarising may simply be making use of the modes of textual construction that he or she knew at school. (Angelil-Carter, 2000, p. 165, as cited in Carroll & Appleton, 2001, p. 15).

Another example is a conversation between a group of Japanese students and a tutor. The tutors questions the students on their failure to cite authors whose work they had used,

... They [students] replied that since what the author said was obviously true, his name did not need to be mentioned. In other words, the author's insights, having achieved the status of common sense, had thereby entered the field of common knowledge, and no longer belonged to him exclusively. (Pecorari, 2001, p. 145, as cited in Sowden, 2005, pp. 226-227)

A further example is an exchange between a lecturer in an Australian University and a Japanese Student by,

When the latter was asked 'What is your opinion about these two conflicting inter-pretations of the reasons for the Great Depression?', his reply, 'But I do not have an opinion - I am student', reflected genuine cultural bewilderment. (Ballard, 1996, p. 155, as cited in Sowden, 2005, p. 227)

The above are a few examples of many where cultural values, academic culture, language and the teacher-student relationship needs to be considered when addressing the issue of plagiarism.

In addition, family pressure and peer pressure may motivate students to plagiarise in order to pass assessments. In certain cultures failure is seen as degrading in the eyes of family and peers. Hence, it is clear that with the increase in the number of foreign students from different cultures, we cannot look at plagiarism from a simple Anglo-Saxon cultural perspective that promotes individual orientation and horizontal relationships. It is crucial that we discuss the cultural aspect when attempting to understand plagiarism.

PLAGIARISM IN DISTANCE EDUCATION

Distance education has become a necessity. The advancement in Information and Communication Technology has afforded the efficient implementation of distance education. Many students prefer to pursue education in a distant institution while residing in their own home, city or country. For example, some UK universities offer distance education degree programmes for students residing in foreign countries. A common format of these degree programmes is that the students spend the first two years of their education in their home countries and during their final year they visit the UK to complete their degrees and submit their dissertation (Joint Information

Systems Committee, 2005). When looking at this issue from the plagiarism perspective, it is suspected that students who spend the first two years in their home country may not have gained the proper academic skills needed by a university student (Joint Information Systems Committee, 2005). This could be due to the student's home country's academic culture, social value systems or simply because they were not educated about the academic conventions of the UK systems. Students especially from Asian cultures that have a hierarchical teacher-student relationship who see reproducing a 'masters' work as acceptable are most likely to face accusations of plagiarism due to their lack of knowledge of adopted countries academic conventions (Anyanwu, 2004; Bamford & Sergiou, 2005).

The teacher's knowledge of student capacity is one of the important attributes a teacher may use to detect instances of plagiarism (Lawhead et al., 1997). In a distance educational context often lack such a strong teacher-student relationship. Teachers and students have limited contact and teachers do not have an opportunity to get to know the student. Therefore, there is less likelihood of the teacher knowing the personality, competencies and capacity of a student.

A further difficulty in distance education is how to address plagiarism once it is detected. If plagiarism were detected, the Teacher/Institution would generally send an official email or letter to the accused student explaining the detection and calling for a meeting or requesting for an explanation. This is much more threatening than a classroom situation where a teacher would talk to the student and the non-verbal expressions would be aimed at a constructive approach rather than a confrontational approach. Official letters and emails inherently lack the ability to transmit emotion and a constructive dialogue is therefore more difficult to create than in a face-to-face interaction. The lack of constant teacher-student contact would further complicate the resolving of the issue at hand.

In addition to these challenges, there is an issue of perception of Web-Based Distance Education (WBDE). Some researchers are of the view that WBDE provides more opportunities for academic dishonesty than the traditional classroom situation. Some go further to state that WBDE even promotes dishonesty (Kennedy et al., 2000, as cited in Baron & Crooks, 2005). However, in their conclusion, Baron & Crooks (2005) state that scarce data that does exist strongly challenges the assumptions of the lack of integrity and the widespread dishonesty in WBDE. This conclusion is further supported by Grijalva et al.'s (2006) study where they conclude that a 3-4 percentage of students cheating in an online classroom is not greater than estimates of cheating in a traditional classroom. Hence, it seems premature to worry about plagiarism being more profuse in distance education although more research has to be carried out in order to ascertain the actual situation with regard to plagiarism in distance education.

TACKLING PLAGIARISM

The previous sections of this chapter have been dedicated to the understanding of plagiarism and how it is affected by social, academic, cultural and educational contexts. In this section we focus on more practical approaches to the issue of plagiarism by discussing opportunities and avenues for plagiarism, detection of plagiarism and finally a collection of good practice guidelines that have been suggested by researchers and academics.

The Catalysts: Opportunities and Avenues for Plagiarism

In order to find solutions and counter plagiarism, we need to understand what leads to plagiarism. Opportunities that leave doors open for students to plagiarise and avenues that lead to plagiarism need to be identified and barred. Following is a list of some of the most common situations that may lead to plagiarism.

Students' Lack of Knowledge and Understanding About what Constitutes Plagiarism and How to Avoid It (Anyanwu, 2004; Carroll & Appleton, 2001; Hart & Friesner, 2004; Marshall & Garry, 2005)

To avoid something one needs to know what to avoid and how to avoid it. Hence it is clear that to avoid plagiarism, students need to know what constitutes plagiarism and what steps they need to take to avoid it. It is common that teachers assume that students understand what plagiarism is and what constitutes it, although this assumption is not always accurate. Hence one of the main reasons for plagiarism is the students' lack of knowledge about plagiarism and lack of awareness on how to avoid it.

Students' Lack of Knowledge of Academic Conventions (Chester, 2001b, Marshall & Garry, 2005; Parlour, 1995, as cited in Evans, 2000; Park, 2003)

Knowledge of academic conventions and how to apply these conventions are skills that every student needs possess in order to succeed academically. The lack of these skills is one of the main avenues that lead to plagiarism. Most institutions offer academic writing and research method courses for postgraduate programs, but lack courses that teach academic conventions to undergraduates. This is a problem for undergraduates since they have to learn these skills on their own. Since they have little or no prior experience in the use of academic conventions it is likely that they will unintentionally plagiarise during their learning process.

Lack of Institutional Policy and Institution Wide Uniformity in Dealing with Plagiarism

Students can interpret the lack of an institutional plagiarism policy as the institution not taking plagiarism seriously and believe that they might not be punished even if they cheat (Chester, 2001b). Furthermore, the lack of a clear institutional policy on plagiarism would cause a problematic situation with administrators, teachers and students not knowing how to deal with a case of breaching of academic integrity (Anyanwu, 2004). The problem of dealing with plagiarism without a well developed and defined policy could not only lead to violation of students' rights, but also to legal issues. The same applies when there is no uniform application of the policies across the institution.

Teachers' Lack of Knowledge on Plagiarism, Lack of Skills to Identify Plagiarism and Uncertainty about How to Deal with It (Anyanwu, 2004)

Similar to students, teachers sometimes lack knowledge and skills needed to detect and act upon issues of plagiarism. The varying level of teacher skills in detecting plagiarism and competence in the use of Information & Communication Technology creates a problem to detect and deal with plagiarism in a uniform manner. It is possible that some students might use these weaknesses of teachers to attempt or justify plagiarism. The lack of teacher knowledge and skills affect the issue of early problem rectification of students who might plagiarise unintentionally.

Lack of a Learner-Centric Academic Environment that Promotes Inclusivity of Students

In an academic environment that does not promote inclusivity, students may feel bored and uninterested. In such an environment students will lack enthusiasm, motivation, ownership of their education and commitment to actively participate in the course (Chester, 2001b). Furthermore, if courses are thought badly or students do not see positive gain, the students may not see a reason to put an effort into the course (Macdonald, 2000; Park, 2003). In such environments it is tempting for students to take shortcuts that might lead to plagiarism.

Bad Assessment Design and Lack of Planning and Coordination

Plagiarism is strongly related to assessment. One of the main factors that leave doors open for plagiarism is the assessment process. Badly designed assessment tasks make plagiarism easy and accessible (Stefani & Carroll, 2001; Ashworth, Freewood & MacDonald, 2003).

With respect to planning and coordination, immense workloads and tight deadlines create time pressure for students (Chester, 2001b; Grijalva et al., 2006 Evans, 2000), thereby tempting students to take shortcuts leaving opportunities for plagiarism. Furthermore, the lack of time for students to read through their work before submitting or follow citation norms stringently might lead to unintentional plagiarism. In this case the issue is not the lack of students' skills on time management, but rather an effect of lack of planning and coordination by teachers within the department and across the faculty.

Students' Lack of Language Proficiency and Writing Skills

Even though language and writing skills are very much beyond the borders of the classroom, it is another contributing factor to student plagiarism. The inability to handle language profusely tempts students to take phrases, sentences or entire paragraphs from other sources. Even with attribution, large chunks of text are unacceptable. Furthermore, students might also be tempted to patchwrite. The problem occurs when students think that, if this is what I want to say, and I cannot say it better, why not use it the way it exactly is (Pennycook, 1996). In addition, thinking in one language and converting that thought into another language takes a lot of effort (more labourous) and a considerable amount of time (Atkinson & Ramanatha, 1995; Silva, 1993; Uzawa, 1996). This is supported by Silva (1993) who states, "in general terms, adult L2 [second language] writing is distinct from and simpler and less effective (in the eyes of L1 readers) than L1 [First Language] writing" (p. 661).

Academic Role Models Setting Bad Examples

There have been incidents in when university teachers, renowned authors and prominent public figures have been accused of plagiarism (e.g. Baron & Crooks, 2005). Students generally tend to follow the type of people mentioned above. It is not possible to enforce a code of conduct across society, but it is viewed as duplicity when teachers who tell students not to cheat and are supposed to enforce the academic integrity, commit plagiarism. It reflects negatively upon all teachers, even the honest ones. Students may use it as an excuse to commit plagiarism.

Lack of Deterrents (Davis & Ludvigson, 1995, as cited in Park, 2003)

Students do a cost and benefit analysis before they plagiarise (Grijalva et al., 2006). Hence, if no big enough deterrent exists that outweighs any benefit of plagiarising students may choose the plagiarism option. Lack of strong and multiple offence deterrents may leave students weighing their options of whether to plagiarise or not.

Detection

Once measures have been taken to bar opportunities for and avenues to plagiarism, the next step is to monitor and investigate if plagiarism still occurs. This is where the teacher needs to know plagiarism detection methods. These detection methods can be broadly divided into traditional and technology aided methods.

Traditional Detection

The first instance of suspicion of plagiarism occurs when the teacher goes through the student's submitted work. Traditional detection uses experience, the knowledge and the sensors of the teacher for detection. Below is a list of traditional detection methods.

1. **Similar Submissions:** A common occurrence is students submitting work that is very similar to another student. In such a situation, both students are accused of plagiarism. Even if one admits guilt, the other is guilty of collusion.
2. Inconsistencies in the Submitted Work:
   a. **Language and Intellectual Capacity:** Teachers in most cases have knowledge of an individual student's language capacities as well as the student's intellectual capacity. This may be from interactions in class or from work submitted on previous occasions. It is natural for a teacher to compare newly submitted work with the known competencies of the student. Any discrepancies in the language in the work and the known language of the student may be an indication of plagiarism. The same applies for the intellectual capacity of the student and the intellectual capacity evident in the submitted work.
   b. **Variation within Document:** The inconsistency in language such as voice and tense in addition to spelling variations for example between American and British English (Culwin & Lanchaster, 2001) and intellectual capacity depicted from section to section within the work might be evidence that some sort of plagiarism has occurred.

    c.   **Formatting:** If there is an inconstancy in the formatting of the document, it may be an indication of plagiarism. Varying of fonts, general document layout, indentations and misplaced RETURN characters are some of the key giveaways of plagiarised work.

    d.   **Citation Style:** If the citation style varies from the citation style specified it might be an indication of plagiarism (UNCA, 2007). In addition, if there are multiple styles used throughout the document and/or if the reference list is formulated according to different citation styles, this too may be an indication that the work is a collection of various cut and pasted resources.

3.   **Outdated References:** The consistence use of old references (UNCA, 2007; Culwin & Lancaster, 2001) and lack in referencing of any new and up to date research work could be an indication that the submitted work is an old composition by someone else.

4.   **Mismatch with Given Task:** If the final submitted work does not tally with the assignment or substantial portions of it are left out (Evans, 2000) it could be an indication that the produced work was not originally intended for this specific assignment or that the student may not have found existing work to match all the outcomes of the assignment.

5.   **Used References are not Readily Available:** When a majority of the reference books are not available in the local library or if some of the referenced articles are unavailable through the local library subscription to electronic library services, it might indicate that the student has indulged in plagiarism.

6.   **Embedded Source Information:** URLs, Stray page numbers, links to paper mill or ghostwriter sites, downloaded dates are "smoking gun" as referred to by Evans (2000). These are clear indications of plagiarism.

7.   **Non-Local Context:** If the work submitted takes examples from non-local context (Culwin & Lancaster, 2001) and/or show evidence that the work refers to events of a specific part of the world, it is likely that the submitted work originated in that part of the world. In such a scenario, it is possible that a student has plagiarised.

An important fact to remember is that a student is 'innocent until proven guilty'. Once a suspicious work is detected, the next step for the teacher is to verify that suspicion. The most effective and convenient way is to use a technological resource to clarify the doubts.

Technology-Aided Detection

"The technological element is the Internet. It has vastly expanded the availability of potential sources for plagiarism, eased the incorporation of plagiarized material into academic productions, and has thus made the detection of plagiarism burdensome" (Thomas, 2008, p. 2). However, the very technologies used to plagiarise are now part of the solution to counter it. Technology aided detection methods and tools mainly rely on the use of Information and Communication technology, and in particular, on the Internet. The Virtual Academic Integrity Laboratory (2002) categorises plagiarism detections software into four main types.

1.   Web Search Engines and other Web resources.
2.   Subscription databases.
3.   Online or remotely located search tools and services.
4.   Stand-alone desktop software.

   Described below are methods of how these tools can be used by a teacher to detect or confirm instances of plagiarism. We can generalise online or remotely located search tools and service and stand-alone desktop software as dedicated plagiarism detection services and software.

Web Search Engines and Other Web Resources (e.g. google.com, yahoo.com, essayprofessor.com, cheathouse.com)

Since most students use these same Internet search engines to look for material on the Web, it is most likely that a teacher would find the suspected materials on the search results page. A common way to look for the material is to take a distinct phrase or sentence and search the Web for it. A teacher is most likely to receive a link to the entire article or to a section if it were copied from the Internet. Scholar. google.com might be a preferred search if teachers are looking for content of high academic inclination. In addition to these Internet search engines if a teacher suspects that the entire work is plagiarised, the teacher can look for such works in paper-mill (essay-mill) sites. These are sites that sell articles and papers to students. If the work is plagiarised, it is likely that the teacher will find the entire paper, with or without some superficial differences such as the article tile and formatting.

Subscription Databases

Sources can be cross-referenced against library databases and subscription databases of academically inclined content. These databases contain eBooks, journals, magazines, and even scanned and indexed versions of physical books. There are two possible ways of using these services. The first is to search for the source document of the suspected plagiarism. The second is to check if the students have access through the local library to the reference material they have listed.

Dedicated Plagiarism Detection Services or Software (e.g. plagiarism.com, turnitin.com and EVE2)

There are free as well as subscribed plagiarism detection services and software. Such detection software can be an online or a stand-alone desktop based version. The teacher needs a digital copy of the work and permission of the student (who holds the copyright for his or her work) as most of these services add the submitted work to their databases. These services generally provide a percentage of how likely or how much content is suspected of being plagiarised. An example at Virginia Commonwealth University (Writing Centre, Virginia Commonwealth University, 2009) gives instructors the following advice on what percentages mean in their SafeAssign system.

Source Scores above 50%... indicate a high degree of text match and suggest excessive quoted or improperly paraphrased, or plagiarized...

Scores between 35 and 50%... perhaps problematic levels of quoting or improper paraphrasing...

Source Scores between 20 and 35%... significant quoted or improperly paraphrased material... scores in this range are likely appropriate, provided... student has correctly documented the source work.

Source Scores below 20%... some quotes or blocks of text in the paper match other documents. This score may indicate a reasonable use of sources or may indicate that a paper needs more outside support...

Upon confirmation that plagiarism has occurred it is important that the teacher acts immediately (Carroll & Appleton, 2001), that the teacher follows the institutional guideline and alerts relevant persons.

Plagiarism Detection Services and Software

The previous section briefly covered the methods of plagiarism detection using technological tools. Some of them are general tools that may be used for plagiarism detection. This section will focus on dedicated plagiarism detection tools.

It is important to point out that plagiarism detection services and software are not a complete solution (Savage, 2004; Carroll & Appleton, 2001; Maruca, 2004) but have to be used in conjunction with pedagogical approaches. The best solution to plagiarism is deterrent and prevention not detection and punishment (Carroll & Appleton, 2001; Evans, 2000; Macdonald & Carroll, 2006). Plagiarism detection services and software are intended for detection, but they are most effective and powerful when used as deterrents.

While certain people have welcomed these technologies (Javis, 2010; Savage, 2004) there are also sceptics and critiques. One issues has been that the services violate the copyright of the student who submits the work when the services add the student's work to their source database (Virtual Academic Integrity Laboratory, 2002; Maruca, 2004). As a solution, the plagiarism detection companies suggested that teachers obtain permission from their students to submit, store and reuse the work. One issue, though, is how likely it is that a student can deny permission within the power-relationship of a classroom situation (Maruca, 2004). Furthermore, the question arises of how ethical it is that the company that offers the services and software use the students' work for commercial gain. There are also issues where the student submission of work to the services is looked upon as the student being 'guilty until proven innocent' (Savage, 2004).

Table 1 summarises the views and opinions of students and teachers in a study conducted by Savage (2004) for the plagiarism detection service turnitin.com

Plagiarism detection services have limitations in their detection capabilities. For example, they cannot provide a definitive response to whether plagiarism has occurred or not and provide only a percentage that the teacher can use as a benchmark

Table 1. Summary of staff and student responses to turnitin (Savage, 2004)

	Positive	Negative
Students	Fairer Assessment, since if a student is cheating, he or she will [might] get caught	Students are suspects until proven innocent
	Students will improve their citation skills	Violation of student's privacy and copyright
	It will act as a deterrent to students who are thinking of plagiarising	Private companies making profit
Teachers	A deterrent against plagiarism	Not a complete solution
	Helpful tool for detection	Limitations in detection and reporting
	Fairness in assessment by discouraging cheating	Might spawn legal action by students
	Improve standards of students work by helping identify bad citation and plagiarism and help students improve	

to scrutinise the work thoroughly. Another limitation is that these services might not identify if a part is cited or not, thereby leaving to a teacher to go through the work thoroughly (Savage, 2004). A further problem is the vastness of the World Wide Web. Having a growth rate of several billion of Web pages per day (Alpert and Hajaj, 2008) it is almost impossible for any service to provide a comparison of a document across the entire content on the World Wide Web. The same issue applies in the context of the 'surface (indexable) Web' and the 'deep Web' (Bergman, 2001). Conventional Internet search engines skim the surface Web, but the deep Web is about five hundred times larger and not searched by most conventional search engines (Bergman, 2001).

In addition to these services and software, there are special systems that help monitor plagiarism and cheating in general and help in remote supervision of examination especially in the distance educational context. A few of these technologies are listed below.

1. Keystroke dynamics for authentication and monitoring of text production process. (Usoof & Lindgren, 2008)
2. Voice recognition systems for remote oral exams. (Hayes & Ringwood, 2008)
3. Video chat and Fingerprint authentication for remote assessment. (Baker, Lee & Hewitt, 2007)

It is important to bear in mind that all services and software used for plagiarism detection have their pros and cons, their limitations and ethical implications.

Good Practice to Deal with Plagiarism

Previous sections have addressed opportunities and avenues for plagiarism created due to bad practice, detection methods, and plagiarism detection tools. This section emphasises good practise to prevent opportunities and bar avenues that may lead to plagiarism with a focus on "The best correction for plagiarism is not punishment, but prevention" (Evans, 2000).

Researchers, Universities and special committees have published guides, documents and Web pages on approaches that may be followed to deter, detect and deal with plagiarism. In the following section we present five examples of good practice recommendations that can be used to deter plagiarism (Carroll & Appleton, 2001; Carroll, 2004; Evans, 2000; Joint Information Systems Committee, 2005; McGowan, 2005; University of Cincinnati Libraries, n.d.; Delta State University Libraries, n.d.; Ferguson, 2007; Information Technology Services, PennState, 2009, Franklin & Marshall College Library, 2009).

Course and Assessment Design

Student plagiarism mainly occurs in relation with assessments. Hence the design of assessment should promote originality and complicate plagiarism. The assessment tasks is closely related to the design of the course as a whole, wherefore both have to be considered in order to prevent plagiarism. Examples of designs that complicate plagiarism are those that imply higher-order thinking skills and promote student originality. A task that requires this is much more difficult to come by, as well as much easier to detect if it does not converge with the student's personality, language capacity and intellectual maturity. Assessments that require knowledge regurgitation are far easier to plagiarise than assessments where a student has to apply her knowledge to analyse and evaluate instances, and to synthesise new ideas.

Another type of assessment is an individualised task, which implies that the task is specific to a student and therefore, the response too is specific to that student. Carroll and Appleton (2001) provide an example; "a general essay on George Elliot could be individualised by asking how an Elliot character dealt with a situation and how a recent public figure did so, leaving the student to select the figure" (p. 10).

Another plagiarism resistant assessment type is interrelated tasks, for example in a project. The first task might be a literature survey and proposal submission, the second task might be a couple of interim reports or a set of drafts and the final task a full report or complete paper. Hence, it is unlikely that a student will find all of these interrelated works to plagiarise. Furthermore, oral presentation session/discussion help discourage plagiarism and/or help detect instances of plagiarism.

Narrow instead of a broad scoped assessment tasks make it unlikely that the student will be able to find a specific work that he or she is able to pass off as his or her own. Narrow scoped assessments also enhance the individuality of a student in the submitted work.

Asking students to submit a signed declaration form during the submission of the assignment (Chester, 2001a; Ashworth et al., 1997; Hart & Friesner, 2004) will not only be a deterrent but a reminder that they are not allowed to plagiarise. A further safeguard is by making sure that the students possess the references by asking them to submit a copy of the page they referred from (Wilhoit, 1994).

In addition there are certain assessment processes that need to be avoided. Avoiding the reuse of past year's assessment task for a new group of students is one example. These tasks are highly prone to plagiarism once students identify the case. In such instances there is unnecessary temptation for students to copy their seniors' work. For such instances of teacher negligence, Carroll and Appleton (2001) forward the question "Why should we [students] make an effort when the lecturer does not?" (p. 9). Furthermore, assessment tasks that are common to all students should be avoided, as they can lead to students paraphrasing other students' work or plagiarising other students' ideas. This creates a scenario where a set of students works hard whilst another set takes shortcuts. If by chance the students who plagiarised are not detected, both groups receive similar grades. This is not only an ethical issue but also an issue that affects the academic quality of the institution.

Thus, assessment is an important issue to consider in relation to plagiarism or as MacDonald (2000), states "plagiarism is going to be a fact of life if the way we assess learning encourages, or rewards, the uncritical use of secondary materials. We need to be more imaginative, while recognising the constraints imposed by large classes and reduced resources." He questions the focus on plagiarism and the student. He states "After years of trying to get students to develop information skills, we are penalising them for using those very same skills on the Internet." He goes on to add, "It is necessary to consider the learning, teaching and assessment strategies used. And this becomes a staff development issue".

Educating Students about Plagiarism and Academic Conventions

This includes educating students about plagiarism in general, the academic conventions, institutional policy on plagiarism and the *Honour Code*. Educating students on these aspects gives student a fair chance to avoid unintentional plagiarism as well as acting as a deterrent to those who might be contemplating plagiarising. Further, it makes it easier for teachers and institutions to deal with incidents. It is unfair to penalise students who have not been taught the skills to avoid plagiarism (Anyanwu, 2004).

Moreover one cannot expect a student to gain all the knowledge from the documents they are receiving when they enter an institution or from the institution's Website. Conducting a series of workshops for students might be a way to educate students about these issues. Sharing experience in class, of plagiarism incidents of the past, reiterating and reinforcing the institutional policy will have a positive effect and act as a deterrent against it. Having a course that is dedicated to teaching the students about academic writing conventions will, in most cases, help to minimise cases of unintentional plagiarism.

Extra attention should be paid to the information of international students from different academic cultures, language constructs and social values. They need to be provided with adequate information and education about the academic culture at hand and values of the new society they are in, the academic writing conventions they are supposed to adhere to and most importantly, the concept of plagiarism.

Furthermore, it is important that students receive clear guideline on collaboration (Wilhoit, 1994). There should not be any disambiguates or gray areas between collaboration and collusion. Students must have a clear perception of when to work together and when to work alone. Hence, providing guidelines and examples of situations will help students avoid unintentional plagiarism.

Institutional Policy and Uniformity in Dealing with Plagiarism

Most institutions include their institutional policy on plagiarism in the student handbook and/or on the institute Website. Furthermore, most institutes have guidelines and educate teachers about how to handle plagiarism. Some Institutes have an *Honour Code*, which is written by the students themselves and commits to academic integrity. As an example, the *Honour Code* of Stanford University was written in 1921 by students and binds not only students but also teachers to academic honesty, by specifically implying that teachers avoid academic procedure that may create temptations for students to violate the *Honour Code*.

Strict institutional regulations help deter plagiarism. PennState University in their Website states "The most severe sanction [for academic dishonesty] is the XF grade which states that the student failed a class specifically because of Academic Dishonesty". In order to act as an example for future offenders, institutions may also expel students or revoke students' degrees.

Incidents of plagiarism should be dealt with in a uniform manner across the institute. It is important that teachers are provided with a set of clear guidelines in order to be familiar with the process and know what to do in case an issue arises. In relation to guidelines, teachers need education about the institution policy, the guideline and action to be taken so that all teachers deal with the plagiarism in the similar manner. There might be a support person in the department to assist teachers if he or she is uncertain of what steps to take. If there is no uniformity, teachers run a risk of being labelled "good" or "evil" by students. A teacher who deals with a plagiarism issue at the classroom level will be labelled as "good" and a teacher who refers a student to the Disciplinary Committee will be labelled as "evil". Teachers are concerned about the fact that they might get a bad student rating and negative feedback (Anyanwu, 2004), which in turn can affect their employment.

One way to ensure uniformity in dealing with breaches of academic integrity is to have a disciplinary committee or a judicial affairs committee. Since these committees are made up of a group of people who are well versed in content of the academic dishonesty policy and since they have experience in dealing with similar cases, it is fair by the student that he or she will be treated as any other student. This also safeguards against student rights violations and legal challenges as the committees do take all of these aspects into consideration (McDonald & Carroll, 2006; Carroll & Appleton, 2001).

Furthermore, the skill of detecting plagiarism needs to be fostered among the teachers, not only because plagiarism needs to be detected but also to ensure that there is fairness in the process of applying the institution's academic dishonesty policy. This will ensure that situations in which one plagiarising student is penalised and another is not are avoided. With the increase in use of Information & Communication Technology by students to plagiaries, teachers too should possess the same skill in the use of this technology. Teachers should be able to use Internet services such as search engines, library services and even paper-mill (essay mill) sites in order to confirm suspicious instances of plagiarism. In addition they should be computer savvy enough to use online services such as turnitin.com, crossrefme.net, articlechecker. com and desktop software such as Essay Verification Engine and CopyCatch Gold.

Creating a Learner-Centred Environment

A learning environment where the student feels a part of will reduce the risk of plagiarism. By creating a learner-centric environment, students will be given the ownership of and a voice in their learning process (Sparrow, Sparrow & Swan, 2000). A student feeling of ownership in learning is important in terms of motivation (Biggs, 1999). Collaborative learning (Watters & Ginns, 2000; Sparrow et al., 2000) and Problem based learning (McLoughlin & Luca, 2002; Sparrow et al., 2000) are just few ways of engaging students and creating active learners. By providing students with opportunities to indulge in higher-order skills avenues for students to express themselves are opened up which make students feel involved in their learning. It further provides them with opportunity to collaborate, reflect and create their learning environment, thereby taking ownership of their own learning (Sparrow et al., 2000). It is also important that tasks are designed for real world relevance and for their authenticity (McLoughlin & Luca, 2002) making education more meaningful and practical. Such an environment will not only make plagiarising tough, but also illogical and counterproductive.

Fostering Language Proficiency and Writing Skills in Students

Lack of language proficiency and writing skills is common among students who follow their education in a language that is not their mother tongue. As a solution some institutions offer language courses as well as academic writing courses in order to foster language proficiency and writing skills among students (Howard, 1995). Another approach to address this issue is for teachers to reassure students that content in assignment is more important than the language used. Furthermore, some students consider themselves as inadequately skilled and are concerned about how others might view their work. A suggested solution to this issue comes from the Penn State University advice page on plagiarism for students; "Maybe you feel that the quality of your work is so poor that you could never pass the class. But, faculty do not expect your work to be 100 percent perfect. The purpose of any assignment is for you to learn and practice new skills... it is far better you discuss your concerns with your instructor..."

CHALLENGES

Even though there are several good practises on how to deal with plagiarism, institutions may face several challenges in the process of implementing them. Outlawing, detecting and dealing with plagiarism can be similar to the scenario where there are police officers to catch criminals and laws to prosecute them, still that does not stop criminals indulging in unlawful acts as long as they think they can get away with them and as long as there are some benefits involved. Similarly, plagiarism is considered wrong, immoral and going against the social value system, but as long as there are opportunities for students to plagiaries, as long as they think they will not get caught and as long as they see some gain in it, it is highly unlikely that plagiarism will disappear from the academic system or from society as a whole. The challenge is to educate students that "crime" does not pay off and that they need to work for their grades.

There is additionally a considerable financial gain from abating academic plagiarism. As long as there is a demand, there will be a supply. There will be paper mills that offer an essay on global warming for 12 – 40 $US, or 'rented' coders in India who will bid 10 - 40 $US to write a computer programme, or a 'ghostwriter' who will write a customised essay for 19.08 – 41.12 $US as long as students are willing to buy them. There is not much one can do to close these businesses down as in the broader judicial system, they are not violating laws. It is up to the institutions and teachers to educate students, not provide them with opportunities to cheat, instate deterrents and punish those who are caught so that the demand may drop and the supply will decrease.

The ease of which plagiarism can be committed is a further challenge. Evans (2000) states that it used to take effort to plagiaries, but now it is a case of "click click click". Even physical books that do not have electronic versions can be copied as a whole. Optical character recognition software will convert the scanned page (or book) into a text document. Again the only options left are to educate, remove opportunities, instate deterrents and punish if caught.

Cooperation among teachers and administrators is important in order to implement the institution's academic dishonesty policy. Any lack of cooperation by either party to enforce the policy will delay the process. This in turn will on one hand cause undue anxiety for the student and on the other, not give the student a chance to correct his or her mistake before the next assessment task (Anyanwu, 2004). Furthermore, there is a need for a collective effort from both teachers and students to improve student knowledge on plagiarism and academic conventions and to device ways to avoid plagiarism. Finding common ground to cooperate on this issue is paramount to ridding the academic domain of plagiarism.

Ethical and legal issues are additional challenges. If the policy and the implementation procedures are not well thought of or if there are flaws in their implementation, students will be left with an opportunity to challenge the system in the judiciary.

SUMMARY

Plagiarism and the fuss behind it are here to stay, at least till some sort of drastic social change occurs. Plagiarism is an ethical and moral issue in the academic domain and when the act of plagiarism infringes copyright, it transforms to being a legal and in some cases a financial issue. It is important to keep in mind that the domain of plagiarism is multi dimensional and complex. It encompasses the moral value system of individuals, the social context, academic cultures, academic disciplines, and legal and financial systems. Standing alone, most of these systems are quite dynamic themselves and when put together the system is complex and unpredictable. Hence, teachers will always have to be alert, innovative and able to adapt to the changing face of plagiarism.

Furthermore, there is lack of understanding of the meaning of plagiarism and what it really constitutes. The vague definition is one of the reasons that plagiarism is hard to tackle. Other factors that contribute to plagiarism are lack of awareness, lack of education, weak teaching and assessment habits and most importantly, lack of a comprehensive institutional Academic Dishonesty policy. It is important that the Academic Dishonesty policy has rules, regulations and a list of appropriate actions, but in addition contains a plan to educate both teachers and students and also monitor the plagiarism situation at the institution.

One of the best ways of avoiding plagiarism is to reduce students' opportunities to plagiarise. This can be achieved by being innovative in teaching and assessment processes. Teaching students the skill needed to observe academic conventions, uplifting their moral values and self-respect, creating student-centred learning environments and creating new assessment models are ways to develop a non-plagiarising learning environment. Another 'weapon' against plagiarism is the deterrent. The cost of getting caught plagiarising must always be greater than the benefits.

Finally like many social issues, plagiarism does not have a 'one fits all' answer, but rather a best practice and a context dependant solution, which needs to be challenged, adapted and re-contextualised in order to provide the best possible solution in different learning environments.

REFERENCES

Alpert, J., & Hajaj, N. (2008, July 25). *We knew the web was big.* Retrieved from http://googleblog.blogspot.com/2008/07/we-knew-Web-was-big.html

Altbach, P., & Knight, J. (2006). The internationalization of higher education: Motivations and realities. In *The National Education Association Almanac of Higher Education* (pp. 27–37). Washington, DC: NAE.

Altbach, P. G., & Peterson, P. M. (1998). Internationalize American higher education? Not exactly. *Change, 30*(4), 36–40. doi:10.1080/00091389809602630.

Anyanwu, R. (2004). Lessons on plagiarism: Issues for teachers and learners. *International Education Journal, 4*(4), 178–187.

Ashworth, P., Bannister, P., & Thorne, P. (1997). Guilty in whose eyes? University students' perceptions of cheating and plagiarism in academic work and assessment. *Studies in Higher Education, 22*(2), 187–203. doi:10.1080/03075079712331381034.

Ashworth, P., Freewood, M., & MacDonald, R. (2003). The student lifeworld and the meaning of plagiarism. *Journal of Phenomenological Psychology, 34*(2), 257–278. doi:10.1163/156916203322847164.

Atkinson, D., & Ramanathan, V. (1995). Cultures of writing: An ethnographic comparison of L1 and L2 university writing/language programs. *Teachers of English to Speakers of Other Languages Quarterly, 29*(3), 539–568. doi:10.2307/3588074.

Baker, T., Lee, S., & Hewitt, J. (2007, June). *The development and testing of a video system for online authentication of assessment.* Paper presented at the Second International Blended Learning Conference. Hatfield, UK. Retrieved from https://uhra.herts.ac.uk/dspace/bitstream/2299/1727/1/901869.pdf

Bamford, J., & Sergiou, K. (2005). International students and plagiarism: An analysis of the reasons for plagiarism among international foundation students. *Investigation in University Teaching and Learning, 2*(2), 17–22.

Baron, J., & Crooks, S. M. (2005). Academic integrity in web based distance education. *TechTrends, 49*(2), 40–45. doi:10.1007/BF02773970.

Bergman, M. M. (2001). The deep web: Surfacing hidden value. *Journal of Electronic Publishing, 7*(1). doi:10.3998/3336451.0007.104.

Biggs, J. (1999). *Teaching for quality learning at university.* Buckingham, UK: SRHE and Open University Press.

Böhm, A., Davis, T., Meares, D., & Pearce, D. (2000). *Global student mobility 2025: Forecasts of the global demand for higher education*. Paper presented at the 16th Australian International Education Conference. Hobart, Tasmania. Retrieved from www.aiec.idp.com/PDF/Bohm_2025Media_p.pdf

Brandt, D. S. (2002). Copyright's (not so) little cousin, plagiarism. *Computers in Libraries*, *22*(5), 39–41.

Buscall, J. (2009, September 21). *Annual report shows influx of international*. Retrieved from http://www.su.se/english/about/news-and-events/annual-report-shows-influx-of-international-students-1.1674

Butterfield, F. (1991, July 3). For a dean at Boston U., a question of plagiarism. *The New York Times*. Retrieved from http://www.nytimes.com

Callan, H. (2000). Higher education internationalization strategies: Of marginal significance or all- pervasive? The international vision in practice: A decade of evolution. *Higher Education in Europe*, *25*(1), 15–23. doi:10.1080/03797720050002161.

Carnevale, D. (1999, November 12). How to proctor from a distance. *The Chronicle of Higher Education*, *46*(12). Retrieved from http://chronicle.com PMID:14598855.

Carroll, J. (2004, November). *Deterring, detecting and dealing with plagiarism*. Retrieved from http://www.brookes.ac.uk/services/ocsd/2_learntch/plagiarism.html

Carroll, J., & Appleton, J. (2001). *Plagiarism: A good practice guide*. Oxford, UK: Oxford Brookes University.

Chester, G. (2001a). *Pilot of free-text electronic plagiarism detection software in five UK institutions*. Retrieved from http://www.jisc.ac.uk/media/documents/programmes/plagiarism/pilot.pdf

Chester, G. (2001b). *Plagiarism detection and prevention*. Retrieved from http://www.jisc.ac.uk/uploaded_documents/plagiarism_final.pdf

Cortazzi, M., & Jin, L. (1997). Communication for learning across cultures. In McNamara, D., & Harris, R. (Eds.), *Overseas Students in Higher Education: Issues in Teaching and Learning* (pp. 76–90). London: Routledge.

Culwin, F., MacLeod, A., & Lancaster, T. (2001). *Source code plagiarism in UK HE computing schools: Issues, attitudes and tools (SCISM Technical Report)*. London: South Bank University.

Cummings, R., Maddux, C. D., Harlow, S., & Dyas, L. (2002). Academic misconduct in undergraduate teacher education students and its relationship to their principled moral reasoning. *Journal of Instructional Psychology*, *29*(4), 286–296.

Delta State University Libraries. (n.d.). *Plagiarism detection & prevention: A guide for faculty.* Retrieved from http://www.deltastate.edu/pages/1270.asp

Dionne, E. J., Jr. (1987, September 17). Biden was accused of plagiarism in law school. *The New York Times.* Retrieved from http://www.nytimes.com

Evans, J. (2000). The new plagiarism in higher education: From selection to reflection. *Interactions Journal, 4*(2). Retrieved from http://www2.warwick.ac.uk/services/ldc/resource/interactions/archive/issue11/evans

Ferguson, J. (2007, July 27). *Faculty plagiarism resources: Prevention and detection.* Retrieved from http://bullpup.lib.unca.edu/library/lr/plagiarism.html

Franklin & Marshall College Library. (2009, August). *Plagiarism: A resource for faculty.* Retrieved from http://library.fandm.edu/plagiarism.html

Gamet, J. (2006, May 7). Samsung caught plagiarizing apple icons. *The Mac Observer.* Retrieved from http://www.macobserver.com/tmo/article/Samsung_Caught_Plagiarizing_Apple_Icons

Grijalva, T. C., Nowell, C., & Kerkvliet, J. (2006). Academic honesty and online courses. *College Student Journal, 40*(1), 180–185.

Harry Potter Publisher Denies Plagiarism. (2009, June 16). *The Telegraph.* Retrieved from http://www.telegraph.co.uk

Hart, M., & Friesner, T. (2004). Plagiarism and poor academic practice - A threat to the extension of e-learning in higher education? *Electronic Journal on e-Learning, 2*(1), 89-96. Retrieved from www.ejel.org/volume-2/vol2-issue1/issue1-art25-hart-friesner.pdf

Hayes, B., & Ringwood, J. V. (2008). Student authentication for oral assessment in distance learning programs. *IEEE Transactions on Learning Technologies, 1*(3), 165–175. doi:10.1109/TLT.2009.2.

Hayes, N., & Introna, L. D. (2005). Cultural values, plagiarism, and fairness: When plagiarism gets in the way of learning. *Ethics & Behavior, 15*(3), 213–231. doi:10.1207/s15327019eb1503_2.

Howard, R. M. (1995). Plagiarisms, authorships, and the academic death penalty. *College English, 57*(7), 788–806. doi:10.2307/378403.

Howard, R. M. (2002). Don't police plagiarism: Just TEACH! *Education Digest, 67*(5), 46–49.

IDP Education Pty Ltd. (n.d.). *The value of international education to Australia*. Retrieved from http://www.idp.com/research/statistics/education_export_statistics.aspx

Information Technology Services. Penn State. (2009, March 3). *Plagiarism prevention resources*. Retrieved from http://tlt.its.psu.edu/plagiarism

Jarvis, J. (2010, January 31). Professors are beating cheating with turnitin.com. *The Cowl*. Retrieved from http://www.thecowl.com/2.7830/professors-are-beating-cheating-with-turnitin-com-1.1103149

Joint Information Systems Committee. (2005). *Deterring, detecting and dealing with student plagiarism*. Retrieved from http://www.jisc.ac.uk/publications/briefingpapers/2005/pub_plagiarism.aspx

Kenny, S. S. (1998). *The Boyer commission on educating undergraduates in the research university: Reinventing undergraduate education: A blueprint for America's research universities*. Stony Brook, NY: The Carnegie Foundation for the Advancement of Teaching. Retrieved from http://naples.cc.sunysb.edu/Pres/boyer.nsf

Knight, J. (1999). Internationalisation of higher education. In *Quality and Internationalisation in Higher Education* (pp. 13–28). Paris: OECD.

Knight, J., & de Wit, H. (1995). Strategies for internationalization of higher education: Historical and conceptual perspectives. In de Wit, H. (Ed.), *Strategies for internationalization of higher education: A comparative study of Australia, Canada, Europe, and the United States of America* (pp. 5–32). Amsterdam: European Association for International Education.

Lancaster, R. C. (2006). *Eliminating the successor to plagiarism? Identifying the usage of contract cheating sites*. Retrieved from http://www.plagiarismadvice.org/documents/papers/2006Papers05.pdf

Lawhead, P. B., Alpert, E., Bland, C. G., Carswell, L., Cizmar, D., & DeWeill, J. et al. (1997). The web and distance learning: What is appropriate and what is not: report of the ITiCSE '97 working group on the web and distance learning. *ACM SIGCUE Outlook, 25*(4), 27–37. doi:10.1145/274382.274383.

MacDonald, R. (2000, November 24). Talking shop: Why don't we turn the tide of plagiarism to the learners' advantage? *The Times Higher Education*. Retrieved from http://www.timeshighereducation.co.uk

MacDonald, R., & Carroll, J. (2006). Plagiarism-A complex issue requiring a holistic institutional approach. *Assessment & Evaluation in Higher Education, 31*(2), 233–245. doi:10.1080/02602930500262536.

MacKinnon, D., & Manathunga, C. (2003). Going global with assessment: What to do when the dominant cultures literacy drives assessment. *Higher Education Research & Development, 22*(2), 131–144. doi:10.1080/07294360304110.

Malinowski, C. I., & Smith, C. P. (1985). Moral reasoning and moral conduct: An investigation prompted by Kohlberg's theory. *Journal of Personality and Social Psychology, 49*, 1016–1027. doi:10.1037/0022-3514.49.4.1016.

Marsh, B. (1997). Plagiarism thread on ACW-L. *Kairos, 3*(1). Retrieved from http://english.ttu.edu/kairos/3.1/binder.html?reviews/marsh/plagintro.html

Marshall, S., & Garry, M. (2005). How well do students really understand plagiarism? In H. Goss (Ed.), *Proceedings of the 22nd Annual Conference of the Australasian Society for Computers in Learning in Tertiary Education (ASCILITE)* (pp. 457-467). Brisbane, Australia: ASCILITE.

Maruca, L. (2004, June). *The plagiarism panic: Digital policing in the new intellectual property regime.* Paper presented at the Conference on new Directions in Copyright. London, UK. Retrieved from http://www.copyright.bbk.ac.uk/contents/publications/conferences/2004/lmaruca.pdf

Matalene, C. (1985). Contrastive rhetoric: An American writing teacher in China. *National Council of Teachers of English. College English, 47*(8), 789–808. doi:10.2307/376613.

Mazzarol, T., Soutar, G. N., & Seng, M. S. Y. (2003). The third wave: Future trends in international education. *International Journal of Educational Management, 17*(3), 90–99. doi:10.1108/09513540310467778.

McCabe, D. L. (1993). Faculty responses to academic dishonesty: The influence of student honor codes. *Research in Higher Education, 34*(5), 647–658. doi:10.1007/BF00991924.

McCabe, D. L. (2001). Why students do it and how we can help them stop. *American Educator, 25*(4), 38–43.

McCabe, D. L., Butterfield, K. D., & Trevino, L. K. (2006). Academic dishonesty in graduate business programs: Prevalence, causes, and proposed action. *Academy of Management Learning & Education, 5*(3), 294–305. doi:10.5465/AMLE.2006.22697018.

McCabe, D. L., & Trevino, L. K. (1993). Honor codes and other contextual influences. *The Journal of Higher Education, 64*, 522–538. doi:10.2307/2959991.

McGowan, U. (2005). Plagiarism detection and prevention: Are we putting the cart before the horse? In Brew, A., & Asmar, C. (Eds.), *Higher education in a changing world* (pp. 287–293). Adelaide, Australia: Higher Education Research and Development Society of Australasia.

McLoughlin, C., & Luca, J. (2002). A learner-centred approach to developing team skills through web-based learning and assessment. *British Journal of Educational Technology*, *33*(5), 571–582. doi:10.1111/1467-8535.00292.

McMurtrie, B. (2009, April 2). Australian universities see increase in foreign enrolments. *The Chronicle of Higher Education*. Retrieved from http://chronicle.com

National Center for Education Statistics. (2008). *Postsecondary degrees conferred by sex and race*. Retrieved from http://nces.ed.gov/fastfacts/display.asp?id=72

Newstead, S. E., Franklyn-Stokes, A., & Armstead, P. (1996). Individual differences in student cheating. *Journal of Educational Psychology*, *88*(2), 229–241. doi:10.1037/0022-0663.88.2.229.

Nilsson, B. (2003). Internationalisation at home from a Swedish perspective: The case of Malmö. *Journal of Studies in International Education*, *7*, 27–40. doi:10.1177/1028315302250178.

Park, C. (2003). In other (people's) words: Plagiarism by university students - Literature and lessons. *Assessment & Evaluation in Higher Education*, *28*(5), 471–488. doi:10.1080/02602930301677.

Pennycook, A. (1996). Borrowing others' words: Text, ownership, memory, and plagiarism. *TESOL Quarterly*, *30*(2), 201–230. doi:10.2307/3588141.

Plagiarism Investigation Ends at Virginia. (2002, November 26). *The New York Times*. Retrieved from http://www.nytimes.com

Plagiarism. (n.d.). *Oxford English Dictionary*. Retrieved from http://dictionary.oed.com

Pratt, M. (2005, April 2). Telegram & Gazette fires sports writer accused of plagiarism. *USA Today*. Retrieved from http://www.usatoday.com

Price, M. (2002). Beyond gotcha! Situating plagiarism in policy and pedagogy. *College Composition and Communication*, *54*(1), 88–115. doi:10.2307/1512103.

Rao, K. R. (2008). Plagiarism - A scourge. *Current Science – Bangalore, 94*(5), 581-586.

Renard, L. (1999). Cut and paste 101: Plagiarism and the net. *Educational Leadership*, *57*(4), 38–42.

Rise in Foreign Students in UK. (2008, January 10). *BBC News*. Retrieved from http://news.bbc.co.uk/2/hi/uk_news/education/7181806.stm

Rovai, A. P. (2000). Online and traditional assessments: What is the difference? *The Internet and Higher Education, 3*, 141–151. doi:10.1016/S1096-7516(01)00028-8.

Savage, S. (2004). *Staff and student responses to a trial of turnitin plagiarism detection software*. Retrieved from http://www.indiana.edu/~tltc/technologies/savage.pdf

Schab, F. (1991). Schooling without learning: Thirty years of cheating in high school. *Adolescence, 26*(104), 839–848. PMID:1789171.

Sheard, J., Dick, M., Markham, S., Macdonald, I., & Walsh, M. (2002). Cheating and plagiarism: Perceptions and practices of first year IT students. *ACM SIGCSE Bulletin, 34*(3), 183–187. doi:10.1145/637610.544468.

Shepherd, J. (2006, March 17). Polls find elite top cheats list. *The Times Higher Education*. Retrieved from http://www.timeshighereducation.co.uk/story.asp?storyCode=201977

Shepherd, J. (2008, May 6). History essay in the making. *The Guardian*. Retrieved from http://www.guardian.co.uk/education/2008/may/06/highereducation.students

Silva, T. (1993). Toward an understanding of the distinct nature of L2 writing: The ESL research and its implications. *TESOL Quarterly, 27*(4), 657–677. doi:10.2307/3587400.

Sowden, C. (2005). Plagiarism and the culture of multilingual students in higher education abroad. *ELT Journal, 59*(3), 226–233. doi:10.1093/elt/cci042.

Sparrow, L., Sparrow, H., & Swan, P. (2000, February). *Student centred learning: Is it possible?* Paper presented at Teaching and Learning Forum. Perth, Australia. Retrieved from http://lsn.curtin.edu.au/tlf/tlf2000/sparrow.html

Stefani, L., & Carroll, J. (2001). *A briefing on plagiarism*. Retrieved from http://www.bioscience.heacademy.ac.uk/ftp/Resources/gc/assess10Plagiarism.pdf

Stevenson, D. (2010, February 16). How schools beat the net cheats. *PC Pro*. Retrieved from http://www.pcpro.co.uk/features/355597/how-schools-beat-the-net-cheats

Student Plagiarism. 'On the Rise'. (2005, February 11). *BBC News*. Retrieved from http://news.bbc.co.uk/2/hi/uk_news/education/4257479.stm

Swain, H. (2005, January 28). Nip double trouble in the bud. *The Times Higher Education.* Retrieved from http://www.timeshighereducation.co.uk

The Plagiarism Plague. (2003, February 7). *BBC News.* Retrieved from http://news.bbc.co.uk/2/hi/uk_news/2736575.stm

Thomas, M. (2008). Plagiarism detection software. In Bonk et al. (Eds.), *Proceedings of World Conference on E-Learning in Corporate, Government, Healthcare, and Higher Education* (pp. 2390-2397). Las Vegas, Navada: Springer.

University of Cincinnati Libraries. (n.d.). *Plagiarism: Prevention and detection strategies.* Retrieved from http://www.libraries.uc.edu/instruction/faculty/plagiarism.htm

Usoof, H., & Lindgren, E. (2008). Who is who and doing what in distance education? Authentication and keystroke dynamics. *Journal of Research in Teacher Education, 3*(4), 173–187.

Uzawa, K. (1996). Second language learners' processes of L1 writing, L2 writing, and translation from L1 into L2. *Journal of Second Language Writing, 5,* 271–294. doi:10.1016/S1060-3743(96)90005-3.

Virtual Academic Integrity Laboratory. (2002). *Faculty and administrators guide: Detection tools and method.* Retrieved from http://www.umuc.edu/distance/odell/cip/vail/faculty/detection_tools/detectiontools.pdf

Watters, J. J., & Ginns, I. S. (2000). Developing motivation to teach elementary science: Effect of collaborative and authentic learning practices in preservice education. *Journal of Science Teacher Education, 11*(4), 301–321. doi:10.1023/A:1009429131064.

Weeks, S. (2001, May 18). Plagiarism: Think before pointing finger of blame. *The Times Higher Education.* Retrieved from http://www.timeshighereducation.co.uk

Wilhoit, S. (1994). Helping students avoid plagiarism. *College Teaching, 42*(4), 161–165. doi:10.1080/87567555.1994.9926849.

Worthen, K. J. (2004). Discipline: An academic dean's perspective on dealing with plagiarism. *Brigham Young University Education and Law Journal, 2,* 441–448.

Writing Centre, Virginia Commonwealth University. (2009, October 4). *SafeAssign: Interpreting SafeAssign scores - For instructors.* Retrieved from http://www.vcu.edu/uc/writingcenter/safeassign/InterpretingForInstructors.html

Zeleny, J. (2008, February 19). Clinton camp says Obama plagiarized in speech. *The New York Times.* Retrieved from http://www.nytimes.com

KEY TERMS AND DEFINITIONS

Academic Cheating: The act of cheating in academic work like using crib sheets, plagiarising, collusion and purchasing questions/answers and other work.

Academic Dishonesty: Also referred to as Academic misconduct is the act of dishonesty in academic work. This includes cheating, plagiarism, collusion and falsification of data.

Distance Education: A field of education focussed on pedagogy, instructional systems and technology in order to deliver education to students who are not physically present in a traditional classroom.

Higher Education: The level of education provided at Universities, Colleges, Institutes of Technology, Vocational Institutes, Community Collages, and other post secondary educational institutes.

Plagiarism: The act of passing off ideas, text, speech or other creative work of another as one's own.

Chapter 4
Creating Online Community:
Challenges and Solutions

Mats Deutschmann
Umeå University, Sweden

EXECUTIVE SUMMARY

The challenges in creating a collaborative environment for online learning are great. This chapter describes some practical examples of community building in online learning contexts and discusses the effects of such activities. It draws its data from six years of online courses in English at Mid Sweden University, where the author was employed from 2003-2009 and worked with development and implementation of their Internet course program.

1. INTRODUCTION

Any teacher that can be replaced by a computer, deserves to be. (Thornburg, n.d.)

There is an increasing awareness of the special challenges posed by online education (see for example Palloff & Pratt 1999; Salmon 2002, 2004; Beetham & Sharpe 2007). While the number of Internet based courses in higher education has increased steadily over the past decades, it is also becoming increasingly clear that these "new" modes of distribution pose new challenges to instructors, students and learning institutions. For example, several studies have shown that attrition from e-learning is higher than in traditional classroom environments (Carr, 2000; Flood, 2002; Diaz, 2002; Westerberg & Mårald, 2006). While there may be several factors contributing

DOI: 10.4018/978-1-4666-4486-1.ch004

to this tendency, one major cause is arguably that the design of online education often has been based on the same models as traditional courses, according to what Svensson (2004) calls the "you do what you did before approach"; academics see their main role as providing the contents of the course. The result has often been online learning environments that merely offer ready-made educational material to be downloaded, after which the individual is left to pursue his or her studies in relative isolation. The problem with this approach is that it disregards a crucial factor – namely the social dimension of any learning experience. Online students often report feelings of isolation, and feature limited contact with instructors and fellow students. The result of this isolation can be unfinished courses or degrees (Shaw & Polovina, 1999).

The importance of social factors in deciding retention is not a new concept. As early as 1975 Tinto's Retention model postulated that whether a learner persists or drops out on a course is strongly predicted by that learner's degree of "academic and social integration." In an ordinary classroom environment, the social context for learning is something that a lecturer more or less can take for granted. Students make friends and enter networks without the interference of academic staff. Similarly, we can assume that discussions about course content and other academic questions take place outside the classroom, over coffees and snacks. As a lecturer, one is thus only providing one of the influences in the total formula making up the "learning context". The rest, however, takes care of itself and perhaps because of this, the importance of the social dimension is often underestimated. When the learning is moved to an online environment, however, this is no longer the case. I would strongly argue that it is not enough just to provide learning materials and instructions on how to use them in an online course. We also have to provide the framework for community building in our courses so that "academic and social integration" becomes possible.

There are other good reasons related to quality for the creation of community on online courses. Learning theories based on socio-cultural theories and situated learning (Vygotsky 1978; Lave & Wenger 1991; Wenger 1998) have long claimed that knowledge is constructed when individuals engage socially in talk and activity about shared problems or tasks. Similarly, in much of the current research into online learning, the social dimension is highlighted as being of primary importance. Palloff & Pratt (1999: 5), for example, maintain that the key to the learning processes in online education is "the formation of a learning community through which knowledge is imparted and meaning is co-created". Similarly, Deutschmann and Lundmark (2008) were able to show that pass rates in online language courses could be directly correlated with the amount of communication that was going on in the courses. Arguably then, creating a community in the online environment does not only affect retention, but also improves the quality of learning. The present online learning paradigm, so called Computer Supported Collaborative Learning

(CSCL) (Salmon, 2004), has thus involved a shift from passive learning to active student-driven participation, collaboration and dialogue between learners. Within the domain of online language education, in particular, this has become evident. According to Ciekanski and Chanier (2008: 163) there has been a shift trend from computer assisted language learning (CALL) to computer mediated communication (CMC) and computer-supported collaborative learning (CSCL) involving "every language skill and area" in recent years. This is also reflected in the types of software that are being developed for online learning. As Kern & Warschauer (2000:11) put it, technology usage has moved on from software that involve "learners' interaction with computers to interaction with other humans via the computer." Online learning is thus being transformed from "silent, solitary acts to lively, meaning-making events rich in discussion" where learning takes place with others in a social context (Bonk & Cunningham 1998: 35).

In practice, however, the challenges in creating a collaborative environment for online learning are great. This chapter will describe some practical examples of community building in online learning contexts and discuss the effects of such activities. It draws its data from six years of online courses in English at Mid Sweden University, where I was employed from 2003-2009 and worked with development and implementation of their Internet course program.

2. BACKGROUND

Mid Sweden University is a small multi-campus university situated in northern Sweden. Due to its rather remote location it has a long tradition of distance learning and an estimated 45 percent of its students study on distance programs. As a result of dwindling numbers of applicants on traditional distance courses with face-to-face meetings, the subject of English started developing Internet courses in 2004, where the aim was to provide all teaching and communication online. Although the motivation for developing the Internet courses was largely economical, the team that worked hands-on with the development also envisaged that the use of ICT could actually improve communication between the students and between the teachers and students. With this in mind, we built our courses on a collaborative learning model.

Two models, in particular, influenced our design of the courses: Salmon's *Five Stage Model* (2004) and Johnson, Johnson, Stanne, and Garibaldi's (1990) *Key Element Model* cited in Beisenbach-Lucas (2004). Salmon's (2004) *Five Stage Model* focuses on both technical and social processes and describes the stages that an online learning community goes through, starting with the Access and Motivation stage. During this first stage the participants engage in trying to access the system and the main role of the e-moderator is to welcome and encourage students. The community then moves onto the second stage – Online Socialisation, whereby participants familiarise themselves with each other and their learning environment. It is also here that the social culture of the community starts being established. During the third stage, the Information Exchange, participants begin to explore the range of information available to them and the interaction at this stage concerns the content and sharing of information. During the fourth stage, Knowledge Construction participants start to become involved in active interaction and knowledge construction, responding and reacting to each others' input. The final stage in Salmon's model constitutes the Development stage where learners become more responsible for their own learning and need less support from the e-moderator. Participants are here likely to challenge the content of the course and start constructing their own knowledge.

Salmon's model is of particular interest since it provides a temporal framework for how an online learning community develops and highlights different aspects that need to be considered during different stages of a course. It thus provides a framework for course design and the role of the teacher, or e-moderator, during the different stages of the course (see Figure 1).

Figure 1. The five stage model (Salmon, 2004, p. 29)

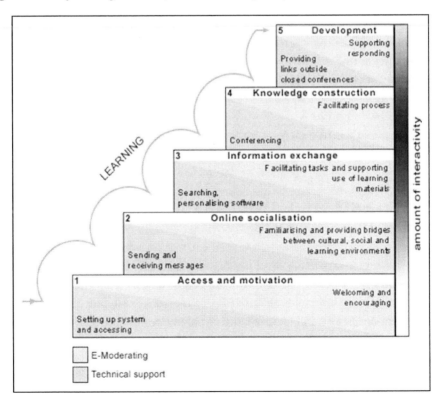

Johnson, Johnson, Stanne, and Garibaldi's (1990) Key Element Model is more focussed on the students' behaviour and how task design can help to promote certain characteristics deemed as essential key elements for collaborative learning. The list includes:

- **Positive Interdependence:** Students organize themselves by assuming roles which facilitate their collaboration.
- **Promotive Interaction:** Students take responsibility for the group's learning by sharing knowledge as well as questioning and challenging each other.
- **Individual Accountability:** Each student is held responsible for taking an active part in the group's activities, completing his/her own designated tasks, and helping other students in their learning.
- **Social Skills:** Students use leadership skills, including making decisions, developing consensus, building trust, and managing conflicts.
- **Self-Evaluation:** Students assess individual and collective participation to ensure productive collaboration (Beisenbach-Lucas, 2004, p. 157).

These basic key elements were worked into task design (see Section 4 below for more examples and details).

We also had some additional starting points when designing the courses which included: clarity in terms of instructions and design, ease of access to learning materials, engaging courses, the possibility of written and oral modes communication, the creation of a 'low anxiety' environment where students would feel free to communicate using informal language, and finally that tasks and written exams would test surface as well as deep structure knowledge. The prerequisites are summarised below in Figure 2.

Having given the framework for the course design, I will now go on to give an account of practical examples of community building in the courses.

3. GETTING STARTED: STUDENT SUPPORTING PROSPECTIVE STUDENTS

Starting to study at university level is a big step for many people and doing so in an online environment perhaps even more so. Many studies from traditional campus environments have shown that the use of peer mentors or student "buddy" systems can help reduce anxiety and facilitate the initial integration process (Heffern, 2003; DuBois et al., 2005; Yorke & Thomas, 2003). We tried to apply this model to our programmes.

Figure 2. Starting points for course design (adapted from Deutschmann, et al., 2006, p. 219)

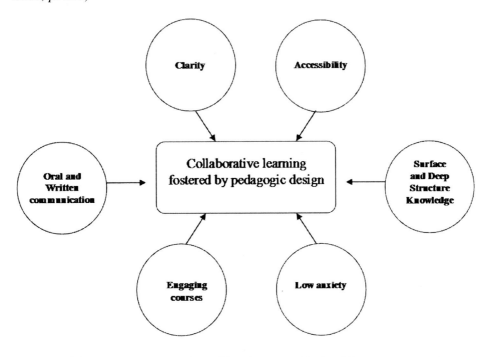

Mature students, in particular women, are overrepresented in the student community at Mid Sweden University. This category of student often has several other commitments apart from their studies – jobs and families are the most obvious. From questionnaires, it has, for example, been brought to our attention that more than 75 percent of our students in English have between 50-100 percent paid commitment apart from their studies. This includes employment and parental leave. In other words, studies often compete with other activities of equal importance. This may result in high drop-out rates, and that many students never actually get started with their studies.

During the first years of running the courses, we were struck by the great discrepancy between the number of students who applied for, and were admitted to, the courses on the one hand, and the number of students who got as far as registering themselves and actually started their studies, on the other. This was especially true for the so-called A-courses, the first term of studies. We were curious as to what was hindering students from fulfilling their initial intentions to study and started enquiring into this question.

There were several issues that came up related to problems in the admission/ registration processes. Students found it hard to find the necessary information and often missed necessary parts of the process. In order to understand these, it is necessary first to give a brief outline of what a student has to do in order to join a course at the university.

Prospective students first apply to a course via a national admission database. In this system students can apply to several courses at the same time, ranking these in order of preference (first choice, second choice etc). If a student has the necessary qualifications, and if there is space on a course, s/he is then sent a letter informing her/him that they have been admitted to their different choices. The students then have to respond to these accepting or rejecting their choices. After this initial stage the local university admission board takes over and communicates the lists of students who have accepted their places on a course to the various departments. It is then departments' responsibility to contact the students with administrative details concerning the course – timetables, course plans, where and when to meet etc. At Mid Sweden University this information is provided on departmental homepages, and letters are sent out to students informing them where to find the information.

The next stage is registration. For online students, this is done via the so-called "student portal". About two weeks prior to course start, admitted students are sent user IDs and passwords by mail and are then asked to activate their profiles by entering the student portal site. It is also here that they find the online forms for formal registration to the courses that they have been admitted to. Registration can, however, only be done four days before course start at the very earliest. It is only once the student has registered on the course formally that s/he gains access to the first module in the Learning Management System (LMS) WebCT, which is also available through the student portal. Furthermore, gaining access to the course platform of the English Courses is a two-stage process: firstly, the students gain access to a general Introduction platform. After having completed an introductory assignment, they are then split into groups and given access to the first course module of the programme. In summary then, the process from applying to a course to actually getting started on the same is quite complex and involves several steps. These are summarised in Figure 3.

In the above process, there are obviously several potential hurdles and students are often daunted by the complexity of the system. After initial enquiries into where the problems lay, two actions were taken to help clarify the process. Firstly, of less interest here, an online site was set up where the students were given an overview of the process as well as specific information and FAQ-lists for each part of the admittance and registration process. Secondly, we decided to use current students as a support resource for students who were in the process of being admitted to the courses. This latter line of action proved very successful and will thus be dealt with in more detail.

Figure 3. Admission and registration process, English online courses at Mid Sweden University

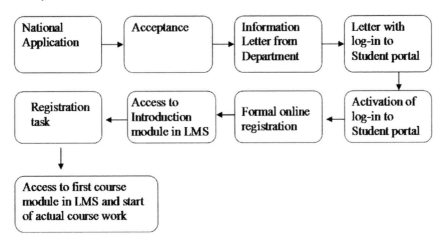

In the "Student Supports Student" project we recruited students from our own courses who would then act as peer mentors for new recruits. These students were chosen on the basis of their activity in the courses and included individuals who had been particularly supportive to their fellow students. On a typical course, there are usually one or two students, especially, who take this role of supportive peer. These students become very active in discussion forums helping others with practical issues related to the course. Our idea was to use this resource more systematically and also to compensate the students for their work. Selected students were thus approached and were then instructed how to support the new recruits.

The student mentors were given contact lists of all the applicants to the courses who had indicated that the English courses were their first, second or third choices of preference. The student mentors were then asked to phone up the applicants on two occasions during the admittance and registration process: The first occasion was early in the process shortly before the applicants had to accept their places on a course. On this first occasion, our student mentors were instructed to answer general queries about the course, such as explaining what tools we used, how the courses were organised, what commitment the courses entailed, what computer facilities the students needed etc. They were also asked to give a brief outline of the registration procedures. The second contact occasion was scheduled for later in the process, shortly before the formal registration (i.e. roughly a week before term start). On this occasion they were to inform the applicants more specifically about the details involved in registering and accessing the learning environment. The student mentors were also asked to note occasions when applicants had decided not to join the course and enquire about reasons for this. Finally, we also asked the student mentors to enquire about the applicants' attitude towards the Student Supports Student project.

The results from this student support activity have been encouraging. Of the approximately 260 applicants that were contacted during the first two terms only one expressed irritation. The rest were positive. Many applicants had wanted to contact the university in order to enquire about details but were uncomfortable about bothering teachers with practicalities. They were thus relieved when they could ask "stupid questions" to a peer. They also appreciated talking to someone who had actually studied on the courses so that they could get a clear idea of content and work load from a student perspective. In other words, students supporting applicants was in many ways more appropriate than teachers doing the same. An additional benefit was that teachers experienced that they received less enquiries regarding practical issues prior to course start, something which had previously been time consuming and taxing.

The most positive result of this activity, however, was observed in the recruitment statistics to the courses. In spring 2007, there were 81 applicants who indicated that the Internet English A course was their first-hand choice. Note here that we do not have access to the statistics concerning how many students had chosen the course as their second or third choice. The same term, 65 students accepted their course places and 64 actually registered on the course. In comparison spring term 2008, only had 68 first-hand applicants. The number of students who actually accepted their places after being approached by the student mentors was, however, 92, which means that many of the applicants who had specified the online English course at Mid Sweden University as their second or third choice, actually went on to choose to study on this course rather than their first-hand choice. Of the 92 students that accepted their places on the course, 88 went on to register spring term 2008. We have observed similar tendencies all the terms that we have been conducting the student mentor system and it is now fully integrated into the course structure. Figure 4 summarises the outcome of the student mentor activity spring 2008 in comparison with spring 2007, when no such support was in place.

4. FOSTERING COMMUNITY BUILDING AND COLLABORATIVE LEARNING THROUGH TASK DESIGN

On the courses, there are a number of types of tasks with different functions. The overall pedagogical aim, however, is to encourage collaborative learning in the different stages of the courses. To this effect, we have used Johnson et al.'s (1990) Key Element Model as a starting point. Key elements here include interdependence, interaction, accountability, social skills and self evaluation (cf. above section 2).

Figure 4. Effects of student mentor activity prior to course start spring 2008

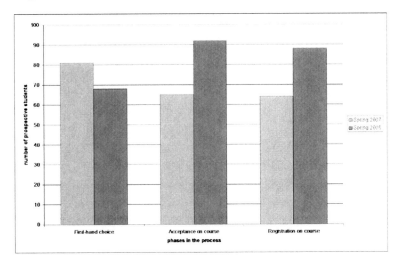

During the initial stages of a course, tasks are primarily aimed at creating contact. So-called warm-up tasks are used to this effect. This type of task is usually quite 'easy' and informal, and tries to cover topics which connect the particular academic subject of the course to the real life experiences of the students. The tasks are formulated in such a way that they should be fun to write and read and there are no strict requirements concerning form or language. Examples of such tasks include the warm-up task of the Grammar course on the A-level – My Past Experiences of Grammar, where students are encouraged to tell each other anecdotes from their school days and the different types of lessons and teachers they have been exposed to. In the Cultural Studies course on the same level, the warm-up task involves discussing stereotypes that the students associate with the United Kingdom and the USA. In the linguistics course on the C-level, a course which deals with various topics of linguistics including semantics, pragmatics and socio-linguistics, the same task involves giving accounts of funny incidents that the students have experienced resulting from mistranslations and other language hitches. The tasks are submitted in public discussion boards and the result is often entertaining reading and adds to process of group building. In this type of task, the main emphasis is thus on the social skills element in the Key Element model above. These tasks can also be seen as adapted for Stage 2, Socialisation processes in Salmon's Five Stage Model.

Once the course gets under way, the typical task tries to incorporate all the key elements in Johnson et al's model and tasks that are adapted for stages 3 and 4, the Information and Knowledge Construction stages, in Salmon's Five Stage Model. In practical terms this entails tasks that include an individual element, a group element (usually involving students reviewing and discussing each other's work), followed by an individual reflection, where the student evaluates his/her own performance and the feed-back received from others. The aims are to create collaboration, but also individual accountability, joint responsibility and the ability to give and take critique in a constructive manner. In addition, self reflection is an added element in this type of task. The following example illustrates these aspects in more detail:

On the Grammar course of the A-level there are four tasks that operate according to the above model. In one of these tasks, students are asked to work with article usage in English and are asked to decide and motivate/explain the use or non-use of the definite, indefinite or zero articles in a number of example sentences. The point here is that many of the examples do not have single correct answers, and it is thus the explanations that are of real grammatical interest. For example, a sentence such as "He got out of (insert "a", "the" or the zero article) bed.", could yield two, arguably three different correct answers, depending on context. Thus the explanation, both in terms of meaning and grammatical structure, is of main interest here.

The first part of this task involves an individual element where the student has to work out the answers and motivations by him/herself (individual accountability). The second stage of the task involves the students posting these solutions in group discussion forums (four members per group) for peer commenting. Important to note here, is that the groups are not predetermined by the teacher, but are decided on the basis of when the students finish the individual element of the task. No student can join a group without posting their individual task solutions, and groups are filled as students finish this part of the task. In other words, a student will join the group where there is space (i.e. less than four members). As students finish the individual part of the task, more and more groups fill up. The effect of this way of grouping students is that: 1. all members in a group have actually provided their individual input for the group task to proceed, and 2. students are in phase with each other, i.e. efficient students do not have to wait for the input of those that are late, since they will not end up in the same groups. Individual accountability is thus a key element here. In the second phase of the task, the students are then asked to comment the solutions of the other three members of the group, discussing differences and similarities. This part of the task involves the key elements interdependence, accountability and social skills. The students thus have to give and receive critique and are challenged to reflect over their own and other students' answers. The final part of the task involves a reflective summary of the peer discussion. Students are asked to summarise comments they have made and received and how these affected the view of their original solution. This document is then sent to the teacher and graded. The final part thus involves the key element self evaluation, but also interdependence and accountability since the summary cannot be completed if students do not comment on each other's work. Excerpt 1 demonstrates the type of discussions that is generated by the tasks. The example is taken from the Mini Mid Sweden Corpus of Computer Assisted Language Learning (Mini-McCall), a pilot corpus currently being constructed at Mid Sweden University, based on communication from the courses (for more information see Deutschmann, Ädel, Garretson & Walker 2009). The names below have been anonymised.

Excerpt 1

Hi Elma!
I've read your work and I think you are making it very clear. I just have some thoughts, in 2.e you say that the use of the article "a" is used because it refers to a specific programme. But I think the use of the article in "a very good programme" is because it's not refering to a specific programme, just a programme, and it's mentioned for the first time? I think the same goes for 2.g. where it doesn't refer to a specific house, they just live in "a house" by the sea. I had some trouble myself with why we don't want to use an article on Italian food in 2.h. Can you help? Take care!
Sofia.

There are also other types of tasks, such as group tasks (students together producing PowerPoint presentations, for example), problem-based tasks and discussion seminars, where different issues are discussed using real time audio. As students get to know each other and 'open up', it is interesting to note how much the content of the courses is enriched by the input of the students themselves. This is in line with the predictions of Salmon's Five Stage Model, where the Development stage (stage 5), involves students becoming more responsible for their own learning and adding to content themselves.

The student groups are often very heterogeneous and the discussions are enriched by the varied personal experiences. In Excerpt 2, for example, a student residing in Africa comments on a task in the literature module based on the Chinua Achebe's *Things fall Apart*. The task involves discussing differences in social structures between Europeans and Africans as illustrated in the novel. The student below draws from her experiences in Africa to illustrate this point further with her own experiences:

Excerpt 2

Socialising in XXXX means visiting your friends, sitting down and leaving after several hours. Marriages take three days. When the great Tabaski feast occurs, I am placed in an impossible situation because I have many friends to visit, but as the guest of honour I cannot leave too early nor arrive too late at the next place, so someone is always bound to feel rejected... Amongst my close friends however, our conversations are never formal, but a typical greeting, whether it be on the phone or in person, always goes as following:

- *Sanu, sanu! (hello, hello)*
- *Ina uni? (How are you)*
- *Lahia lo! (Very well!)*
- *Ina gajiya? (How is your tiredness?)*
- *Ba' gajiya! (Don't have any tiredness)*
- *Ina guida? (how is the family?)*
- *Lahia lo! (Very well!)¨*
- *Ina aiki? (How is work?) -*
- *Alhamdulai! (God be thanked!) -*
- *Ina rana? (How is the sun? = How are you coping with the sun?)*
- *Ina iska? (How are you coping with the wind?)*
- Ah, akway iska dayawa! Akway rana dayawa! (Oh, there is a lot of wind! There is a lot of sun!)

By then, you've already spent two minutes talking to one another, and since you were just passing, you bid farewell.

Other examples of student input enriching the course content include an occasion of oral discussion on gender and language, when a student studying from prison told the rest of his colleagues about male language norms in American prisons. The student in question had spent twelve years in this environment and obviously knew what he was talking about! On another occasion a woman of Indian decent told her fellow students about her experiences from England, and how she was treated depending on what accent she used, Standard English or Indian English, both of which she mastered perfectly. The point here is that collaborative tasks of this nature draw on the knowledge capital of the student body itself so that he students themselves become part of the source of the content adding to subject relevance. This adds to engagement.

5. TEACHER ROLE AND MODELS OF COMMUNICATION

The traditional situation, where teachers act in the role of providers of knowledge through one-way communication is becoming less and less valid. In collaborative models of learning, knowledge is instead negotiated through social processes where people must define their roles, build trust, and identify common goals and expectations (Palloff & Pratt, 1999). The tool used in all these processes is language and the social signals transmitted through this medium arguably constitute the "oil" of the collaborative machinery. The initial communication between teachers and students sets the communicative culture on a course, and we have tried to take this into consideration in our courses.

As mentioned earlier, it is clear that the educator has to be more than a mere source of information. The e-moderator also has an important role in the process of community building. Salmon (2004: 52) lists a number of tasks that an online educator has to deal with apart from lecturing and evaluating work, including many social aspects such as giving encouragement, dealing with insecurities, installing confidence, building bridges for communication, giving guidance about online behaviour, encouraging the sharing of information etc. Especially in the initial stages of a course, the educator's most important task is arguably to orchestrate the prerequisites for learning, to set the scene for a collaborative learning environment. It is thus reasonable to expect the efforts of the teacher, both in terms of quality and quantity, to be of decisive importance for the future success/failure of a particular course. In an e-learning environment, these efforts are largely manifested linguistically, in the educators' everyday communication with the students.

Further challenges in this respect are represented by the mode of interaction; communication in the digital environment is often primarily dependent on asynchronous written text. This mode of interaction is lacking in such key elements as intonation, facial expressions, eye contact and body language – social elements of communication that we heavily rely upon (Palloff & Pratt, 1999). Such non-referential meaning instead has to be embedded in the written text, leading to a situation that demands special language skills, both in relation to production and interpretation.

Formality is one such linguistic aspect. Formality is generally associated with communicative situations where there is great power difference and/or social distance between the communicators (cf. Brown and Levinson 1987). Formal style is, however, very hard to define, even though most native speakers intuitively have a feeling for when something is formal or not. Many researchers, however, make a distinction between formal and informal based on the factor of 'involvement', i.e. how language signals distance or closeness between communicators (see Biber 1988 and Heylighen & Dewaele 1999, for example). Given this presupposition, we have tried to create a learning environment that signals involvement rather that formality, and this has been worked into the communicative model.

Another factor related to communication and the teacher role, especially in the early stages of a course before the students have formed a community, is the quantity/frequency of communication. Students often feel insecure and uncertain that they are actually doing what they are supposed to and need reassurance. Waiting a few days before answering queries, without explicitly explaining that you answer mails on certain days of the week, for example, might be devastating and cause unnecessary anxiety and frustration. As the course progresses it is, however, also important to point out that greater responsibility has to be placed on students to communicate with each other instead of relying on the teacher.

In a study of teacher-student communication in the early stages of our online courses (Deutschmann & Lundmark 2008), we explored these two factors – the quantity and quality of teacher communication and the consequences that these variables had on student performance. We were able to show that there was a positive correlation between how active the teacher was in communicating with the students and how active the students were in communicating with each other. Student activity in its turn seemed to affect pass rates; the more active students were in communicating on the courses, the more likely they were to pass. In addition, we were able to show that teachers that used involved language were more successful in creating an active communicative environment. The results suggest that two important factors that affect the level of student activity in the initial stages of an online course include how much the teacher communicates with the class and the manner in which he or she does so. The optimal prerequisites for an active class seem to be a teacher who communicates frequently with the students and shows involvement through his/her language use.

Synchronous audio communication is introduced on our courses during the second term, as learners become more confident with the technology involved. Synchronous online audio environments deserve a special mention here. One problem with online audio environments is that many of the cues available in ordinary face-to-face communication are missing. As humans we depend on these cues for communication. If, for example, we are met with total silence in a conversation and/ or a listener who shows no facial or bodily expression that he or she is listening, chances are that we will stop talking. In an ordinary conversation these interactional cues and supportive moves can be quite subtle – a nod or a smile is often enough. In an online situation, however, they have to be more obviously expressed. One way of doing this is through so-called minimal responses – *uhuh, hmm, okay, yeah, I see* and other minimal forms "which encourage a speaker to continue talking" and which "indicate that the listener is paying attention and is interested in hearing more" (Holmes, 1995:56).

In a study (see Deutschmann & Panichi 2009 and Deutschmann et al 2009) based on an Action Research mode of investigation, we investigated the teacher's role in encouraging active student participation in online oral proficiency classes conducted in the virtual world environment Second Life. Action research represents (see also Figure 5), a "framework for thinking systematically about what happens in social situations, implementing action for change and monitoring and evaluating the effects of the action with a view to continuing development" (Hudson, Owen, & van Veen, 2006: 581).

Figure 5. The moments of action research (from Hudson, Owen, & van Veen, 2006, p. 581)

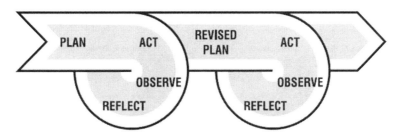

Under our research framework the course *Oral Competence for Doctoral Students* was first conducted in spring 2008, with the ambition to bring doctoral students together in order to practice presenting and discussing their research in English with other post graduates from around the world. When we first started the course, we had little experience of this type of course and the results as far as encouraging active oral participation on behalf of the students were quite discouraging. As it turned out, it was mainly the teachers who did the talking and this was obviously not the aim of the course. We then redesigned the course and did a re-run. Special attention was paid to task design, which was made more student focussed and we also evaluated and discussed our roles as teachers in managing and encouraging active oral participation. The results were encouraging: During the first course the students' contributions represented less than 20 percent of the floor time, the rest being made up of 'teacher talk'. On the second course occasion this trend was reversed and the students' contributions made up roughly 65 percent of the floor space (see Figure 6).

The key to managing online conversation included teachers actively signalling interest and managing the conversation through the use of elicitors – comments and questions, that are uttered in order to elicit a response in the dialogue. This type of teacher behaviour could specifically be shown to be important in contributing to student activity. For example, we correlated the number of minimal responses uttered by teachers to the turn lengths produced by the individual students and signalling active listening seemed to have a direct effect on the turn lengths produced by the students (see Table 1). It was also interesting to note that this linguistic behaviour was imitated by the students, who started supporting each other in a similar fashion as the course progressed.

In summary then, communicative models in an online course is something that we should be aware of as educators. Increased teacher awareness of the specific discourse pragmatics of online communication and the importance of facilitating learner interaction via linguistic involvement may lead to greater learner autonomy

Figure 6. Floor space taken up by teachers and students during sessions 1 of courses 1 and 2 (T1-T3 represents teachers, F1-4 represents female students and M1-3 represent male students) (from Deutschman, et al., 2009, p. 218)

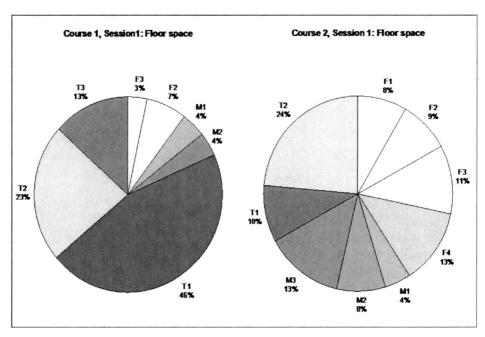

and initiative within these new learning environments. It may also be important for the teacher to be prepared to change his/her role as the course progresses, taking a less prominent position in the latter stages of a course so that students themselves gain control of their learning situation.

Table 1. Correlation coefficients floor time students/responses per minute SL first session (Deutschmann & Panichi, 2009, p. 324)

	F1	F2	F3	F4	M1	M2	M3	Cor. Coeff
Floor time	3:42	2:37	2:22	1:22	1:47	1:33	1:23	
Supportive moves from Teacher per minute	8.65	6.13	6.36	7.35	3.37	4.52	3.62	0,67
Supportive moves from Students per minute	1.89	0.00	1.69	0.00	0.56	0.00	0.00	0,75
Supportive moves total per minute	10.54	6.13	8.05	7.35	3.93	4.52	3.62	0,78

6. CREATING CONTEXTS BEYOND THE CLASS

One important additional factor affecting student engagement and retention is, according to many studies, students' involvement with the subject that goes beyond the specific goals of the course, i.e. to create meaning in the learning experience that can be related to the 'real world'. Language education is no exception and one of the traditional challenges has been to provide meaningful contexts for learning. Few language educators would disagree with the claim that one of the most significant triggers of motivation in learning a foreign language is not an interest in the object itself, the language, but the yearning to communicate via the language. In spite of this, the traditional language classroom is all too often "make-believe"; second language learners are forced into constructed, artificial communicative situations on more or less relevant topics, where they can easily revert to their mother tongue. Consequently, one of the main motivational forces for language learning is not exploited, namely the need and wish to communicate.

In bringing together learners from different language backgrounds, online environments can increase the scope for cross-cultural interaction to the extent that the target language becomes the only viable option for meaningful communication. In a language learning setting, this thus becomes an authentic learning situation, an occasion when learners are forced to use their skills in order to make themselves understood. Authenticity is a primary issue mentioned in online task design. According to Hampel (2003: 24) "meaningful tasks include "the use of authentic materials and authentic settings". She goes on to quote Warschauer (1997: 487) who "demands" that students be given the opportunity to "conduct actively 'meaningful tasks and solve meaningful problems in an environment that reflects their own personal interests as well as the multiple purposes to which their knowledge will be put in the future'"

In an online language course setting, there is really nothing stopping us from creating this type of situation; modern e-learning tools offer the possibility to open up the language classroom to a more global arena with relative ease. In a project involving the online courses, we created tasks where students from other universities around the world collaborated with students from Mid Sweden University in mutually beneficial exchanges, and where the students themselves became part of the source of input for the course content. E-learning tools such as Second Life, online video conferencing tools, voice-blogs, wikis and blogs were used to enable this collaboration.

Some examples of tasks included oral presentations aimed at doctoral students (see section 5). The meetings were held in the virtual reality world of Second Life, which allowed us to simulate a conference environment where the students could present their research in English to other doctoral students situated in various parts of the world. The students appreciated the experiment, as it was an authentic situation where they had to use English in order to communicate their research to others with similar interests. In another course, we used so called voice blogs for asynchronous oral discussions in a literature class. We managed to connect our students in a Global Literature class with students from Central Missouri University who were studying a course of African American literature. Both courses included literature of Alice Walker, and students discussed tasks using the voice blog. The asynchronous nature of the tool meant that time differences did not pose a problem. Students could simply record their thoughts at their leisure and then enter the tool later to see what responses they had received. It was exciting to see how the different perspectives of the two student groups led to a more complete understanding of the books they were reading, and the students appreciated the task. A final example from this project includes the use of blog tools for written discussions on various current topics in our Written Proficiency courses. We set up blogs posts on various topics such as immigration, drugs, prostitution, abortion etc, and students from Pisa University, Italy, studying a similar proficiency course were invited to discuss these topics with our students. Again the students thought the tasks were particularly meaningful as they felt that they were using English in an authentic communicative situation. Some of the comments from the evaluation of these projects are listed below:

I got some really nice input from the Italian Students and it was pretty obvious that we live in different parts of Europe. Our conditions and thoughts differ and the chance to see things from another angel was very interesting.

It's always interesting to be able to discuss issues with people from a different society then your own. It broadens your mind and makes you realise that what we take for granted here in Sweden can be far away from the reality in other countries.

I think this collaboration was a really good way of interchange some ideas and opinions. It was really interesting to hear about what they had to say about my topic and how it was like in their country. This project helped me write my essay because I had been given some more background about the topic!

I think that the thought of this project was brilliant since it involved the skills in talking and listening as well as in reading.

I thought the project was great, I got to try something new which I really enjoyed. Voice blogging, if I can call it that, is fun and quite scary, but very rewarding. Not only do you get to hear yourself talking (good for improving pronunciation!) but you also get to listen to the other student's comments. It made it a lot more personal rather then just reading all the time. And it was great to hear students from Missouri!

Although rewarding, the challenges involved in building up a meaningful international collaboration should not be underestimated. This type of collaboration often involves taking various cross-institutional variables into account and it is often difficult to match one's own course content and learning goals with those of the partner universities. Designing learning activities that are meaningful to all involved thus often requires careful planning. As an illustration of how this can be done we can use *Avalon Debating*, which was conducted under the EU- financed AVALON project, two-year multilateral project aimed at testing and developing models for using virtual worlds in language teaching funded under Key Activity 3 (ICT) of the EU EACEA Life Long Learning Programme (LLP).

Avalon Debating was offered in the spring semester of 2009 and was lead by instructors under the AVALON project. The course was a collaboration between four universities and the learning goals addressed rhetorical skills and argumentation techniques. Special care had to be taken to address what Engström (2001, p.133) calls the four central questions of any theory of learning, namely: 1) Who are the learners? 2) Why do they learn and make the effort? 3) What do they learn, what are the contents and outcomes of learning? and 4) How do they learn? When designing the course, these questions had to be addressed from the different prerequisites presented by the four distinct educational contexts of the different participants involved. In the planning the learning activities, the educators involved thus all contributed to the content so that it would be relevant for the program of their own student group, while at the same time taking the needs of the other student groups into consideration.

In *Avalon Debating* students came from four separate academic programmes at four universities in England, Sweden, Italy and the U.S.A. The English students were teacher trainees and were attending the course as part of an elective on online learning. From these students' point of view the main interest in the course lay in partaking in an online learning event of this nature in order to gain experience and ideas for their future professional lives. The Swedish participants were all students on an Internet English language program. They partook in *Avalon Debating* as part of a ten-week course unit that involved academic presentation and oral proficiency. As such, the Swedish students' motivation for joining the course thus consisted of practicing oral academic discourse in an authentic setting with native speakers. The Italian students were attending PhD programs and their motivation for participating in *Avalon Debating* was primarily to improve their oral proficiency. An acceptable level of English is a prerequisite for any PhD student within the Italian system. The American students were attending Avalon Debating as part of an electorate composition class on the theme of Cyber Culture and were offered extra credits in their ordinary course if for partaking in the collaboration. In addition, they were encouraged to use the debating topics as starting points for their future compulsory compositions, but did not have to do so if they did not want to. From this student group's perspective, the course activities under *Avalon Debating* were thus entirely conducted on a voluntary basis.

Given these, in many ways, disparate profiles the course activity had to be designed with the different learner groups in mind. Three main learning objectives were included in the course description:

- **Technical:** Learning to use virtual worlds for learning, both as a tool for communication and a source of information.
- **Social:** To get to know friends from other countries and being able to collaborate with them in an online environment towards a common goal.
- **Academic:** How to present ideas in a convincing manner, looking at issues such as structure, cohesion, presentation techniques etc.

The first of these learning objectives was designed to appeal to the English and American students' academic interests in particular. Both of these groups had an interest in the digital medium itself and the English students, in particular, also had an interest in how the actual learning processes were affected by the medium. For the Swedish students this objective also made sense since they were attending an Internet course and *Avalon Debating* represented a new way of approaching e-learning.

The social objective was mainly included as a way of addressing the fourth question in Engtröm's list, namely "How they learn?" The course was designed according CSCL-model (Computer Supported Collaborative Learning model – Salmon, 2004) and as such it was important to include this in the overall objectives.

The academic objective was included primarily with the Swedish and American students in mind. Both of these students groups were actually studying courses that involved academic presentation. In order to accommodate the English students' (and American students') subject interest, the topics chosen for the debate all dealt with matters related to various aspects of Internet culture, subjects which were also of general interest for all the students involved. In summary then, the learning activities in the course were designed baring the different academic objectives of the students groups in mind, and thus fits into a design model where each participant's motivation and objectives are key issues in the design of the collaboration. Figure 7 gives an illustration of the design involved in *Avalon Debating*.

In summary, all the above activities described in this section can be seen as part of the fifth stage in Salmon's Five Stage Model, what Salmon refers to as "providing links outside the closed conference". Arguably, this type of activity fosters learner autonomy and places the learning experience in a greater context.

Figure 7. Avalon debating in relation to the student groups' academic programmes

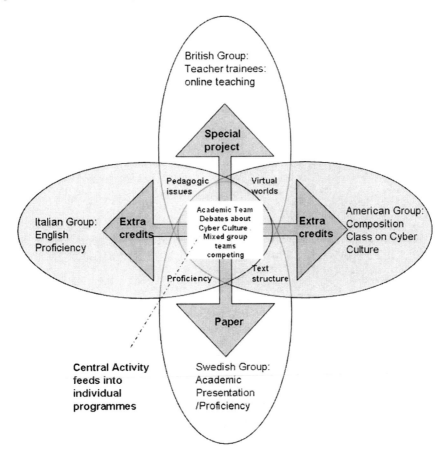

7. SUMMARY AND CONCLUSION

The examples provided in this chapter illustrate how pedagogical research and models can be translated into practical design of online learning environments. Reflecting over issues such as communication and social aspects in a course and finding ways of incorporating models for these in task design and the communicative culture on courses has, in our experience, improved our product. We have managed to retain a front position as a provider of online courses in English in Sweden and our retention rates are quite high, comparable to our campus course (between 65-80%). Course development, however, is a never-ending process and constant monitoring of what goes on in the learning environments is necessary in order to stay ahead. One of the key factors to our modest success is arguably that we acknowledge pedagogics as a serious science, and that we try to apply it in our everyday activity. We have, over the past few years, not only provided courses, but also studied the same in depth. This model of action learning/research, i.e. a framework for thinking systematically about what happens in social situations, implementing action for change and monitoring and evaluating the effects of the action with a view to continuing development, is in my view a serious way to approach any learning product. We are, after all, operating in a domain of constant change and development, and what may be a good model today, might be less so tomorrow.

ACKNOWLEDGMENT

We are grateful to Forum for Flexible Learning at Mid Sweden University, who initially funded this activity.

REFERENCES

Beetham, E., & Sharpe. (2007). *Rethinking pedagogy for a digital age – Designing and delivering e-learning*. London: Routledge.

Biber, D. (1988). *Variation across speech and writing*. Cambridge, UK: Cambridge University Press. doi:10.1017/CBO9780511621024.

Biesenbach-Lucas, S. (2004). Asynchronous web discussions in teacher training courses: Promoting collaborative learning—or not? *AACE Journal, 12*(2), 155–170.

Bonk, C. J., & Cunningham, D. J. (1998). Searching for learner-centered, constructivist, and sociocultural components of collaborative educational learning tools. In Bonk, C. J., & King, K. S. (Eds.), *Electronic collaborators: Learner-centered technologies for literacy, apprenticeship, and discourse* (pp. 25–50). Mahwah, NJ: Erlbaum.

Brown, P., & Levinson. (1987). *Politeness: Some universals in language use*. Cambridge, UK: Cambridge University Press

Carr, S. (2000). As distance education comes of age, the challenge is keeping the students. *The Chronicle of Higher Education, 23*, A39.

Ciekanski, M., & Chanier, T. (2008). Developing online multimodal verbal communication to enhance the writing process in an audio-graphic conferencing environment. *ReCALL, 20*(2), 162–182. doi:10.1017/S0958344008000426.

Deutschmann, M. Dyrvold, Gregersdotter, McIntyre, & Sheppard. (2006). Kollaborativ inlärning som startpunkt för utveckling av Internetkurser inom ämnet engelska. In P. Svensson (Ed.), Från vision till praktik: Språkutbildning och informationsteknik. Nätuniversitetet.

Deutschmann, M., & Lundmark. (2008). Let's keep it informal guys – A study of the effects of teacher communicative strategies on student activity and collaborative learning in Internet-based English courses. *Tidskrift för Lärarutbildning och Forskning, 2*.

Deutschmann, M., & Panichi. (2009). Talking into empty space? Signalling involvement in a virtual language classroom in Second Life. *Language Awareness, 18*(3-4), 310–328. doi:10.1080/09658410903197306.

Deutschmann, M., Ädel, Garretson, & Walker. (2009). Introducing mini-McCALL: A pilot version of the Mid-Sweden corpus of computer-assisted language learning. *ICAME Journal, 33*, 21-44.

Deutschmann, M., Panichi, & Molka-Danielsson. (2009). Designing oral participation in second life – A comparative study of two language proficiency courses. *ReCALL, 21*(2), 206–226. doi:10.1017/S0958344009000196.

Diaz, D. P. (2002). Online drop rates revisited. *The Technology Source*. Retrieved from http://technologysource.org/article/online_drop_rates_revisited/

DuBois, D. L., & Karcher. (2005). *Handbook of youth mentoring*. Thousand Oaks, CA: SAGE Publications Ltd.

Engström, Y. (2001). Expansive learning at work: Toward an activity theoretical reconceptualization. *Journal of Education and Work, 14*(1), 133–156.

Flood, J. (2002). Read all about it: Online learning facing 80% attrition rates. *TOJDE, 3*(2).

Hampel, R. (2003). Theoretical perspectives and new practices in audio-graphic conferencing for language learning. *ReCALL, 15*(1), 21–36. doi:10.1017/S0958344003000314.

Heffern, L. (2003). *Improving student drop-out rates through student observations and peer contacts*. Retrieved from http://www.pde.state.pa.us/able/lib/able/lfp/lfp03heffern.pdf

Heylighen, F., & Dewaele, J.-M. (1999). *Formality of language: Definition, measurement and behavioral determinants*. Brussels, Belgium: Free University of Brussels.

Holmes, J. (1995). *Women, men and politeness*. New York: Longman.

Hudson, B., Owen, D., & van Veen, K. (2006). Working on educational research methods with masters students in an international online learning community. *British Journal of Educational Technology, 37*(4), 577–603. doi:10.1111/j.1467-8535.2005.00553.x.

Johnson, D. W., Johnsson, R. T., Stanne, M., & Garibaldi, A. (1990). The impact of leader and member group processing on achievement in cooperative groups. *The Journal of Social Psychology, 130*, 507–516. doi:10.1080/00224545.1990.9924613.

Kern, R., & Warschauer. (2000). Theory and practice of networkbased language teaching. In M. Warschauer & R. Kern (Eds.), *Networkbased language teaching: Concepts and practice*, (pp. 1–19). Port Chester, NY: Cambridge University Press.

Lave, J., & Wenger, E. (1991). *Situated learning - Legitimate peripheral participation*. Cambridge, UK: Cambridge University Press. doi:10.1017/CBO9780511815355.

Palloff, R. M., & Pratt. (1999). *Building learning communities in cyberspace: Effective strategies for the online classroom*. San Francisco, CA: Jossey-Bass.

Salmon, G. (2002). *E-tivities – The key to active online learning*. London: Kogan Page Ltd..

Salmon, G. (2004). *E-moderating: The key to teaching and learning online* (2nd ed.). London: Routledge. doi:10.4324/9780203465424.

Shaw & Polovina. (1999). Practical experiences of, and lesson learnt from, internet technologies in higher education. *Journal of Educational Technology & Society, 2*(3), 16–24.

Svensson, P. (2003). Virtual worlds as arenas for language learning. In Felix, U. (Ed.), *Language learning online: Towards best practice*. Lisse: Swets & Zeitlinger.

Thornburg, D. (n.d.). *Quote*. Retrieved from http://thinkexist.com/quotation/any_teacher_that_can_be_replaced_by_a_computer/203766.html

Tinto, V. (1975). Dropout from higher education: A theoretical synthesis of recent research. *Review of Educational Research, 45*, 89–125. doi:10.3102/00346543045001089.

Vygotsky, L. S. (1978). *Mind in society*. Cambridge, MA: Harvard University Press.

Warschauer, M. (1997). Computer-mediated collaborative learning: Theory and practice. *Modern Language Journal, 81*(4), 470–481. doi:10.1111/j.1540-4781.1997.tb05514.x.

Wenger, E. (1998). *Communities of practice: Learning, meaning, and identity. Cambridg,e UK*. Cambridge University Press.

Westerberg, P., & Mårald. (2006). *Avbrott på nätutbildningar – En studie av när och varför studenter hoppar av alternativt fullföljer IT-stödda distanskurser* [Interrupted net courses: A study of when and why students drop out or finish IT-supported distance courses]. Umeå, Sweden: Umeå University, Umeå Centre for Evaluation Research.

Yorke, M., & Thomas, L. (2003). Improving the retention of students from lower socio-economic groups. *Journal of Higher Education Policy and Management, 25*(1). doi:10.1080/13600800305737.

Chapter 5
Introducing Peer Collaboration in a Networked English Writing Class

Huahui Zhao
Umeå University, Sweden

EXECUTIVE SUMMARY

This chapter proposes a model of introducing networked peer assessment to an online course. In the organisation background, the benchmark model of peer assessment is introduced in terms of its theoretical and empirical bases. The discussions about Dadaelous Integrated Writing Environment (DIWE) and empirical studies on its use in language classes set the stage of the model of networked peer assessment. The model is then described in detail in terms of its structure and its use within DIWE. Challenges for using networked peer assessment are then discussed in the light of learners' technological skills, online collaboration skills, and shifted teachers' and students' role in online learning. This chapter ends with solutions and recommendations in dealing with the three challenges mainly in terms of training students in technological use and in developing online collaboration skills and training teachers in using networked peer assessment.

DOI: 10.4018/978-1-4666-4486-1.ch005

ORGANISATION BACKGROUND

In the past decades, peer assessment has been increasingly used and extensively examined in the field of second language (L2) writing, mainly through the lens of socio-cultural theory. In this theoretical framework, human activities, including language learning, is suggested to be socially and culturally mediated via tools such as language, external sources and others (e.g. peers and teachers) (Vygotsky, 1978). Further, socio-cultural theory suggests that social mediation is most conducive for learning when it is provided within a learner's Zone of Proximal Development (ZPD) (Aljaafreh and Lantolf, 1994; Guerrero and Villamil, 2000; Lantolf, 2000; Weissberg, 2006). ZPD refers to "the distance between the actual developmental level determined by independent problem solving and the higher level of potential development determined through problem solving in collaboration with more capable peers or seniors" (Vygotsky, 1978, pp.86). In the field of L2 learning, ZPD was adapted by Foster and Ohta (2005) as "the distance between the actual developmental level determined by individual linguistic production, and the level of potential development determined through language produced collaboratively with a teacher or peer" (p.144). As far as peer assessment in L2 writing is concerned, ZPD "recognises the importance of peer assistance in the solutions of tasks and, consequently, in learning" (Villamil and Guerrero, 1996, pp.54) and thus is presented as the concept that best explains social interaction and social mediation in peer assessment for the development of an individual's writing skill (Villamil and Guerrero, 2006). The discussion of ZPD indicates that collaborative peer assessment could assist L2 learners to achieve a higher developmental level of writing skills than that determined by an individual writing activity. This has been substantiated in empirical studies on peer assessment.

Tables 1, 2, and 3 summarise key studies on the use of peer assessment in L2 writing classes, based on literature search of key journals on L2 learning and teaching. The scope of the review was narrowed to those published after 1990, four years before the special issue on peer assessment in Modern Language Journal (1994, winter) which seemed to launch increasing discussions about peer assessment. Key words used to search the literature included peer feedback, peer response, peer review, peer interaction and peer revision.

From Tables 1, 2, and 3, we could observe the following key findings of peer assessment for L2 writing:

1. L2 learners were capable of providing feedback on both local and rhetorical areas (e.g. Mendonca and Johnson, 1994; Hu, 2005).
2. Peer assessment played a complementary role to teacher assessment by focusing on different language aspects of writing and covering areas unaddressed by teachers (e.g. Caulk, 1994; Tsui and Ng, 2000).

Table 1. Studies examining learners' performance in peer assessment for L2 writing

Study	Research focus and main theoretical ground	Participants	Data collection approach	Key findings
(1) Carson and Nelson (1994, 1996)	The influence of learners' culture background on their behaviours in group writing through the lens of socio-cultural theory	11 advanced ESL (English as a Second Language) college students	Videotaping peer response; Interviews	1. Chinese students' primary goal of maintaining group harmony in group work affected the nature and type of interaction in their group discussions. 2. Chinese students were reluctant to criticize drafts or disagree with peers because they thought they were lack of authority and expertise as readers, compared to their teachers. 3. Chinese students accepted peer comments without negotiation and did not force peers to accept their comments either.
(2) Connor and Asenavage (1994)	A comparison of focus and effectiveness of peer and teacher feedback through the lens of process-approach writing (i.e. writing is socially and culturally embedded act.)	8 ESL college freshmen in two groups	Three audio-recorded peer interaction on the first draft; Teacher feedback on the second draft	1. Five percent of revisions were based on peer feedback, against 35% and 60% based on teacher feedback and other resources, respectively. 2. Collaborators' commitment to interaction played an important role in the effectiveness of peer feedback. 3. Learners' previous English learning experiences, especially the teacher's role in classroom influenced learners' use of peer feedback in revisions.
(3) Guerrero and Villamil (1994)	Interaction during peer revisions through the lens of socio-cultural theory	54 intermediate ESL college students	40 tape-recorded peer interaction sessions, consisting of 17 on narrative essays and 23 on persuasive essays	1. L2 learners helped peers with their writing in a symmetrical or asymmetrical interaction pattern. 2. Genres of writing influenced the development of social relationships during interaction. 3. Learners took risks and struggled to comply with peer revision tasks despite their linguistic and rhetorical limitations. 4. Teachers should provide learners with opportunities to interact with a range of peers.

continued on following page

Table 1. Continued

Study	Research focus and main theoretical ground	Participants	Data collection approach	Key findings
(4) Hu (2005)	Provision of peer feedback by Chinese ESL college students through the lens of process-approach writing	Three different groups of Chinese ESL college students in Singapore in a three year action research project	Questionnaires investigating learners' perceptions of the effectiveness of peer feedback; Analysis of peer feedback and its use in revisions	1. Learners responded to both rhetorical and local issues. 2. Many valid suggestions made by learners were not addressed by the teacher. 3. Learners claimed to learn more by reading others' work than by providing feedback on peers' writing. 4. Providing training in offering peer feedback and teacher intervening in peer assessment were suggested to be important for peer assessment.
(5) Lockhart and Ng (1995)	Interaction in ESL peer response groups through the lens of socio-cultural theory	27 dyads of ESL freshmen English majors in Hong Kong	Audio-recorded interactions in labs	1. Learners approached the same task in different ways. 2. Focus and effectiveness of peer interaction differed from collaboration patterns. 3. Teachers could influence learners' perceptions of peer response and shape their ways of engaging in peer response activities. 4. Learners' previous experiences of writing and feedback, their personalities, and the classroom context influenced collaboration patterns.
(6) Mendonca and Johnson (1994)	Peer negotiation and use of peer feedback; Learners' perceptions of peer responses; Through the lens of socio-cultural theory	12 advanced ESL college learners in dyads	Audio-recording peer response; Revisions with feedback; Interviews with learners	1. Different types of negotiation were observed. 2. Learners focused on both local and global issues. 3. Peer feedback led to 53% revisions. 4. All learners indicated to benefit from both peer and teacher responses.
(7) Nelson and Murphy (1993)	Effects of peer responses on revisions through the lens of collaborative learning and process-approach writing	4 intermediate ESL college students	Videotaping peer feedback; Learners' revisions with peer feedback	1. Learners made a mean 3.2 of revisions with peer responses (total score: 5). 2. Learners were inconsistent in the use of peer feedback. 3. Learners who interacted with peers in a collaborative manner were more likely to incorporate peer feedback in redrafts.

continued on following page

Table 1. Continued

Study	Research focus and main theoretical ground	Participants	Data collection approach	Key findings
(8) Storch (2001, 2002, 2005)	Collaborative paired writing of ESL learners through the lens of socio-cultural theory	ESL college students in dyads (most from Asia) (2001-three pairs; 2002- ten pairs; 2005-23 students in pairs or by themselves)	Audio-taping interaction data	1. Collaborative dyads produced the longest and the most accurate texts. 2. Language proficiency and the length of time spent on the task impacted the effectiveness of peer collaboration for the improvement of writing quality.
(9) Villamil and Guerrero (1996) and Guerrero and Villamil (2000)	Revision activities; Mediating strategies; Social behaviours; Through the lens of socio-cultural theory	54 intermediate ESL college students	Interaction data; Revisions with feedback	1. Mutual scaffolding occurred between two novice writers. 2. Peer oral interaction provided learners with the chance to explain, defend, and clarify their viewpoints. 3. First language appeared to be a natural crutch for peer interaction. 4. The institutional context was tightly related to the nature of collaboration.
(10) Villamil and Guerrero (1998, 2006)	Impact of peer revisions on learners' final drafts of narration and persuasion essays through the lens of socio-cultural theory	14 intermediate ESL college students	Audio-recorded interaction; Revisions with feedback	1. Seventy-four percent of peer commentary was incorporated. 2. The rhetorical modes influenced the effectiveness of peer assessment. 3. Seven percent of students' revisions with peer feedback were incorrect.

Table 2. Studies examining learners' perceptions of peer assessment for L2 writing

Study	Research focus	Participants	Data collection approach	Key findings
(1) Jacobs et al (1998)	Learners' preference for peer feedback	121 EFL (English as Foreign Language) college learners from Hong Kong and Taiwan	Questionnaires	Ninety-three percent of learners preferred to have peer feedback for their writing because it increased feedback sources and helped them to spot the mistakes that they themselves could not find.
(2) Leki (1990) Cited in Ferris (2003a) and Guerrero and Villamil (2000)	Learners' perceptions of reading others' papers, reading and hearing other learners' comments	20 ESL college writing students	Students' responses to two questions concerning reading peers' papers and reading/hearing peer feedback on their writing	1. Sixteen of seventeen students made positive comments about the helpfulness of reading peers' papers. 2. The majority of learners expressed positive attitudes towards peer feedback: 15 positive, 5 negative and 2 mixed reactions.
(3) Mangelsdorf (1992)	Learners' perceptions of the type and value of peer feedback provided during peer oral interaction	40 ESL college freshmen in a composition course; 5 ESL teachers	In-class discussion	1. Most students and teachers held positive attitudes towards peer response. 2. Peer response helped learners obtain different ideas about a topic, develop and clarify ideas, foster audience awareness, and provided models to follow. 3. Seventy-seven percent of students were concerned about their limited language proficiency as critics and thus lacked trust in peer feedback on their texts. 4. Most negative comments came from students with an Asian background.
(4) Zhang (1995, 1999)	Students' preference for peer and teacher feedback	81 ESL college learners with exposure to peer, teacher and self-assessment	Questionnaires	Learners overwhelmingly preferred teacher feedback to peer feedback, irrespective of gender, ethnicity and ESL proficiency.

Table 3. Studies examining the effects of training on peer assessment for L2 writing

Study	Research focus	Participants	Data collection and analysis approach	Key findings
(1) Berg (1999)	Effects of training on students' revision types and writing quality	46 intermediate ESL students in an American university	Experimental design: comparing the trained and untrained group in terms of the quality of revisions and the quality of writing	1. The trained group generated more meaning changes than the untrained group. 2. The trained group made greater improvement of writing quality than the untrained group. 3. Language proficiency appeared not to significantly influence training effectiveness.
(2) Min (2005)	Effects of training on the quantity and quality of peer comments	18 second-year students in her composition class in Taiwan	Comparison design: collecting peer response data before and after training	The provision of training resulted in a significantly increased number of comments on global issues, more specific and focused ways in elaborating writers' ideas, and a higher level of confidence for less-advanced students.
(3) Stanley (1992)	Effects of training time on peer assessment	31 ESL college freshmen most from Asia	Experimental design: providing 7 hours of training with one group of 12 students and 1 hour of coaching with another group of 19 students	The more extensively coached group made more conversations about their drafts with a higher level of motivation, confidence and engagement, and, as a result, generated more specific peer comments on peers' writing and more revisions with peer feedback.
(4) Zhu (1995, 2001) and McGroary and Zhu (1997)	Effects of training on peer comments and peer interaction	145 native English speakers and 24 non-native English speakers	Experimental design: comparing experimental and control groups with respect to the quantity and quality of feedback generated on peer writing and in peer interaction	1. Training students in peer response led to significantly more and better quality peer feedback. 2. Trained learners were more engaged in interaction and negotiation of meaning. 3. Peer responses did not necessarily lead to beneficial social interaction and mediation for learners' writing quality.

3. Peer feedback triggered revisions in learners' subsequent drafts, to a varied extent (e.g. Nelson and Murphy, 1993; Mendonca and Johnson, 1994; Villamil and Guerrero, 1998).

4. Individual differences in approaches to peer assessment existed among L2 learners (e.g. Guerrero and Villamil, 1994; Mendonca and Johnson, 1994; Lockhart and Ng, 1995).

5. Peer collaboration patterns influenced the quantity and quality of peer feedback (e.g. Storch, 2001, 2002, 2005).

6. Learners made positive comments on peer assessment (e.g. Jacobs, et al., 1998; Ferris, 2003b) but no evident preference for peer assessment was made when they were asked to compare peer and teacher assessment (Zhang, 1995, 1999).

7. Factors affecting the efficacy of peer assessment also included learners' English language proficiency (e.g. Mangelsdorf, 1992; Storch, 2001, 2005), learners' previous English learning experiences (e.g. Carson and Nelson, 1994, 1996), the nature of writing tasks (e.g. Guerrero and Villamil, 1994; Villamil and Guerrero, 1998, 2006), and teachers' perceptions of and intervention in, peer assessment (Lockhart and Ng, 1995).

8. Training learners to do peer assessment could increase the quantity of peer feedback and enhance the efficiency of peer assessment (e.g. Stanley, 1992; Zhu, 1995; McGroarty and Zhu, 1997; Zhu, 2001; Min, 2005).

With reference to socio-cultural theory and empirical evidence of peer assessment, a case study research was conducted to explore how peer assessment facilitated learners developing their L2 writing capacity in a traditional face-to-face English writing class. Eighteen second-year English majors in a university in China were involved in the study for 16 weeks. Peer assessment was examined in terms of peer written feedback, peer oral interaction and learners' perceptions of peer assessment, by using teacher assessment as the comparison baseline. Table 4 provides an overview of the research design.

Based on the findings in the case study, a model of introducing peer assessment into a face-to-face L2 writing class was proposed, as shown in Figure 1.

As shown in Figure 1, the model consists of six steps.

Step 1: Introduces peer assessment into the class, inviting students to discuss their understanding of peer assessment, possible values and problems of peer assessment, and ways to solve the problems. This step aims to familiarise students with the concept of peer assessment and motivate them to participate in peer assessment through clarifying the value of peer assessment and inviting them to address their concerns about peer assessment.

Table 4. Overview of research design

Stage 1: Pre-Assessment Phase
Research Questions
RQ1: What were the students' perceptions of peer assessment for the development of their English writing before they were involved in peer assessment in their writing class?   **RQ2:** What were the tutor's perceptions of peer assessment for the development of students' English writing before he used it in his writing class?
Data Collecting Methods
1. Student questionnaires and interviews (for RQ1)   2. Student learning diaries on peer assessment (for RQ1)   3. Teacher interviews (for RQ2)
Data Size
1. 16 student questionnaire and 11 student interview data sets
2. 43 diary entries
3. one writing teacher interviewee
Stage 2: Assessment Phase
Research Questions
RQ3: Were there differences in written feedback provided by the peer assessors and the writing tutor? If there were, what were the differences?   **RQ4:** Were there differences in oral feedback provided by the peer assessors and the writing tutor? If there were, what were the differences?   **RQ5:** Were there differences in learners' responses to peer feedback and teacher feedback? If there were, what were the differences?
Data Collecting Methods
1. Collecting peer and teacher feedback on the first drafts (for RQ3)   2. Recording peer oral interaction in class (for RQ4)   3. Recording teacher-student conferencing (for RQ4)   4. Collecting students' revised drafts (for RQ5)   5. Conducting stimulated recall interviews to examine learners' understanding of feedback (for RQ5)
Data Size
1. 79 written assignments containing 1552 teacher feedback instances and 620 peer feedback instances
2. 26 peer and teacher-student oral interaction data
3. 26 stimulated recall interview data
Stage 3: Post-Assessment Phase
Research Questions
RQ6: What were the students' perceptions of peer assessment for the development of their English writing after they were involved in peer assessment in their writing class?   **RQ7:** What were the tutor's perceptions of peer assessment for the development of students' English writing after he used it in his writing class?   **RQ8:** What were the factors that emerged to influence the use of peer assessment in the writing class?
Data Collecting Methods
1. Student questionnaires and interviews (for RQ6 and RQ8)   2. Student diaries (for RQ6 and RQ8)   3. Teacher interviews (for RQ7 and RQ8)

continued on following page

Table 4. Continued

Data Size
1. 17 student questionnaire and 11 student interview data sets
2. 34 learning diary entries
3. one teacher interview data

Figure 1. Model of introducing peer assessment (PA) into a face-to-face writing class

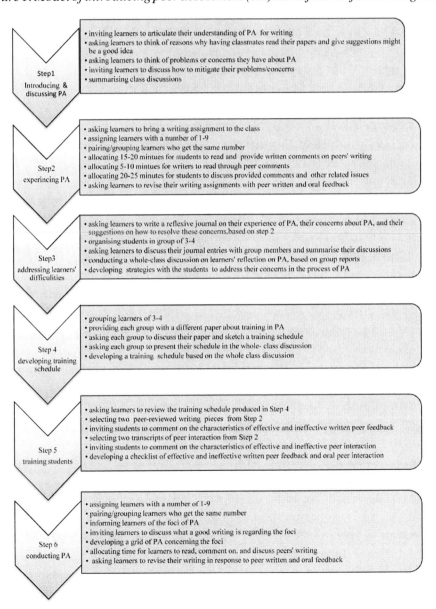

Step1
Introducing &
discussing PA
- inviting learners to articulate their understanding of PA for writing
- asking learners to think of reasons why having classmates read their papers and give suggestions might be a good idea
- asking learners to think of problems or concerns they have about PA
- inviting learners to discuss how to mitigate their problems/concerns
- summarising class discussions

Step2
experincing PA
- asking learners to bring a writing assignment to the class
- assigning learners with a number of 1-9
- pairing/grouping learners who get the same number
- allocating 15-20 mintues for students to read and provide written comments on peers' writing
- allocating 5-10 mintues for writers to read through peer comments
- allocating 20-25 minutes for students to discuss provided comments and other related issues
- asking learners to revise their writing assignments with peer written and oral feedback

Step3
addressing learners'
difficulties
- asking learners to write a reflexive journal on their experience of PA, their concerns about PA, and their suggestions on how to resolve these concerns,based on step 2
- organising students in group of 3-4
- asking learners to discuss their journal entries with group members and summarise their discussions
- conducting a whole-class discussion on learners' reflection on PA, based on group reports
- developing strategies with the students to address their concerns in the process of PA

Step 4
developing training
schedule
- grouping learners of 3-4
- providing each group with a different paper about training in PA
- asking each group to discuss their paper and sketch a training schedule
- asking each group to present their schedule in the whole- class discussion
- developing a training schedule based on the whole class discussion

Step 5
training students
- asking learners to review the training schedule produced in Step 4
- selecting two peer-reviewed writing pieces from Step 2
- inviting students to comment on the characteristics of effective and ineffective written peer feedback
- selecting two transcripts of peer interaction from Step 2
- inviting students to comment on the characteristics of effective and ineffective peer interaction
- developing a checklist of effective and ineffective written peer feedback and oral peer interaction

Step 6
conducting PA
- assigning learners with a number of 1-9
- pairing/grouping learners who get the same number
- informing learners of the foci of PA
- inviting learners to discuss what a good writing is regarding the foci
- developing a grid of PA concerning the foci
- allocating time for learners to read, comment on, and discuss peers' writing
- asking learners to revise their writing in response to peer written and oral feedback

Step 2: Creates the chance for students to experience peer assessment. In this step, the teacher collects written peer feedback and records oral peer interaction for the training purpose in Step 5. This step is to familiarise learners with the procedure of peer assessment. Their experiences will also help them to reflect on difficulties they have encountered or might encounter in providing peer feedback and communicating with peers, apart from benefits from peer assessment.

Step 3: Invites students to write a reflexive journal based on their experiences of peer assessment in step 2. They are then requested to address their concerns over peer assessment in groups then in the whole class. This step shares similar aims to that in Step 1 such as solving learners' concerns over peer assessment to motive them to conduct peer assessment. However, in this step, learners' concerns over peer assessment are based on their true experiences. Individual learners may have different problems of peer assessment as suggested in Guerrero and Villamil (1994), Mendonca and Johnson (1994) and Lockhart and Ng (1995); therefore, this step is indispensible to introducing peer assessment into a particular student group.

Step 4: Involves students in producing a training schedule of peer assessment in groups then in the whole-class discussion by providing them with papers on training in peer assessment. To involve students in the design of the training schedule helps to foster their ownership of the whole process of peer assessment. In addition, the students could refer to their own experiences in Step 2-3 to design a training schedule which catering for their own needs.

Step 5: Follows the schedule produced in Step 4 and provides training on how to offer constructive peer feedback. Samples of written feedback and oral interaction from Step 2 are used as the basis. Using feedback and interaction data from the students themselves should be more effective those from other student groups because the nature of feedback and characteristics of interaction data might vary somewhat from different student groups. Using feedback and interaction data from the students themselves also creates opportunities for learners to reflect on their performance, reaching the development of metacognitive skills of how to provide productive peer assessment.

Step 6: Uses peer assessment in writing classes formally.

We could see that five of the six steps are regarding preparing students for peer assessment. This is because the model is oriented to students who have limited experiences of peer assessment. The importance of training has been exemplified in key studies in Table 3; however, the way of providing training depends on the ecological characteristics of the local instruction context such as students' language proficiency and the nature of the assessment task. In this sense, the model deems to be flexible. We could also see that each step requires students' involvement, aiming to motivate them to participate in peer assessment and foster their ownership of peer assessment (i.e. it is the students themselves rather than the teacher who design the procedure of peer assessment.). However, this does not mean the teacher's role in peer assessment is not essential. This model does not cover teacher facilitation in peer assessment in order to keep it succinct; however, course tutors' guidance on and intervention in peer assessment are essential. For example, in Step 1, the teacher could refer to empirical studies on peer assessment to clarify students' misunderstanding of peer assessment and to provide supplementary comments on the advantages and pitfalls of peer assessment. In Step 2 and Step 6, the teacher shall remind students of timing duration for each assessment task and provide assistance in solving disagreement among students.

This model was built in the setting of a face-to-face writing class but it is not confined to face-to-face writing classes. This chapter explores how the model could be utilised in an online distance course which requires written reports and encourages peer assessment on the reports. The computer-mediated learning environment is created by the software called Dadaelous Integrated Writing Environment (DIWE).

SETTING THE STAGE

This chapter aims to propose a model of integrating peer assessment into a computer-mediated environment wider than DIWE. The reasons to choose DIWE are twofold. For one thing, DIWE aggregates tools for writing drafts (i.e. Invent and Write), for commenting on peers' writing (i.e. Response), for discussing writing or feedback (i.e. InterChange) and for communicating (i.e. Mail). It will be more illustrative of the network-based model by using one software package with multiple functions (i.e. DIWE) than by using several software packages with each having one function. For another thing, DIWE was once the most popular software among language teachers in particular writing instructors (Warschauer, 1996b). Till 1999, it had been used in over 600 high schools, colleges, and universities in the United States, France, Greece, Middle Eastern institutions and Asian countries and areas including Japan, Taiwan, and Hong Kong (Butler, 1999). In this sense, DIWE might be better known than other similar software packages; therefore, it might be much easier to understand the model if it is explained with DIWE.

DIWE was developed in 1988 by a group of graduate students and professors at the University of Texas at Austin, United States who aimed to create software aiding both the writing process and collaborative learning (The Daedalus Group, 1988). The latest version of DIWE (7.0) comprises six components to support different stages of writing: Invent, Write, Response, Mail, InterChange and BiblioCite.

1. **Invent:** Was designed to assist students to gestate topic ideas through providing them with pre-writing prompts which were varied from writing topics. Writing instructors can create new prompts best fitting their curriculum, pedagogy and students' needs through the use of an instructor utility called PromptManager.
2. **Write:** Works like a streamlined word processor with simpler formatting and spell checking. It can be used at various stages including composing drafts, preparing peer comments, summarising group discussions, revising, editing, and proofreading.
3. **Respond:** Provides the space where students review and provide written feedback on peers' writing. Similar to Invent, a number of prompts for peer response were provided and the number and the focus of prompts differed from writing tasks. The instructors could create their own prompts to guide students on commenting peers' writing.
4. **Mail:** Was designed to enable students to send mails during writing process, via 'private' or 'public' options. It is for asynchronous communications between/among teachers and students or between/among students.
5. **InterChange:** Creates a platform for real-time synchronous computer-mediated communication. InterChange is the most significant and most frequently used feature of DIWE in terms of collaborative writing (Brown, 1992). It could be used for different purposes such as pre-writing, discussions of course, and peer review workshops.
6. **BiblioCite:** Helps learners organise their bibliographic information by providing simple forms such as MLA Works Cited and APA Reference pages.

DIWE could be used in a local area network or online. The local area network base broadens the availability of DIWE in particular for the institutions with no or unstable wide-area networks.

DIWE has been extensively examined by language teachers and researchers since its first use in an English literacy course during 1980s and in L2 teaching by 1991. As the most significant module of DIWE, InterChange was examined most extensively. Table 5 summaries key studies on the use of InterChange in language teaching and learning, deriving from literature in key journals on computer-assisted language learning.

We can observe in Table 5 that DIWE has been used in all aspects of language teaching (most in French teaching), although it was designed for writing originally. A comparative approach was predominated in the studies in Table 5 (8 out of the 12 studies) and the following advantages over face-to-face classroom oral discussions were observed:

Table 5. Studies examining class interaction through using InterChange

Study	Main research focus	Participants	Data collection	Findings
(1) Beauvois (1992)	Examining student interaction in networked French instruction via InterChange	Intermediate level university French learners	Transcripts of InterChange discussions; Learners' self-report data	1. InterChange increased students' language production and peer interaction in class. 2. InterChange created a free environment for negotiation of meaning and motivated learners to discuss in French. 3. Students reported positive affective responses to InterChange.
(2) Beauvois (1994)	Examining the effectiveness of InterChange for reading in a French as a Foreign Language class	41 university French learners	Attitude questionnaire and follow-up interviews before and after the use of InterChange; Researcher field notes including classroom observation notes	1. Students expressed overwhelmingly positive attitudes toward InterChange. 2. A lower frequency of code switching was observed in InterChange than in oral interaction because of the possibility of time-delayed responses. 3. Students' positive attitudes and possibility of time-delayed responses led to increased student participation and increased use of French in InterChange sessions.
(3) Beauvois (1998)	Comparing class interaction in InterChange and in traditional French class	41 Intermediate university French learners	Classroom discussions; Network discussions; Classroom observation notes	1. Students produced more responses with a higher quality in networked than in classroom discussions. 2. Students produced more complete and complex sentences in InterChange discourse. 3. Students used first language less frequently in InterChange than in classroom discussions.
(4) Burley (1998)	Comparing the effects of word processing software and conferencing software on writing (i.e. InterChange)	53 college students	Classroom discussions; Electronic discussions; Writing papers	1. The InterChange group achieved a significant higher score than the other two groups. 2. Fewer errors were made in the InterChange group than the other two groups. 3. InterChange fostered learners to become a more expert writer.
(5) Bump (1990)	Comparing students' perceptions of InterChange (synchronous) and CONTACT (asynchronous) in university classes	18 freshman and 33 senior English literature learners; 12 graduate students in humanities computing class	Questionnaires consisting of 50-70 multiple choice questions regarding computer-assisted class discussions at the beginning and end of each semester	1. InterChange was more popular than face-to-face class discussions and contact among students. 2. InterChange increased student participation and generated more democratic, more individualised, and anonymous comments. 3. InterChange led to less coherent discourse, loss of controlling instructors and technological stress.

continued on following page

Table 5. Continued

Study	Main research focus	Participants	Data collection	Findings
(6) Chun (1994)	Using InterChange to develop German learners' interactive competence	first-year university German learners	Transcripts of Inter-Change discussions	1. InterChange increased discourse complexity. 2. Students engaged in a wide variety of discourse functions in InterChange discussions. 3. InterChange might enhance learners' writing ability.
(7) Huang (1998)	Comparing the type of speech produced in face-to-face and InterChange peer response	17 university students in English composition class at a university in Taiwan	Transcripts of face-to-face discussion; Transcripts of electronic discussions	1. Face-to-face environment generated a larger number of revision suggestions on peers' writing and more extensive discussions on peer feedback. 2. InterChange produced a smaller proportion of speech devoting to expressing agreement or disagreement with collaborators' comment. 3. InterChange entailed a greater proportion of praises.
(8) Kelm (1992) (cited in Kern, 1995)	Exploring the use of Inter-Change in Portuguese class	Intermediate level university Portuguese learners	Transcripts of Inter-Change discussions	1. InterChange increased language production and student interaction. 2. InterChange promoted more democratic distribution of conversational power. 3. Interchange developed learners' capacity of reading Portuguese text quickly and reading for meaning. 4. Students reported positive affective response to InterChange.
(9) Kern (1995)	Comparing the difference in InterChange and oral class discussions	40 students in an elementary French class	Transcripts of Inter-Change discussions; Transcripts of oral discussions; Attitude questionnaire	1. Students took more turns and followed a more democratic way in InterChange discussions. 2. Students produced a larger number of words and sentences in InterChange sessions. 3. InterChange encouraged student interactions. 4. Less teacher control in InterChange sessions might result in anarchistic student discussions. 5. Students overwhelmingly favoured InterChange discussions but the tutors expressed less enthusiastic views on it.

continued on following page

Table 5. Continued

Study	Main research focus	Participants	Data collection	Findings
(10) Sullivan and Pratt (1996)	Comparing student's attitudes towards writing with computers, the type of discourse and the improvement of writing quality in face-to-face and InterChange writing class	38 intermediate Spanish learners	Pre- and post-test on writing comprehension; Transcripts of InterChange; Audio/video tape of classroom discussion	1. Writing environment had no effect on attitudes toward writing with computers or writing apprehension. 2. InterChange interaction was more focused and generated more oral discussions. 3. All student participation was found in online discussion. 4. Sixty-five percent of class talks were made by the teacher in oral discussion against 15% in InterChange sessions. 5. More turns were taken by students in face-to-face discussions.
(11) Schultz (2000)	Comparing the effects of computer-based and face-to-face peer interaction on French earners' writing	108 intermediate university students	InterChange transcripts; Tape recordings of oral interaction; 93 essays with first and revised drafts; Attitude questionnaire	1. Face-to-face peer interaction resulted in a larger number and more massive changes. 2. Face-to-face interaction was more preferred by learners. 3. A mixed venue of InterChange and oral interaction was suggested to benefit students' French writing most. 4. Learners' language proficiency affected the effects of different interaction venues on writing.
(12) Warschauer (1996b)	Comparing student participation equality, students' attitudes, the language use in face-to-face and InterChange writing class	16 international students enrolled in an advanced ESL college composition class	Audio recording face-to-face interaction; InterChange transcripts; Survey data; Classroom observation data	1. Electronic discussions as a whole were twice as equal as the face-to-face discussions. 2. Electronic discussions involved significantly more complex target language, longer turns and more formal expressions. 3. Students reported they were freer, more comfortable, more creative and less stressed in InterChange. 4. Nationality, cultural factors, oral fluency and discomfort in speaking out could be important factors in determining relative participation in the two modes.

1. Increase learners' participation in class interaction (Study 1, 3, 5, 9, 10, and 12), except Huang (1998) and Schultz (2000).
2. Generate a more democratic distribution of conversation power (Study 5, 8, 9, 10, and 12).
3. Amplify learners' use of target language (i.e. any language that learners are trying to learn in addition to their native language) in class discussions (Study 1, 2, 3, 8, and 12).
4. Stimulate learners' motivation for class discussions (Study 1, 2, 5, 8, 9, and 12).
5. Possibly improve learners' writing, reading and speaking ability in target language (Study 4, 6, 8, and 11).

Increase Student Participation in Class

A higher level of learners' participation has been observed in InterChange than in face-to-face discussions (Study 1, 3, 5, 9, 10, and 12) (e.g. Bump, 1990; Faigley, 1992; Beauvois, 1997; J. Liu and Sadler, 2003; Warschauer, 2007). This is mainly because InterChange creates a less stressful interaction environment than face-to-face classroom, owing to its features including the possibility of keeping message senders anonymous, the relative absence of teacher evaluation, and waiting time for students to think before responding. For example, in Kelm's study (cited in Kern, 1995) (Study 8), the first study exploring the use of InterChange in foreign language learning, reported that student interaction was increased in InterChange sessions. A higher level of student participation was also reported in Warschauer (1996b) (Study 12): The 16 students in his advanced English composition class made electronic discussions by a whole twice as equal as face-to-face discussions. Similarly, Kern (1995) (Study 9) also observed that all students participated in InterChange class discussions whereas only five students were actively involved in classroom discussions. Further, he observed that the students in InterChange discussions produced 2-3.5 times more turns than in oral discussions. Likely, Sullivan and Pratt (1996) (Study 10) observed 100% student participation in InterChange group discussions against 50% in oral group discussions.

Generate More Equally Distributed Participation

Increased student participation in class discussions contributes to the equal distribution of power in class, in particular between teachers and students. Beauvois (1998) (Study 3) reported in her study that the 21 students in InterChange sessions made 186 messages against 35 messages made by the teacher; by contrast, in classroom discussions, the teacher answered 11 of the 13 questions she asked and only 5 students were actively involved in class discussions. Similarly, in Sullivan and Pratt (1996), the teacher made 65% of oral classroom talk whereas only 15% of InterChange talk was made by the teacher. Kern (1995) also observed a pivotal teacher's role in classroom discussions who took 54% of turns and furthermore, a significant number of teacher turns devoted to selecting the next speaker; however, the teacher's role in InterChange was attenuated where the teacher took only 4% of turns and students responded to messages freely and simultaneously. The more equal distribution of power between teachers and students was described by Faigley (1992) as follows:

By allowing everyone to "talk" at once, the use of networked computers for teaching writing represents for some teachers the realisation of the "student-centred" classroom. The utopian dream of an equitable sharing of classroom authority, at least during the duration of a class discussion, has been achieved. (p.167)

In addition, InterChange also promotes an equal distribution of power between students and generates the multiplicity of voices in class talk. Burley (1998) observed in his InterChange class that class discussions were no longer dominated by the most confident and vocal students but every student including those shy students had the chance to articulate their opinions and get responses. This is agreed by Beauvois (1998) who argued that InterChange made typically reticent students participate in discussions more readily and more abundantly in the less threatening InterChange environment than in the face-to-face classroom.

Amplify the Use of Target Language

InterChange allowing learners to think before responding to messages reduces learners' anxiety of using target language in conversation. As a result, it increases students' use of target language in class discussions. As exemplified in Beauvois (1994) (Study 2), the university French learners did less code-switching between their first language (English) and target language (French) in InterChange than in oral discussions because of the possibility of time-delayed responses in InterChange discussions. A similar finding was reported in her later 1998 study where her students used the target language (i.e. French) almost exclusively in InterChange discussions. Moreover, the target language used in InterChange appears to possess more complex morphosyntactic features and serve a wider variety of discourse functions than that used in face-to-face discussions. Beauvois (1998) (Study 3) found that students made more complete and complex sentences in target language in the InterChange discourse than in face-to-face oral discourse. Chun (1994) (Study 6) observed that after using InterChange for one semester, the ratio of simple sentences to complex sentences was raised from 3:1 to 3:4; in addition, she observed that InterChange exposed students to a wider variety of discourse functions than face-to-face discussions. A similar finding was reported in Warschauer (1996a) (Study 12). He ascertained through analysing transcripts in terms of type-token ratio and coordination index that a significantly more complex target language was used in InterChange than in face-to-face oral discussions. The development of learners' target language proficiency through InterChange resonates with socio-cultural theory that language learning is a tool mediated activity and in this case, InterChange is a useful tool of developing learners' second/foreign language proficiency (Vygotsky, 1978; Lantolf, 2003).

Improve Learners' Writing, Reading, and Speaking Ability in Target Language

The increased use of target language in InterChange discussions is suggested to have the potential to improve learners' target language proficiency in reading and speaking apart from writing. Beauvois (1992) claimed that InterChange electronic discussions created a favourable environment for negotiation of meaning and as a direct consequence of student interaction via InterChange, students' reading, writing, and even speaking ability in target language could be improved. Her claim has been confirmed by students in her later study where students articulated an improved target language proficiency (French) via InterChange (Beauvois, 1994). A similar assertion was made by students in Kern (1995): 78% students (n=40) articulated that InterChange requested them to conduct written discussions in French which improved their writing as well as speaking ability in French. The more complex structure of target language used in InterChange than face-to-face discussions discussed above could be another important evidence for the improvement of learners' target language proficiency.

Stimulate Students' Motivations for Class Discussions

InterChange is believed to stimulate learners' motivation to involve in class discussions because of students' affective advantage of InterChange over traditional classroom discourse. In Kern (1995) (Study 9), the 40 students overwhelmingly favoured InterChange over face-to-face interaction (93%) because the former broke the classroom routine, allowed more student-to-student interaction, changed class dynamics in a positive way, allowed time to compose messages, and improved their writing ability in French. The eleven writing instructors in the same study, although were not as enthusiastic as the students, were mostly positive towards InterChange because it made their students more attentive and active than face-to-face interaction and it significantly improved the depth and strength of students' argumentation. In Warschauer (1996a) (Study 12), the students also expressed their preference for InterChange because it was less threatening and more comfortable than face-to-face discussions.

Apart from the advantages above, InterChange should also share the following advantages with regard to all computer-mediated communication software packages. The interactive negotiation of meaning in InterChange discussions could enhance learners' understanding of peer feedback and thereby improve their long-term language proficiency (Braine, 1997; Tuzi, 2004; Ware and Warschauer, 2006). The printouts of InterChange discussions could be used to train students to provide effective peer assessment, to remind students of the main points that were discussed, and to serve as the basis for follow-up discussions (Schultz, 2000; Guardado and Shi, 2007; Warschauer, 2007). Teachers could convene and moderate peer discussions more closely in InterChange than in face-to-face classrooms (DiGiovanni and Nagaswami, 2001; M. Liu, Moore, Graham, and Lee, 2003) because they are able to offer intervention in front of the computer screen. Finally, in the networked classroom where students do not see each other and where they could make anonymous comments, students could be more honest and much fairer to comment on peer's writing and feel less upset when receiving critical comments (Guardado and Shi, 2007).

CASE DESCRIPTION

The aforementioned advantages of networked peer assessment and the increasing use of distance courses in tertiary education call for a network-based model for peer assessment for writing.

Greene (2000) outlined three key tenets to design a computer-assisted course model, namely: underlying theories, stakeholders/users, and technological considerations. For this model, the underlying theory is socio-cultural theory in general and writing as a social process activity in particular (e.g. Flower and Hayes, 1981; Zamel, 1983; Flower, 1989; Susser, 1994; Lockhart and Ng, 1995; Hayes, 1996). Socio-cultural theory has been widely viewed as the primary theoretical underpinning of peer assessment and of computer-assisted learning (See Table 1). Writing, as one of the most important language learning activities, is deemed to be socially and culturally mediated (e.g. Nelson and Murphy, 1993; Connor and Asenavage, 1994; Hu, 2005). Villamil and Guerrero (1996) interpreted Vygotsky's notion of the ZPD in relation to the collaborative peer assessment of writing as follows:

His concept of 'zone of proximal development' which recognises the importance of peer assistance in the solutions of tasks and, consequently, in learning, seems particularly applicable to the kind of collaborative instructional activity that occurs during peer revisions. (p.54)

This quotation reveals the importance of peer revisions in the development of learners' writing abilities. In line with this, Gere also proposed the necessity of collaboration for writing activities, highlighting the importance of the social context for writing:

Writing fits comfortably in the domain of collaborative learning because writing demands a dialogue between writer and context. Writing can succeed only when it adheres to the conventions of "normal discourse" for a given community, and writers can learn this discourse through using it in the kinds of conversations that occur in collaborative learning. (cited in Lockhart and Ng, 1995, p.145)

Likewise, Hamp-Lyons and Kroll argued that:

Writing is an act that takes place within a context, that accomplishes a particular purpose, and that is appropriately shaped for its intended audience. (cited in Weigle, 2002, p.19)

These assertions fit well with the core ritual of socio-cultural theory that human knowledge is constructed and shaped by the social and cultural context, and context and capacity are intricately intertwined (Lee and Smagorinsky, 2000). Secondly, this model is oriented to course tutors who embark on introducing peer assessment to a networked class consisting of learners inexperienced in peer assessment; therefore, this model, adherent to the original version of classroom-based peer assessment, underlines the importance of raising learners' awareness of peer assessment and training students to undertake peer assessment. Finally, in order to make the model more succinct and accessible, this model does not discuss training in how to use DIWE, assuming learners have been provided technological guidance on using them. Technological considerations will be further discussed when challenges of introducing peer assessment in a networked class are discussed at the end of this chapter.

Figure 2 presents the model of introducing peer assessment into a networked class. Before applying the model to the class, students are grouped randomly or purposefully (e.g. based on student gender, language proficiency, familiarity, etc.). Group members could remain stable or vary from tasks. Both ways of organising students have their own advantages. In an online course, students get fewer op-

Figure 2. Model of introducing peer assessment into a networked class

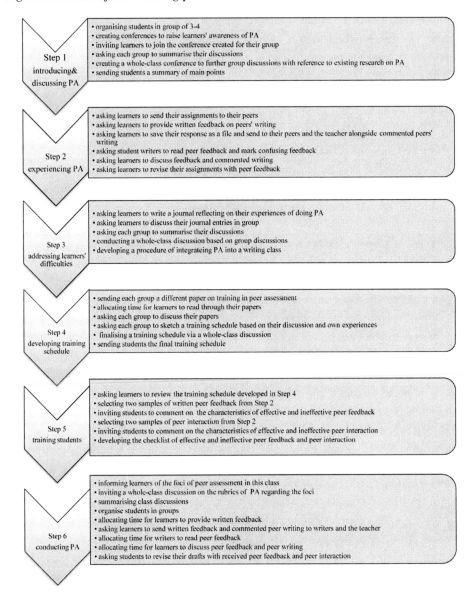

portunities of meeting each other and less frequent personal communications than they do in traditional face-to-face classes. As a result, it takes a longer time for students to get to know each other, to get used to each other's collaborative style, and to foster a sense of writing community in a group. Keeping group members stable enables students to foster positive interdependence with group members and thereby facilitates group collaboration (Biesenbach-lucas, 2004). On the other hand, varying group members from each task allows students to learn different things from different peers and helps to avoid boring students by working with the same partner. No matter which way is followed, students need acknowledging explicitly which group they belong to.

The model consists of six steps.

Step 1: Introducing and discussing peer assessment.

This step aims to get student acquainted with peer assessment and to raise their awareness of what peer assessment is and how it might work. To fulfil this aim, the writing teacher needs to create online conferences in InterChange where students are asked to discuss the following four questions:

1. What is your understanding of peer assessment?
2. Could you think of any reasons why having classmates read your papers and give suggestions might be a good idea?
3. Could you think of any problems or concerns you have about peer assessment?
4. Could you think of any possible ways to mitigate these problems, assuming you were the course teacher?

Instead of conducting whole-class discussions, students are organised to small groups in order to make class discussions more intensive and turns more equally distributed. It could also help to avoid overwhelming students with massive messages on screen when they respond to the conference theme simultaneously (Beauvois, 1994; Kern, 1995). Small group discussions also enable the teacher to notice and address the 'silent' students more easily than in whole class discussions.

The teacher creates a number of conferences corresponding to the number of groups. The conference for each group can be distinguished with a different name (e.g. by colour or fruit). Students are then invited to join the conference designed for their group. To improve the efficiency of group discussions, the teacher shall moderate it in at least three ways. They should control the time duration and remind students of covering all the four questions. They could further group discussions by raising issues emerging from students' ongoing discussions, possibly referring to findings in existing studies on peer assessment. They shall also notice the 'silent' students and invite them to join the discussion forum so that each student could have his/her 'voice' in online conferences.

At the end of group discussions, each group is asked to summarise their discussions for the following whole-class conference. This step is essential because (a) it poses pressure on students to stick to the task so that they could make points in the summary of group discussions and (b) it provides students with the chance of reflecting on what they have discussed to strengthen their understanding of peer assessment. Based on the whole-class discussion, the teacher synthesises the main points and sends them to students via 'public' Mail for their reflection.

Step 2: Experiencing peer assessment.

This step aims to create the chance for students to experience peer assessment whereby they can get realistic ideas of their difficulties in doing peer assessment and corresponding help they would like to get.

In this step, students are asked to send their writing assignments to their peers via the 'Private" Mail. The teacher allocates time for students to provide written feedback on their partners' report in response to the prompts provided in Response or created by the teacher in Response. It is important to encourage students to comment and provide specific suggestions on problematic areas of peers' writing, apart from its strengths. Comments on other aspects different from the prompts shall also be encouraged. After providing feedback in Response, the students are asked to save their feedback as a separate file and send it with commented peers' report to their peers and the teacher via the 'Private' Mail option. The reasons for asking students to send feedback and commented peers' writing to the teacher are twofold. For one thing, it will make students take the peer response task more serious because the teacher will review their commentary afterward. For another thing, peer response and commented student's writing will be used for the training purpose in Step 5. After receiving peer feedback, give writers time to read peer feedback. Ask them to question why a feedback instance is provided and to mark the instances they feel confused or inappropriate for their writing. The marked peer feedback instances are used as the main basis for the following peer interaction session via the InterChange module. In the end, ask learners to revise their writing with reference to peer feedback and peer interaction, using the Write module.

Step 3: Addressing learners' difficulties in doing peer assessment.

This step aims to mitigate students' difficulties and to release students' concerns about networked peer assessment in order to stimulate students' motivation to conduct peer assessment and enhance the efficacy of peer assessment. In addition, students should be encouraged to articulate their technological difficulties with the teacher or their peers.

Students are asked to write a reflexive journal via the Write module to record their feelings about peer assessment by revisiting the four questions in Step 1 and their peer assessment experiences in Step 2. They are then requested to discuss their journal entries in groups via the InterChange module. Similar to Step 2 and for the similar purpose, each group is asked to submit a summary of their discussions for the follow-up whole-class discussions. The teacher synthesises the whole-class discussions and send the main points to students via the 'public' email option. The whole-class discussions set up the basis of developing a plan of how to train students in Step 4.

Step 4: Developing a training schedule of peer assessment.

This step aims to involve students in developing a training schedule of peer assessment. Each group is provided with a different paper on training via Mail. Time is allocated for students to read papers before discussing them with their teammates. Two questions are posed for students to read the paper and conduct group discussions: Why is training important and how should training be provided? In addition, students are encouraged to integrate their own ideas of training based on their experiences in the previous three steps. At the end of group discussions, each group is expected to produce a training schedule. This serves as the basis of developing the final training schedule via a follow-up whole-class discussion in the InterChange module. The teacher finalises the training schedule by reviewing InterChange transcripts of group and whole-class discussions. The final training schedule is sent to the whole class via the "Public" Mail.

Step 5: Training students in peer assessment.

This step aims to improve the efficacy of peer assessment in a networked class through training students to provide constructive peer feedback and conduct productive peer interaction. The importance of training in peer assessment has been stipulated in studies in Table 3.

Students are asked to review the schedule designed in Step 4 before training is provided. The teacher selects two samples of anonymous written peer feedback and commented student writing from Step 2 (or more samples depending on the available class time). Ask students to comment on the effectiveness of peer feedback in the two samples, focusing on both effective and ineffective examples of peer feedback. Based on discussions, a list of characteristics of effective and ineffective peer feedback is produced. The teacher then selects two InterChange transcripts of peer interaction produced in Step 2 for the students to comment on the effectiveness of peer interaction. As a result, a summary of the characteristics of effective and ineffective peer interaction is produced. Based on class discussions on the effectiveness of peer feedback and peer interaction, the teacher generates the checklist of effective and ineffective peer feedback and peer interaction. The list is sent to the whole class via the 'Public' Mail option. Students are asked to closely attend to the checklist when doing peer assessment in Step 6.

Step 6: Conducting peer assessment.

In this step, the students are informed of the foci of peer assessment in this class because the time limitation for each class makes it more realistic to focus on one or two language aspects of writing (e.g. grammar, wording, organisation, content or style) or on one or two paragraphs. The foci of peer assessment in the class could be notified via Class Assignment.

Invite students in whole-class discussions via InterChange to develop a guideline on peer assessment. The necessity of guidance on peer assessment has been restated in the mainstream of studies on peer assessment, although the debate about its procedure is still ongoing (Nelson and Murphy, 1993; Lockhart and Ng, 1995; a less structured peer assessment suggested by researchers including Hyland, 2000) (a structured peer assessment suggested by researchers including Berg, 1999; Patri, 2002; Tuzi, 2004; Rollinson, 2005). The guideline could be provided by the teacher or could be developed collaboratively by the teacher and students, depending on the complexity of assessment foci, learners' readiness to comment on the foci, and the availability of the class time.

The guideline is then integrated into the prompt in the Response module. Time is allocated for students to provide written feedback on peers' writing. Students are then asked to send peer feedback and commented peers' writing (if it contains peer feedback) to writers and the teacher. Time is allocated for student writers to read peer feedback and highlight the feedback instances that need further clarifications. Students then discuss peer comments and writing via InterChange. Students revise their drafts in response to peer feedback and peer interaction. In this step, the teacher shall moderate the process, for example, timing each stage and probing comments in peer discussions.

The model might last for one or several consecutive classes, depending on students' readiness for peer assessment and the available time in each class. For instance, Step 1-2 could be conducted in one class; Step 4-5 regarding training could be fulfilled in one class; and Step 6 could be done in one class. Course tutors could also modify the model by adding or reducing steps according to their own teaching context. For instance, after the students become more acquainted with peer assessment, Step 2 might be eliminated from the process.

CHALLENGES FOR NETWORKED PEER ASSESSMENT

Although networked computer technology has been observed to greatly facilitate peer assessment and consequently its effectiveness for helping learners revise their writing assignments, it has also its pitfalls that pose challenges against networked peer assessment. Here, three challenges are discussed in detail: students' technological skills, students' online discussion skills, and the shifted teachers' and students' role in networked peer assessment.

Students' Technological Skills

As Warschauer (1999) argued, the use of computer technology in literacy teaching has made literacy no long discrete language knowledge. It has extended literacy to literacies such as cultural literacy, critical literacy, visual literacy, media literacy and computer literacy (Monteith, 2002). Among them, computer literacy is obviously a necessary skill for learners to be involved in computer-mediated learning, as Greene (2000) asserts that "the need for an acquisition of computer skills is an *ipso facto* necessity: students cannot learn writing with computers unless they can use computers!" (p. 243). This has been exemplified by studies on DIWE where students' concerns about their computer literacy and the problems rising from students' insufficient computer skills were reported. Beauvois (1997), for example, suggested that unskilled computer users might become frustrated in InterChange class discussions. DiGioVanni and Nagaswami (2001) noted that students in their study spent time in discussing how to use software and hardware when doing their online peer response activities. Likewise, through questionnaires with 167 English learners in Hong Kong, Taiwan and the USA, Warschauer (1996c) suggested that student motivation to write with computers was closely related to their self-report knowledge of computers. We therefore should cast attention to the necessity of developing learners' computer and telecollaboration skills when applying networked computer technology for online peer assessment. The technological barriers might make students end up giving in the online course and make course tutors feel stressed to continue the course.

Students' Online Discussion Skills

Networked peer assessment also involves problems of data management, time control, delayed response and alike. The equal participation in electronic discussions generates the multiplicity of voices in class discussions on one hand and results in massive messages on screen on the other. Further, freedom to participate in discussions at any time without revealing identities might even cause anarchist. Kern (1995) reported that 55% of the 40 participants in his study claimed difficulty in reading everything that everyone wrote in InterChange discussions. A similar problem was reported in Beauvois (1994). Massive massages on computer screens could lead to students' ignorance of responses. This will hamper students' motivation to participate in the following peer assessment sessions. Moreover, electronic peer discussions are very often unwieldy and the text under discussions is not always explored in the same way as in a teacher-driven face-to-face classroom. In the classroom, the teacher provides a more thorough analysis of the text and control the direction of peer discussions (Beauvois, 1997). By contrast, as indicated in studies in Table 5, electronic discussions decentralise and attenuate the teacher's role in class interaction. Due to the unsettled discussion threads, although a larger amount of peer interaction is generated in electronic than face-to-face discussions, students unnecessarily benefit more from electronic discussions.

Shifted Teachers' and Students' Role

As discussed above, the teachers' and students' role in a networked course is very different from traditional face-to-face classrooms. The use of networked technology changes learning culture. The teacher's dominant role in traditional classrooms is attenuated in networked classrooms. Teachers can no longer select the next speaker in a networked class because the students could type their 'voices' simultaneously or at their own convenient time without teachers' permission and they can also choose the messages that they want to respond. In addition, the absence of teachers in networked classrooms could cause at least two negative effects. It might make students lose the impulse to involve in class interaction; however, if waiting time for peers' response on writing is too long, learners might lose the motivation to continue conducting peer assessment. Absence from class makes teachers unable to provide timely help to solve learners' uncertainty about partners' writing or peer feedback, which may lead to learners' hesitation of using and providing peer feedback. The absence of teachers from classes requires learners to be active and independent learners; however, learners might not be ready to manage their learning without teachers' guidance. Further, individual learners adapt to networked courses differently, which requires the course tutors to conduct analyses of learners' needs for participating in networked peer assessment. As Salmon (2000) suggests, the use of networked technology in learning calls for a new way of teaching. The use of networked technology in education also calls for a new way of learning.

SOLUTIONS AND RECOMMENDATIONS

In response to the three challenges, training should be provided to improve learners' technological skills, online collaboration skills and teachers' skills of using networked peer assessment.

Training in Technological Use

Technological training could be provided based on the analysis of learners' need via learners' self-report data (e.g. through questionnaire) or classroom discussions. The analysis of learners' need helps to design tailor made training. Training in technological use could be provided in the form of workshop. If the students have courses in computer use in the department curricula, the course tutor could get information about learners' current level of computer use capacity from the computer tutor and discuss the possibility of integrating the technological training to the computer course with the computer tutor. Catering to students' different levels of computer use capacity, course tutors could create different versions of user manuals for the training purpose. In addition, the course tutor could create frequently asked questions (FAQs) in the online environment (Salmon, 2000) whereby the learners could get useful tips for how to solve commonly encountered problems without waiting for teachers' response. The tutor could also create a forum regarding the use of software where students could seek assistance in the use of software from their teachers and/or their peers.

Training in Online Collaboration Skills

Because the students in networked environment are no longer passive note takers but active participators, they have to acquire knowledge of online collaboration skills. One of the most important online learning skills is of data management: The tangled massive postings on varied themes in the computer screen require students to possess skills in sifting useful messages. The students might look to their teachers to provide direction through the overloaded information and help them to develop seeking, searching and selecting information skills (Salmon, 2000). Therefore, training in data management is necessary and important. Training in data management could be started with the printouts of students' electronic discussions. Ask students to describe their ways to sift messages from a sample discussion transcript. Comment on their ways. Develop a rubric for efficient data management skills. Another important aspect of online collaboration skill is time management. As Cates stated, the students need to know how to estimate the length of time a task will take to complete (cited in Savenye, Olina, and Niemczyk, 2001). For inexperienced online peer assessment participants, the teacher may help them to time each task (e.g. how long to provide peer feedback and how long to discuss peer feedback) and reminding students of the remaining time for each task until they are able to control time by themselves. If peer assessment is conducted in an asynchronous environment such as BlackBoard, the course tutor should publish the deadline of each task and email students when the deadline is approaching. To create a friendly working environment, course tutors shall give students guidance on turn-taking behaviours if synchronous and manners of responding to messages. Finally, to solve the unsettled issues in ongoing or completed online peer interaction, the teacher could ask learners to highlight them by using the text editing tool in the forum whereby the tutors could provide suggestions when they review student interaction later on. Alternatively, the students could record the unsettled issues in a forum designed for teachers' responses to unsettled issues. Teachers' assistance in settling disagreed issues helps to settle the nerve of the students who are not confident in their own or their partners' subject knowledge thus hesitate to provide or use peer feedback, being aware that the tutors will provide help to avoid inappropriate peer commentary misleading them.

Teacher Training in Using Networked Peer Assessment

The essential role of teacher moderation in electronic peer assessment raises the importance of teacher training in conducting networked peer assessment. As Breuch and Racine (2000) stipulated, the networked writing instruction environment forces writing instructors to appreciate text-only environment, to develop procedures for responding to online comments and to work as appropriate online facilitators. Breuch and Racine (2000) provided a description of how to train writing instructors in networked writing environment, including involving course tutors in (a) discussing advantages of text-only electronic environment, (b) exploring the characteristics of electronic written dialogues, (c) developing a procedure for online response, and (d) practising online dialogue by imitating the role of online student writers and peer reviewers. Apart from their suggestions, the writing tutors could also be encouraged to design their own technology-enhanced teaching model with reference to literature on online course design such as Savenye, Olina and Niemczyk (2001) and Salmon (2000). Savenye, Olina and Niemczyk provided guidance on how to design an online writing course from both theoretical and practical perspectives. Salmon (2000) viewed online course tutors as e-moderators and outlined a five-step model for computer-mediated communication in education and learning, consisting of (a) assess and motivation, (b) online socialisation, (c) information exchange, (d) knowledge construction and (e) development. This model has been widely used in CMC courses. It is also essential to develop course tutors' skills in diagnosing whether their students are ready for an online course in terms of technological skills and subject knowledge. The importance of conducting analyses of learner needs is particularly outstanding in an online course consisting of learners from varied cultural backgrounds, as Warschauer (1996a) argued that learners' motivation and performance in networked class discussions were closely related to their cultural backgrounds. In addition, how to design the networked writing class should be shaped within teaching goals. Kern (1995) suggested that "questions about the 'effectiveness' of InterChange use must be therefore be framed in terms of particular goals" (p.470) because InterChange encouraged student participation and generated discourses of an overall greater level of sophistication but InterChange discourse suffered from grammatical accuracy which exposed students to defective target language use.

REFERENCES

Aljaafreh, A., & Lantolf. (1994). Negative feedback as regulation and second language learning in the zone of proximal development. *Modern Language Journal, 78*(4), 465–483. doi:10.1111/j.1540-4781.1994.tb02064.x.

Beauvois, M. H. (1992). Computer-assisted classroom discussion in the foreign language classroom: Conversation in slow motion. *Foreign Language Annals, 25*(5), 455–464. doi:10.1111/j.1944-9720.1992.tb01128.x.

Beauvois, M. H. (1994). E-talk: Attitudes and motivation in computer-assisted classroom discussion. *Computers and the Humanities, 28*(3), 177–190. doi:10.1007/BF01830738.

Beauvois, M. H. (1997). High-tech, high-touch: From discussion to composition in the networked classroom. *Computer Assisted Language Learning, 10*(1), 57–69. doi:10.1080/0958822970100104.

Beauvois, M. H. (1998). Conversations in slow motion: Computer-mediated communication in the foreign language classroom. *Canadian Modern Language Review, 54*(2), 198. doi:10.3138/cmlr.54.2.198.

Berg, E. C. (1999). The effects of trained peer response on ESL students' revision types and writing quality. *Journal of Second Language Writing, 8*(3), 215–241. doi:10.1016/S1060-3743(99)80115-5.

Biesenbach-Lucas, S. (2004). Asynchronous web discussions in teacher training courses: promoting collaboration learning - Or not? *AACE Journal, 12*(2), 155–170.

Braine, G. (1997). Beyond word processing: Networked computers in ESL writing classes. *Computers and Composition, 14*(1), 45–58. doi:10.1016/S8755-4615(97)90037-2.

Breuch, L.-A. M. K., & Racine. (2000). Developing sound tutor training for online writing centers: Creating productive peer reviewers. *Computers and Composition, 17*(3), 245–263. doi:10.1016/S8755-4615(00)00034-7.

Brown, L. F. (1992). The daedalus integrated writing environment. *Computers and Composition*, *10*(1), 77–88. doi:10.1016/S8755-4615(06)80021-6.

Bump, J. (1990). Radical changes in class discussion using networked computers. *Computers and the Humanities*, *24*(1-2), 49–65. doi:10.1007/BF00115028.

Burley, H. (1998). Does the medium make the magic? The effects of cooperative learning and conferencing software. *Computers and Composition*, *15*(1), 83–95. doi:10.1016/S8755-4615(98)90026-3.

Butler, W. M. (1999). *Writing and collaborative learning with the Daedalus integrated writing environment*. Retrieved May 29, 2009, from www.greek-language.gr/greekLang/files/document/conference-1999/01_Butler.pdf

Carson, J. G., & Nelson. (1994). Writing groups: Cross-cultural issues. *Journal of Second Language Writing*, *3*(1), 17–30. doi:10.1016/1060-3743(94)90003-5.

Carson, J. G., & Nelson. (1996). Chinese students' perceptions of ESL peer response group interaction. *Journal of Second Language Writing*, *5*(1), 1–19. doi:10.1016/S1060-3743(96)90012-0.

Caulk, N. (1994). Comparing teacher and student responses to written work. *TESOL Quarterly*, *28*(1), 181–188. doi:10.2307/3587209.

Chun, D. M. (1994). Using computer networking to facilitate the acquisition of interactive competence. *System*, *22*(1), 17–31. doi:10.1016/0346-251X(94)90037-X.

Connor, U., & Asenavage. (1994). Peer response groups in ESL writing classes: How much impact on revision. *Journal of Second Language Writing*, *3*(3), 256–276. doi:10.1016/1060-3743(94)90019-1.

DiGiovanni, E., & Nagaswami. (2001). Online peer review: An alternative to face-to-face? *ELT Journal*, *55*(3), 263–272. doi:10.1093/elt/55.3.263.

Faigley, L. (1992). *Fragments of rationality: Postmodernity and the subject of composition*. Pittsburgh, PA: University of Pittsburgh Press.

Ferris, D. (2003a). Responding to writing. In Kroll, B. (Ed.), *Exploring the dynamics of second language writing*. Cambridge, UK: Cambridge University Press. doi:10.1017/CBO9781139524810.010.

Ferris, D. (2003b). *Response to student writing: Implications for second language students*. Mahwah, NJ: Lawrence Erlbaum Associates.

Flower, L., & Hayes. (1981). A cognitive process theory of writing. *College Composition and Communication*, *32*(4), 365–387. doi:10.2307/356600.

Flower, L. (1989). Cognition, context and theory building. *College Composition and Communication, 40*(3), 282–311. doi:10.2307/357775.

Foster, P., & Ohta. (2005). Negotiation for meaning and peer assistance in second language classroom. *Applied Linguistics, 26*(3), 402–430. doi:10.1093/applin/ami014.

Greene, D. (2000). A design model for beginner-level computer-mediated EFL writing. *Computer Assisted Language Learning, 13*(3), 239–252. doi:10.1076/0958-8221(200007)13:3;1-3;FT239.

Guardado, M., & Shi. (2007). ESL students' experiences of online peer feedback. *Computers and Composition, 24*(4), 443–461. doi:10.1016/j.compcom.2007.03.002.

Guerrero, M., & Villamil. (1994). Social-cognitive dimensions of interaction in L2 peer revision. *Modern Language Journal, 78*(4), 484–496.

Guerrero, M., & Villamil. (2000). Activating the ZPD: Mutual scaffolding in L2 peer revision. *Modern Language Journal, 84*(1), 51–68. doi:10.1111/0026-7902.00052.

Hayes, J. R. (1996). A new framework for understanding cognition and affect in writing. In Levy, C. M., & Ransdell, S. (Eds.), *The Science of writing* (pp. 1–28). Hoboken, NJ: Lawrence Erlbaum Associates.

Hu, G. (2005). Using peer review with Chinese ESL student writers. *Language Teaching Research, 9*(3), 321–342. doi:10.1191/1362168805lr169oa.

Huang, S.-Y. (1998). *Differences in the nature of discussion between peer response sessions conducted on networked computers and those conducted in the traditional face-to-face situation.* Paper presented at the Annual Meeting of the International Writing 98 Conference. New York, NY.

Hyland, F. (2000). ESL writers and feedback: Giving more autonomy to students. *Language Teaching Research, 4*(1), 33–54.

Jacobs, G. M., Curtis, Braine, & Huang. (1998). Feedback on student writing: Taking the middle path. *Journal of Second Language Writing, 7*(3), 307–317. doi:10.1016/S1060-3743(98)90019-4.

Kern, R. G. (1995). Restructuring classroom interaction with networked computers: effects on quantity and characteristics of language production. *Modern Language Journal, 79*(4), 457–476. doi:10.1111/j.1540-4781.1995.tb05445.x.

Lantolf, J. P. (2000). *Sociocultural theory and second language learning.* Oxford, UK: Oxford University Press.

Lantolf, J. P. (2003). Intrapersonal communication and internalization in the second language classroom. In Kozulin, A. (Ed.), *Vygotsky's educational theory in cultural context* (pp. 349–370). Cambridge, UK: Cambridge University Press. doi:10.1017/CBO9780511840975.018.

Lee, C. D., & Smagorinsky. (2000). Introduction: Constructing meaning through collaborative inquiry. In C. D. Lee & P. Smagorinsky (Eds.), *Vygotskian perspectives on literacy research: Constructing meaning through collaborative inquiry* (pp. 1-18). Cambridge, UK: Cambridge University Press.

Liu, J., & Sadler. (2003). The effect and affect of peer review in electronic versus traditional modes of L2 writing. *Journal of English for Academic Purposes*, *2*(3), 193–227. doi:10.1016/S1475-1585(03)00025-0.

Liu, M., Moore, Graham, & Lee. (2003). A look at the research on computer-based technology use in second language learning: Review of literature from 1990-2000. *Journal of Research on Technology in Education*, *24*, 250–273.

Lockhart, C., & Ng. (1995). Analysing talk in ESL peer response groups: Stances, functions and content. *Language Learning*, *45*(4), 605–655. doi:10.1111/j.1467-1770.1995.tb00456.x.

Mangelsdorf, K. (1992). Peer reviews in the ESL composition classroom: What do the students think? *ELT Journal*, *46*(3), 274–284. doi:10.1093/elt/46.3.274.

McGroarty, M. E., & Zhu. (1997). Triangulation in classroom research: A study of peer revision. *Language Learning*, *47*(1), 1–43. doi:10.1111/0023-8333.11997001.

Mendonca, C. O., & Johnson. (1994). Peer review negotiations: Revision activities in ESL writing instruction. *TESOL Quarterly*, *28*(4), 745–769. doi:10.2307/3587558.

Min, H.-T. (2005). Training students to become successful peer reviewers. *System*, *33*(2), 293–308. doi:10.1016/j.system.2004.11.003.

Monteith, M. (2002). *Teaching primary literacy with ICT*. Buckingham, UK: Open University Press.

Nelson, G., & Murphy. (1993). Peer response groups: Do L2 writers use peer comments in revising their drafts? *TESOL Quarterly*, *27*(1), 135–142. doi:10.2307/3586965.

Patri, M. (2002). The influence of peer feedback on self- and peer-assessment of oral skills. *Language Testing*, *19*(2), 109–133. doi:10.1191/0265532202lt224oa.

Rollinson, P. (2005). Using peer feedback in the ESL writing class. *ELT Journal*, *59*(1), 23–30. doi:10.1093/elt/cci003.

Salmon, G. (2000). *E-moderating: The key to teaching and learning online.* London: Kogan Page limited.

Savenye, W. C., Olina, & Niemczyk. (2001). So you are going to be an online writing instructor: Issues in designing, developing, and delivering an online course. *Computers and Composition, 18*(4), 371–385. doi:10.1016/S8755-4615(01)00069-X.

Schultz, J. M. (2000). Computers and collaborative writing in the foreign language curriculum. In Warschauer, M., & Kern, R. (Eds.), *Network-Based Language Teaching: Concepts and Practice* (pp. 121–150). Cambridge, UK: Cambridge University Press. doi:10.1017/CBO9781139524735.008.

Stanley, J. (1992). Coaching student writers to be effective peer evaluators. *Journal of Second Language Writing, 1*(3), 217–233. doi:10.1016/1060-3743(92)90004-9.

Storch, N. (2001). How collaborative is pair work? ESL tertiary students composing in pairs. *Language Teaching Research, 5*(1), 29–53.

Storch, N. (2002). Patterns of interaction in ESL pair work. *Language Learning, 52*(1), 119–158. doi:10.1111/1467-9922.00179.

Storch, N. (2005). Collaborative writing: Product, process and students' reflections. *Journal of Second Language Writing, 14*, 153–173. doi:10.1016/j.jslw.2005.05.002.

Sullivan, N., & Pratt. (1996). A comparative study of two ESL writing environments: A computer-assisted classroom and a traditional oral classroom. *System, 24*(4), 491–501. doi:10.1016/S0346-251X(96)00044-9.

Susser, B. (1994). Process approaches in ESL/EFL writing instruction. *Journal of Second Language Writing, 3*(1), 31–47. doi:10.1016/1060-3743(94)90004-3.

Tsui, A., & Ng. (2000). Do secondary L2 writers benefit from peer comments? *Journal of Second Language Writing, 9*(2), 147–170. doi:10.1016/S1060-3743(00)00022-9.

Tuzi, F. (2004). The impact of e-feedback on the revisions of L2 writers in an academic writing course. *Computers and Composition, 21*(2), 217–235. doi:10.1016/j.compcom.2004.02.003.

Villamil, O. S., & Guerrero. (1996). Peer revision in the L2 classroom: social-cognitive activities, mediating strategies, and aspects of social behaviour. *Journal of Second Language Writing, 5*(1), 51–75. doi:10.1016/S1060-3743(96)90015-6.

Villamil, O. S., & Guerrero. (1998). Assessing the impact of peer revision on L2 writing. *Applied Linguistics, 19*(4), 491–514. doi:10.1093/applin/19.4.491.

Villamil, O. S., & Guerrero. (2006). Socio-cultural theory: a framework for understanding the socio-cognitive dimensions of peer feedback. In K. Hyland & F. Hyland (Eds.), *Feedback in second language writing: Contexts and issues* (pp. 23-41). Cambridge, UK: Cambridge University Press.

Vygotsky, L. S. (1978). *Mind in society: The development of higher psychological process*. Cambridge, UK: Cambridge University Press.

Ware, P. D., & Warschauer. (2006). Electronic feedback and second language writing. In K. Hyland & F. Hyland (Eds.), *Feedback in Second Language Writing: Contexts and Issues* (pp. 105-122). Cambridge, UK: Cambridge University Press.

Warschauer, M. (1996a). Comparing face-to-face and electronic discussion in the second language classroom. *CALICO Journal, 13*(2), 7–26.

Warschauer, M. (1996b). Computer assisted language learning: An introduction. *Multimedia Language Teaching*. Retrieved May 29, 2009, from http://www.ict4lt.org/en/warschauer.htm

Warschauer, M. (1996c). Motivational aspects of using computers for writing and communication. In Warschauer, M. (Ed.), *Telecollaboration in foreign language learning* (pp. 29–48). Hawaii, HI: University of Hawaii Press.

Warschauer, M. (1999). *Electronic literacies: Language, culture, and power in online education*. Mahwah, NJ: Lawrence Erlbaum Associates.

Warschauer, M. (2007). Technology and writing. In Cummis, J., & Davison, C. (Eds.), *International Handbook of English Language Teaching* (*Vol. 15*, pp. 907–930). New York: Springer US. doi:10.1007/978-0-387-46301-8_60.

Weigle, C. S. (2002). *Assessing writing*. Cambridge, UK: Cambridge University Press. doi:10.1017/CBO9780511732997.

Weissberg, R. (2006). Scaffolded feedback: Tutorial conversations with advanced L2 writers. In Hyland, K., & Hyland, F. (Eds.), *Feedback in second language writing: Contexts and issues* (pp. 246–265). Cambridge, UK: Cambridge University Press. doi:10.1017/CBO9781139524742.015.

Zamel, V. (1983). The composing processes of advanced ESL students: six case studies. *TESOL Quarterly, 17*(2), 165–187. doi:10.2307/3586647.

Zhang, S. (1995). Reexamining the affective advantage of peer feedback in the ESL writing class. *Journal of Second Language Writing, 4*(3), 209–222. doi:10.1016/1060-3743(95)90010-1.

Zhang, S. (1999). Thoughts on some recent evidence concerning the affective advantage of peer feedback. *Journal of Second Language Writing, 8*(3), 321–326. doi:10.1016/S1060-3743(99)80119-2.

Zhu, W. (1995). Effects of training for peer response on students' comments and interaction. *Written Communication, 12*(4), 492–528. doi:10.1177/074108839501 2004004.

Zhu, W. (2001). Interaction and feedback in mixed peer response groups. *Journal of Second Language Writing, 10*(4), 251–276. doi:10.1016/S1060-3743(01)00043-1.

Chapter 6

Listening and Learning through ICT with Digital Kids:
Dynamics of Interaction, Power, and Mutual Learning between Student Teachers and Children in Online Discussion

Dianne Forbes
University of Waikato, New Zealand

EXECUTIVE SUMMARY

The following case reports on the involvement of children in online discussion with student teachers within initial teacher education in New Zealand. The focus is on listening to children, with wider implications for listening as a professional capability extending beyond the teaching profession. In this case, student teachers and pupils communicated online, exchanging ideas, debating, and engaging in co-construction of understandings around the place of Information and Communication Technologies in teaching and learning. The case explores the interaction and social dynamics observed and mutual learning experienced, with links to theoretical perspectives including constructivist and democratic pedagogies. Implications for improved practice are considered. It is argued that there is a need to explicitly teach listening skills and to encourage professionals in training to listen to clients. It is argued that the online environment is an excellent training ground for developing effective listening skills as it lends itself to reflective practice and to meta-listening awareness.

DOI: 10.4018/978-1-4666-4486-1.ch006

BACKGROUND

The Bachelor of Teaching (Mixed Media Programme) is a distance education degree offered by the University of Waikato, School of Education, in Hamilton, New Zealand. The degree results in professional accreditation as a primary (elementary) school teacher in NZ, so that graduates are qualified as beginning teachers of pupils aged 5-14 years. The Mixed Media Programme (MMP) has been operating since 1997, and is designed to cater for tertiary students whose commitments prevent them from participating in a traditional on-campus teacher education programme (http:www.soe.waikato.ac.nz/mmp). MMP students are geographically dispersed throughout the country, often from rural areas, and complete their initial teacher education at a distance, by studying online using Moodle as a Learning Management System (http://www.moodle.org.nz/). Online study is combined with time spent in base schools in each student's local area. Students spend one day each week in a base school, where they receive support from an experienced teacher, and have opportunities to observe and participate in school life, and to teach. Students travel to on campus meetings several times a year, and complete a block practicum of 4-8 weeks each year in order to gain intensive teaching experience.

In 2002 the MMP programme was recognised by the Tertiary Teaching Excellence Awards (New Zealand), for excellence in innovation. At that time, the programme was offered via ClassForum, a customised elearning system. More recently, in 2008, the university transitioned to Moodle as a Learning Management System. Within either ClassForum, or more recently Moodle, students' online study usually requires participation in asynchronous online discussion, alongside completion of assignment work, across a range of curriculum and professional areas of study.

The case presented here reports on the experience of involving children in online discussion with student teachers within the Bachelor of Teaching (MMP), with a focus on listening to children, and with wider implications for listening as a professional capability, extending beyond the teaching profession.

SETTING THE STAGE

As a Senior Lecturer in the Department of Professional Studies in Education, I have taught in the Mixed Media Programme (MMP) since 2002, coordinating classes focused on professional practice in the context of teaching, learning theory, pedagogy, assessment, and learning through Information and Communication Technology (ICT).

This case represents an authentic educational example, stemming from an initial experience in 2004, when I first invited 12-year old pupils to join the MMP teacher education students in online discussion. As a result of the success and mutual learning experienced during this initial trial, I have involved children (aged between 10 and 15 years) in online discussion at least twice a year during the past five years.

The case focuses on one instance in which middle school children were involved in online discussion with first year teacher education students. The objective of the exercise was to encourage the class of fifty-seven teacher education students to listen to a group of nineteen year 8 pupils (12 year olds). The focus of the discussion was on Information and Communication Technology (ICT), how ICT can be used to enhance learning both within the classroom and outside of school as we know it, and how teachers and children might learn together through ICT. For two weeks, the student teachers and pupils communicated online, exchanging ideas, debating and engaging in co-construction of understandings around the place of ICT in teaching and learning.

This chapter explores the interaction and social dynamics observed between the two groups, focusing in particular on how the student teachers "listened" to the children in the context of the online discussion. Key points are illustrated by quotes from the participants in the discussion, which serve to bring the interaction dynamics to life. The dynamics of power are also examined, along with comment on how the subject matter and the online environment may have impacted on the distribution of power between the adults and the children. Mutual learning experienced by both parties is highlighted, with links to theoretical perspectives including constructivist and democratic pedagogies. Finally, implications for improved practice are considered. It is argued that there is a need to explicitly teach listening skills and to encourage teacher education students to listen to children. By implication, there is a need to encourage other professionals to examine the role of listening in their professional practice. Indeed, there is a need for all of us engaged in online interactions to examine the effectiveness of our own listening practices. It is argued that the online environment is an excellent training ground for developing effective listening skills as it lends itself to reflective practice and to meta-listening awareness. Participants can think about and plan the best ways to show they are listening responsively and actively to partners in discussion, and can evaluate their performance in this regard, leading to ongoing improvements in listening and learning.

The quality of a professional distance degree may be judged by how well the degree program prepares professionals for participation in key areas of their profession. Communication, listening and learning are key competencies in most professions. As such, this case holds wide relevance for those coordinating professional distance degrees. Any professional distance degree program could be enhanced by the practice of connecting potential clients and experienced professionals with students through asynchronous online discussion. In doing so, the aim is to develop and enhance listening and constructive communication skills, in preparation for ongoing professional discussions.

CASE DESCRIPTION

The online discussion between teacher education students and middle school pupils took place within the context of a first year online class in which the teacher education students were enrolled. The subject of the class was ICT so Information and Communication Technology was both the focus and the medium for this online class. As a requirement for the class, students are expected to actively engage in online discussion. Three-quarters of the way through the semester, a group of middle school children joined the teacher education students for an online discussion. The learning intention of this exercise was that the teacher education students would listen to the pupils' perspectives on the use of ICT for teaching and learning. This intention stemmed from the author's observation that at this early stage of their professional preparation, the teacher education students tend to emphasize teachers' roles in transmitting information to pupils and controlling the class. It was hoped that listening to the pupils would challenge these early emphases so that teacher education students might come to appreciate that teaching is not merely about one-way transmission but rather that children have valuable perspectives to share and that children's voices need to be listened to rather than controlled. In this particular instance the 'listening' took place online as part of the teacher education class.

It was hypothesized that the children, as "Digital Natives" (Prensky, 2001) have a great deal to teach adults about growing up with ICT. In addition, it was thought that the pupils would benefit from engaging in an academic online discussion since they had not experienced this form of interaction previously. Most of the children had some experience with MSN chat but not as part of an asynchronous academic discussion. Finally, it is argued here that asynchronous online discussions lend themselves particularly well to listening because it is impossible to interrupt another participant in an online asynchronous discussion as messages are posted consecutively, so all participants can have their say. Furthermore, participants decide when they will contribute, and are not forced into immediate responses. For this reason, online responses are often more reflective and considered than those occurring face-to-face. Participants do, however, need to actively show each other that they are listening since in the absence of body language and other paralinguistic clues, it is necessary to use other means to convey active listening.

In this case, the teacher education students were a selected sample of students who were enrolled in the author's class. The middle school pupils were selected through contact with their ICT teacher, who was interested in offering some of her pupils the opportunity to engage in an asynchronous online discussion for the first time. The pupils who were invited to participate were regarded by the teacher as socially mature, competent communicators, and eager to take part. The reasoning behind these selection criteria was that pupils should be more likely to make high quality contributions to online discussion if they are able to take the 'netiquette' and 'cybersafety' requirements seriously, if their written communication skills were adequate, and if they were computer literate enough to work with the software. Finally, it was hoped that choosing "those who were keen" would safeguard the voluntary nature of the project (informed consent), and would increase the likelihood that the pupils would contribute regularly to the discussion. These selection criteria are not unusual as children's linguistic competence and motivation are often considered when they are to be engaged in research activities (Dockrell, Lewis and Lindsay, 2000).

The online class consisted of fifty-seven teacher education students organized into five groups of eleven-twelve students for the purpose of online discussion. Original student-groupings were retained as the teacher education students had spent 8 weeks engaging in discussion within these groups and it would have be unsettling to rearrange the groups. Twenty middle school pupils were invited to take part in the online discussion project, so that this would enable four pupils to join each group. It was hoped that having four pupils in each group would provide pupils with peer support and alleviate the pressure on fewer pupils who might be expected to participate more often than they could manage.

Leading up to the discussion, face-to-face sessions were held with both the middle school pupils and the teacher education students. For the teacher education students, the project was explained, permission to participate was sought, and further advice was given to the students online regarding how to interact appropriately with the middle school pupils. For the middle school pupils, the face-to-face session was used to establish a rapport with the author, to establish some guidelines for cybersafety and netiquette, to introduce the online discussion topic specifically and the process of contributing to academic discussion online more generally, and to give technical guidance for using the software. Informed consent to participate had previously been obtained from the pupils' school principal, parents and from the pupils themselves. University ethical approval was also gained.

For two weeks prior to the commencement of the online discussion between the pupils and the students the middle school pupils participated in a "private" online area with the author in order to try out the tools and become familiar with online discussion. During this time, a series of "ice-breakers" online, following Salmon's (2002) e-tivities, were facilitated in order to build rapport and to introduce the pupils to asynchronous online discussion. The importance of building rapport with research participants is widely emphasized in the literature (Anderson and Kanuka, 2003; Lewis and Lindsay, 2000). The familiarization phase also enabled coaching and encouragement of the pupils' first efforts online. This was deemed necessary even for "Digital Natives" due to the academic nature of the discussion ahead. Following these two weeks in the "practice area", the real discussion began.

As a starter for the discussion the following questions were asked:

- How is ICT used in schools to promote and enhance learning?
- How is ICT used outside of school to promote and enhance learning?
- How can teachers help children to learn through ICT?
- How might teachers and students learn together?

As is usually the case with asynchronous online discussions the five discussion groups pursued different directions as they worked to address the above questions. These interactions across the five groups generated 425 messages, so for the sake of manageability much of the subsequent analysis has focused on just one group (107 messages). There is room here to explore only a small number of highlights from the online discussion that occurred within this group, in order to examine something of the social dynamics between the discussion participants. Firstly, it is pertinent to consider how the teacher education students listened to the pupils online, and indeed why listening is a necessary focus.

Listening

Why Focus on Listening?

In people-oriented professions, including but not limited to teaching, listening is of central importance. Indeed, in any context where interpersonal interaction is a priority, listening must also occupy a central place.

Beginning in the arena of education, it has long been accepted that one must listen in order to learn. In addition, it is now widely held that one must listen in order to teach effectively. It is imperative that teachers listen to students. In Charlton's (1996) view, "Listening to pupils is a fundamental component of good teaching" (p.51). Similarly, Galloway and Davie (1996) point out, "effective teaching is interactive and involves seeking, listening to and valuing children's experiences" (p.140). With this in mind, it is sensible to ensure that pre-service teacher educators encourage student teachers to listen to children, so that the need to listen to children is understood by new teachers, and so that these teachers in training learn the skills necessary to actively and sensitively listen to children. The current case investigates patterns of interaction, in order to develop insights that will assist in the development of teacher education students' listening skills, along with their awareness of the importance of listening to children.

There are a number of reasons for listening to children. These include moral reasons, educational arguments and pragmatic benefits (Galloway and Davie, 1996). On moral grounds, there is "an ethical imperative that children have a basic right to be heard" (Lloyd-Smith and Tarr, 2000, p.60). Listening is fundamentally a mark of respect. If children's voices are overlooked, they become just one more marginalized group in society. In educational terms, listening enables children to participate in democratic pedagogies (Taylor, 2000), and learning often improves (Charlton, 1996). When children participate in matters concerning them they develop a sense of personal autonomy (Lloyd-Smith and Tarr, 2000). As Marland (1996) points out, "to be listened to, participate, and have views taken into account and acted upon is to become more understanding of society, decision-making and self" (pp.68-69). In addition, listening to children often makes good practical sense when their views shed light on what would otherwise be unknown to adults. Children can give valuable feedback to teachers. For this reason, we should listen to children and allow them to teach us about their perceptions of problems and environments that they experience (McLaughlin, Carnell and Blount, 1999). As Charlton (1996) explains, "By listening to their views we extend our knowledge of their perceptions of those experiences. If we listen carefully we may learn more about our own successes and failures; and we should be prepared to consider changes in our provisions and practices in the light of such comment" (p.50).

Of course many of these arguments for listening to children can be readily applied to human beings of all ages, and in diverse contexts. If we accept that it is imperative that teachers listen to students, then this is no less important for online teachers and students than it is for those who work predominately face-to-face. The notion of effective listening online therefore has implications at numerous levels: As online teachers, how do we listen effectively to our students? As online teacher educators, how do we teach our student teachers to listen effectively to their pupils? How can all professionals working online listen effectively to clients, and for that matter to any partner in online communication, in any context?

What Does Listening Look Like?

Drawing together practical ideas from literature on children's perspectives, counselling skills and oral language/literacy, it is possible to assemble a range/catalogue of listening behaviours. In this way, a definition of what it means to listen actively and effectively can be derived. Literature in the area of Rogerian client-centred counselling, focusing on trying to understand another person's perspective is particularly useful here (Ivey, Bradford-Ivey, and Simek-Downing, 1987). Key microskills from this approach are supported in the field of teaching listening as a component of oral language within *English in the New Zealand Curriculum* (Ministry of Education, 1994). [See Endnote]. In turn, these ideas are supported by those who advocate active listening to children's perspectives (e.g. Charlton, 1996; Nesbitt, 2000).

In summary, listening skills or attending behaviours include staying on the topic, taking turns, encouraging, paraphrasing, questioning, reflections of meaning or feelings, self-disclosure, feedback, and summarization (Ivey et al, 1987).

Looking more closely at each of these skills in turn, it is apparent that staying on the same topic of discussion as the person we are listening to, and avoiding changing topics abruptly is a feature of effective listening (English online, 2004; Ivey et al, 1987). Taking turns to speak is also a feature of listening (English online, 2004; Ministry of Education, 1996). In an online context, however, this is predetermined by the environment, as it is not technically possible to interrupt or overlap the comment of another participant in asynchronous discussion. Encouraging, or restating what a person has said involves directly repeating their comments, or making short statements like "tell me more..." (Ivey et al, 1987, p.72). Paraphrasing is an encapsulated repetition back to the person using their own main words and thoughts. This can help to clarify the essence of what has been said, to bring together recent comments or threads of discussion, and to concisely present ideas in order to make sure key facts are understood (Ivey et al, 1987). Questioning may involve closed or open questions. The former are often used to check out a person's meaning. For example, one might ask "Does this make sense?" or "Is that right?" Open questions, on the other hand, show interest in a variety of responses and are effectively an invitation to talk (Dockrell, Lewis and Lindsay, 2000; Ivey et al, 1987; McGee, 2001). In addition to asking questions in order to show active listening, effective listening also involves replying when someone asks a question (English online, 2004). Reflection of meaning or feelings provide the listener with an opportunity to "check out" where the other participant/s in the discussion are on an issue, either in terms of what a situation means to them, or in emotional terms (Ivey et al, 1987). These are variations of paraphrases. While paraphrases tend to focus on facts, reflections focus on either meaning for the individual, or emotions associated with the facts and meanings. Self-disclosure involves relating ones own experience to that of the person we are listening to (Ivey et al, 1987). Relating to personal experience is a key component of listening, according to the English curriculum (Ministry of Education, MOE, 1994). Feedback may occur when a participant comments directly on the actions of another person in the discussion. This is often evaluative (MOE, 1996). To listen critically and evaluate is considered a component of listening within the English curriculum (MOE, 1994). Summarization involves gathering together verbalizations, facts, feelings and meanings and presenting them in outline form (Ivey et al, 1987). To summarise shows effective listening because it can enable clarification and suggests a structure that the other participants can then respond to (Ivey et al, 1987). This gives the listener a chance to hear if their thinking is accurate.

It is important to recognize that this initial list of listening behaviours is by no means exhaustive. Furthermore, as Ivey et al (1987) point out, "attending behaviour varies from culture to culture and from individual to individual" (p.52). The literature also emphasizes non-verbal listening behaviours such as eye contact and body language, and nuances of verbal interaction, such as tone of voice (Charlton, 1996; Ivey et al, 1987; Nesbitt, 2000). These aspects are absent or altered in an online context.

How Does Listening Occur Online?

The assumption that it is possible and worthwhile to listen effectively online requires examination. The current case is premised on two key assumptions about online discussion. Firstly, it is assumed that people interacting online do "listen" to each other. Although there is no auditory stimulus involved, the assumption is made that the type of interaction that occurs online is analogous to "listening" if it involves close attention and responsiveness to what another person has to say. Furthermore, it is assumed that effective listening online must be demonstrated as active listening, rather than as "lurking" while reading discussion.

Listening behaviours may be fundamentally altered online, as visual and social cues are differentiated in the context of asynchronous, text-based online discussion. In the online environment, eye contact is not possible, and there is no body language or tone of voice. Some of the aspects of emotion and tone can, however, be conveyed online through the use of emoticons or symbols that represent non-verbal behaviours like smiling, frowning, or looking puzzled (Anderson and Kanuka, 2003; Harris, 2001). A possible limitation of emoticons is that "the emotion that is implicit in our ordinary communication only gets communicated by first making it explicit. Consequently, the receiver has to be on guard when accepting the emotion, as there is virtually no means to check the sincerity of the sender" (Westera and Sloep, 2001, p.127). While this is important for the receiver of a message, it also serves as a reminder that the sender must overtly show emotion if they are intending to communicate it, as this will not automatically be transmitted just because the sender is sincere. In order to convey listening, one has to do so actively.

Despite the devices for enriching communication online, much of the literature on online interaction is dominated by what Hine (2000) refers to as "the reduced social cues model" (p.14). According to this model, online communication is stripped of social, visual, and auditory context cues and is altogether a less human form of communication (Bullen, 1998, online). However, as Hine (2000) notes, the reduced social cues model for understanding online communication has come under attack from more context-based approaches. For example, it is suggested that a great deal depends on the extent to which participants think of themselves as part of a group. A group identity is likely to have formed in an online class, and this can be facilitated by social rapport building (Haynes, 2002), as occurred when the participants in the current project met online. Introductions were made and both the pupils and the students shared a little of their diverse backgrounds and experiences, accompanied by the posting of their photographs online, which conveyed a sense of personal presence.

Increasingly, online communication also has its own system of social cues in the form of "netiquette" or Internet Etiquette (Wilkinson, 2000; Palloff and Pratt, 2001; Haynes, 2002). All participants in the current project had some familiarity with netiquette due to their prior experiences in the online course (students) or ICT classroom (pupils). The participants' preparation for engaging in this research project included a reminder about some basics of netiquette – e.g. greetings, use of peoples' names, appropriate use of emoticons, clarity of messages, responding to others, and how to disagree politely.

The Focus of this Case

Within the local professional situation, this project began as a learning experience for the teacher education students and pupils involved. The decision to research this experience came from the wish to explore the existing situation with regard to teacher education students' listening skills. Exploring the current skill levels would provide a baseline from which to work on developing the readiness to listen to pupils' perspectives.

The intention was that the research would attend to the way the student teachers convey that they are "listening" to pupils, and how they encourage the children to express their ideas, in an online context. In order to open up inquiry, the broad research question asked here was 'What listening behaviours are evident in the contributions of teacher education students, when they are engaged in online discussion with middle school pupils?'

How Analysis Occurred

In order to make the concept of listening more concrete and less abstract, use was made of the listening behaviours drawn from the literature. These behaviours were used as initial categories for classifying or coding the data online. In this way, a "hypothetic-deductive" approach was adopted, where "a preconceived and formatted set of categories can be used to guide qualitative coding" (Anderson and Kanuka, 2003, p.176). The analysis involved more than simple sorting into predetermined categories, however. The listening behaviours drawn mainly from the counselling arena are not an exhaustive list of categories, as noted earlier. In addition, it was deemed important to note variations in the online context and to avoid being entirely constrained by preconceived categories. Scope for inductive classification was allowed so that new categories and classifications for use in the analysis could stem from the data.

In order to further clarify each category of behaviour, a guiding question was formulated to assist in focusing attention on each behaviour. The questions were as shown in Table 1.

To assist with this classification, the following definitions of open and closed questions were used:

- **Open Questions:** Usually begin with "what", "how", "why", "could", or "would". Questions that begin with these words usually require the client to provide a longer, more open response and not easily answered with a "yes" or "no". An open question is an invitation to talk (Ivey, Bradford-Ivey and Simek-Downing, 1987, p.71).
- **Closed Questions:** Usually begin with the words "is", 'are", "do", or "did". A closed question can be answered with a "yes" or "no" or just a few words (Ivey et al, 1987, p.72).

To demonstrate how the teacher education students' postings were coded and their listening behaviours categorized, the following is a particularly good example of a single contribution from a student, containing six distinct listening behaviours:

Table 1. Questions

Staying on the same topic	To what extent did the teacher education students stay on the same topic as the children they were listening to, avoiding abrupt changes of topic?
Encouraging	To what extent did the teacher education students encourage by restating or directly repeating the comments of the children, or by otherwise encouraging the children to tell them more?
Paraphrasing	To what extent did the teacher education students provide an encapsulated repetition back to the children, where they brought together recent comments?
Questioning	To what extent did the teacher education students ask open or closed questions of the children? Did they reply when the children asked a question?
Reflection of meaning or feelings	To what extent did the teacher education students check out where the children are on an issue, in terms of meaning or feelings?
Self-disclosure	To what extent did the teacher education students relate their own experiences to those of the children?
Feedback	To what extent did the teacher education students comment directly on the actions of the children in discussion?
Summarization	To what extent did the teacher education students summarise the children's comments in the discussion by systematically gathering together disparate themes?

Hi all, I am a digital immigrant but spend so much time on here that I must be close to being a native. I have always loved maths and believe I have a very logical mind which has made ICT fun for me. Reading these posts are really awesome all these new terms digital immigrants, digital natives, learning through ICT not about it, referring to the computer as just another tool from your pencil case is an excellent description. J, M can you give us some more examples they make so much sense. I have learnt how to use a computer and the Internet through trial and error and having fun with it. I want to use the skills I have now and the skills I will gain over the next three years, in the classroom when I become a teacher. I would really like to know what makes a good ICT teacher?

The above entry would be classified as follows:

Staying on the same topic, as the topics of digital immigrants/natives, and how the students learned to use ICT were raised previously by the children.

- **Encouraging:** "J, M can you give us some more examples they make so much sense." (Could also be classified as a closed question.)
- **Paraphrasing:** "All these new terms digital immigrants, digital natives, learning through ICT not about it, referring to the computer as just another tool from your pencil case."
- **Open Question:** "What makes a good ICT teacher?"
- **Self-Disclosure:** "I am a digital immigrant but spend so much time on here that I must be close to being a native. I have always loved maths and believe I have a very logical mind which has made ICT fun for me… I have learnt how to use a computer and the Internet through trial and error and having fun with it. I want to use the skills I have now and the skills I will gain over the next three years, in the classroom when I become a teacher."
- **Feedback:** "Reading these posts are really awesome… referring to the computer as just another tool from your pencil case is an excellent description… can you give us some more examples they make so much sense."

Possible other categories that could be generated from the above example may include use of commonly understood language to convey attention to previous comments (e.g. "digital immigrant", "digital native"). This category would be similar to the notion of staying on the same topic but could enable more detailed awareness of whether the nuances of word use were picked up on by a listener in the discussion.

The above example also highlights some of the complexity of coding the listening behaviours, as it is noted that the behaviour classified as encouraging could also be classified as a closed question. There are overlaps between categories in numerous instances and a decision must be made about how to classify the behaviour. In this instance the behaviour is regarded as 'encouraging' since it would seem to be "encouraging the children to tell more" as per the guiding question for encouraging. Conversely, the statement is not regarded as a closed question, despite the fact it begins with the word "Can". This is because the statement lacks a question mark and is clearly an invitation to tell more rather than to just reply briefly to the request. Such judgments made in analysis are highly subjective and based on the researcher's interpretation. However the guiding questions for each category proved helpful here and there was an effort made to be consistent.

KEY FINDINGS

In this section, each category of listening behaviour is reviewed in turn, and occurrences are illustrated by quotes from the participants in discussion. Findings are then summed up in relation to the evidence and key patterns of listening found in this case.

Staying on the Same Topic

Rather than staying on the same topic as the previous contributor who posted immediately before each teacher education student, there was a far more prevalent tendency to refer back to earlier contributors. Often the teacher education students deliberately chose to refer back to the comments of a child, rather than to focus on the more recent comments of their own peers. No abrupt changes of topic were noted in the first half of the discussion. In the second half, changes of topic did occur as adults questioned the children without otherwise responding to them, or introduced new topics of discussion, and then pursued these through adult-to-adult interactions.

Encouraging

Encouraging took two distinct forms in the discussion. It either involved direct restatements or repetitions of children's ideas, with reference made directly to the child by name. For example, "It was a very interesting statement that both M and J discussed, about how "we don't learn about ICT, we learn through ICT" (TE stu, #43). Alternatively, encouraging involved asking for more from the children in the discussion. For example,

Would love to hear your comments. (TE stu, #54)

I am very interested to find out more information from a child's perspective. (TE stu, #60)

Looking forward to your reply. (TE stu, #72)

A noticeable tendency was for the first form of encourager (restatement/repetition) to be used in conjunction with self-disclosure, so that the teacher education students referred to the children's comments before making links with their own experiences. For example, "J discussed how it must have taken a while to finish projects as there were no computers back in the day. This is very true. Even when I was at school we would have to spend a lot of time searching through the library to find relevant information" (TE stu, #7). As the discussion continued, it became apparent that restatements linking to own experience were often accompanied by affirmative evaluative feedback. For example, "J I totally agree with you. I hope books never die out, they are an important part of our lives." (TE stu, #85). Another student picked up and affirmed the comments of two children by linking them to her own learning within the course:

It was a very interesting statement that both M and J discussed, about how we don't learn about ICT, we learn through ICT. So many people, including myself at the start of this paper, assume that ICT is something that is learnt on its own, something you learn about. (TE stu, #43)

Paraphrasing and Summarizing

It proved difficult to distinguish paraphrasing, encouraging and summarizing in the discussion. This is because all three categories of behaviour often involve some repetition of another contributor's ideas. In the first half of the discussion, encouraging was the prevalent form, as discussed. During the second half of discussion, the teacher education students did paraphrase by drawing together some of the new terminology and new learning they had experienced. These were paraphrases rather than summaries as the teacher education students tended to focus on one or two aspects of the discussion to highlight, rather than systematically gathering together disparate themes. For example, "I learnt a lot of new words and what they mean for example ergonomics and about digital natives and digital immigrants" (TE stu, #97)

The only summarization that occurred in the discussion was performed by the lecturer, which of course has implications for researcher-effect in this study.

Questioning

When the teacher education students asked questions of the children, which they did frequently, there was an overwhelming tendency for them to ask more than one question at a time. During the first 50 entries there was a tendency to combine open and closed questioning. For example, "On a normal day at school, does your teacher allow you to use the Net at specific times throughout the day or can you use the computer whenever you like? And how do you make it fair so that everyone in the class gets a turn?" (TE stu, #11). During the second phase of the discussion, there was a tendency to use multiple open questions within an entry, or multiple closed questions, rather than combining the two questioning types.

When children asked questions, which occurred far less frequently than teacher questions did, these questions usually yielded multiple replies. Responses to questions were very direct, so that the teacher education students often prefaced their replies with "In response to..."

Reflection of Meaning and Feelings

Reflections of meaning and feelings occurred infrequently as the teacher education students occasionally shared their interpretations of the pupils' messages. It was notable, however, that when such reflections did occur they served as very good illustrations of the tendency for people engaged in online discussion to use language usually attributed to oral communication and to "listening". For example, one student commented "It sounds like you are all getting good things out of your school" (#19).

Self-Disclosure

Self-disclosure was very frequent throughout the discussion, and particularly during the first half of the entries. Teacher education students frequently linked their own experiences directly to those of the children in the discussion. It is important to note here that this is an assessment criterion for the discussion, and that students' discussion contributions are partially marked on whether they "shared aspects from [their] own personal experience." Again, this raises issues of lecturer/researcher effect. As the discussion drew to an end, some of the students' final comments were of an "I have learned..." form of self-disclosure, which may also have been prompted by the lecturer's moderation of the discussion.

Feedback

Feedback to the children in the discussion took three forms, as the teacher education students either commented generally that they were enjoying the discussion and finding it interesting, or they picked up more specifically on an individual child's statement and commented evaluatively on this. For example, a general statement was "I have read through all this group's contributions and it is very interesting so far" (TE stu, #19). More specifically, a student commented by referencing a child's description when they affirmed that "referring to the computer as just another tool from your pencil case is an excellent description" (TE stu, #52). The third type of feedback was to directly thank the children for their answers or input. For example, "Thanks to J, M and J for answering my question." (TE stu, #53). It is important to note here that although the teacher education students' feedback to the pupils was certainly evaluative, it tended to be non-specific, and would not necessarily inform the pupils of why their statements or questions were particularly deserving of praise or thanks.

Additional Categories

Additional categories of behaviour stemming from the data include the use of commonly understood language, which could be interpreted as conveying listening. For example, terminology like "digital native" and "digital immigrant" were eagerly seized upon by the students. A further example occurred when a teacher education student continued a metaphor proposed by one of the children in the discussion. The child had compared ICT to tools in a pencilcase (#26), and the teacher education student later asked "How do you make the computer use fair for everyone needing to do research? (so you're not all racing for the pencil sharpener at once)" (#42).

In addition, the teacher education students would often either agree or disagree with a child in the discussion, which also demonstrated that they were listening to the points made. Agreeing was far more prevalent than disagreement was, and debate of issues raised by the pupils was fairly limited, although this did occur in respect of a books versus computers issue briefly:

Just going back to the issue of computers vs books (J, #65), what's wrong with books dying out? I mean the only real reason we need books is to learn to read right? Well every time we sit down at our computers and surf the Internet we are continuously reading! (TE stu, #78)

On at least one occasion a teacher education student also acknowledged that she had revised her previous views after listening to the pupils' comments, indicating that the listening was occurring at a deeper level. This was a particular form of self-disclosure, where the disclosure related to the learning that the student was experiencing, rather than to an anecdote linking to a pupil's experience. For example, "J, I like your comparison of computers being like something in your pencil case! I can now understand how computers can be tools and not distractions" (TE stu, #50)

Patterns of Listening Online

Referring to the research question, 'What listening behaviours are evident in the contributions of teacher education students, when they are engaged in online discussion with middle school pupils?' this case suggests that many listening behaviours from a face-to-face context are transferable to online discussion, in that students use many of the listening behaviours they would be expected to use in face-to-face encounters. It is possible to encourage, paraphrase, question, reflect meaning or feelings, self-disclose, and to give feedback to pupils online. There are, however, some interesting differences in the way some of the listening behaviours exhibited online.

For example, there is a tendency for contributors to respond to any previous speaker, rather than the most recent comments. This is likely to be influenced by the asynchronous character of the online discussion since the earlier messages are preserved and are not displaced by more recent comments. The pattern noted online is consistent with what Williams and Robson (2004) refer to as "threading" (p.27). Participants engage in threading when they simultaneously conduct, and maintain distinctions between, multiple topics of conversation. This pattern has also been referred to as a "multilogue" (Shank and Cunningham, 1996, p. 37), "polylogue" or "telelogue" (Voiskounsky, 1998, p.33). In the current case, behaviour was compatible with threading rather than with staying on the same topic as a previous contributor. However, this did not constitute abrupt change of topic as the teacher education students who threaded their contributions were still observed to be "staying on the same topic as the children they were listening to" in accordance with the listening behaviours outlined within this paper. This is a good example of where a listening behaviour was altered in the online context, and where it would not be fair to judge the online contributions by the same criteria as face-to-face interaction. Because the teacher education students engaged in threading does not imply that they were not listening.

As a further example, it is apparent that encouragers used online often take the form of an overt and direct request to tell more, as when a contributor writes "Looking forward to your response" at the close of their statement. This type of comment is often used online and in written communication (e.g. email, memos, letters), where the interaction is asynchronous and a response may not be immediately forthcoming. This would not usually be said to a discussion partner face-to-face, but perhaps might be replaced by a silence and an expectant look. Online, the expectancy, and encouragement to talk further, can be conveyed by overtly "asking for more". The need to be overt, conscious and purposeful in the demonstration of listening makes the online environment an excellent training ground for developing effective listening skills as it lends itself to reflective practice and to meta-listening awareness. Participants can think about and plan the best ways to show they are listening responsively and actively to partners in discussion, and can evaluate their performance in this regard, leading to ongoing improvements in listening and learning.

CURRENT CHALLENGES

E-Listening?

The findings in this case suggest that listening behaviours do vary to some extent online, as compared with face-to-face contexts. Since language does differ in an online context, it is tempting to assign a new label, as Mann and Stewart (2004) do when they refer to "electronic paralanguage" (p.386), or as Gibbs (2000) does with her reference to "cyberlanguage" (p.11). One could refer to 'e-listening', in keeping with the trend that labels work in an online context as 'e-learning', 'e-teaching', 'e-research', and so on. However, I am mindful of the wisdom of a senior colleague who has stated that she longs for the day when we will stop talking about 'e-learning' and simply get back to talking about 'learning' (Campbell, personal communication). Anderson and Kanuka (2003) also make this point rather cleverly when they refer to their fears of being criticised by the "Society for the Preservation of the other 25 letters" (p.4). The contention here is that listening online need not be given a new name just because it occurs in a different context. Face-to-face interaction, or the hearing world, does not have exclusive claim to listening, and experimenting with listening in new contexts can usefully extend the concept.

Beyond Listening Behaviours

The initial focus on listening behaviours is helpful to the extent that it enables constructive guidance for future online teacher education students regarding listening behaviours to work with online. In this way, the case informs the cycle of professional development, since it stemmed from an interest in online learning and interaction, and serves to guide further online learning and interactions. However, the focus on listening behaviours is also problematic and requires deconstruction when critically reflecting on this case. Of principle concern is the possibility that behaviour alone may not be evidence of listening. It may be that research needs to focus more closely on peoples' perceptions of listening. The intentions of the listener and the perceptions of their partner in the conversation could both be pertinent here. The implications for further research are that rather than focus exclusively on the listening behaviours exhibited by the teacher education students online, there is also a need to consider the intentions of the teacher education students and the perceptions of the children in the online discussion. In future, it would be of interest to ask the students "When were you listening?" "How did you try to show you were listening?" "When you were not listening what were you doing?"

In addition, it would be useful to ask the pupils "When did you feel listened to, and why?" "When did you feel that you were not being listened to, and what gave you this impression?"

In addition to noting the observable behaviour from the researcher's point of view, it would make sense to explore how participants respond to the behaviour – for example what position did it offer them to respond from? What kind of invitation to contribute did they hear? (Drewery, 2004). A limitation of this research in its current form, therefore, is that the focus on observable behaviours means the study explores "inferred experience" without actually checking with the participants to ensure that interpretations of listening are accurate from their perspectives (Lloyd-Smith and Tarr, 2000). With this in mind, new study is currently being undertaken to examine perspectives of participants engaged in asynchronous online discussion (Forbes, 2009).

Dynamics of Power

As the patterns of listening are examined, it is useful to consider also the distribution of knowledge and power between the two groups involved in this discussion. There is evidence that the power balance between the adult teacher education students and the 12 year old pupils was indeed challenged, as a result of the subject matter of the discussion, the children's superior expertise and confidence, and the disinhibiting tendencies of the online environment. On the other hand, however, this was far from a panacea for equitable relations as there is still ample evidence that existing social relations are reproduced, and that student teachers hold firmly to a traditional stance, just as children continue to harbour traditional attitudes toward authority.

This mixed picture of both perpetuation and challenge of existing social relations is supported by literature examining power dynamics in online contexts. In Kowal's (2002) view, "the rise of the Internet as a democratic communication technology ... has resulted in the opening of new opportunities for "speaking" as well as being "heard"" (p.105). This statement is in keeping with what Crawford (2002) depicts as a "techno-populist" stance, whereby "online speech communities are free of social hierarchies, privilege, and oppression, which characterize embodied life, and can function as realms of radically egalitarian debate and conversation" (Crawford, 2002, p.94). That is, the online discussion is seen as "a pluralist democracy where all voices could be heard equally" (Crawford, 2002, p.93). Although some writers, like Willson-Quayle (1997) do offer some qualified support for the notion of cyber-democracy, others like Crawford (2002) dismiss the idea that the Internet necessarily flattens hierarchies, and creates participatory democracy as "techno-populist rhetoric" (p.89). Gimenez (1997) argues that virtual communities reproduce the stratified relations of the larger society, and offer no real challenge to the social relations of non-virtual life.

One identifiable pattern in the literature is that power relations are more likely to be challenged where there is greater anonymity among online participants. That is, where there is a "lack of awareness among participants of the social status of others" (Willson-Quayle, 1997, p.237). This lack of social status awareness is, however, largely inapplicable to the current study as participants' identities were not disguised, and it was clear from the outset that participants were either teacher education students or middle school pupils. Despite this transparency of teacher-pupil status, however, there is still evidence of challenge to traditional power dynamics.

In the current case, traditional power dynamics were challenged when the pupils challenged the student teachers' use of language and their underlying assumptions. The pupils directed the student teachers' learning, and pupils later reflected with pride that they were "teaching the teachers". This was affirmed by those student teachers who acknowledged that they were learning from the pupils. The pupils' challenge to the teachers was exemplified in a strand of discussion where the pupils encouraged the teacher education students to think about the distinction between learning about ICT and learning through ICT. This strand commenced when teacher education students posed the following questions for the pupils:

What aspects of ICT do you learn about at school? (TE stu, #33)

Do you think learning about ICT in your school has helped you with other things outside of your school and how? (TE stu, #39)

A pupil entered the discussion to challenge the teacher education students' use of language and their underlying assumptions:

A, we don't learn about ICT, we learn through ICT. Yes we do come to the computer room and we do use computers, but we don't learn about computers, we learn social studies, or science, or English. It's kind of like I said before, computers are like something in your pencil case. We don't learn about our ruler; we use our ruler to extend our work (excuse the pun). But as the years go by we learn how to use the ruler better, hold it straighter; but we still don't learn about the ruler, we use the ruler... We don't go on the Internet to learn how to hit the back key, we go on the Internet to learn about the hardships of a World War One soldier. You see? We don't learn about ICT, we learn through ICT. (pupil, #40)

The distinction between learning about ICT and learning through ICT became pivotal in the discussion, and was referred to as a key instance of learning by many of the teacher education students. As one teacher education student commented,

Until this discussion I didn't understand how computers could be used to their full potential in the classroom… Reading your explanation of learning through ICT has helped me understand that ICT is just a tool to support new ways of learning.

Similarly, another student teacher commented,

What it highlighted for me was that teaching students is not necessarily showing them how to use a computer but giving them opportunities to use a range of ICT tools to enhance their critical thinking skills

This example serves to illustrate the point that the pupils were able to challenge the teacher education students' thinking, and that the pupils' voices were indeed powerful.

Nevertheless, there were occasions when the perpetuation and reproduction of traditional power dynamics was clearly evident. This was the case when the teacher education students resorted to remarks that could be deemed patronizing, or belittling of the pupils' identities as independent learners and thinkers. For example, "It's great to see you children are so well informed. Your teacher has done a wonderful job, I hope you appreciate her" (TE stu, #80).

In addition, the pupils admitted to 'holding back' from challenging the student teachers due to fear of consequences. As one pupil commented,

I didn't want to write that I disagree because I felt I shouldn't disagree with adults and couldn't tell them if they were wrong. You might get in trouble for being cheeky and one day in the future they might be your teacher and then you'd really be in trouble because they'd be out for revenge. Perhaps we need secret identities.

Obviously, there is still a long way to go if pupils think they need to hide their true identities in order to safely challenge their teachers. As Ess (1996) reminds us, "technology does not necessarily transform, much less liberate us from, cultural assumptions" (p.7). Teachers need to be willing to listen, and to effectively demonstrate this to pupils before the democratizing effect of online discussion can be fully realized and the traditional hierarchical structures of authority leveled. Online discussions such as the one that occurred in this study, should serve to both encourage and to challenge teachers to listen.

Mutual Learning

Throughout the online discussion between the teacher education students and the middle school pupils, knowledge was constructed through interaction. There is ample evidence, already quoted, to suggest that the student teachers' listening led to re-examination of their initial preconceptions, and to further reflective thinking prior to sharing their own insights.

The learning for the student teachers occurred on two levels: In the first instance, they engaged in some deeper thinking about the role of ICT in teaching and learning; and in addition, they learned something of the importance of listening in order to learn. This learning was evident in the evaluative comments made by the student teachers at the conclusion of the discussion, as they reflected on their own learning. For example, the teacher education students commented,

How might teachers and students learn together? I think that this discussion has just completely answered that! You students and us student teachers have learnt together I feel, and that is through discussion, this discussion this week has taught me that to learn effectively communication is vital. I think it is a fantastic way for students and teachers to learn together!

I believe that students must take a major part in their own learning and I have found out through this course, ways in which I can help them do this.

[The pupils showed us] critical thinking skills in action.

[I learned] that we are never too old to learn things and to be humble enough to accept good information from those who are much younger than ourselves.

I learned that kids are sometimes capable of more than we think, we too often underestimate kids. Kids understand things really quickly, and sometimes they are more open-minded.

For the pupils' part, they learned to think reflectively about their own learning in order to share their insights with others. The pupils learned that they themselves have a great deal to offer as 'teachers of teachers' and that their voices are powerful when others are prepared to listen and learn. These ideas are demonstrated by the following comments by pupils:

Before this project some of us hadn't thought about how we use ICT in school and now we have.

We know more about ICT than we think we do.

... the thing that has surprised me most is the insight that me, J and M have got into the minds of teachers. This conversation has been one of the most interesting things I have participated in throughout my schooling years because instead of being taught maths or English, students and future teachers were brought together to interact and post in a very stimulating discussion about ICT.

Teaching the teachers made me feel important.

The challenge inherent here is to ensure that any partnership whereby guests are involved in online discussion with students should ensure that there are reciprocal benefits to both parties, in terms of learning gains and empowerment.

IMPLICATIONS

This case offers insight into how listening may occur online and how particular face-to-face listening behaviours may transfer and be modified to an online context. It is clear that it is possible to encourage, paraphrase, question, reflect meaning or feelings, self-disclose, and to give feedback online. It is also clear that patterns of response may differ online, as compared with face-to-face interactions, as threading or multiloguing is prevalent online. In addition, listening behaviours must be overtly expressed online, in order to compensate for absence of non-verbal cues. In this case, students also demonstrated listening online by adopting common language to the pupils, where understandings were 'taken as shared', via agreement and disagreement, and by acknowledging the revision of their views.

The findings provide a starting point for working with staff and students to further examine their own listening practices. For example, students in this case could be guided to summarise and to reflect meaning and feelings more frequently in order to check with their discussion partners. Their listening and learning may be enhanced by revising their questioning practice, so that they ask fewer, more intentional questions, rather than delivering a barrage of closed questions. Their feedback to the children could have been more specific, in order to move beyond vague statements expressing teacher approval. This latter point raises the issue of power dynamics between adults and children working together online. Further work of this kind is needed in order to convince teacher education students that they can and should learn by listening to children, and in order to convince pupils that it is safe to challenge their teachers without fear of repercussions. When children do challenge and when teachers do listen, the mutual learning is clearly evident.

It would be useful to involve students and pupils more closely in examining their own listening behaviours, and their own attitudes towards power. The online environment is an excellent training ground for developing effective listening skills as it lends itself to reflective practice and to meta-listening awareness. Students can think about and plan the best ways to show they are listening responsively and actively to partners in discussion, and can evaluate their performance in this regard, leading to ongoing improvements in listening and learning.

The implications for improving practice in online instruction extend beyond the arena of teacher education, and beyond interactions with children online. In any people-oriented field, a great deal of good could come from considering the need to listen, and how well listening occurs online.

CONCLUSION

In conclusion, in the case reported, teacher education students were encouraged to listen to children, in the context of asynchronous online discussion. Listening behaviours demonstrated by the student teachers throughout the discussion were monitored, and consideration was given to how listening behaviours transfer to an online context, and how these are necessarily altered online. In some respects the power dynamics between the adult students and the children in the discussion were challenged, although in other respects perpetuation of some traditional attitudes was still evident. Mutual learning resulted for both student teachers and pupils, in relation to the topic under discussion (teaching and learning through ICT), and to the importance of listening and dialogue for learning. There are implications for improved practice when working online as discussion partners and when guiding others to listen effectively online, and offline in their professional practice. There are implications for professional distance degree programs as the quality of such programs can be judged by how well the learning within the program prepares students for professional challenges such as those posed by the need to actively communicate, listen and learn while engaged in professional practice. Any professional distance degree program could be enhanced by the practice of connecting potential clients and experienced professionals with students through asynchronous online discussion.

ACKNOWLEDGMENT

The former New Zealand curriculum for the teaching of English has been a source of information here; however, readers are likely to find similarities when considering any English language curriculum internationally. It seems likely that there will be global similarities regarding the demonstration of listening. Of course, there will also be cultural differences, and listening in languages other than English may raise many new issues. Whether and how listening behaviours differ across languages other than English would certainly be an interesting consideration for future study.

REFERENCES

Anderson, T., & Kanuka, H. (2003). e-Research: Methods, strategies and issues. Boston: Pearson Education, Inc.

Bullen, M. (1998). Participation and critical thinking in online university distance education. *Journal of Distance Education, 13*(2). Retrieved on 24 April 2003 from http://cade.icaap.org/vol2013.2002/bullen.html

Charlton, T. (1996). Listening to pupils in classrooms and schools. In Davie, R., & Galloway, D. (Eds.), *Listening to children in education* (pp. 49–63). London: David Fulton Publishers.

Crawford, A. (2002). The myth of the unmarked net speaker. In Elmer, G. (Ed.), *Critical perspectives on the Internet* (pp. 89–104). Oxford, UK: Rowman & Littlefield Publishers, Inc..

Dockrell, J., Lewis, A., & Lindsay, G. (2000). Researching children's perspectives: A psychological dimension. In Lewis, A., & Lindsay, G. (Eds.), *Researching children's perspectives* (pp. 46–58). Buckingham, UK: Open University Press.

Drewery, W. (2004). *Why we should watch what we say: Everyday speech and the production of relational subjectivity*. Unpublished manuscript.

English Online. (2004). *Listening strategies*. Retrieved on 28 August 2004 from http://english.unitecnology.ac.nz/resources/units/listening/strategies.html

Ess, C. (1996). Introduction: Thoughts along the i-way: Philosophy and the emergence of CMC. In Ess, C. (Ed.), *Philosophical perspectives on computer-mediated communication* (pp. 1–12). Albany, NY: State University of New York Press.

Galloway, D., & Davie, R. (1996). A way forward? In Davie, R., & Galloway, D. (Eds.), *Listening to children in education* (pp. 137–142). London: David Fulton Publishers.

Gibbs, D. (2000). Cyberlanguage: What it is and what it does. In Gibbs, D., & Krause, K. L. (Eds.), *Cyberlines: Languages and cultures of the Internet* (pp. 11–29). Australia: James Nicholas Publishers Pty Ltd..

Giminez, M. E. (1997). The dialectics between the real and the virtual: The case of the progressive sociology network. In Behar, J. E. (Ed.), *Mapping cyberspace: Social research on the electronic frontier* (pp. 79–104). New York: Dowling College Press.

Harris, D. (2001, July 9). Be nice: David Harris's guide to good manners online. *Computerworld New Zealand*, 18-19.

Haynes, D. (2002, April). *The social dimensions of on-line learning: Perceptions, theories and practical responses.* Paper presented at the Distance Education Association of New Zealand Conference. Wellington, New Zealand.

Hine, C. (2000). Internet as culture and cultural artifact. In *Virtual Ethnography* (pp. 14–40). London: Sage Publications.

Ivey, A. E., Bradford-Ivey, M., & Simek-Downing, L. (1987). *Counseling and pyschotherapy* (2nd ed.). Boston: Allyn and Bacon.

Kowal, D. M. (2002). Digitizing and globalizing indigenous voices: The Zapatista movement. In Elmer, G. (Ed.), *Critical perspectives on the Internet* (pp. 105–126). Oxford, UK: Rowman & Littlefield Publishers, Inc..

Lewis, A., & Lindsay, G. (2000). Emerging issues. In Lewis, A., & Lindsay, G. (Eds.), *Researching children's perspectives* (pp. 189–197). Buckingham, UK: Open University Press.

Lloyd-Smith, M., & Tarr, J. (2000). Researching children's perspectives: A sociological dimension. In Lewis, A., & Lindsay, G. (Eds.), *Researching children's perspectives* (pp. 59–70). Buckingham, UK: Open University Press.

Mann, C., & Stewart, F. (2000). *Internet communication and qualitative research: A handbook for researching online.* London: Sage Publications Ltd..

Mann, C., & Stewart, F. (2004). Introducing online methods. In Hesse-Biber, S. N., & Leavy, P. (Eds.), *Approaches to qualitative research: A reader on theory and practice* (pp. 367–401). Oxford, UK: Oxford University Press.

Marland, M. (1996). Personal development, pastoral care and listening. In Davie, R., & Galloway, D. (Eds.), *Listening to children in education* (pp. 64–76). London: David Fulton Publishers.

McGee, C. (2001). Classroom interaction. In McGee, C., & Fraser, D. (Eds.), *The professional practice of teaching* (2nd ed., pp. 106–133). Palmerston North, Australia: Dunmore Press Ltd..

McLaughlin, C., Carnell, M., & Blount, L. (1999). Children as teachers: Listening to children in education. In Carolin, B., & Milner, P. (Eds.), *Time to listen to children: Personal and professional communication* (pp. 97–111). London: Routledge.

Ministry of Education. (1994). *English in the New Zealand curriculum*. Wellington, New Zealand: Learning Media.

Ministry of Education. (1996). *Exploring language: A handbook for teachers*. Wellington, New Zealand: Learning Media Ltd..

Morrow, V. (1999). It's cool… 'cos you can't give us detentions and things, can you?!: Reflections on research with children. In Carolin, B., & Milner, P. (Eds.), *Time to listen to children: Personal and professional communication* (pp. 203–215). London: Routledge.

Nesbitt, E. (2000). Researching 8 to 13-year-olds' perspectives on their experience of religion. In Lewis, A., & Lindsay, G. (Eds.), *Researching children's perspectives* (pp. 135–149). Buckingham, UK: Open University Press.

Palloff, R., & Pratt, K. (2001). *Transforming courses for the online classroom: Lessons from the cyberspace classroom*. San Francisco, CA: Jossey-Bass Inc..

Prensky, M. (2001). Digital natives, digital immigrants. *On the Horizon, 9*(5), 1-6. Retrieved on 15 January 2005 from www.marcprensky.com/writing/default.asp

Salmon, G. (2002). *E-tivities: The key to active online learning*. London: Kogan Page.

Shank, G., & Cunningham, D. (1996). Mediated phosphor dots: Toward a post-cartesian model of computer-mediated communication via the semiotic superhighway. In Ess, C. (Ed.), *Philosophical perspectives on computer-mediated communication* (pp. 27–41). New York: State University of New York Press.

Taylor, A. S. (2000). The UN convention on the rights of the child: Giving children a voice. In Lewis, A., & Lindsay, G. (Eds.), *Researching children's perspectives* (pp. 21–33). Buckingham, UK: Open University Press.

Voiskounsky, A. E. (1998). Telelogue speech. In F. Sudweeks, McLaughlin, & Rafaeli (Eds.), Network and Netplay: Virtual Groups on the Internet (pp. 27-40). Cambridge, MA: The MIT Press.

Westera, W., & Sloep, P. B. (2001). The future of education in cyberspace. In *Cybereducation*. Larchmon, NY: Mary Ann Liebert Inc..

Wilkinson, I. (2000). *Building collaborative learning communities in an online course environment for human service education*. Paper presented at the Distance Education Association of New Zealand 2000 Conference. Dunedin, Australia.

Williams, M., & Robson, K. (2004). Reengineering focus group methodology for the online environment. In Johns, M. D., Chen, S. S., & Hall, G. J. (Eds.), *Online social research: Methods, issues, and ethics* (pp. 25–45). New York: Peter Lang Publishing, Inc..

Willson-Quayle, J. (1997). Cyberspace democracy and social behavior: Reflections and refutations. In Behar, J. E. (Ed.), *Mapping cyberspace: Social research on the electronic frontier* (pp. 229–244). New York: Dowling College Press.

Chapter 7
Culturally Responsive Online Learning for Asian/Pacific Islanders in a Pacific Island University

Catherine E. Stoicovy
University of Guam, USA

EXECUTIVE SUMMARY

This chapter examines the socio-cultural contexts of Asian/Pacific islanders in a Western Pacific island to identify key components for culturally responsive online course development. A model for constructing an online learning environment is proposed using McLoughlin and Oliver's (2000) principles as design frameworks for designing a culturally inclusive instructional design that will support Asian/Pacific islanders' learning in blended courses.

INTRODUCTION

The University, a land-grant institution accredited by the Western Association of Schools and Colleges, is the major institution of higher education in the Western Pacific. In a student population of just over 3,000, 90% are of Asian-Pacific islander ethnicity from Guam and the Northern Mariana Islands, the Philippines and the Micronesian islands of Chuuk, Palau, Pohnpei, Kosrae, Yap, and the Marshalls. The remaining population includes a small contingent of white and other ethnic groups. Inherent in the open-door policy of the University is the responsibility of meeting the needs of a culturally and linguistically diverse student population. While the

DOI: 10.4018/978-1-4666-4486-1.ch007

University faculty honors and addresses cultural diversity in the regular classrooms, no studies have been conducted to determine the degree to which cultural inclusivity is addressed, if at all, in the University's online learning environments.

The purpose of this chapter is to examine the socio-cultural contexts of Asian/Pacific islanders in a Western Pacific island to identify key components for culturally responsive online course development. Given that Chamorro Pacific Islanders and Filipinos comprise the largest percentage of students attending the University, the chapter will focus on these two cultural groups. Chamorros make up 43% of the student population, while Filipinos comprise 37%. We will begin with a discussion of culturally responsive education, to include online learning environments. We will then introduce Guam and the Chamorro indigenous population, Chamorros' shared colonial history with the Philippines, and the core cultural values of the Chamorro islanders and Filipinos. Finally, we will examine McLoughlin & Oliver's (2000) principles as design frameworks for designing a culturally inclusive instructional design that will support Asian/Pacific islanders' learning in blended courses. Blended courses integrate online with traditional face-to-face activities.

CULTURALLY RESPONSIVE EDUCATION

Culturally responsive education is not a new concept. For over two decades, educators and researchers have looked at ways to develop a closer fit between students' home culture and the school as a response to the growing diversity in classrooms across the United States. This work has had a variety of labels including "culturally appropriate" (Au & Jordan, 1981), "culturally congruent" (Erickson & Mohatt, 1981), "culturally responsive" (Cazden & Leggett, 1981), "culturally compatible" (Jordan, 1985; Vogt, Jordan, & Tharp, 1987), culturally relevant (Ladson-Billings, 1992, 1995) and culturally sensitive (Banks, 1999). The idea behind culturally responsive instruction is that teaching approaches build upon the strengths that students bring from their home cultures, instead of ignoring these strengths or requiring that students learn through approaches that conflict with their cultural values (Au, 2001, p. 3). In doing so, culturally responsive pedagogy places other cultures alongside middle class mainstream culture at the center of the instructional paradigm (Smith, 1991).

Most educators would agree with Au (1993) that for educational experiences to be relevant, they must connect with the students' particular life experiences and perspectives. Students learn in different ways and under different conditions, many of which are governed by their cultural socialization. The more a teacher understands the cultures and other aspects of diversity in a classroom, the more likely the teacher can provide a classroom context that is culturally responsive and that will result in successful, high-quality education for culturally and linguistically diverse students (Au, 1993; Gay, 1988; Gilbert & Gay, 1985; Ladson-Billings, 1992, 1995; Smith, 1991; Vogt, Jordan, & Tharp, 1987). For example, the Kamehameha Early Education Program (KEEP), established in Hawaii in the early 1970s as a research and development center to meet the educational needs of native Hawaiian children, provides an example of how an educational program can develop academic skills if it is compatible with the culture of the children it serves. These children, ethnic minority group speakers of Hawaiian Creole English, were not achieving well in school, particularly in reading (Au & Jordan, 1981).

Efforts at the KEEP school have shown that with an approach that is culturally responsive, these children do learn to read. Co-narration, or "talk story," a familiar feature of the native Hawaiian storytelling tradition, was incorporated into reading lessons (Au, 1980; Au and Kawakami, 1985; Au and Mason, 1983). According to the researchers, one student does not do all the talking, but rather various speakers enthusiastically "jump in" and provide their descriptive and contextual enhancement to the story. Group performance, rather than individual performance, is the focus of this cultural pattern of communication. Through an understanding of children's home and community experiences, cultural congruence was established success-fully in the classroom context through KEEP, and literacy learning flourished. As a result, reading achievement scores increased and remained at national norm levels for over a decade (Tharp & Gallimore, 1988, p. 116).

When working with a culturally diverse student population, it's important to recognize differences in patterns of thought, communication styles, and learning. To illustrate, Pacific Islanders may not speak out or openly challenge their teacher with questions. They may remain quiet if a question is directed to them, even if they know the answer. Teachers instructed in the Anglo-European style of extensive questioning techniques in their classrooms often conclude that these students are shy or do not understand the question. The expectation that students will question knowledge or the teacher is a not a universally accepted form of interaction (Reeves & Reeves, 1997).

CULTURALLY RESPONSIVE ONLINE LEARNING

Both theorists and practitioners in online education are paying increasing attention to the cultural dimension in the design process by emphasizing the need to provide culturally sensitive learning environments responsive to the needs of culturally and linguistically diverse students (Reeves & Reeves, 1997; Collis, 1999; McLoughlin & Oliver, 2000). To develop culturally responsive distance education courses, it is important for distance learning providers to understand what is meant by culturally responsive education and its implications for successful online learning experiences.

Researchers who have written about and advocate culturally responsive online learning emphasize the relationship between culture and learning and the need for equity and inclusion of all learners. McLoughlin (2001) maintains that culture pervades learning, with respect to factors such as language and semantics, learning style differences, and educational values. When planning the learning environment, instructional designers should assess whether the needs of culturally diverse learners are being addressed. According to Branch (1997), educational technologists can use plurality of the learners' preferences, backgrounds, and experiences to make instruction more meaningful and contextualized. Instructional designers and educators must incorporate the students' culture into instructional practices and relate the curriculum to student experiences (Powell, 1997). Collis (1999) points out that it is important to consider the cultural backgrounds of learners when designing because culture shapes learners' values, perceptions and goals and determines how they respond to computer-based learning. McLoughlin and Oliver (2000) also echo this when they state that "the acceptance, use and impact of WWW sites are affected by the cultural backgrounds, values, needs and preferences of learners" (p.58).

One of the limitations in current instructional design models is that they do not fully contextualise the learning experience, and are themselves the product of particular cultures (McLoughlin & Oliver, 2000; Henderson, 1996). Web-based instruction often appears to be tailored to the needs of a particular cultural group, recognising the specific learning needs, preferences and styles of a single, perhaps homogeneous, group of learners (McLoughlin, 1999). Western-designed, prepackaged computer courseware often isolates the learner from his or her peers (Smith & Ayers, 2006). This creates advantages for those whose cultural backgrounds emphasize the desirability for individual autonomy, while presenting marked disadvantages for learners socialized in field-dependent cultures – such as those of Asia and Latin America (Bowers, 1988). According to Marcus and Gould (2000), online courses that rely on working alone and competing against others will inherently appeal to individualistic learners, but when technology is used to communicate and collaborate, it may appeal to the more collectivistic learner.

Henderson (1996), proposes a multiple cultures model which is not culturally exclusive, one that incorporates multiple ways of teaching and learning and best suited for use with diverse populations. This model takes on an eclectic approach that allows for variability and flexibility in the design of learning resources. Using the multiple cultural model, McLoughlin (1999) conducted a study to understand the cultural implications for the development of an online learning community for indigenous students in Australia. She found that culturally sensitive or appropriate on-line instruction can be provided if designers are aware of the socio-cultural background and learning styles of their learners, and if an appropriate institutional paradigm is applied to the process of development (p. 241). The creation of an online community of practice was built through electronic messaging, communication forums and asynchronous communication tools such as email and bulletin boards. The "Yarning Place", a virtual meeting space or informal chat room, encouraged students to discuss community topics related to their studies. A news component gave students access to information outside their community, as well as direct links to tutors and mentors, who served to guide students throughout their learning process.

Yet even when educators attempt to address some of the problems associated with cultural diversity and distance learning – such as encouraging collaborative work through online discussion forums- cultural problems can still ensue (Smith and Ayers, p. 407). For example, the expectation to initiate discussion, to critique the ideas of others, and to question knowledge or the instructor is inconsistent with cultural traditions that stress harmony and respect for authority (Joo, 1999; McLoughlin, 2000; Reeves & Reeves, 1997). In an online learning environment, this may manifest itself as discomfort in challenging the ideas of others and misunderstanding the instructor's use of the Socratic method as confrontational (Stanton, 2006).

In adult indigenous education, the instructional design of educational programs must use the skills and values of the community, its cultural traditions and its problems and issues in order to create a unified and authentic learning environment. Subject matter that is relevant to these communities must be taught. In Australia and North America, research conducted with indigenous adults shows that purely cognitive based approaches have had limited success, while interactive, dialogic approaches have been found to equip indigenous students with the analytic and verbal skills they need to succeed in the contemporary world (McCarthy, Lynch Wallace, & Benalla, 1991; Ryan, 1992; McDonald, 1993). Successful implementation and initiation of the on-line course delivery for indigenous learners depended on the adoption of an appropriate framework and educational paradigm that builds a network of learners through a community based focus on shared goals, interests and space.

CULTURALLY RESPONSIVE ONLINE LEARNING IN THE PACIFIC

In a study of distance learning courses in Micronesia, Rao (2007) found that Pacific Island participants valued the face-to-face mode of communication. A culturally responsive solution was to use a Web-based conferencing software to replace the face-to-face interaction. As a result, the blended or hybrid model of distance learning incorporating both synchronous and asynchronous distance learning worked well for the participants. Rao & Giuli (2008) noted that the lack of in-person interactions posed an obstacle for successful distance learning programs in the Micronesia region. Participants desired closer and more continuous contact with their colleagues.

Moreover, the demands of family, community, and work responsibilities made the quick pace of course work extra challenging for participants. To address these issues, Rao and Giuli recommend scaffolding strategies such as stress management, advisors to help navigate bureaucracy, assigned buddies to ease the instructional demands, and Web-based conferencing software for real-time interaction with class members and instructors. In a study of Maori students, Zepke and Leach (2002) found that Maori cultural preferences included face-to- face contact and working in groups. Studies of Native Hawaiian and Pacific Island students enrolled in online courses revealed similar findings in that social isolation was a significant barrier to successful online learning (Menchaca, Yong, & Hoffman (2008). In another study, Menchaca and Hoffman (2008) describe this barrier as cultural:

It is not surprising that students lamented the lack of personal contact with the instructor. While this finding is typical with many students, it is even more prevalent among Pacific Rim students where personal interaction plays a significant cultural role. Hawaii is a society based on human interaction and the isolation of online courses must be addressed when working with students from this background (p. 13).

In a research study of Pacific Island online learners from institutions in New Zealand, one key finding was that participants found similarities between e-learning class and family relationships (Koloto, Katoanga, & Tatila, 2006). They felt responsible for their roles within the class, as in a family. The study indicates that face-to-face academic support and team-building sessions should be integral elements of blended courses offered to Pacific peoples. Online support also improved students' motivation and achievement in the e-learning environment.

INTRODUCTION TO GUAM

Guam, the westernmost unincorporated territory of the United States, is the largest and southernmost island of the Marianas archipelago. Located between Hawaii and the Philippines, Guam is "where America's day begins" because it is 12 hours ahead of the U.S. West Coast. Guam is the closest American soil to Asia. The island is the gateway to Micronesia and a crossroad to the Far East. Hong Kong, Korea, the Philippines, Japan, Okinawa, and Taiwan are just a three to four hour jet flight away.

The island is approximately 30 miles long, four to eight miles wide, and has a total of 212 square miles. It is situated 13 degrees north of the equator in the Western Pacific, 6,000 miles west of San Francisco, 1,500 miles southeast of Tokyo, 2,100 miles east-southeast of Hong Kong, and 1,500 miles east of Manila. The southern part of Guam is made up of volcanic hills that range in altitude up to 1,300 feet, while the central and northern parts have limestone plateaus with steep cliffs that drop down to narrow coasts. The climate is tropical, with a usual temperature range of 74 to 92 degrees Fahrenheit. There are two seasons, rainy and dry, with the rainy season from June to November, and the dry season from December to May. Because of its location in the typhoon belt, Guam experiences the devastating effects of typhoons, including several commonly referred to as Super Typhoons, with winds in excess of 190 miles per hour. The island's amazing ability to prepare for and rebuild after a Super Typhoon is testimony not only to the resiliency of the people, but also to their respect for the forces of nature.

There are approximately 180,000 people residing on Guam – including military dependents. Registered voters of Guam can vote for their governor, a unicameral 15-seat legislature, municipal mayors, and a local (non-voting) delegate to represent the island at the U.S. House of Representatives. English is the official language on Guam with Chamorro the native tongue. Both languages are taught in local and private schools. Much like the Hawaiian language, there is a movement to have Chamorro spoken by younger generations. The Chamorro language has a 5,000-year-old origin. It joins the western group of the Austronesian languages, which includes languages from Indonesia, Malaysia, Palau, and the Philippines.

INDIGENOUS CHAMORROS

The Chamorro people are the indigenous inhabitants of the Mariana Islands who came to Guam approximately 4,000 years ago and were part of the migration in the Pacific from Southeast Asia. Anthropologists believe that the ancient Chamorros came from Southeast Asia because of physical and cultural similarities between the people of the Mariana Islands and the people of Coastal Southeast Asia, Indonesia, and the Philippines.

By nature, the Chamorros were a carefree, laughing people, very fond of festive dancing and singing, of storytelling, and legend-spinning, of contests of great strength and skill (Beardsley, 1964). There were festivities where the people sang or recited legends and stories of their ancestors. The best storytellers competed to see who could speak or sing the most couplets in long epic poems. Perhaps one of the most distinctive features of the ancient Chamorro culture was their ability to create poetry on the spot. They sang poems of four line stanzas that they just made up as they went along. Today this art form is the chamorrita (Cunningham, 1997; Thompson, 1969).

The Chamorros also enjoyed engaging in debate. Adults trained children, as young as five years old, in the art of debate. Mari is the Chamorro word for this skill of competitive debate (Cunningham, 1992). Although they could be serious when the occasion demanded, they took great delight in jokes, playing tricks, and mockery. They enjoyed boasting and playing practical jokes on those people outside their clan.

The temperament of the ancient Chamorros, according to early accounts, may be described as playful friendliness tempered with stubborn persistence. A Franciscan missionary who lived in the Mariana Islands and had an opportunity to observe the early Chamorros at first hand, related that they were a "tractable and kindly people, who regaled him and his companion and showed them much respect" (Beardsley, 1964). In 1602, Fray Juan Pobre de Zamora, a Spanish missionary, reported that the Chamorros were so naturally kind to one another (Cunningham, 1997). As Cunningham explains, there was so much love among the Chamorros and so little among the Spanish Christians that Fray Juan could not explain it. The way the Chamorros shared with one another and the hospitality they showed strangers particularly impressed Fray Juan.

In 1598, Spain claimed the Mariana Islands and stayed for the next two centuries. In 1898, the Spanish-American War ended the Spanish Era and Spain ceded Guam to the United States. The United States military administered Guam until the outbreak of World War II. Japan invaded Guam in 1941 and remained in power for the next three years. The island was retaken by the US three years later in 1944.

COLONIAL INFLUENCE ON EDUCATION ON GUAM

Education on the island of Guam cannot be discussed without reference to the influences of colonial powers in Guam's history. For over four hundred years, the education of the Chamorro people has been the replication of educational models created by and for other people. Colonial powers have made a significant impact on schools and schooling on the island. During the Spanish Era, schools on Guam were used to acquire only the bare essentials of literacy. The greatest influence of the Spanish over Guam's culture was through the Catholic Church which has, since the 17th century been the center of village activity. Today, every village has its patron saint whose feast day is celebrated with a fiesta, to which the entire island is invited. A culturally sensitive teacher will note the significance of the Chamorro/Catholic identity of a majority of the students. The Catholic Church guides the daily lives of most Chamorros. The implications of these interactions on schooling are at times significant. For example, school absences to attend funeral masses for immediate and extended family, sleepiness during class because of attendance at nightly rosaries for the deceased, the importance of Catholic holidays, baptismals and fandangos, any of which may contribute to school absences or failure to complete homework.

When the Americans took control in Pre-War Guam (1899-1941), the U. S. military introduced the American culture and schools were established to teach basic education skills. Japan invaded Guam in December 1941 and occupied the island until July 1944. Like the Spanish, the Japanese colonial objectives were to claim control of the island and exercise political authority over the Chamorros. The Japanese imposed their language and culture, implementing an educational program using the Japanese language. As Underwood (1998a) explains, with the return of the Americans in 1944, the agenda of the U.S. military was the Americanization of the Chamorro people through compulsory education, an English-only policy in the schools and the workplace, and the emulation of American culture.

GUAM AND THE PHILIPPINES: SHARED COLONIAL HISTORY

Guam has always enjoyed a special relationship with the Philippines. Because Guam and the Philippines share a strong Spanish influence in their respective cultures, Guam has traditions similar to its Filipino neighbors. In addition to geographical proximity, Filipinos make up 27 percent of Guam's total population, the second largest ethnic group on the island following Guam's native Chamorros. Both Guam and the Philippines were subjected to a long history of Spanish rule from 1521 to 1898 and both were subjected to American colonialism. Filipino culture was significantly shaped by the values of the foreign powers which have dominated it. Nearly four centuries of colonization by the Spanish and the Americans have given Filipinos a decidedly 'Western' orientation which sets them apart from other Asian traditions (Gochenour, 1990). Catholicism is the predominate religion.

CHAMORRO CORE VALUES

The core of Guam culture, the Chamorro, is characterized by a complex social protocol centered upon respect, caring, accepting and helping one another. Inafa'maolek, or interdependence, is a central value in Chamorro culture which depends on a spirit of cooperation. Historian Lawrence Cunningham in 1992 wrote:

In a Chamorro sense, the land and its produce belong to everyone. This is the armature, or core, that everything in Chamorro culture revolves around. It is a powerful concern for mutuality rather than individualism and private property rights. The culture is visibly manifested in the kissing of the hands of elders, passing of legends, music, dance, chants, courtship rituals, handicrafts, burial rituals, preparation of herbal medicines, and requesting forgiveness from spiritual ancestors when entering a jungle (The Culture of Guam n.d. p. 1).

Underwood (1998b) writes that in order to grasp the essence of what it means to be a Chamorro, it is important to examine the nature of the ancient Chamorros and the core values by which they lived their lives. The Chamorro value system can be related to a set of core values that have their origins in pre-contact Guam (Cunningham, 1997; Underwood, 1998b). The Chamorro core values of Inafa'maolek, Family, Respect for Elders, Nature, and Mamahlo, as described by Underwood (1998b) are presented in greater detail in the following section.

Inafa'maolek

The core value in Chamorro culture is inafa'maolek (interdependence) with the extended family (inafa'maolek: making it good for each other or helping each other in an agreeable fashion). Inafa'maolek is a sense of mutuality and togetherness. The ancient Chamorros valued harmony through group consensus, rather than individual decision-making. It was not appropriate to express personal opinion directly because this would slow down the group consensus process. Interdependency is more important than personal independence. Shared work requires cooperation within the group and always accomplishes more than individual work. Chenchuli (the giving of gifts in the form of money and goods to assist the costs of a feast) is used in virtually every social activity, even to this day.

Family

The ancient Chamorros organized themselves into interdependent extended families. "The family was the most important socializing and nurturing force in an ancient Chamorro's life" (Cunningham, 1997, p.31). The family was always more important than the individual. Today, extended families continue to be an important part of life on Guam. The extended family includes father, mother and children, as well as aunties, uncles, tata-bihu (grandfather), nana-biha (grandmother), cousins, nieces, and nephews. Extended families celebrate and overcome challenges and hardships by working together for the common good.

Respect for Elders

Respect for elders and authority figures is a core cultural value. Since pre-contact days and up to the present, Chamorros equate old age with wisdom. Any elderly person, no matter who he or she happens to be, deserves respect. In addition, responsible persons always respect social position and the social situation.

Nature

Chamorros have a great respect for the forces of nature. The culture is rich with legends that emphasize respect for nature. For example, many Chamorros continue to respect ancestral spirits that are said to inhabit the jungle. Respect the spirits and their land or face the possibility of a stroke of bad luck.

Mamahlo

The attitude of deference for others can be referred to as behaving in a mamahlo manner to maintain harmony. This is the reason it is not polite to correct another person. An ancient Chamorro would never correct an older or higher status person. A sense of mamahlo continues to guide Chamorros in their daily behavior.

The Chamorros underwent many significant changes in their lifestyle during the periods of colonization. However, despite the introduction to new lifestyles, the belief system of the Chamorro people, rooted in their ancient ancestors, remains relatively intact. That the culture and language continues to this day is a testament to the resiliency and determination of the Chamorro people.

FILIPINO CORE VALUES

The core cultural values of Filipino people can be defined as follows (Asian Pacific Islander Populations n.d. p. 3).

Family

The Philippines is known to be a family centered nation. Faithfulness to the family is a tradition that is characteristic of Filipino society. The Filipinos recognize their family as an important social structure that one must take care of, especially with regard to the safety and unity of one's family.

Reciprocal Obligation (Utang Ng Loob)

Relationships are cemented by the giving and receiving of favors or services. For example, small gifts are given as a token of appreciation for someone's time. Honor requires that if a favor or service has been received, it must also be returned at some point.

Shame (Hiya)

The shame of the individual brings shame on the family. The threat of letting one's family down helps enforce societal norms. Gossip, rather than open disagreement, may be used as a means to encourage a community member to start behaving properly.

Going Along with Others (Pakikisama)

To Filipinos, it is often more important to maintain group harmony than to conclude business that leaves some people with hard feelings (Gochenour, 1990). In organizational settings, this might mean that it will take longer to complete tasks, as the primary emphasis is not on time but on reaching consensus and maintaining relationships. Maintaining smooth personal relationships governs every facet of Filipino behavior (Agbayani-Siewert, 1994, 1997).

Protection of self-esteem (amor propio). Filipinos are highly sensitive to criticism and may even feel humiliated (Lynch, quoted in Agbayani-Stewart & Revilla, 1995). Rather than raise an issue directly, Filipinos tend to use a third party to speak on their behalf (Gochenour, 1990).

The core cultural values of Chamorros and Filipinos interface in several ways. Both cultures recognize family as an important social structure which includes extended family members. Children are taught at a young age to honor parents and elders and to respect social positions, situations, and authority figures. Maintaining group harmony is also a common thread in both cultures, with interdependency more important than personal independence (see Figure 1).

Figure 1. (a) Chamorro and (b) Filipino core values

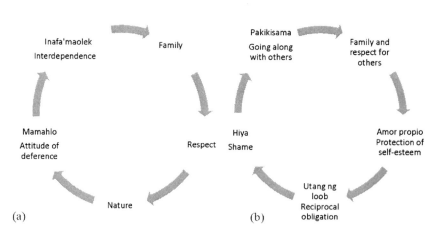

FOCUS GROUPS: CULTURAL VALUES REVEALED BY PARTICIPANTS

In Spring 2008, a cohort of Asian/Pacific Islanders consisting of Chamorro and Filipino graduate students in the University's graduate literacy program participated in focus groups to discuss their experiences in blended online courses. Focus groups have the advantage of allowing people more time to reflect and to recall experiences; also, something that one person mentions can spur memories and opinions in others (Lofland & Lofland, 1995, p. 21). The students' responses were analyzed for emerging patterns and their relationship to the core cultural values of Chamorros and Filipinos. The next section illuminates the following emergent themes: 1) respect, 2) collaboration, 3) family, and 4) oral tradition.

Respect

A key theme that emerged from the focus groups is the importance of respect for one another. One participant describes an uncomfortable experience with an online classmate who was not an Asian/Pacific Islander. "Maybe it's a cultural thing. Some of them could be pretty forward in their comments. So I'm thinking they're not Asians, not Pacific islanders, I'm sure. It makes me apprehensive to answer or give my honest opinions and comments because you can have someone who's pretty forward and he just shoots out the answer to you and writes "you're wrong." Another participant adds, "It deals a lot with your ethnic background and how you're brought up. With us, we were taught how to be courteous and how to respect others and the other person's feeling or thoughts, but this individual wasn't born and raised here. He didn't realize what he was doing was disrespectful." One participant handles similar situations by not responding to the perpetrator. She explains, "I'm the type of person that will not respond back. My parents always taught me it doesn't matter what people say, you don't respond because you are just adding fuel to fire." Another adds, "In our university, we're not overly critical. We're more considerate of the other person's feelings." Agreeing with her colleague, a participant explains. "I do get paranoid at times, because I feel that what I'm writing may be misinterpreted and I may offend the reader or readers."

A final comment from a participant sums up the feeling of the group. "Be humble," she advises. When asked how the instructor should handle incidents such as this in an online learning environment, one participant offers this suggestion, "The professor should email the disrespectful student individually so as not to embarrass the student and they won't drop out of the class. Set the tone." This participant showed concern for her classmate, despite the perceived infraction.

Collaboration

Participants consistently commented on how much they enjoy working together as a group. As one participant points out, "I enjoyed working with classmates in group activities. We had no problem with the amount of work contributed because we seem to work great as a team and if we needed help we were an e-mail or phone call away. We had excellent teamwork and cooperation." The participants felt that they were not alone in the learning process and could count on their classmates for the support needed. "Working as a group helps you understand the concepts better. The assignments that we were given in class, helping each other out, really helped me because I didn't feel like I was in this alone." Another participant adds, "When I was first told about online learning I was really confused, I was really terrified by it. But I had the support from the professor and the classmates where it was step by step. Every time I went to them and said I really don't understand they didn't look down on me."

Family

Family and social obligations that require students' attendance at school and church functions place demands on students' time. While school work is important, family and church remain top priorities. The blended courses help them to balance these obligations with the responsibilities of graduate studies. All of the participants agreed with their classmate who remarked, "The blended courses are convenient because I can now attend more of the rosaries that are usually scheduled at 6:00 pm in the church. My family is happier, too, because I can spend more time with them."Several participants have the added responsibility of caring for an elderly parent when they return from their university courses at night. The online activities allow more at-home time for taking care of elderly parents and tending to other family responsibilities.

Oral Tradition

Pacific islanders come from a traditionally oral society. Other cultures may rely more heavily on the written mode for learning, whereas oral cultures are more rooted in the oral mode of communication. For example, one participant's brother received an online degree in education from a university in the US mainland that required only written assignments. The participant describes his brother's experience below:

He was born here on island but he did his undergraduate work in the mainland. So he's used to doing an activity and then synthesizing it in a way that he can present it in a paper. That's how they did it. They presented it in a paper and the professor assessed whether they reached their objectives just purely through the paper. It's totally doable but there they are more familiar with that method... just writing a paper and turning it in. That's just the way the culture is set up. That's all they expect from the professor and that's all they get from the professor. But for us, we're more willing to share it verbally as opposed to in text.

For those participants who speak English as a second language, communicating in writing can be an arduous task. Equipped with oral native-like English speaking skills their academic writing skills may be weaker. One participant explains the difficulty she experiences when translating her first language into English. "There are some words in my language that can't be explained in the standard English written language. I find it hard to express what I am thinking because of this barrier. I enjoy the times we meet face-to-face so that I can express myself better when I talk instead of writing."

Students appreciate the face-to-face interactions afforded in a blended online learning environment. "With the blended courses, at least we know each other by face, we know each other's personality. It's more personable," says one participant. We get to talk about course content, not just write about it." Another participant explains that the face-to-face sessions allow the instructor to more fully assess a student. "Blended is good in a sense because the face-to-face classes play to my strengths. I thought that you were better able to assess my strengths as opposed to what I just was able to contribute on online.... you're not going to get a full idea about your students through just a pure online medium."

Participants also express their desire to know their instructors on a personal, face-to-face relationship, rather than only through writing. As one participant explains:

If I were to talk to you through Internet only I wouldn't know how sweet, how sensitive, how supportive you actually are. If all the interaction I had with you were online I wouldn't have been able to catch that character. The students get a strong feel for who they are going to be working with. It makes a big impact to know you deeper than just as a professor.

Another participant agrees, adding the following comments:

You would be sacrificing a bit of your own classroom experience by providing fully online courses because you do provide a very relaxed atmosphere in the face-to-face sessions where we can talk about stuff we do know and stuff we don't know. We can say, Doc, I don't understand how this works in the classroom setting. And you're more than willing to help.

DISCUSSION

The major findings of the focus groups suggest that the participants' core cultural values of respect, family, and working together in a collaborative, harmonious fashion, are also valued by the participants in their interactions with one another in blended courses. Participants believe that respect is especially important during online written communication. They were uncomfortable with classmates whom they perceived as aggressive and confrontational during online discussions. Participants attributed this type of behavior to students who are not Asian/Pacific islanders and who do not understand island culture. Pacific islanders and Filipinos stress harmony and collaboration and may not appreciate the frankness and line of questioning that other cultures find appropriate. This finding is consistent with previous studies (Joo, 1999; McLoughlin, 2000) which found that the expectation to initiate discussion, to critique the ideas of others, and to question knowledge or the instructor is inconsistent with cultural traditions that stress harmony and respect for authority. The Chamorro core culture inafa'maolek, making it good for each other or helping each other in an agreeable fashion, and the Filipino core culture of pakikisama "going along with others" was evident in the participants' emphasis on the importance of working together in a harmonious way.

Another major finding from the focus groups is that Pacific islanders continue to feel rooted in the oral tradition. Pacific islanders in Guam and other Micronesian islands are at various stages between orality and literacy. While the degree to which they are influenced by patterns of literate thought will vary (Dunn, 2001), their cultural roots remain grounded in the traditions of orally held knowledge. Supporting this notion is Sachuo's (1992) argument that, "Oral discourse constitutes the sociolinguistic frame of island societies and is always an inherent characteristic of Micronesian languages even in written form" (Sachuo, 1992, p. 406). With regard to the Filipino students who come from a written society, interestingly enough they too seem to value the oral, face-to-face tradition over a predominately written mode. That they value the oral tradition is not surprising as the Filipino participants were born and raised on Guam, or came to Guam during their early years.

CONCLUSION

Culturally sensitive or appropriate on-line instruction can be provided for Asian/Pacific Islanders if designers are aware of the socio-cultural background of their target learners and if an appropriate instructional framework is applied. It is important for educators and designers to respect the cultural values and expectations of learners. In their case study of online learning for indigenous Australian learners at the university level, McLoughlin and Oliver (2000) draw from constructivism and culturally responsive learning to advocate ten design principles for culturally inclusive instructional design. These principles can serve as design frameworks as well as indicators of success for evaluating a culturally responsive learning environment (Ngeow & Kong, 2002). The following is a summary of these principles (McLoughlin & Oliver, 2000 pp. 5-8):

1. Recognize students' capacity to construct their own knowledge, bring prior experience and culturally preferred ways of knowing to learning.
2. Design authentic learning activities that build on prior knowledge, and incorporate the skills and values of the community, its cultural traditions and its values.
3. Create flexible tasks and provide online tools for knowledge sharing to reinforce the collaborative nature of learning (i.e., bulletin boards, discussion forums) to discuss assignments, offer peer support and feedback.
4. Provide multiple forms of support for online learners including mentors and frequently asked questions through Web based tools.
5. Provide clear communication of learning outcomes and navigation tools to scaffold novices until they develop the skills and competence for online learning.
6. Ensure access to multiple channels of communication and social interaction through chat rooms, discussion forums or other virtual meeting places.
7. Create tasks for self-direction, ownership and collaboration through online journals, shared workspaces, and the exploration of the Web to augment resources provided.
8. Ensure that instructors and mentors have an online presence that is visible, with help features and discussion forums providing learners with rapid feedback and scaffolding.
9. Create access to varied resources to ensure multiple perspectives.
10. Allow students to select topics for research, and the pace and sequencing in which they access the resources. Provide flexibility in assessment to address the needs of mature age learners with diverse life experiences and close community ties that need to be maintained while studying at the university level.

Drawing from Chamorro and Filipino core cultural values and McLoughlin and Oliver's guidelines, the following recommendations are provided to support Asian/Pacific islanders' learning in blended online courses.

1. The following guidelines should help maintain harmony in online environments with culturally diverse students. To promote respect and professionalism for one another during online forums and chat rooms, instructors should set the

tone by establishing guidelines for communication etiquette. Post guidelines on the discussion forums reminding students that typical communication etiquette also applies online. For example, advise students to respond to each other's comments in a timely and considerate way and to avoid dominating the conversation.

2. To foster collaboration and support during online activities, maximize the use of online tools found in most course management systems. Utilize discussion forums, chat rooms, and bulletin boards. Group learning activities can easily be incorporated into the online activities through the grouping feature. Assign online buddies for those who need additional support with technology skills. Instructors should make themselves available to students via email, discussion forums, phone calls (i.e., Skype). The synchronous chat feature found on course management systems allows for students and instructor to meet online at the same time to ask questions about course content and to seek advisement. Online office hours should be posted on the online course room.

3. As a culturally responsive alternative to face-to-face sessions, consider incorporating the use of a Web-based conferencing system such as Eluminate Live! Rao (2007) found that Pacific Islanders enjoy this synchronous Web-based system that allows instructor and participants to interact via audio, text, and whiteboard.

4. Recognize that family and community obligations in Asian/Pacific islander cultures may require some flexibility in establishing deadlines for submission of assignments.

5. To scaffold academic writing skills the instructor should provide clear and explicit feedback on students' writing, how to make use of feedback, and how to revise and edit their work. A writing software can be incorporated into the online program.

REFERENCES

Agbayani-Siewert, & Revilla, L. (1995). Filipino Americans. In *Asian Americans: Contemporary Trends and Issues*. Thousand Oaks, CA: Sage Publications.

Agbayani-Siewert, P. (1994). Filipino American culture and family: Guidelines for practitioners: Families in society. *Families in Society*.

Agbayani-Siewert, P. (1997). The dual world of Filipino Americans. *Journal of Multicultural Social Work*, 6(1/2), 59–76. doi:10.1300/J285v06n01_05.

Au, K. H. (1980). Participation structures in a reading lesson with Hawaiian children: Analysis of a culturally appropriate instructional event. *Anthropology & Education Quarterly, 11*(2), 91–115. doi:10.1525/aeq.1980.11.2.05x1874b.

Au, K. H. (1993). *Literacy instruction in multicultural settings.* Orlando, FL: Harcourt Brace College Publishers.

Au, K. H. (2001, July/August). Culturally responsive instruction as a dimension of new literacies. *Reading Online, 5*(1). Retrieved January 12, 2009, from http://www.readingonline.org/newliteracies/lit_index.asp?HREF=/newliteracies/au/index.html

Au, K. H., & Jordan, C. (1981). Teaching reading to Hawaiian children: Finding a culturally appropriate solution. In Trueba, H., Guthrie, G., & Au, K. (Eds.), *Culture and the bilingual classroom: Studies in classroom ethnography* (pp. 69–86). Rowley, MA: Newbury House.

Au, K. H., & Kawakami, A. J. (1985). Research currents: Talk story and learning to read. *Language Arts, 62*(4), 406–411.

Au, K. H., & Mason, J. (1983). Cultural congruence in classroom participation structures: Achieving a balance of rights. *Discourse Processes, 6*(2), 145–167. doi:10.1080/01638538309544560.

Banks, J. A. (1999). *An introduction to multicultural education.* Boston: Allyn & Bacon.

Beardlsey, C. (1964). *Guam past and present.* Tokyo: Charles E. Tuttle Company, Inc..

Bowers, C. (1988). *The cultural dimension of educational computing.* New York: Teachers College Press.

Branch, R. M. (1997). Educational technology frameworks that facilitate culturally pluralistic instruction. *Educational Technology, 37*(2), 38–41.

Cazden, C., & Leggett, E. (1981). Culturally responsive education: Recommendations for achieving Lau remedies II. In Trueba, H., Guthrie, G., & Au, K. (Eds.), *Culture and the bilingual classroom: Studies in classroom ethnography* (pp. 69–86). Rowley, MA: Newbury House.

Chase, M., Macfadyen, L., Reeder, K., & Roche, J. (2002). Intercultural challenges in networked learning: Hard technologies meet soft skills. *First Monday, 7*(8-5). Retrieved April 10, 2009, from http://firstmonday.org/htbin/cgiwrap/bin/ojs/index.php/fm/article/view/975/896

Collis, C. (1999). Designing for differences: Cultural issues in the design of WWW-based course support sites. *British Journal of Educational Technology*, *30*(3), 201–217. doi:10.1111/1467-8535.00110.

Cunningham, L. (1992). *Ancient chamorro society*. Honolulu, HI: The Bess Press, Inc..

Cunningham, L. (1997). The ancient Chamorros of Guam. In Carter, L., Wuerch, W., & Carter, R. (Eds.), *Guam history: Perspectives volume one* (pp. 11–36). Mangilao, Guam: Richard Flores Taitano Micronesia Area Research Center.

Curtis, D. D., & Lawson, M. J. (2001). Exploring collaborative online learning. *Journal of Asynchronous Learning Networks*, *5*(1), 21–34.

Dunn, M. (2001). Aboriginal literacy: Reading the tracks. *The Reading Teacher*, *54*(7), 678–686.

Dziuban, C. D., Hartman, J. L., & Moskal, P. D. (2004). Blended learning. *Educause Center for Applied Research, Research Bulletin, 7,* 1-12. Retrieved December 10, 2008, from http://www.educause.edu/ir/library/pdf/ERB0407.pdf

Erickson, F., & Mohatt, G. (1981). Cultural differences in teaching styles in an Odawa school: A sociolinguistic approach. In Trueba, H., Guthrie, G., & Au, K. (Eds.), *Culture and the bilingual classroom: Studies in classroom ethnography* (pp. 105–119). Rowley, MA: Newbury House.

Gay, G. (1988). Designing relevant curricula for diverse learners. *Education and Urban Society*, *2*(4), 327–340. doi:10.1177/0013124588020004003.

Gilbert, S., & Gay, G. (1985). Improving the success in school of poor black children. *Phi Delta Kappan*, *67*(2), 133–137.

Gochenour, T. (1990). *Considering Filipinos*. Yarmoth, ME: Intercultural Press, Inc..

Henderson, L. (1996). Instructional design of interactive multimedia. *Educational Technology Research and Development*, *44*(4), 85–104. doi:10.1007/BF02299823.

Joo, J. (1999). Cultural issues of the internet in classrooms. *British Journal of Educational Technology*, *30*(3), 245–250. doi:10.1111/1467-8535.00113.

Jordan, C. (1985). Translating culture: From ethnographic information to educational program. *Anthropology & Education Quarterly*, *16*(2), 105–123. doi:10.1525/aeq.1985.16.2.04x0631g.

Koloto, A., Katoanga, A., & Tatila, L. (2006). *Critical success factors for effective use of e-learning by Pacific learners*. Retrieved December 15, 2008, from elearning. itpnz.ac.nz/files/Koloto_Critical_Success_Factors.pdf

Ladson-Billings, G. (1992). Reading between the lines and beyond the pages: A culturally relevant approach to literacy teaching. *Theory into Practice, 31*(4), 312–320. doi:10.1080/00405849209543558.

Ladson-Billings, G. (1995). But that's just good teaching! The case for culturally relevant pedagogy. *Theory into Practice, 31*(3), 159–165. doi:10.1080/00405849509543675.

Lofland, J., & Lofland, H. (1995). *Analyzing social settings.* Belmont, CA: Wadsworth Publishing Company.

Marcus, A., & Gould, E. (2000). Crosscurrents: Cultural dimensions and global web user interface design. *Interaction, 7*(4), 32–46. doi:10.1145/345190.345238.

Mathur, R., & Oliver, L. (2007). Developing an international distance education program: A blended learning approach. *Online Journal of Distance Learning Administration, 10*(4), 1-10. Retrieved August 10, 2008, from http://www.westga.edu/~distance/ojdla/winter104/mathur104.html

McCarthy, T. L., Lynch, R. H., Wallace, S., & Benalla, A. (1991). Classroom inquiry and Navajo learning styles: A call for reassessment. *Anthropology & Education Quarterly, 22*(1), 42–59. doi:10.1525/aeq.1991.22.1.05x1172b.

McDonald, H. (1993). Aboriginal and Torres Strait islander creativity and the affirmation of identity: Educational potentials. In Loos & Osanai (Eds.), Indigenous Minorities and Education. Tokyo: Sanusha Publishing Co Ltd.

McLoughlin, C. (1999). Culturally responsive technology use: Developing an online community of learners. *British Journal of Educational Technology, 30*(3), 231–245. doi:10.1111/1467-8535.00112.

McLoughlin, C. (2000). Cultural maintenance, ownership, and multiple perspectives: Features of web-based delivery to promote equity. *Journal of Educational Media, 25*(3), 229–241.

McLoughlin, C. (2001). Inclusivity and alignment: Principles of pedagogy, task and assessment design for effective cross-cultural online learning. *Distance Education, 22*(1), 7–29. doi:10.1080/0158791010220102.

McLoughlin, C., & Oliver, R. (2000). Designing learning environments for cultural inclusivity: A case study of indigenous online learning at a tertiary level. *Australian Journal of Educational Technology, 16*(1), 58–72. Retrieved August 22, 2008, from http://www.ascilite.org.au/ajet/ajet16/mcloughlin.html

Menchaca, M., & Hoffman, E. (2008). *Qualitative analysis of student experiences with distance education in the Pacific Rim.* Paper presented at University of Hawaii Manoa Campus. Honolulu: HI.

Menchaca, M., Yong, L., & Hoffman, E. (2008). Understanding barriers to native Hawaiian participation in distance education. In *Proceedings from Distance Learning and the Internet Conference.* Retrieved May 15, 2009, from http://www.waseda.jp/DLI2008/program/proceedings/session7-9.html

Ngeow, K., & Kong, K. Y. S. (2002). *Designing culturally sensitive learning environments.* Retrieved April 20, 2009, from https://secure.ascilite.org.au/conferences/auckland02/proceedings/papers/055.pdf

Powell, G. C. (1997). On being a culturally sensitive instructional designer and educator. *Educational Technology, 37*(2), 6–14.

Rao, K. (2007). Distance learning in Micronesia: Participants' experiences in a virtual classroom using synchronous technologies. *Innovate Journal of Online Education, 4*(1), 1-10. Retrieved January 20, 2009, from http://www.innovateonline.info/index.php?view=article&id=437

Rao, K., & Giuli, C. (2008). *What works in distance learning: Early indicators from an evaluation of REMOTE, an online master's degree program for Micronesia and American Samoa.* Paper presented at the 13th ANNUAL TCC Worldwide Online Conference. New York, NY.

Reeves, T. C., & Reeves, P. M. (1997). Effective dimensions of interactive learning on the world wide Web. In Kahn, B. (Ed.), *Web Based Instruction* (pp. 5–18). Englewood Cliffs, NJ: Educational Technology Publications.

Ryan, J. (1992). Aboriginal learning styles: A critical review. *Language, Culture and Curriculum, 5*(3), 161–183. doi:10.1080/07908319209525124.

Sachuo, S. (1992). Impact of communication technology on traditional discourse in the culture of Micronesia. In D.H. Rubinstein (Ed.), *Pacific History: Papers from the 8ᵗʰ Pacific History Association Conference* (pp. 405-418). Pacific History.

Smith, D., & Ayers, D. (2006). Culturally responsive pedagogy and online learning: Implications for the globalized community college. *Community College Journal of Research and Practice, 30*, 401–415. doi:10.1080/10668920500442125.

Smith, G. P. (1991). *Toward defining a culturally responsible pedagogy for teacher education: The knowledge base for educating the teachers of minority and culturally diverse students.* Paper presented at the Annual Meeting of the American Association of Colleges for Teacher Education. Atlanta, GA.

Stanton, C. (2006). Diversity challenges in online learning. In Rahman, H. (Ed.), *Empowering marginal communities with information networking* (pp. 1–15). Hershey, PA: Idea Group Publishing. doi:10.4018/978-1-59140-699-0.ch001.

Tharp, R., & Gallimore, R. (1988). *Rousing minds to life: Teaching, learning and schooling in social context*. New York: Cambridge University Press.

The Culture of Guam. (n.d.). Retrieved March 15, 2009, from http://ns.gov.gu/culture.html

Thompson, L. (1969). *Guam and its people*. Westport, CT: Greenwood Press.

Topping, D. (1992). Literacy and cultural erosion in the Pacific islands. In Dubin, F., & Kuhlman, N. (Eds.), *Cross-cultural literacy: Global perspectives on reading and writing* (pp. 19–31). Englewood Cliffs, NJ: Prentice Hall.

Truluck, J. (2007). Establishing a mentoring plan for improving retention in online graduate degree programs. *Online Journal of Distance Learning Administration, 10*(1), 1-7. Retrieved November 20, 2008, from http://www.westga.edu/~distance/ojdla/spring101/truluck101.htm

Underwood, R. (1998a). *English and Chamorro on Guam*. Mangilao, Guam: University of Guam, College of Education Book of Readings.

Underwood, R. (1998b). *Hispanicization as a socio-historical process on Guam*. Mangilao, Guam: University of Guam, College of Education Book of Readings.

Vogt, L., Jordan, C., & Tharp, R. (1987). Explaining school failure, producing school success: Two cases. *Anthropology & Education Quarterly, 18*(4), 276–286. doi:10.1525/aeq.1987.18.4.04x0019s.

Zepke, N., & Leach, L. (2002). Appropriate pedagogy and technology in a cross-cultural distance education context. *Teaching in Higher Education, 7*(3), 309–321. doi:10.1080/13562510220144806.

Chapter 8

A Case Study of Online MBA Courses:
Online Facilitation, Case–Based Learning, and Virtual Team

Rich Magjuka
Indiana University, USA

Xiaojing Liu
Indiana University, USA

EXECUTIVE SUMMARY

This chapter presents a case study that examines the perceptions of online students and instructors regarding their their experiences in a reputable online MBA program. The findings indicate that both the instructors and students exhibited a high level of satisfaction with their online experiences in the program and positive attitude toward online learning in general. This study also explores the in-depth views of the online participants on several key components of online business education, including online learning facilitation and interaction, virtual teamwork, and Case-Based Learning (CBL). The issues and challenges identified in the study indicate a need for the instructors and students to receive more guidance and support, technologically and pedagogically, in order to create a more engaging and fruitful online learning environment.

DOI: 10.4018/978-1-4666-4486-1.ch008

BACKGROUND

In this article, online education (or online learning) is broadly defined as the type of education that primarily uses the Web and online communication technologies in order to enhance the delivery of courses, improve learners' access to learning opportunities and success (Australian Flexible Learning Framework, 2004).

Along with prominence on online education, online learning offerings have increased since the turn of the century. According to the most recent Sloan Consortium report (Allen & Seaman, 2008), more than 60% of schools that provide face-to-face courses have offered graduate courses online. Almost 3.9 million students took at least one online course during the fall 2007 term, a nearly 12% increase over the number reported in the previous year.

Business schools have been aggressively following this online learning trend as education via online technology is considered to be one of the key delivery modes for MBA programs (Phillips, 1998). With the increasing acceptance of online graduate degrees in the workplace, students with full-time jobs have become the fastest growing market segment in Internet-based management training (Smith, 2001). It is estimated that $40 billion is spent annually by corporations and governments on training, and a growing portion of this training is accomplished through online technology (Magjuka, Min, & Bonk, 2005).

The field of business requires diversified practices for real-world problems as much as or more than any other field. Questions and concerns remain regarding whether online learning can fulfill the promise of providing prospective MBA students with application skills and knowledge similar to the knowledge gained by traditional business professionals (Lee, Lee, Liu, Bonk, & Magjuka, 2009). The tremendous growth of online MBA programs has not been accompanied by adequate research with which to address the quality of online business education relative to classroom-based courses. The available research on the effectiveness of online management education is not only limited, but is also inconclusive. Some of the evidence suggests comparable or superior performance and a higher level of satisfaction of online MBA students compared to traditional MBA students (Hay, Peltier, & Drago, 2004; Kretovics & McCambridge, 2002). Other studies have documented that such programs create feelings of isolation and a lack of interaction in online MBA courses (Arbaugh, 2002; Hay et al., 2004).

Giving the inconsistent findings in regard to the effectiveness of online management education, there is a pressing need to examine the critical factors influencing the successful delivery of online management education. The purpose of this article is to report on a case study, the goal of which was to identify success factors and barriers in regard to online business education from the perspectives of online instructors and students.

Interaction and Facilitation

Previous research has suggested that learning is a social process in which communication and interaction between the participants are vital to the learning process (Caine & Caine, 1997). Weston and Cranton (1986) suggested that interactive learning strategies promote higher-order learning, including analysis, synthesis and problem solving. Fulford and Zhang (1993) found that student perception of the level of interaction was a critical predictor of learner satisfaction. Swan (2001) found a significant correlation between the students' reported levels of activity in the course and the reported satisfaction and learning. The more interaction that the students believed they had with the instructors and other students, the more they were satisfied with their courses, and the more that they thought they had learned (Swan, 2001).

The close relationship between interaction and learning effectiveness is also demonstrated in business literature. A study which compared the interactions in both online and traditional learning communities in an online MBA program suggested that interaction is an important predictor in regard to the effectiveness of an MBA course regardless of the mode of delivery (Ponzurick, France, & Logar, 2000). Some researchers have suggested that online learning may stimulate higher levels of interaction than the large lecture classes typical of business schools (Hay, Hodgkinson, Peltier, & Drago, 2004). However, studies have also reported that many instructors and students still express concerns about the lack of networking and interaction in online MBA classes due to inadequate course design (McGorry, 2002).

Smith and Dillon (1999) noted the importance of having a teacher for a course who would "guide the learner through the learning quest, keeping learners on track, fostering meaning-making and providing support and motivation" (p.18). High quality online instruction requires that instructors have effective online moderation skills. A study comparing the perceptions of MBA students regarding the role of online instructors in reflective learning in traditional and online courses found that the instructor plays a more important role in developing critical thinking in online courses than in traditional classroom courses (DeLacey & Leonard, 2002).

Often, a variety of pedagogical, technical and social roles have to be performed by an instructor in order to facilitate higher order thinking skills (Berge, 1995). Berge (1995) summarized the four roles that online instructors may play in online learning: (1) pedagogical roles in which they encourage students to share and build knowledge through interactive discussions, design a variety of educational experiences, provide feedback and refer to external resources or experts in the field; (2) social roles in which they take measures to develop harmony and group cohesiveness; (3) managerial roles, such as coordinating assignments, managing online discussion forums and handling overall course structure; and (4) technical roles, such as addressing technical concerns and allowing students sufficient time to learn new programs.

Case-Based Learning

Similar to several other areas of professional education, including law and medicine, Case-Based Learning (CBL) has been extensively used in business education as a substitute for the traditional lecture as an instructional method (Marcus, Taylor, & Ellis, 2004; William, 2004). In CBL, students study actual or hypothetical business situations typically written as an in-depth situation of a company, its market, and its strategic decisions – in order to improve a student's problem-solving ability. Typically multiple issues are considered and many viable alternatives to solve the case issues are presented (Helms, 2006).

CBL is regarded as suitable for traditional classrooms because it allows learning to take place through discussions and experiential learning arising from an exchange of ideas (Christudason, 2003). Implementing CBL in an asynchronous online learning environment presents both advantages and challenges to online business education. Research has indicated that solving cases in asynchronous online courses increases group process gains, promotes in-depth reflection on topics, integrates external expertise, and increases decision quality. Procrastination and anxiety caused by delays or different participation rates and feelings of impersonal mediums are among the major issues surrounding CBL in online business education (Nunamaker, Dennis, Valacich, Vogel, & George, 1991; Benbunan-Fich & Hiltz, 1999). For example, Benbunan-Fich and Hiltz (1999) observed that groups of MBA students working in an asynchronous networked environment produced better and longer solutions to the case study, but were less satisfied with the interaction process due to the nature of asynchronous interactions, characterized by delayed feedback and "login-lags."

Instructors can play a critical role in motivating students' participation in CBL. Williams (2004) posits that successful CBL requires instructors to skillfully use questioning techniques and moderate the online discussions through feedback and scaffolding. Without the appropriate design and facilitation, some students may reach only a superficial level of knowledge, even in a contextually-rich learning environment (Marcus, Taylor, & Ellis, 2004).

Advances in computer-mediated communication technology have allowed online instructors to integrate a variety of technological tools (e.g., email, discussions and video conferences) into their online CBL. A study conducted at Harvard Business School indicated that students are enthusiastic about using video during cases studies in online courses. CBL Video is cited as having multiple advantages, such as commanding more interest than text, conveying subtleties about personalities and allowing for the visualization of places and activities. In short, video is closer to the real experience than written text and, therefore, makes learning more accessible (DeLacey & Leonard, 2002).

However, the use of technology itself does not generate an effective learning experience. Instead, the way in which the technology is used in order to scaffold the process of learning creates the effective learning experience. Experts advocate that the design of tools should allow students to generate and display conceptual links and debate key points, as well as allow for counter-cases, expert commentary, role-playing and the display of chains of reasoning (Bonk, Hara, Dennen, Malikowski, & Supplee, 2000).

Virtual Teams

Teamwork has been widely utilized as an effective instructional method in residential higher education environments. During the past several years, numerous studies have indicated the value of teamwork in online learning, including assisting in student knowledge generation, helping students to prepare for the real world, triggering deeper processing of content and promoting transformative learning by developing critical thinking skills (Duart & Snyder, 1999; Palloff & Pratt, 2005).

Although extensive research has investigated a variety of factors that affect the success of virtual teams in organizations (Maznevski, & Chudoba, 2001; Martins, Gilson, & Maynard, 2004), limited research is available with respect to the importance and effectiveness of virtual team learning in online business education. Only a few studies found in business literature provide useful insights into the uses of virtual teams in online MBA programs. In a study that explored learning in an online MBA program and the structures necessary to support and enhance that learning from the perspective of the learners, the results indicated that the collaborative nature of the teamwork required in this online MBA program provided major benefits to the learners, which included decreased feelings of isolation, the development of support systems, authentic "real world" learning and an improved ability to communicate clearly online. However, virtual teamwork also challenged the learners to learn how to deal with different learning styles, academic goals and varying time commitments to the program by the various team members (Gabriel & MacDonald, 2002).

A few studies consistently found a close relationship between virtual teamwork and the learning outcomes of MBA students. Huang, Luce and Lu's (2005) study found that virtual team learning was significantly correlated with the learning outcome. Alavi (1994) conducted an experiment in order to compare the learning processes and outcomes of an MBA information science course that utilized both a traditional classroom setting and a groupware-supported synchronous setting. She reported that the groupware-supported synchronous virtual teams achieved a higher level of perceived learning, learning skill development and learning interest than the student teams who did not utilize the groupware software. Williams, Duray and Reddy's (2009) study indicates that both teamwork orientation and group cohesiveness predict student learning, with group cohesiveness mediating the relationship between teamwork orientation and student learning.

Case Study of Online MBA Programs

The College of Business at San Diego State University embarked on a pilot program to introduce an online version of its MBA program in the spring of 2000. Student response to the online courses was positive. A majority of the students responded that convenience was the greatest benefit of the online format. The students felt a high level of discussion occurred both in class and through email because the instructors asked more probing and in-depth questions. The sense of community was evident through the student's use of jargon and sidebar conversations. Nearly all of the faculty members reported that they felt that the online delivery of the course material was as effective as the traditional approach. However, many of the faculty members voiced concerns about the challenges for online teaching such as workload issues, compensation, technical training, administrative support, applicability toward tenure and promotion and lack of release time for course development (Hergert, 2003).

Another study presented the results of research on the first year of an innovative program to create a hybrid online MBA program for busy executives from one organization. Although faculty were initially unsure about the best way to approach online teaching and the methods that they chose to use did not always turn out to be successful, their overall reaction to teaching online courses has been extremely positive. The faculty cited program support, initial technical and pedagogical training as well as ongoing support as major factors in their success as program instructors. Students cited the responsiveness of the faculty, the ability to manage the workload, an effective use of teamwork and attention to student concerns as the key factors in their success. The ability of the students to react honestly to their experiences and the willingness of the faculty to respond and adapt has been one of the most important aspects of the program (Schrum & Benson, 2000).

SETTING THE STAGE

E-learning Direct Programs (ED) is an online MBA program in business school at a large Mid-western University, which is responsible for the design, development and delivery of online business education. During the 2007-2008 academic year, ED offered MBA and MS degree programs, as well as Certificate programs. The program was founded in 1999 with only 14 students, and has grown to include approximately 1,500 students. ED attracts a diverse group of students from around the world, including India (0.8%), China (2.5%), Europe (1.3%), the Middle East (0.7%), South America (0.36%), Canada(0.87%), Mexico (0.65%), and all regions of the United States (90.3%).

Presently, ED offers 48-credit online MBA programs [1] and 30-credit MS programs. Students come on-campus for a one-week in-residence course each year. The online courses are delivered in an asynchronous mode via Internet technologies in order to offer greater flexibility to the professionals who want to learn while remaining employed full-time. The program operates on a quarterly system of 12 weeks each quarter. Students are typically able to complete an MBA program in two years and an MS program in just over one year.

The instructor pool is drawn from the business school and contains full-time, tenured professor as well as clinical professors. ED policy limits enrollment to 40 students per teaching section. Many courses offered during the year attract an enrollment greater than 40 students. In these instances, multiple sections are offered for the same course and the same instructor will teach multiple sections of a course.

ED's philosophy toward instruction is straightforward. The instructional goal of the instructors when teaching an ED course is to provide an educational experience comparable to what is learned by students enrolled in the residential MBA degree programs in the business school. This philosophy has exerted a profound influence on the pace and direction of ED's instructional efforts. From the inception of the program, policy has been to directly support the instructional efforts of faculty and assist them in creating diverse personal strategies with which to teach their courses online. There are few guidelines or regulations in place to restrict professors in their efforts to build an online course. The Faculty Committee has declined to endorse any effort to develop a teaching template or standard for the online instruction. The underlying goal for the instruction is to facilitate the instructors in their attempt to transfer their knowledge of how to effectively teach in a face-to-face environment in to the online environment

THE CASE STUDY

Although this online MBA program has maintained a very high growth rate in regard to the enrollment and student retention rates since its inception, the need for a systematic approach to evaluate the program for quality assurance in regard to learning was raised due to an increasingly competitive e-learning market for online MBA programs. Therefore, a case study was designed in order to explore the perceptions of the online students and instructors on their experiences in the ED online MBA program so as to identify critical success factors and issues affecting the delivery of the program.

Research Questions

In addition to examining the overall satisfaction of the students and instructors, the study explored the in-depth views of the online participants on several key components of online business education, including online learning facilitation and interaction, virtual teamwork and CBL. Therefore, this study focused on the following research questions:

- How were the participants satisfied with their overall teaching or learning experience in the ED online MBA program?
- What were the key strategies used by the online instructors in facilitating the online learning of the MBA students in the ED program (in regard to the three aspects)?
- How did the students perceive the effectiveness of their learning experiences in regard to the three aspects?
- What challenges and issues did the students and instructors perceive in regard to the three aspects in the ED online courses?

Data Collection and Analysis

Interview

This study conducted semi-structured one-on-one and focus group interviews with selected instructors and students in order to discuss their perceptions of their teaching or learning experiences. Twenty-six online course instructors, with between one and four years of online teaching experience, were interviewed face-to-face. Each interview took approximately 45 to 75 minutes. Twenty-seven semi-structured questions were asked during the instructor interview. The interview questions focused on the participants' background information as well as their perceptions of the issues and challenges facing online facilitation, delivering case based learning online, interactions in online settings and facilitating virtual teams.

Ten second-year online MBA students participated in one-on-one interviews with each interview lasting 30 to 45 minutes. In addition to the one-to-one interviews, 10 second-year online MBA students participated in two focus group interview sessions (i.e., five students per session). The focus sessions each lasted about 60 minutes and were facilitated by one external specialist in online learning and two to three doctoral students. The investigators used an interview protocol, which included information associated with the purpose of the interview, and confidentiality of their responses as well as 15 leading interview questions. Every interview was recorded and later transcribed for analysis.

For the qualitative data analysis, the constant comparative method (Merriam, 1998) was used in order to triangulate the data from the different data sources and summarize the emerging themes. According to Patton (1990), Strauss and Corbin's (1990) constant comparison method was appropriate when analyzing the responses because we cross-case grouped the answers. We followed the steps below when analyzing the interview data.

- Three interview transcripts were selected for initial coding by two independent researchers.
- Each researcher reviewed each transcript carefully and made notes of the important patterns, themes and categories that emerged from the data.
- The transcripts reviewed later by the researcher were compared with his previous summaries of key categories and themes. Similar themes or categories were grouped together. The frequencies of each theme or category were marked.
- After each researcher completed his independent analysis, two additional researchers validated and discussed their coding decisions until a common set of codes based on all of the transcripts was determined.
- Two researchers used the established set of codes to finish coding the rest of the transcripts. New codes were added if the themes could not be categorized under the existing codes.

Survey

A survey was administrated to second year MBA students about their perceptions of online learning experiences. The survey consisted of 67 closed items under 8 categories including pedagogical and instructional presence, pedagogy and learning tools, online facilitation, CBL, use of resources, virtual teaming, and sense of community, assessment and satisfaction, and four open questions. 102 valid responses were collected from the students during their in-residence week. The return rate was 100%. The students came from a variety of backgrounds and varied in their ages, genders, locations, professional experiences and online learning experiences.

For the quantitative data analysis, the survey data was entered into SPSS. Various statistical analyses, including descriptive statistics and correlation analyses, were employed.

Content Analysis

A content analysis was also conducted on 27 courses in order to assess the status of the uses of instructional activities. The content coding scheme included a list of activities used for facilitating online interaction and collaboration.

For the content analysis of the 27 courses, the archived transcripts of the asynchronous discussions, synchronous chats, course announcements and other course materials posted in the course management system were collected and analyzed in order to determine how the courses were designed and the learning activities used. Descriptive data were obtained by counting the frequencies of the occurrences of the activities based on the coding scheme. Two investigators analyzed the data independently and compared their results in order to check for inter-reliability of the data analysis.

THE FINDINGS

Overall Satisfaction

In general, the students exhibited positive attitudes toward online learning. In response to a survey question about the general satisfactions with the ED online courses, approximately 93% of the respondents agreed that they were satisfied with the quality of the online courses. In addition, the majority of the students felt that they had learned a lot from the courses (M=4.33, SD=.72, where 1 = "strongly disagree" and 5 = "strongly agree"), had improved skills at work (M=4.22, SD=0.73) and would recommend the program to others (M=4.54, SD=0.61).

The students also exhibited positive attitudes toward online learning general. In the survey, 90.2% of the students agreed that taking online courses had more advantages than the residential course equivalents. 84% of the students agreed that online learning fits into their learning styles.

All of the instructor participants expressed a high level of satisfaction with the online teaching experience. In addition to receiving an appreciable amount of compensation for teaching online courses in the program, the instructors were intrinsically motivated due to the convenience and flexibility of online teaching and, more importantly, the satisfaction of interacting with highly self-motivated and engaged online students. For instance, one instructor commented that "I think there is a sense of satisfaction that my online students learn more knowledge from the textbook than maybe the average live student."

Interaction and Facilitation

Strategies to Promote Interaction

The online instructors consistently agreed that student-instructor and student-student interaction were vital to a successful online learning experience. For example, two instructors noted that:

The emphases on two-way communications I think are the most important things.

If it's truly an experience that I want them to learn together then it may be more of an opened answer than a specific answer to promote more discussion among the students.

Table 1 summarizes the major instructional activities were used by the instructors to facilitate online interactions. It suggests that answering email, making announcements and providing feedback were the routine strategies used to foster teacher-

Table 1. Summary of the use of instructional activities for online interactions (N=27)

Type of Interaction	Instructional Activities	Courses used	Percentage of Usage
		(count)	(%)
Teacher-Student	Answering inquiries through email	27	100%
	Announcements	27	100%
	Feedback on assignments	27	100%
	Summary of class key points/concepts	26	96%
	Instructor participation in asynchronous class discussions	12	44%
	Instructor participation in synchronous class discussion	3	11%
	Virtual office hours	3	11%
Student-Student	Virtual teamwork	22	78%
	Online asynchronous class discussions	18	85%
	Small team discussions	11	41%
	Peer evaluation	5	19%
	Team-team interaction	9	33%
	Student online café	2	7%
	Bulletin board used to express student expectations	4	15%

student interactions. According to the instructor interviews, the instructors highly preferred to use email for daily communications and to answer student inquiries because of its immediacy in reaching the students and convenience in providing personalized instructional support when requested by the students. Announcements were frequently used to broadcast important notices, lecture notes, directions on assignment, clarifications on issues and course schedule related information such as reminders of due dates.

The instructors unanimously agreed on the importance of giving timely and quality feedback to the online learners. In addition to carefully selecting and designing the course content, giving feedback was the next important step in assuring the quality of learning. The instructors used a variety of strategies to enforce resourceful and effective feedback in facilitating learning. For example, one instructor mentioned that giving detailed feedback on the submitted assignments was "where some of the learning comes in." Another instructor mentioned that she gave the feedback in a way that forced the students to use the feedback given by her rather than only "spending five minutes reading over it and then forgetting it". Some of the instructors also redesigned assignments to be smaller and more frequent so that more feedback could be given so that more attention could be focused on the process of learning and engagement.

Asynchronous discussion was used in 85% of the courses. In 44% of the courses the instructors actively facilitated online discussions. The instructors agreed that online discussion was key to fostering student-student interaction. The instructors also noted that an online discussion provided a common framework for the online students to share their professional growth and collaboratively construct knowledge, whereas the instructors needed to take an "interaction facilitator" or "consultant" role in order to scaffold the discussion. For example, one instructor commented that he felt comfortable putting himself in a similar discussant role to that utilized by the students, but was able to provide more insight as to company relationships than the students were able.

The instructors emphasized the importance of providing clear instructions and course structures in order to improve the efficiency of online interactions. For example, one instructor described his observations in regard to providing instruction guidelines in his courses:

My other observation is that the level of precision that you need in the on-line world is probably five or six times the level of precision that you need in the classroom, because, again, you have visual cues to tell you yes or no people [in traditional classrooms], they either understand or don't understand; whereas [in online courses] you have to be going through much more specific detail, not even sure that they're understanding, but at least you've made the attempt to reduce any ambiguity.

Challenges in Facilitating Interactions

Promoting Effective Online Discussion

One of the key issues associated with online facilitation is promoting deep levels of cognitive discourse in the online discussions. The students noted that a variety of facilitating skills levels existed among the online instructors and that the instructors who exhibited effective facilitation skills in the online discussions significantly enhanced the students' learning experiences. For example, two students noted:

Some of them lead very insightful discussions and some don't lead any discussions. You're just expected to read the case, come to the solution and write a paper on what your solution is. In other courses, the cases are discussed exhaustively until there is nothing left to discuss. I feel that is a very rich experience ... It really depends on the course and the instructor.

I was interested to see how involved [instructor name] was, he's very involved in the class because you would post and, a matter of hours later, he would counter with something else, with new ideas or new questions for you to answer.

A number of the student interviewees indicated that they felt pressured to contribute fresh ideas in a constantly expanding discussion forum. The students attributed this dilemma to the lack of skills of some of the instructors in renewing discussions so that conversations progressed in such a way as to widen a topic in order to allow new ideas and thoughts to enter the discussion. For example, one student stated:

The one problem I had with that class specifically was the weight was so heavy on posting things, so everybody was scrambling to get in there and, like we say, part of the reason we're in this program is we're traveling. You know, we might not be able to get there Monday and then you get in there and you read what you have already prepared and you feel very usurped by that.

Making sure that all students had equal opportunities to participate in online learning activities in their courses was a key concern for online instructors. In the present study, the instructors noted that the time lag in asynchronous communication or differing levels of backgrounds and experiences could cause the dominance of some students in online discussions. A few the instructors addressed the importance of providing guidelines in order to ensure that each of the students had an equal opportunity to contribute to the discussions. For example, some of the instructors limited the length of each student's posting messages. Although the students may become more "disciplined" by conforming to the rules of the online participation, the instructors were uncertain whether such participation limits discourage students' learning motivations.

The extensive time commitment to facilitating online discussions was another significant challenge the online instructors had to deal with. They stated that answering daily emails and regularly moderating the online participation required significant time investments. For example, one instructor commented that facilitating online discussions was very labor intensive and, when he went abroad, he had to find an Internet café and use a dial-up connection which cost him even more time.

The Development of Social Presence in Online Environments

For many instructors, developing a social rapport with online students remained one of the greatest challenges for the instructors. A few instructors noted that, in their minds, the students were just lists of names as they never really got to know the students. The student survey indicated that only 43% of the students agreed that they got to know the other students in their online courses quite well, while 25% of the students still felt lonely or isolated when they took the online courses.

A review of content analysis indicated that few instructors developed social activities which would be helpful in establishing personal relationships. Only two out of the 27 courses (see Table 1) used some simple social ice-breaking activities or introduction forums, which allowed students to become familiar with each other.

Some instructors didn't recognize the need to build a social presence or sense of community in the online courses because they were concerned that the extra effort required to build social relationships might pose a burden on both the instructor and students amid their busy professional lives. For example, one instructor commented:

It's not necessary. It's irrelevant. Most of these [students] are people working by themselves. They are people who hold down a regular job and are really not interested in trying to build social connections or anything like [that]...I don't have time for that stuff.

However, many students stated their preference for an increased social presence in the online interactions. One student said:

Well, it is more difficult definitely than face-to-face, but the pictures help. I think that it would help in our class, operations management, if the professor actually asked everybody to write a couple of paragraphs about themselves and post it for everybody to see that so we kind of knew what everybody's background was. It is easier to remember the person when you know some facts about them versus just looking at pictures or a name. I think that would be helpful if it was available for all of the classes.

The Tension between the Demand for Synchronous Technologies and Accessibility

Table 1 indicates that synchronous discussions were rarely used by the instructors. Although initially attracted by the interactive features of synchronous tools, such as chat rooms and video conferencing, many instructors later gave up these tools for two reasons. First, they found that there was a difficulty in scheduling class meeting times online when the participants were located in different regions of the United States or the world. Some instructors perceived that scheduling frequent synchronous discussions simply defeated the purpose of online learning which is flexibility and convenience. Second, moderating a group of over 10 individuals in the synchronous conference proved to be an obstacle because of limited bandwidth and a lack of skills in online moderation. For example, one instructor had to turn off the two-way audio during a synchronous live video conference because of the limited bandwidth. He then had to ask his students to submit their questions and comments through the small text box. In this session, the interactive nature of the Web was not fully taken advantage of. In addition, some students in the course were not satisfied with the experiences during which the instructors mainly used the tools as lecture presentation tools.

However, the students indicated that the effective use of chat rooms in several courses enhanced the sense of community and afforded rich interactive learning experiences. For example, one student noted that:

Every Wednesday night he had a chat session with everybody on, and that ... made you feel like you were almost in the classroom, that worked out real good, I mean, after a couple of weeks you kind of knew some of the people ... so you would be throwing some comments back and forth, so that worked, that was a good way to get to know each other.

Another student expressed his desire for the inclusion of interactive conferencing technologies to be used for teamwork:

It would be nice if we all could have some type of a computer screen or TV where everybody could see each other and kind of have a conference call... If people live in all different parts of the world and you're not physically able to get everybody together to talk about things, then that's the best you can do. I think it's fairly effective, but it can always be improved.

Satisfactions with Online Facilitation

Overall, the instructors' facilitations in the online courses were well acknowledged by the students. According to the survey, 84.4% of the students agreed or strongly agreed that the instructors played a role of facilitator, guide or coach rather than simply of lecturer. In addition, 81.3% agreed or strongly agreed that the instructors made announcements and gave feedback to the students on a regular basis, while 90.2% agreed or strongly agreed that the learning activities in the online courses fostered their understanding of key concepts. 76.4% of the students agreed or strongly agreed that the way the instructors facilitated the class fostered their learning.

However, we noticed that about one-fifth of the students showed a neutral attitude toward the way of the instructors' facilitation in the online courses. The interview findings suggested that this attitude may be associated with few uses of synchronous activities or other methods to promote social cohesiveness in the courses.

Virtual Teaming

The Uses of Team Activities

78% of the courses used virtual team activities. The majority of the courses required the students to submit team products so as to encourage close collaboration and intensive knowledge sharing among the team members. In order to facilitate the teamwork process, one-third of the courses required the teams to participate in small team discussion activities. Private team workspaces were set up in these courses. One-third of the courses encouraged the teams to give feedback and critique to the other teams, or share their team products or conclusions with the other teams.

In order to meet the needs of different learning styles, all of the courses that used the virtual teams combined the use of team and individual work. 22% of the ED courses gave the students choices as to whether to choose team or individual work for their projects. 48% of the courses allowed the students to choose their own team members. Most of the courses required the students to be in the same teams throughout the duration of the course in order to avoid the cost of team coordination.

The Benefits of Teamwork

The instructors agreed that teamwork contributed to building a sense of community in the online courses. By establishing a common goal, the team members were forced to engage in extensive interactions in order to accomplish the task. For example, one instructor initially did not use teams in his course, but after observing that the students in his class informally collaborated with each other on the assignments, he decided to use teams.

I think that [a sense of community] could be done with the team stuff... I'm just going to get some assignments that are interesting... and make them a team based on that and just open it up...I think that they want to work together with the other students and they want the camaraderie that comes along with working in a team.

Some instructors noted that the teamwork provided an authentic activity that allowed the students to practice their leadership, critical thinking and problem-solving skills. For example, one instructor said:

... I do think that at the graduate level, the importance of group learning has to be emphasized. These people are here to get an advanced degree in management, and you cannot be good managers if you don't know how to discuss and develop ideas in a group setting. That is why I thought it was important to improve the groups and the critiquing of each other because that's much more like real life, where you're going to present ideas and people are going to critique them.

In addition to acknowledging the importance of teamwork, both the students and instructors noted the benefit of developing virtual team skills in online courses, particularly in an increasingly globalized business environment. As was stated by one student:

Virtual teaming is good. Just for one reason, you know companies are global and especially my company. We have some business units, but in different platforms and each platform is within [a country] like North America, Asia, or wherever ... they form a peer team, but they're spread out all over fifty countries ... I'm sure a lot of businesses are doing that too so that's the way we do our teamwork here.

Facilitating Virtual Teams

One of the key decisions that the online instructors had to make in facilitating teamwork was to determine whether to let students choose their own teams or assign student teams. Some of the instructors observed that the students tended to prefer forming their own teams and believe that the trust built from the bonding experiences would contribute to the effectiveness of the teams. However, other instructors were concerned that the self-forming of teams may not reflect real world experiences and, therefore, would not be helpful in developing teamwork skills. The students were similarly split into two different perspectives. For example, the below comments represents two instructors' different perspectives:

That experience in ED, in bringing them on campus, creates a bit of a bonding experience and it creates a trust experience that even though they're only here for a week they create a trust in working with somebody else. And they want to work with that person and they trust that person to help them out, to pull their own weight and they like working with that person.

… I got an email [from a student] saying well now 'shouldn't we align these geographically' and I respond well we could do a lot of things but most of you are growing your careers in an environment where you have to deal with people 12 hours … so view this as an opportunity to practice skills in a real world.

For online instructors, the design and facilitation of teamwork mainly focused on providing clear directions, setting up workspaces and designing tasks. Once these items were complete, the instructors stepped aside and allowed the students to take control of the team processes. The instructors intervened only when the team conflicts could not be resolved within the team. For example, one instructor commented on how he advised a troubled team in regard to confronting team issues:

To this troubled team for instance, I said, if this behavior happened on a QM [company pseudonym] project and became visible in the company, the issue wouldn't be who performed and who didn't. Instead, QM would fire all of you because you're dysfunctional and getting in the way of good people doing good stuff. You're in a safe environment here and this conflict is an opportunity to find a solution.

Challenges in Teamwork

The students cited one critical barrier to effective teamwork was the lack of sense of identity of team members. Due to the short duration of online courses and constant shuffling of team compositions, it was difficult for the students to get to know each other on a personal level. A few students indicated that the team members may be easier to get involved in an argument due to a lack of social rapport. For example, two students commented:

The people that I communicate and work with the best are the people that I've met here face-to-face. I know who they are and where they're coming from. It seems to be a lot more difficult to get to know your team members solely in an online environment.

About two-thirds of the way through the class, one of the members accused me of being, not so much domineering, but kind of strong arming, the rest of the team because we don't understand each other's personalities and we've only had a very short amount of time to meet one another. For me, the most difficult and worst part of the class is trying to understand who these other people are.

The students mentioned that one of the pitfalls of virtual teamwork was that they could easily fall in the game of "divide and conquer" and, therefore, ran the risk of superficial collaboration. Some of the courses built higher interdependency into the teamwork, which seemed to effectively foster higher levels of collaboration. For example, one student noted:

What it does is you run a small business. Everybody is in charge of one particular area and you're competing amongst other teams. We placed 5th out of 6th, but it doesn't matter how we actually did. It was the experience that was so good. It was very engaging and, like I said, it was the one that required the phone calls that we all get together, it was the one that really required teamwork and interaction. But the other ones, you've got a homework assignment and 5 people are supposed to turn in these 5 problems together. All right, you've got 1, you've got 2, you've got 3, okay, and it's all due on Thursday, talk to you on Friday. And that would be the extent of some of the "group work" that had been done in the courses.

Satisfaction with Teamwork

Overall, the students had positive attitudes toward the teamwork in the online MBA program. Approximately 93% of the respondents felt that sharing information and giving peer feedback during the team projects contributed to student learning (M=4.17, SD=.63). One student noted:

I like the teamwork aspect of it because I don't know everything about the topics and a lot of times, I get alternate perspectives from others. So the fact that we all work in teams a lot of times kind of enhances the experience for me. I like it.

Approximately 86% of the students surveyed agreed that working in teams was helpful to their learning (M=4.22, SD=.91), while about 94% of the respondents stated that interacting with the other students or the instructors created a more meaningful learning experience.

Case-Based Learning (CBL)

The Importance of CBL

CBL was used as a key instructional method in the online courses of the MBA program. According to the survey results, the majority of the students (86.3%) agreed that CBL was a critical teaching and learning technique. As was revealed by the interviews, both the instructors and students agreed that CBL provided valuable lessons due to its high relevance to real world experiences. For example, one student noted:

I think it is [important] because it gives you real world examples of what the professor is trying to teach you. So I think that was, that's a valuable lesson with using case-based study.

One instructor stated:

[T]hese cases are important because they are real world and you know that is working when the students will say, this is like job, or this is like my company. I want them to identify with the situations that the managers in these various cases have.

In addition to real world relevance, CBL was regarded by the students as one of the key learning tools to fostering the understanding of concepts and theories and providing opportunities to develop critical thinking skills. During the interviews, some of the students noted that unlike some problems that had right or wrong answers, the ambiguities embedded within the case studies forced them to think much more deeply into the issues. For example, one student commented:

The case based learning is definitely a better way, I think, because it forces you to think and, for the other ones, like, for example, the courses were just problematic problems and answers, right... But in the case based learning you are learning, trying to understand the situation, understand the theory, and then apply the theory to that situation. And in real life, that is what you have to do. In real life, there are no problems that are simple. You always have to apply a solution to a situation, which is why I think it's very useful to have case based and I quite enjoy them.

Redesign CBL for Online Courses

The lack of real-time feedback in asynchronous online learning environments posed challenges to the instructors because the live discussions and presentations that traditional CBL heavily relies upon cannot be easily implemented online. In the ED program, the instructors took deliberate considerations in the design of the course in order to suit to the nature of the online environments and motivate the students into active online participation.

To Select Cases to be Relevant to the Real World

Although a majority of the instructors continued to use classical text-based Harvard cases, many of the instructors chose to mix traditional cases with new, updated and relevant cases in order to stimulate the interests of the online students. One instructor noted:

I try to pick cases within the past three years because the problem with strategy is it can lose relevance if you get dated because trying to analyze the strategy of a case 10 years ago, you always have to deal with hindsight issues, so I try to keep it relatively current, and interesting.

Personalize the Case

Unlike traditional MBA students who usually lack practical work experiences, the online MBA students brought with them a wealth of personal experiences and valuable lessons from their diversified professional work experiences. Many of the instructors took advantage of this learning resource in order to create a rich learning experience. One instructor stated:

They have to write about a situation that they have in their life, in their work life and how they can make it better with operations. It might be a quality problem, it might be a capacity problem, it might be a customer service problem, and they are to identify the problem, tell me about the problem, and then what their own solution is. They can't say, this is what my company did. No, no, unless you're going to criticize it, I want your point of view about this operation.

Choice on Cases

Many of the instructors considered giving choices to the students on their ways of participations in the online case discussions, which they wouldn't normally do in their traditional courses. For example, due to the convenience of the asynchronous text-based learning environments, many ED instructors set up concurrent discussion forums in order to allow the students to choose their preferred topics whereas in the local face-to-face courses, they would do the discussions case-by-case in a chronological order. The choices on the discussion topics not only allowed the class to be broken down into several smaller discussions in order to avoid information overload in a large class discussion, but also, enhanced the students' motivations in participating in the online discussions. One instructor commented:

I'll have 6 easy articles that we're going to discuss in a discussion forum or cases and I'll assign people to 2 of those discussion forums. So there are 2 of those that they have to participate in, and that's primarily what I'm grading. The ones they're not assigned to they can participate in after the assigned people have already made their initial comments.

Design Technology to Enhance

CBL In the ED program, a few of the instructors took the initiative to renovate existing ANGEL course management system tools for CBL. Several of the tools were developed with the assistance of the technical staff in order to meet the specialized needs of the online business instructors. For example, one instructor developed a case builder tool that was capable of streamlining all of the resources and learning activities into one tool. With the case builder tool, text, videos and audio files can be uploaded easily to the case builder so as to enrich the descriptions of the case contexts. The students can hold discussions within the tool, which removes the need for the utilization of an additional tool for the discussions.

A few customized discussion forums were developed in order to structure different dynamics in regard to the online discussions. For instance, one type of forum was designed so that a student could not see the postings from the other students until that particular student had posted his own comment. This tool was very useful in regard to allowing the instructors to assess the students' abilities to think independently before allowing them to share their perspectives.

The role-based forum was designed to allow the visualization of the students' identities as they took on a personality or professional role and interacted with their peers in a simulated learning environment. For example, a business law professor used a Role Play forum in order to simulate the experience of a court debate. The students were given roles as the "judge," "plaintiff" and "defendant" and debated in the forum as if they were really in a court situation. The students gave positive feedback on the use of the role-based forum in the course. The visualization of the roles enhanced the students' awareness of the responsibilities of each role and, therefore, fostered consistent levels of interactions.

Challenges in CBL

Transition to CBL

The major challenge associated with CBL in the program was the approach itself. For many of the students who came from engineering or science backgrounds, CBL represents a different style of learning. The initial adjustment period to CBL at the beginning of their program seemed difficult for some of the students. For example, one student shared his experience:

It is a bit intimidating at first cause it's a different style of learning and …it doesn't reinforce the same method that doing multiple problems does like we saw in finance [courses] where they were much more driven about just solving problems and getting good at using the techniques in different ways. So if you're not used to case-based learning, it can be intimidating or at least take awhile to get used to. There's a learning curve to go through … I think obviously we've all made it through it so it just may have been a little bit more frustrating for others.

Format of the Case Presentation

In the program, 41% of the courses maintained traditional text-based case packages, while 37% of the courses used Web-based text. Only 9% of the courses used audio or video clips to supplement the text-based materials. The students expressed a desire for more cases that utilized multi-media features or sophisticated technology that could deliver interactions close to face-to-face experiences.

This [case] could be delivered via live video or the lab instead of just plain text. That's too primitive.

The only thing that is really difficult about some types of cases is how you discuss something that you would normally draw a diagram like when you're trying to motivate people to think in the same direction you are.

Satisfaction with CBL

The student survey indicated that 88.3% of the students agreed or strongly agreed that the interactive activities designed for CBL were helpful in regard to deepening their learning. 89% of the students agreed or strongly agreed that the technology used in the online courses were effective in supporting CBL. 81% of the students agreed or strongly that the format and complexity of the business cases were well-suited to the online courses.

Summary of Findings

The findings of this case study suggest a successful implementation of an online MBA program is in place in ED. Both the instructors and students exhibited a high level of satisfaction with their online experiences. The key findings of this study are summarized as follows:

- Both the instructors and students displayed a high level of satisfaction with their teaching or learning experiences in the program. They also exhibited positive attitudes toward online learning environments in general.
- The online instructors implemented a variety of learning activities in the online courses in order to facilitate the student-instructor and student-student interactions, which are key to the success of online business education.
- The online students acknowledged the efforts of the instructors in regard to implementing a variety of learning activities in the online courses, stating that the instructors fostered their understanding of the key concepts and their learning overall in the online courses. However, the participants cited a lack of facilitation skills as well as time management, equal participation, lack of social presence and accessibility of technology as barriers for the success of online learning in the program.
- CBL was used as a key instructional method in the online courses of the MBA program. The instructors used various approaches to redesign CBL in their online courses in order to provide a rich learning experience. The instructors also explored the potential of technology in order to enrich CBL. However, the study indicated that some of the students may become frustrated when initially making the transition to CBL if they are not provided with the proper orientation to this instruction approach. Text-dominated case presentations represent a bottleneck for enriching online learning experiences in CBL.
- The student survey indicated that the majority of the students strongly agreed upon the important role that the teams played in their learning. Several benefits were identified with this strategy including: fostering high levels of interaction and sense of community among the students and instructors, bridging the gap between the online learning environments and real world business and providing opportunities to develop leadership skills. However, the study revealed that weak social bonds and the tendency of superficial collaboration were potential barriers to the success of virtual teamwork in the student teams in the program.

SOLUTIONS AND RECOMMENDATIONS

Although this study did not paint a full picture of the ED program, it did suggest that the an online MBA program can be successfully implemented in an online environment that was mostly conducted in asynchronous environments. These findings indicate that the success of the ED online program was grounded in the effective facilitation of online learning activities used to foster student-instructor and student-student interactions, and on the deliberate effort of the online instructors to redesign key instructional approaches (e.g., team activities and CBL) in order to make the approaches suitable for the nature of online learning environments. This study partly validated Leidner and Jarvenpaa's (1995) work which implied that a collaborative learning model is the best fit for Internet-based MBA courses because of the asynchronous nature of the online medium and the relatively high level of the students' professional experiences.

Similar to other online MBA program case studies which have pointed out the need for high level instructor training and support (Schrum & Benson, 2000; Hergert, 2003), the findings of this study revealed uneven skills in regard to online facilitation among the instructors. These uneven skills suggest a need for instructor training in order to improve the skills of online instructors in the program. Although the online instructors may be aware of how their roles change in the online learning environment compared to the traditional classrooms, they still need critical guidance regarding how to design learning tasks for an effective online discourse.

Garrison, Anderson, and Archer (2003) described cognitive presence as the extent to which learners are able to construct and confirm meaning through sustained reflection and discourse. Existing research suggests the discussions do not reach high level of cognitive presence is related to the role of instructors (Celentin, 2007). Sustained development and progression of the discourse to higher levels of cognitive presence require well designed learning activities, facilitation and direction. Questions that direct students to engage in practical applications can better stimulate discussions in such a way as to progress them to a higher level of cognitive thinking, such as synthesis and resolution. A collaborative task that requires a sharable artifact is more likely to facilitate the development of solutions (Garrison & Arbaugh, 2007).

The lack of a social presence in the online courses is worth attention. In the present study, some of the instructors and students felt that it was difficult to develop a social rapport with the other individuals in the courses due to the incapability of the media to project emotions and social identities. The rare use of synchronous tools and non-instructional social interaction strategies often worsened the situation (See Table 1). Garrison, Anderson and Archer's (2003) theoretical work implies that social presence may not have a direct effect on learning, but is helpful in establishing a positive learning environment that may eventually foster learning. In the study, the lack of social presence did not affect the overall satisfaction and perceived learning of the online students, but we suspect that it may have had varying effects on each individual student, particularly those attuned to collaborative learning styles. Hergert's (2003) MBA program case study suggests that a sense of community can be developed through enhanced social interactions. In the present ED program, we focused on the need for instructors to develop social skills in order to foster a positive social climate to promote the high quality of online learning.

Teamwork plays an important role in online business education. This study suggests that teamwork can be structured in a variety of ways in order to foster student-student interaction. The benefits of teamwork as addressed in this study by the participants are consistent with previous research findings on virtual teams (Duart & Snyder, 1999; Palloff & Pratt, 2005). However, as to the benefits of facilitating a sense of community via teams, research suggests that utilizing virtual teams facilitates a sense of community within a team far more quickly than within a course (Hill, Raven, & Han, 2002). In the ED program, many of the instructors kept the students in one team throughout the semester for long-term projects. Such a strategy should be coupled with other activities that would promote team-team or team-class interactions in order to engage the students in interactions with other students outside of the team. Otherwise, the sense of community would only be developed at the team level instead of at the class level.

The study revealed two key issues in virtual teams - weak social bonding among team members and surface-level collaboration – that created challenges in regard to the effectiveness of the virtual teams in the online MBA courses. The findings revealed that the students perceived that increased familiarity and knowledge of team members could have enhanced the effectiveness of the virtual teamwork. Previous research suggests that social presence has been found to moderate the effect of virtual interaction on team outcomes (Maznevski & Chudoba, 2001; Martins, Gilson, & Maynard, 2004). Although online students are typically described as need driven and task focused (Bonk, 2000), this finding implies that appropriate social interaction is needed to start up teamwork in online courses in order to enhance the effectiveness of teamwork.

The divide and conquer pattern of online collaboration indicates the tendency of virtual teams to seek efficiency rather than effectiveness in learning, another indicator of the task-focused nature of online learners. The work processes of some teams exhibited a minimal collaboration pattern of dividing the work into individual parts and then coordinating to compile the work for submission. Other studies have found that in online courses that encourage team work, the students tend to divide their tasks, complete them individually and then combine the independent parts into a final product (Kitchen & McDougall, 1999; Hathorn & Ingram, 2002). Putting student into a group does not necessarily mean that they are going to collaborate, particularly when distance creates an additional barrier for close collaboration. This issue should be of particular importance to online instructors as such instructors need to design team tasks that build positive interdependencies among team members.

As a core pedagogical method, CBL provided authentic learning environments in which learning is situated in real world business contexts. Garvey, O'Sullivan, and Blake (2000) concluded that in order to bring out an extensive learning transfer through online CBL, it is essential for online instructors to be creative when designing the instructional activities and dedicate adequate time to the online facilitation of student learning activities. The findings of the present study demonstrated the instructors' creativity in regard to designing tools and learning activities for CBL which may have contributed to the success of the CBL in the ED program.

However, the findings of the present study also indicate that students who enrolled in the ED program without a background in business education needed support in order to make the transition to CBL. Martinez, Bunderson, Nelson and Ruttan (1999) found that students who were accustomed to highly structured environments featuring clear-cut solutions and a large amount of strictly guided instruction were unlikely to be comfortable learning in a loosely structured, flexible environment that promoted challenging self-discovery. An orientation to the CBL method in online learning would be helpful in causing the students to have a quicker adaptation to the new learning style.

Since in online business courses, most communications are delivered via technology and course management systems, the appropriate choice of the technology and technical assistance can be a key success factor in online teaching and learning. However, with the fast-paced development and utilization of advanced technology in the business industry, the expectations for highly interactive technology implemented in online business education have become increasingly high for students. Although efforts have been made in the ED program to integrate more interactive technology into the course, a gap exists between the expectations and current technology level. The program made a special effort to create technologies that would address the need for more multi-media components in CBL. For example, the case-builder tool was developed in order to facilitate multi-media use in CBL.

The program experiences suggest that the participants desired more sophisticated technology beyond what the course management system was able to offer. However, concerns prevailed among the instructors as to the accessibility and flexibility of such technology. How to balance the tension between accessibility and technology is a significant and growing challenge in regard to technology integration in online learning. Every instructor needs to be aware of potential accessibility issues, but still needs to try to maximize the interaction by using a combination of asynchronous and synchronous technology.

Overall, the issues and challenges point out a need for the instructors and students to receive more guidance and support, technologically and pedagogically, in order to create a more engaging and fruitful online learning environment. Based on the findings, several recommendations were made to the program administrators in terms of training and program support:

- Improve the instructor's skills in promoting a deep level of cognitive discourse in the online facilitation.

In-depth scaffolding strategies should be used in order to encourage the students to articulate, cognitively elaborate or reflect on what they have recently learned in order to foster student motivation. For example, a variety of prompting strategies (e.g., questioning, prompting, praising, modeling, etc.) can be used in order to promote fruitful online discourses. Guest lectures, role playing and debates are some examples of effective strategies for promoting peer interactions.

- Provide instructional assistance in order to foster social familiarity and strong human bonds.

Instructors should structure social interactions and model effective social skills in order to promote a friendly environment and community that contains a positive collaborative atmosphere. Social interaction strategies (such as online personal profiles, ice-breaker activities, occasional chat discussions, peer feedback and social acknowledgements in online discussions) can be used regularly in ED courses at the overall class level as well as at the small group level.

- Improve virtual team effectiveness by assessing the process as well as the product of the teamwork.

Assessment of the teamwork process could help both the instructors and students understand what makes virtual teams effective. Peer evaluations and assessing online team discussions are examples of online assessment strategies.

- Provide opportunities for instructors to share online best teaching practices with each other.

The program administrators should encourage exemplar instructors to demonstrate and share their experiences and knowledge of online teaching with other faculty members. Assigning a faculty mentor to a new instructor, planning regular and structured brownbag meetings and showcasing exemplar course designs are among the many ways to encourage the sharing of knowledge and experience among the ED instructors.

- Foster a higher level of technology integration by encouraging a balanced use of asynchronous and synchronous technology.

Technology training should be provided in order to raise instructors' awareness of various interactive technologies and effective ways of using them.

- Provide substantial training support for online faculty development.

The program needs to continuously provide instructors with substantial regular training sessions (e.g., regular presentations from internal e-learning consultants, invited talks of external experts, debriefings on future trends of online education, etc.).

As a program level case study, the generalizations from the results of this study are limited. However, the success, issues, and challenges presented in this study on the effective facilitations of online learning in regard to MBA students may provide useful insights and lessons for distance educators of other similar online MBA programs in the U.S. in regard to conducting strategic planning and refining practices to provide more satisfactory educational experiences in online learning environments.

REFERENCES

Alavi, M. (1994). Computer-mediated collaborative learning: An empirical evaluation. *Management Information Systems Quarterly, 18*(2), 159–174. doi:10.2307/249763.

Allen, I. E., & Seaman, J. (2008). *Staying the course: Online education in the United States.* The Sloan-C Report. Retrieved January 1, 2010, from http://www.aln.org/publications/survey/pdf/staying_the_course.pdf

Arbaugh, J. B. (2002). Virtual classroom characteristics and student satisfaction with Internet-based MBA courses. *Journal of Management Education, 24*(1), 32–54. doi:10.1177/105256290002400104.

Australian Flexible Learning Framework. (2004). *Cross-cultural issues in content development and teaching online.* Retrieved August 23, 2007, from http://www.flexiblelearning.net.au/flx/Webdav/site/flxsite/users/kedgar/public/quick_guides/crosscultural.pdf

Benbunan-Fich, R., & Hiltz, S. R. (1999). Education applications of CMCS: Solving case studies through asynchronous learning networks. *Journal of Computer-Mediated Communication, 4*(3). Retrieved on Jan 2nd, 2010 from http://jcmc.indiana.edu/vol4/issue3/benbunan-fich.html

Berge, Z. L. (1995). *Facilitating computer conferencing: Recommendations from the field. educational technology.* Retrieved on Feb 11, 2009, from http://www.emoderators.com/moderators/teach_online.html

Bonk, C. J. (2000). My hat's on to the online instructor. *e-Education Advisor. Education Ed., 1*(1), 10–13.

Bonk, C. J., Hara, N., Dennen, V., Malikowski, S., & Supplee, L. (2000). We're in TITLE to dream: Envisioning a community of practice: The intraplanetary teacher learning exchange. *Cyberpsychology & Behavior*, *3*(1), 25–39. doi:10.1089/109493100316201.

Caine, R. N., & Caine, G. (1997). *Education on the edge of possibility*. Alexandria, VA: ASCD.

Celentin, P. (2007). Online training: Analysis of interaction and knowledge building patterns among foreign language teachers. *Journal of Distance Education*, *21*(3), 39–58.

Christudason, A. (2003). A case for case-based learning. *Ideas of Teaching*, *1*, 18–19.

DeLacey, B. J., & Leonard, D. A. (2002). Case study on technology and distance in education at the Harvard Business School. *Education Technology and Society*, *5*(2), 13–28.

Duarte, D., & Snyder, N. (1999). *Mastering virtual teams: Strategies, tools and techniques that succeed*. San Francisco, CA: Jossey-Bass Inc..

Fulford, C. P., & Zhang, S. (1993). Perceptions of interaction: The critical predictor in distance education. *American Journal of Distance Education*, *7*(3), 8–21. doi:10.1080/08923649309526830.

Gabriel, M. A., & MacDonald, C. J. (2002). Working together: The context of teams in an online MBA program. *Canadian Journal of Learning and Technology*, *28*(2), 49–65.

Garrison, D. R., Anderson, T., & Archer, W. (2003). A theory of critical inquiry in online distance education. In Moore, M. G., & Anderson, W. G. (Eds.), *Handbook of distance education* (pp. 113–125). Mahwah, NJ: Erlbaum.

Garrison, R. D., & Arbaugh, J. B. (2007). Researching the community of inquiry framework: Review, issues, and future directions. *The Internet and Higher Education*, *10*(3), 157–172. doi:10.1016/j.iheduc.2007.04.001.

Garvey, M. T., O'Sullivan, M., & Blake, M. (2000). Multidisciplinary case-based learning for undergraduate students. *European Journal of Dental Education*, *4*(4), 165–168. doi:10.1034/j.1600-0579.2000.040404.x PMID:11168482.

Hathorn, L. G., & Ingram, A. L. (2002). Online collaboration: Making it work. *Educational Technology*, *42*(1), 33–40.

Hay, A., Peltier, J. W., & Drago, W. A. (2004). Reflective learning and on-line management education: A comparison of traditional and online MBA students. *Strategic Change, 13*(4), 169–182. doi:10.1002/jsc.680.

Hay, A. M., & Hodgkinson, J. W., Peltier, & Drago W. A. (2004). Interaction and virtual learning. *Strategic Change, 13*(4), 193–204. doi:10.1002/jsc.679.

Helms, M. M. (2006). Case method of analysis. In M. M. Helms (Ed.), *Encyclopedia of management*. Detroit, MI: Thomson Gale Group, Inc. Retrieved June 3, 2007 from http://www.enotes.com/management-encyclopedia/case-method-analysis

Hergert, M. (2003). Lessons from launching an online MBA program. *Online Journal of Distance Learning Administration, 6*(4).

Hill, J. R., Raven, R., & Han, S. (2002). Connections in web-based learning environments: A research based model for community building. *The Quarterly Review of Distance Education, 3*(4), 383–393.

Huang, W., Luce, T., & Lu, Y. (2005). Virtual team learning in online MBA education: An empirical investigation. *Issues in Information Systems, 4*(1), 258–264.

Kitchen, D., & McDougall, D. (1999). Collaborative learning on the internet. *Journal of Educational Technology Systems, 27*(3), 245–258.

Kretovics, M., & McCambridge, J. (2002). Measuring MBA student learning: Does distance make a difference? *International Review of Research in Open and Distance Learning, 3*(2), 1–18.

Lee, S.-H., Lee, J., Liu, X., Bonk, C. J., & Magjuka, R. J. (2009). A review of case-based learning practices in an online MBA program: A program-level case study. *Journal of Educational Technology & Society, 12*(3), 178–190.

Leidner, D., & Jarvenpaa, S. (1995). The use of information technology to enhance management school education: A theoretical view. *Management Information Systems Quarterly, 19*(3), 265–291. doi:10.2307/249596.

Magjuka, R. J., Min, S., & Bonk, C. (2005). Critical design and administrative issues in online education. *Online Journal of Distance Learning Administration, 8*(4). Retrieved January 4, 2006, from http://www.westga.edu/~distance/ojdla/articles/winter2005/magjuka84.htm

Marcus, G., Taylor, R., & Ellis, R. A. (2004). Implications for the design of online case based learning activities based on the student blended learning experience. In R. Atkinson, C. McBeath, D. Jonas-Dwyer, & R. Phillips (Eds.), *Beyond the comfort zone: Proceedings of the 21st ASCILITE Conference* (pp. 557-586). Perth, Australia. Retrieved online on December 1st from http://www.ascilite.org.au/conferences/perth04/procs/marcus.html

Martinez, M., Bunderson, C. V., Nelson, L. M., & Ruttan, J. P. (1999). *Successful learning in the new millennium: A new web learning paradigm.* Paper presented at the annual meeting of WebNet, International Conference. Honolulu, HI.

Martins, L. L., Gilson, L. L., & Maynard, M. T. (2004). Virtual teams: What do we know and where do we go from here? *Journal of Management, 30*(6), 805–835. doi:10.1016/j.jm.2004.05.002.

Maznevski, M., & Chudoba, K. (2001). Bridging space over time: Global virtual team dynamics and effectiveness. *Organization Science, 11*(5), 473–492. doi:10.1287/orsc.11.5.473.15200.

McGorry, S. Y. (2002). Online, but on target? Internet-based MBA courses: A case study. *The Internet and Higher Education, 5*(2), 167–175. doi:10.1016/S1096-7516(02)00089-1.

Merriam, S. B. (1998). *Case study research in education: A qualitative approach.* San Francisco, CA: Jossey-Bass Publishers.

Nunamaker, J., Dennis, A., Valacich, J., Vogel, D., & George, J. (1991). Electronic meeting systems to support group work. *Communications of the ACM, 34*(7), 41–61. doi:10.1145/105783.105793.

Palloff, R., & Pratt, K. (1999). *Building learning communities in cyberspace: Effective strategies for the online classroom.* San Francisco, CA: Jossey-Bass Publishers.

Patton, M. Q. (1990). *Qualitative evaluation and research methods.* Thousand Oaks, CA: Sage.

Phillips, V. (1998). Online universities teach knowledge beyond the books. *HRMagazine, 43*(8), 120–126.

Ponzurick, T. G., France, K. R., & Logar, C. M. (2000). Delivering graduate marketing education: An analysis of face-to-face versus distance education. *Journal of Marketing Education, 22*(3), 180–187. doi:10.1177/0273475300223002.

Schrum, L., & Benson, A. (2000). Online professional education: A case study of an MBA program through its transition to an online model. *Journal of Asynchronous Learning Networks*, *4*(1), 52–61.

Smith, L. J. (2001). Content and delivery: A comparison and contrast of electronic and traditional MBA marketing planning courses. *Journal of Marketing Education*, *23*(1), 35–44. doi:10.1177/0273475301231005.

Smith, P. L., & Dillon, C. L. (1999). Comparing distance learning and classroom learning: Conceptual considerations. *American Journal of Distance Education*, *13*(2), 6–23. doi:10.1080/08923649909527020.

Strauss, A., & Corbin. (1990). *Basics of qualitative research*. Thousand Oaks, CA. Sage (Atlanta, Ga.).

Swan, K. (2001). Virtual interaction: Design factors affecting student satisfaction and perceived learning in asynchronous online courses. *Distance Education*, *22*(2), 306–331. doi:10.1080/0158791010220208.

Weston, C., & Cranton, P. A. (1986). Selecting instructional strategies. *The Journal of Higher Education*, *57*(3), 259–288. doi:10.2307/1981553.

Williams, E. A., Duray, R., & Reddy, V. (2006). Teamwork orientation, group cohesiveness, and student learning: A study of the use of teams in online distance education. *Journal of Management Education*, *30*(4), 592–616. doi:10.1177/1052562905276740.

Williams, M. (2004). *Exploring the effects of a multimedia case-based learning environment in pre-service science teacher education in Jamaica*. (Unpublished doctoral dissertation). University of Twente, Twente, The Netherlands.

ENDNOTES

[1] The US College Credit system is different from Europe ECTS credit system. The former is based on class contact hour (Ground rule for US credit system is for every hour in class students need to spend two outside of class) and the latter on student load. The conversion between ECTS and US College Credit is the following: 1 ECTS = 0.6 US Credit Hour, 75ETS = 45 credit hours, 50 ETS=30 Credit hours.

Chapter 9

A Case Study of a Distance Degree Program in Vietnam:
Examples from a Learner-Centered Approach to Distance Education

Kristy Beers Fägersten
Söderstorn University, Sweden

EXECUTIVE SUMMARY

The English Department at Högskolan Dalarna, Sweden, participates in a distance-learning program with the Faculty of Education at Vietnam National University. Students who enroll in this program are teachers of English at secondary or tertiary institutions, and will study half time for two years to complete a Master's degree in English Linguistics. The distance program, adapted specifically to accommodate the Vietnamese students in terms of cultural differences as well as inexperience with distance methodology, is characterized by three design features: testing, technical training, and fostering a community of learners. The design of the courses also reflects a learner-centered approach that addresses common problem areas in distance education by promoting interactivity. Central to the overall program is the maintenance of different channels of communication, reflecting an effort to support the students academically and socially, both as individuals and members of a learning community. In this way, the effects of physical and cultural distances are minimized.

DOI: 10.4018/978-1-4666-4486-1.ch009

1. INTRODUCTION

The principles and techniques of distance education enable the processes of teaching and learning without the requirement of shared physical space. In other words, education can be delivered across great distances, and historically, distance education has meant that learning need not be confined within geographical or political borders. Significant advances in information technology have also greatly facilitated interpersonal interaction, awarding distance education the potential to be a more communicative experience. Consequently, distance programs are increasingly serving as forums for intercultural communication and exchange.

Accounting for different cultural traditions of education, however, can pose a challenge to the administration of any academic program, and distance programs are certainly no exception. Not only do instructors need to develop their teaching methodology and course content for the distance platform (or, indeed, adapt existing techniques and materials), they must also consider the profile of their students in terms of how familiar they are 1) with the educational culture specific to the degree program and 2) with distance education practices in general. The combination of distance-oriented methodology, disperse geographical locations, and different cultures or traditions of education can be likened to a pedagogical perfect storm. Course and program design should therefore reflect an effort to prevent the demands of teaching from being compounded by physical and cultural distances.

The English Department at Högskolan Dalarna, Sweden, participates in a distance learning program with the Faculty of Education at Vietnam National University. Students who enroll in this program are teachers of English at secondary or tertiary institutions, and will study half-time for two years to complete a Master's degree in English Linguistics. The program includes a total of six graduate-level courses in applied linguistics, and encompasses a Master's thesis, which the students write during their last term of study. The program is run as a modified, or hybrid, distance program, with students and Högskolan Dalarna's linguistics teachers and course coordinators participating in semi-annual visits at the VNU-Hanoi campus. Coinciding with the start of each academic term, these visits serve both to introduce new courses to existing cohorts of students, and to administer a new intake of students, approximately 25-30 students per semester.

This chapter presents Högskolan Dalarna's Master's degree in English Linguistics as a case study of a distance degree program. The focus of the chapter includes both the creation of the program and design of the distance courses, each of which illustrates a learner-centered approach to distance education. In creating the degree program, several features emerged as defining characteristics; these are presented in section 3 of the chapter. Section 4 is a presentation of general course design, in particular how technology can be used in distance courses to deliver content, facilitate communication, and foster a learning community. While the chapter is based on experiences specific to Högskolan Dalarna's distance degree program for students in Vietnam, the issues, concepts and practices presented can be applied to other distance programs, in particular those which are administered in Asia or in an intercultural context.

2. BACKGROUND TO THE STUDY

The Vietnamese education system is overseen by the Ministry of Education and Training (MOET), the resulting governmental institution after the combination of the Ministry of Education and the Ministry of Higher Education in 1990. One of the directives of MOET was to require a minimum of a Master's degree for all teachers in higher education and ultimately even a PhD for teachers at the university level. After the issuing of this directive, a number of university graduates found themselves in need of a post-graduate education. Teachers of English, for example, were required to earn a Master's degree in English in order to retain their current teaching positions. To this end, many Vietnamese university administrators turned to foreign universities for the provision of qualified and reputable degree programs in English.

A representative for the Faculty of Education (FoE) at Vietnam National University (VNU) initiated collaboration with the English Department of Högskolan Dalarna (HD) in March 2006, via VNU colleagues who had contacts within another department at Högskolan Dalarna. The Faculty of Education at VNU had, at that time, collaborated for many years with a university in Australia, but were interested in finding a Master's program that better suited the needs of their students and was more economically feasible.

The Master's degree program in English at VNU's Faculty of Education would ideally target teachers of English at colleges or universities with non-English major students. The FoE was therefore interested in offering their students a Master's degree which reflected a focus on applied linguistics, and could complement the students' TEFL backgrounds. However, the FoE was looking to avoid the high costs incurred via the existing degree program in Australia. The basic program design proposed to Högskolan Dalarna was to host HD teachers in Hanoi for extended periods of on-site teaching. Due to professional schedules as well as personal commitments, this solution was not accepted. Instead, Högskolan Dalarna proposed a Web-based, distance degree program. By 2006, the linguistics courses offered by the English Department at HD were nearly all Web-based, in that materials were available online, and both campus and distance students participated in Web-based coursework. Making the entire degree program Web-based would require very little adjustment or redesign. Furthermore, the Web-based nature of the collaboration would represent a cost effective alternative, as tuition in Sweden is free.

The Faculty of Education was reluctant to accept this proposal: Web-based education was an unfamiliar concept, and the FoE students had no experience of this kind of learning. The system of education in Vietnam is similar to other communist-influenced systems in that it is centrally controlled via a ministry, such as Vietnam's Ministry of Education and Training, and stipulates intense student-teacher contact. The proposed Web-based program thus posed a threat to the traditional system, and the FoE was skeptical if not fearful of foregoing face-to-face instruction and the personal contact of on-site teaching.

It was important to convince the FoE administration of the feasibility of the distance, Web-based format, and assure them that personal contact would not be significantly compromised. The solution which was eventually negotiated between Högskolan Dalarna and VNU's Faculty of Education was to run a hybrid distance program, with two-week, on-site visits to the Hanoi campus at the beginning and end of each term, regular (weekly) Web-based lessons for each course throughout the term, as well as additional Web-based support and interaction. To facilitate and optimize Web-based contact, students admitted to the program are required to arrange for regular access to a computer with a high-speed Internet connection and audio-video capabilities.

The Master's degree in English Linguistics accepted its first cohort of VNU students in the Autumn term of 2006. The cooperation has since seen 6 cohorts accepted, three of which have already graduated. The collaboration contract period will come to an end in the Autumn term of 2010.

3. CREATING THE DISTANCE DEGREE PROGRAM

On-campus instruction and face-to-face communication no longer constitute the only modus operandi of universities and other institutions of education. Advances in technology have enabled and facilitated distance education practices, many of which have been integrated into the design of traditional courses. In fact, examples of distance education practices[1] in classroom-based courses (e.g., chat, as discussed in Abrams, 2003; Chun, 1994; Sanders, 2006) are so common that they may not be immediately recognizable as hallmarks of distance teaching: assignments are delivered by email, post-lecture discussions are conducted on online message boards, or course literature is accessed via the Internet. The first step in the creation of a distance course or program, or the transformation of existing, campus-based courses or programs, is therefore often (mis)understood as an exercise in fully incorporating these and similar practices into the course or program design. It is important, however, to avoid making the mistake of equating the creation of a distance program with simply devising a way to package and deliver course content. While the ever-increasing usability of information technologies encourages a focus on the *how*, this should not be at the expense of the *who*, in other words, the students, who, after all, are the very reason for educational programs.

Traditionally, distance courses and degree programs assume a generic adult learner, so the primary design focus remains on course content and delivery (Sherry, 1996). It is only recently that distance programs have begun targeting specific and varying student groups, ushering in the trend of learner-centered design and methodology. Thus, while technology continues to be singled out as a key component to distance education, meeting the instructional needs of students is increasingly recognized as the key to success in distance programs (Howard et al, 2003; Schamber, 1988; Sherry, 1996, Strauss, 2002).

In the case of the MA program in English Linguistics offered by Högskolan Dalarna to students at Vietnam National University, program design and structure are learner-centered. Prior to VNU's initiating cooperation, the MA degree in English Linguistics was not offered by distance, nor was it learner-centered in terms of being designed for a specific, homogenous student group. Furthermore, the degree included courses in both theoretical and applied linguistics, and stipulated a number of pre-requisite courses as well. In its original state, the program was not suitable for the VNU students. As certified teachers of English as a foreign language, the VNU students wished to enroll in an MA program primarily to receive practical training in applied English linguistics. Högskolan Dalarna's MA program in English Linguistics thus needed not only to be redesigned as a distance program, but also reconfigured to meet the professional needs of the VNU students.

In terms of content, the reconfiguration process required very little effort. Only one preparatory course was created specifically for the VNU students. This course is mandatory during the first term of study, ensuring a shared knowledge-base at an early point in the program. No other new courses were created, and choice among electives was limited. In this way, the program curriculum could be oriented towards applied linguistics, and the content changes to the program were in effect limited to the addition of one preparatory course. The total number of required courses and the total credit hours for the degree remained constant, as did individual course requirements. Content had not been compromised, and no program requirements had been relaxed. Accreditation and approval of a new degree program were therefore not an issue. Furthermore, most of the course material was already Web-based, with basic distance-learning practices also in use. Thus, the general redesign of the program for distance learning did not prove to be problematic.

The most challenging aspect of creating the distance degree program was determining which methods and techniques would be appropriate for the VNU students, which in turn meant knowing the learners. It has been argued that distance education programs should reflect a focus on the learners' instructional needs (Sherry, 1996;

237

Shneiderman, 1992), taking into consideration personal information such as their ages, interests, and levels of education, but more importantly, their familiarity with distance education methods and cultural backgrounds (Schamber, 1988). These last two learner qualities, familiarity with distance methods and cultural background, were particularly influential in the creation of HDa's distance program for VNU students.

3.1. Defining Features of HDa's Distance Degree Program

Before launching the MA degree in English Linguistics with Vietnam National University, little was known among the program teaching staff about Vietnamese culture and traditions of education. Additionally, among the Vietnamese students, there was little familiarity with distance education methods. In recognition of the importance of knowing the learners and engaging them in active involvement in the learning process (Webster and Hackley, 1997), the distance program was designed to accommodate cultural differences as well as inexperience with distance methodology. The most significant cultural differences between Western and Eastern systems of education include the level of independent thinking required of students, the degree of autonomy that is expected or cultivated, and the social distance of student-teacher relationships. Western systems of education encourage more independence of thought and autonomous learning behavior, resulting in greater social distance between students and teachers. The Web-based format of instruction lends itself well to these circumstances, but does not correspond as well with the Eastern culture of education, which, on the contrary, values conformity of thought, group mentality and close student-teacher relationships much more highly (Brislin, 1993; Hofstede, 1991; Smith & Bond, 1993; Triandis, 1995). The difference in educational philosophy might best be expressed in terms of the amount of independence that Web-based learning either *affords* students or *requires* of them. In acknowledgement of the different approaches to education as well as the advantages of each, the distance degree program was designed to accommodate the students' cultural backgrounds while maintaining the hallmarks of Western education. Three design features thus emerged as the cornerstones of the program: testing, technical training, and fostering a community of learners.

3.1.1. Testing

The cooperation with Vietnam National University has ensured a steady supply of students to the MA degree program in English Linguistics, and each term approximately 25-30 students enroll. Eligible students are those who are certified teachers of English at secondary or tertiary institutions. The nature of the coursework, however, requires that each accepted student also have a high level of proficiency in English, as well as good analytical skills. Potential students are therefore tested in order to assure that each participant in the program is in fact capable of understanding and performing the assignments and completing course requirements.

The Faculty of Education students have all completed a Bachelor's degree program in English. However, teachers of English in Vietnam are traditionally non-native speakers, and thus their students (who may become teachers themselves, as in the case of the VNU students) often receive little to no exposure to native-speaker English. Although the Bachelor's degree fulfills a formal requirement for acceptance to Högskolan Dalarna's Master's degree program, there are practical aspects to consider for these non-native speakers, most significantly their ability to adjust to the linguistic level of instruction among the native-speaker teachers of the program.

Since the distance program began in 2006, testing has always been done on site at the VNU campus in Hanoi. Teaching staff from Högskolan Dalarna travel to Hanoi to meet potential students, all of whom are prepared to take part in testing over a 2-day period. In addition to testing linguistic proficiency and analytical skills, potential candidates to the program are interviewed, primarily to assess their oral production and comprehension skills, but also to inquire about their living and work situations as an indication of their personal commitments, professional goals, connectivity capabilities, and potential to cope with the demands of and ultimately succeed in a 2-year distance program. Testing and interviewing also help to preserve the integrity of the degree program, such that only those candidates who are judged to have sufficient academic qualifications and the potential to complete the program are ultimately admitted. Finally, once the testing is completed and students are notified of their acceptance to the program, there is an opportunity for the new cohort members to meet with each other and the teachers, while still on site in Hanoi.

Since the inception of the program, testing has proven to be critical for assuring a shared level of proficiency and similar capabilities in each cohort, which in turn positively affect the overall completion rate and general success of each student. In the early stages of the program, several students were accepted at the encouragement of the VNU administrative staff despite test scores which were below the desired level for admittance. These students struggled from the beginning, needing increasing amounts of guidance and tutoring from their teachers. They were ultimately unable to perform adequately, fell behind the rest of the cohort, and eventually discontinued their studies. This is not to suggest that testing can categorically weed out students who are incapable of successfully completing the program, as other students have also found themselves unable to continue their studies, even despite quite good performances. Nevertheless, the testing methods for acceptance into the program have proven to be reliable as a means of achieving relative stability in the student cohorts, predicting overall success among individual students, and maintaining integrity in the MA program.

3.1.2. Technical Training

Acceptance to the program is a testimony on behalf of Högskolan Dalarna to each student's capabilities and potential to succeed in the program. Participation and commitment are both supported and fostered by membership in the program, the program cohort and the cohort sub-group. Despite these favorable conditions for success, taking part in a distance program also requires a certain amount of familiarity with information technology. As a minimum requirement, each student accepted to the MA program must have access to a computer with reliable, high-speed Internet capability, and be able to perform basic Internet navigation. This requirement applies to all students enrolled in Web-based courses.

The degree program utilizes a number of different Web interfaces for disseminating program information, providing access to literature and other course materials, submitting assignments, participating in seminars, and conducting research. For example, program information, course materials, and bulletin boards are available via the online learning platform Fronter, which is accessible by teachers and students via a login name and password. Lectures are available for downloading as PowerPoint files with audio recording. Seminars are conducted as text chats via Skype, and occasionally students may take part in video-conferences using Marratech software, including whiteboard and chat capabilities. Research can be conducted via the Internet, but also through Högskolan Dalarna's library services, including access to e-books and online journals. For someone new to distance education, this combination of information technology may be overwhelming and perhaps difficult to navigate. For this reason, all new students attend a training session while on site in Hanoi, where each of the interfaces is presented, detailed instructions are provided, and hands-on exercises are supervised. In fact, participation in similar training sessions are required of all students of Web-based courses offered by the English Department (see Figure 1).

Technology training builds confidence in one's abilities to utilize and interact with technology (Compeau and Higgins, 1995), which in turn "plays a significant role in user's expectations and performance." (Webster and Hackley, 1997:1284) Students' opinions of and attitudes towards technology and its use in distance education may also affect their performance (Webster and Hackley, 1997; Davis et al, 1989; Zoltan and Chapanis, 1982). Common training sessions allowing the students to familiarize themselves with the technologies used in the program help to improve their capabilities, ultimately raising their confidence levels and fostering positive attitudes towards distance education practices.

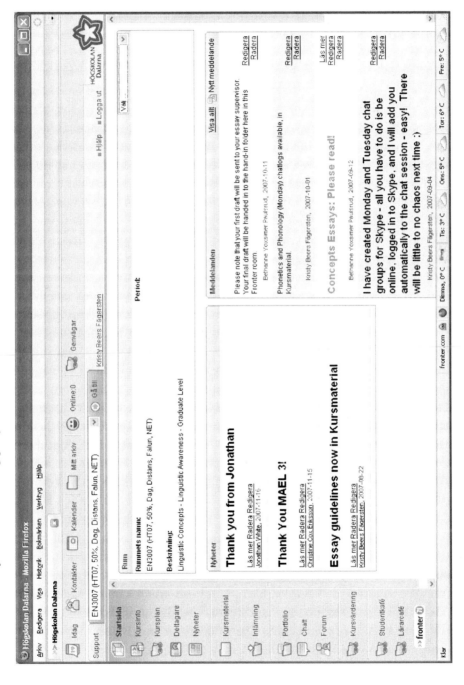

Figure 1. A screen-shot of the web learning platform, Fronter

3.1.3. Fostering a Community of Learners

Pursuing a Master's degree is demanding, even without the challenges of participating by distance, in a foreign language, and while juggling work and family responsibilities. While testing the VNU students helps to identify candidates who will most likely be able to cope with this conglomeration of demands, it is important to create a favorable environment of learning that is conducive to success and, ideally, does not in any way add to or intensify the challenges of the program. The organization and administration of the MA distance program endeavors to promote independence and individual accountability in each of the students, but it is just as critical that measures are taken to foster a cooperative, supportive learning community.

The support systems that are available to students in traditional campus-based education are often absent in a distance learning program. In the traditional classroom, for example, the teacher is present, and students interact as classmates, rendering the learning process a socially embedded experience. Furthermore, through the habit of meeting face-to-face in a regular place at a regular time, classmates reinforce their own and each other's commitment to the course (McBride and Beers Fägersten, 2008). Distance education programs must somehow provide students the kind of support that promotes this sense of connection with a distinct learning community.

In Högskolan Dalarna's Master's program in English Linguistics, the sense of belonging to a community is created via group membership, and students are members of at least three different groups. One cohort of 25-30 Vietnamese students is accepted to the program per semester. Admission to the program is announced after testing, while students are still present at the Hanoi campus. Upon admittance to the program the students are collectively welcomed to the Master's Degree in English Linguistics and, more specifically, as members of a program cohort. Thus, from the moment of admission to the program, group membership is established on two levels: overall program membership and specific cohort membership. Each cohort is named systematically, according to the program call-letters and the numerical position of the cohort in the program, e.g. MAEL1 is the name of the first group to be accepted to the MA in English Linguistics distance degree program. Each cohort is further divided into four sub-groups of six to eight students per group. Sub-groups are named after the seasons: Spring, Summer, Autumn, and Winter. Cohort and sub-group naming greatly facilitates administration of the program and student identification, but also contributes to fostering a sense of community. The students can easily identify themselves by group membership, and can immediately enjoy a sense of belonging in a social network. Ceremony is valued in the Vietnamese culture, and the act of naming and formally welcoming the students into the different groups is a gesture of respect for their new status. The different groups of which they are members constitute communities of learning, while membership encourages cooperation, mutual support and commitment to the program.

Finally, the practice of establishing a culture of groups and fostering learning communities is a way of acknowledging the students as members of a pre-existing group, namely, the Vietnamese student speech community. According to Gumperz (1968/71:114), a speech community is "any human aggregate characterized by regular and frequent interaction by means of a shared body of verbal signs set off from similar aggregates by signficant differences in language usage." In other words, a speech community involves a group of people who partake in regular interaction which can be characterized by linguistic features. A further feature of speech communities is the aspect of shared rules "for the conduct and interpretation of speech, and rules for the interpretation of at least one linguistic variety." (Hymes 1967/72:54-5). The Vietnamese students thus represent a speech community by virtue of their shared ideas for language usage in the context of education and learning.

Should cultural differences or linguistic difficulties give rise to confusion, insecurity, or other problems during the program, the VNU students can consult each other for discussion and support. In-group communication is facilitated by the appointing of a group leader, whose responsibility it is to establish and maintain contact among their group members throughout the duration of the Master's program. The group leaders also act as liaisons between their fellow group members and the teacher. In effect, group leaders are the spokespeople for their groups. If a student feels uncomfortable, insecure, or embarrassed approaching the teacher with a problem, the group leader can represent the student, or the group as a whole.

4. DISTANCE COURSE DESIGN

Although distance education is not a particularly new concept in the field of pedagogy, it enjoys a state of steady renewal, due to the rapid pace at which distance education technologies are developing. It is thus a dynamic form of education, in particular when compared to traditional forms of teaching and learning. As the newer, less conventional form, distance education is easily assumed to be the inferior one, and particulary disadvantageous to students. Galusha (1997) identifies five problem areas and barriers to success in distance education in particular, including "costs and motivators, feedback and teacher contact, student support and services, alienation and isolation, and lack of experience and training." (p. 6) Costs refer to both financial burdens as well as the amount of time a distance program requires, which may be at the expense of the student's work or family responsibilities. Demands on time and resources combined with a lack of personal or professional support for one's distance studies may result in insecurities about learning (Knapper, 1988) and low motivation. The "perceived lack of feedback or contact with the teacher" (Galusha, 1997:6) is a concern among distance students who may not be able to self-evaluate, in turn leading to insecurity about their performance. Furthermore, the lack of regular face-to-face contact with the teacher can be perceived to impair communication and serve to isolate the student. The third problem area identified by Galusha, lack of support and services for the distance student, refers to the need to involve tutors, academic planners, and technical assistance into distance programs. Without this network of support, the distance student is believed to be put at an unfair disadvantage. Similarly, the lack of a tangible learning community can lead to the distance student experiencing a lack of social support, ultimately leading to alienation and isolation. Finally, the fifth problem applies to new distance students, or students faced with new technologies, who may not have the technical skills necessary to participate and be productive in their distance courses.

Sherry (1996) identifies successful distance education systems as ones which "involve interactivity between teacher and students, between students and the learning environment, and among students themselves, as well as active learning in the classroom" (p. 342). The design of the courses offered by distance in Högskolan Dalarna's MA in English Linguistics reflects a learner-centered approach that addresses common problem areas in distance education by promoting interactivity. Central to the overall program is the maintenance of different channels of communication, reflecting an effort to support the students academically and socially, both as individuals and members of a learning community. In this way, the effects of physical and cultural distances can be minimized, and the experience of a meaningful, professionally relevant, and socially embedded education is maximized.

4.1. Community Platform

Many distance students can be disadvantaged by geographical isolation, such that basic administrative tasks, such as contacting teachers and administrators or accessing course materials, are difficult to perform (Meacham & Evans, 1989). The isolation resulting from physical distance can also contribute to a feeling of social isolation, putting distance students at risk of becoming solitary students, with no connection to a scholarly community (Galusha, 1997; Kirkman et al, 2002). Social integration is therefore key to success in distance education (Tinto, 1975). The feelings of inadequacy and insecurity resulting from a lack of social stimulation are particularly relevant to the Vietnamese students, who may already be coping with insecurities about cultural differences and language proficiency. Combined with the physical distance between Sweden and Vietnam, the different time zones, and the general dispersion of fellow students throughout Vietnam, a 'solitary student syndrome,' in other words, the lack of motivation which can accompany a feeling of isolation, is all too likely to affect the Vietnamese students. To prevent them from feeling isolated from their teachers and from each other, it is important that the MA program cultivate a learning community to facilitate contact and encourage communication.

Vital to the maintenance of the learning community for the MA in English Linguistics distance program is the use of Fronter, an online, open learning platform. Fronter serves as a virtual meeting place, where students and teachers can post news items or messages, course materials can be downloaded, assignments can be uploaded, questions can be posted to a forum, or chats can be conducted. Fronter is also the main locus of general-interest interaction for the students and teacher outside of their courses and, together with email, serves the majority of asynchronous communication needs.

The training session, which is offered on site in Hanoi to the newly admitted students, includes an introduction to using the Fronter learning platform. Students receive hands-on instruction as well as the opportunity to click-and-see by accessing Fronter pages for MA program courses. This kind of practice session with supervision reflects the ideology that "technical barriers must be made a non-issue" (Galusha, 1997:6), by minimizing the problem of a lack of experience or training. As students become more familiar with and competent in using Fronter and its various features, their confidence levels increase and, consequently, individual Fronter activity increases. The more individual activity there is, the more Fronter becomes a community platform.

All students are encouraged to check Fronter several times a day for news, important updates, course materials, or new discussion threads. Students can see which other students have been active, or even who is currently online. The use of Fronter as a community platform can be thought of as providing distance students with a virtual campus, a place to visit on a regular basis and conduct normal school business, such as check the bulletin board for new information, take part in an on-going discussion, pick up course materials, turn in assignments, or chat with fellow students. It is these activities which contribute to the experience of being part of a learning community. Fronter represents an educational tool which can provide "a sense of personal involvement between the student and the institution," (Galusha, 1997:5) thereby addressing the solitary student syndrome, that is, the problem of alienation and isolation which may affect many distance students (Huang, 2002; Spitzer, 1998).

As a community platform, Fronter offers social support and encourages both productivity and commitment. The different kinds of communicative activities available via Fronter are examples of what Nipper (1989:63) identifies as the "third generation" of distance education, characterized by the use of computer-mediated communication technology, which "enables greater communication with learners and among learners." (Harry and Khan, 2000:124)

4.2. Lectures

The courses in the distance MA program are run as series of lectures complemented by seminars (see section 4.3). Each lecture consists of a PowerPoint presentation with audio recording, varying in length from 20-45 minutes. Students can download the lectures from Fronter once they are made available, which is normally two to three weeks before the teacher-led seminar. The PowerPoint lectures can be controlled entirely by the student. They can be stopped and re-started at any time, and any part of the lecture can be replayed as often as the student likes. The audio recording lets the students hear their teachers' voices, which personalizes the experience and, in the case of the VNU students, provides training in aural proficiency and exposure to native-speaker English.

Lecture viewing is not time-tabled, nor is it possible to enforce viewing. Instead, the lecture phase of the program courses awards the students control over their own studies, determining for themselves how, when, and how often they want to view the lecture. In this way, the program encourages autonomy, vital to the development of the students as individuals and critical to their success in distance education (Beers Fägersten, 2008; McBride and Beers Fägersten, 2008).

4.3. Pre-Seminars and Seminars

In addition to PowerPoint lectures, the distance MA program courses are designed to include a schedule of pre-seminars and seminars. Pre-seminars are student-led meetings, attended only by members of cohort sub-groups. They are conducted as text chats, using Skype, and are required to last between 60 and 90 minutes. Before the pre-seminar, the students are to view the lecture individually and on their own time. During the pre-seminar, the students work together to complete an assignment based on the lecture, which generally consists of application of theory to linguistic data. Group work has been shown to have pedagogical value (Bhattacharya and Chatterjee, 2000; Long and Porter, 1985; Shaban and Head, 2003) and places learning in a social context (Vygotsky, 1978). Long and Porter (1985) also suggest pedagogical arguments for the use of group work in second language learning; this can certainly be applied to the VNU students as speakers of English as a foreign language. Group work has furthermore been found to be conducive to collaborative learning (Apple, 2006; Huang, 2002; Kitade, 2000), an important principle of social constructivism, where learning is viewed as a natural outcome of negotiation and interaction with other people (Bonk and Cunningham, 1998; Jonassen, 1994; Petraglia, 1998).

At the end of each pre-seminar, one student saves the entire chatlog and then uploads it onto Fronter. Once the chatlog is available on Fronter, both the teacher and the students can access it to review the discussion. The students' work, ideas, and pre-seminar discussions are then developed further in the teacher-led seminars. Timetabled by the teaching staff, the teacher-led seminars are conducted using text chat via Skype and attended by individual cohort sub-groups. The seminars allow the teachers a chance to comment on the pre-seminar chatlog, not just in terms of addressing student questions and concerns, but also by confirming or correcting answers, discussing individual student's ideas and opinions, and giving praise or positive feedback.

The distance courses in the MA program were initially conceptualized as a series of synchronous, online, voice-chat seminars, but text chat was later introduced to complement voice chat, and eventually replaced it entirely due to limited connectivity between the students' homes or workplaces and the campus in Sweden. The program-wide adoption of the text-chat format has entailed added benefits to teaching and learning. First, text chat can be beneficial to students communicating in a foreign language in that the text-chat environment minimizes inhibition. In their study of classroom and online interaction, Hudson & Brockman (2002) identified inhibition as an obstacle to participation in the foreign language setting. The text-chat environment, however, has been shown to minimize inhibition and increase student participation (Hudson and Brockman, 2003; Roed, 2003; Suler, 2004; Warschauer, 1996).

Second, chat frequently results in more equitable participation. Students who are quiet during face-to-face classes tend to produce more in chat (Beauvois, 1992; Bump, 1990; Kern, 1995; Warschauer, 1996), and students in general have been found to take greater initiatives to communicate in chat (Beauvois, 1992; Chun, 1994; Darhower, 2002; Deusen-Scholl et al, 2005; Kern, 1995). Given the increased number of student turns in the online environment, as compared to the classroom environment in which student turns may be fewer due to teacher dominance, text chat represents a form of interaction which can be characterized as "egalitarian participation" (Hudson & Bruckman, 2002:121).

Third, the text-chat format produces a written record of both pre-seminar and seminar activity. Turoff et al (in Howard et al, 2003) note that, particularly in advanced level courses with "high pragmatic content [...], students are required to utilize problem-solving approaches to evaluate the tradeoffs between conflicting objectives. [...] Reviewing the transcripts of class discussions can provide insight into the approaches students are taking to master the material." (p. 2) During pre-seminars, students collaborate in a type of collective scaffolding (Donato, 1994). This, in turn, prepares them for the application of knowledge and independent participation in teacher-led seminars, where they will receive feedback on their performance. For this reason, the seminars are of particular importance to the VNU students, who see their teachers as ultimate authority figures. As representatives of expert knowledge, teachers have much to offer through their presence –real or implied– in chat sessions, particulary in the foreign language setting (Ene et al., 2005; Goertler, 2006).

The students look forward to the seminars as opportunities for social contact with their teachers and a chance to be acknowledged and appraised (Beers Fägersten, 2008; McBride and Beers Fägersten, 2008). This regular contact between the teacher and the students in the seminars serves to remedy the problem of the "perceived lack of feedback or contact with the teacher" (Galusha, 1997:4) that many distance students may experience.

Both the pre-seminars and seminars create and maintain a link between the teacher and students. The recording of the chatlogs awards the teacher a pseudo-presence in the pre-seminars, and students are therefore more likely to engage in discussions which are meaningful and useful. The seminars render teacher presence more salient, reflecting "overt institutional efforts" (Galusha, 1997:4) to re-establish the link that the separation of students and teacher imposes on distance education programs (Keegan, 1986). Even if students are encouraged to learn from each other in the pre-seminars, the subsequent teacher-led seminars ensure that they are not made responsible for teaching each other.

The lack of student support with regards to academic planners and tutors which Galusha (1997) identifies as one of the five barriers to success in distance education is addressed by the combination of individual lecture viewing, student-scheduled pre-seminars and staff-scheduled seminars in the distance program course design. The three phases offer the students flexibility in and control over their studies while assuring a steady progression via deadlines and time-tabled meetings. Although proper tutors are not involved in the program, the inclusion of pre-seminars gives students the chance to meet in a socially embedded context, and learn from each other in a supportive environment. Questions and uncertainties can be aired during these sessions, and students can either receive answers and explanations from their fellow students, or find company among others with similar concerns. Seminars ensure that students have regular contact with the teacher, receive feedback on their work, and, ultimately, achieve an understanding of the course content.

5. DISCUSSION

The creation and initial broad design of Högskolan Dalarna's distance MA program in English Linguistics for students of the Faculty of Education at Vietnam National University were primarily influenced by organizational and administrative concerns, which ultimately affected a number of standard program features. The most influential factor of the program, however, has been the target group of students, whose rather homogenous composition has encouraged a learner-centered approach to specific program and course design. The Vietnamese students all share the same culture and educational background, and they all have similar goals with regards to enrolling in the MA program. The design of the program reflects a conscious effort to acknowledge and accommodate the VNU students in terms of their educational backgrounds, professional goals, and, significantly, their culture.

A noteworthy feature of East Asian cultures is their tendency towards a collectivist orientation (Brislin, 1993; Hofstede, 1991; Smith and Bond, 1993; Triandis, 1995). Whereas individualists focus on self-actualization, a feature associated with Western cultures, collectivists tend to see themselves as members of a group and prioritize group needs before their own (Littlewood, 1999). Collectivist cultures are typically composed of members who more often exhibit interdependent than independent behavior, such as conforming to group opinion, supporting group goals, cooperating with group members, respecting social status differences, and preserving face (Markus and Kitayama, 1991). East Asians tend to perceive themselves as interdependent.

In a cautiously general characterization, the Vietnamese culture and people can be said to exhibit collectivist orientation and interdependent tendencies (see Jamieson, 1993; Kramsch and Sullivan, 1996). This is perhaps an even more reliable statement in the context of education, where students are expected to work together and help each other. In their study of English language teaching in Vietnam, Kramsch and Sullivan (1996) identify the notion of 'classroom-as-family' as one of three defining aspects of Vietnamese educational culture:

[S]tudents are placed into classes of approximately twenty or thirty when they enter the university. Members of these classes often live, study, and play together. The associations students form are more akin to Western notions of 'family' than 'classmate'. In many cases students in the same class will continue close relationships throughout their lives, forming ties that encompass financial, familial, and social obligations (p. 203).

The VNU students of Högskolan Dalarna's distance MA program could be similarly described. Each cohort consists of approximately 25 students, who, throughout the course of the two-year program, spend a significant amount of time interacting. During this time, classmate relationships can become friendships, and group membership indeed takes on aspects of belonging to a family. The VNU students do not, however, live together, and only seldom do they meet face-to-face. Furthermore, the majority of communication, in particular the synchronous chatting, takes place only among sub-group members. As participants in a distance program, the students receive no regular, face-to-face interaction within their cohort or even sub-group. The distance format can therefore represent a challenge or even a threat to Asian collectivist orientation or student interdependence. The learner-centered design of Högskolan Dalarna's distance MA program reflects a prioritizing of a culture of groups and a learning community specifically to minimize this risk. The program is designed to foster a learning community composed of students who are academically equal and trained to participate actively in the Web-based environment. As a whole, the program reflects an effort to maximize the chances for communication, thereby avoiding the imposition of a Western individualist orientation, and preventing students from feeling isolated. Different technologies are incorporated into course design, facilitating interaction, collaborative learning, and group work.

Interestingly, it has been observed that Vietnamese students prefer to act as members of one large group rather than be divided into smaller groups, which can "be divisive and inhibit learning." (Kramsch and Sullivan, 1996:203) This kind of sub-grouping, however, seems to refer to in-class grouping, which can be more conspicuous and thus more disruptive than in distance education. In the case of Högskolan Dalarna's MA program, meaningful communication, for example interaction via text chat, would be nearly impossible to accomplish if it were to include entire cohorts. The sub-groups furthermore enable a greater amount of participation by each student, without necessarily compromising the collectivist orientation. Collectivism and interdependence are acknowledged via collaborative learning and student teamwork – both of which were identified in studies by Hiltz (1994) and Hiltz and Wellman (1997) as features of the educational methodology which most significantly contributed to eblishing distance education as "good as or better than face-to-face courses." (Turoff et al, in Howard et al, 2003:3)

Course and program evaluations from the Vietnamese students enrolled in Högskolan Dalarna's Master's of English Linguistics program reveal two significant strengths of the program design: availability of materials, and accessibility of staff. The orientation towards Web-based course administration prioritizes availability and accessibility. In terms of course materials, it is a general rule of the Master's in English Linguistics degree program that only electronic books and articles accessible through the university library (e-brary) be assigned as course literature. Furthermore, course syllabi, handouts, lectures, feedback, and administrative materials are all provided in electronic form, assuring availability as well as convenience to all students. Having such materials available online increases student autonomy while (ideally) reducing the amount of administrative contact with teachers or other staff.

The Web-based administration of the program in general provides for reliable communication between students and teachers or staff via the establishment of asynchronous communication as the standard, out-of-class communication type. The expectation of immediate contact with staff or with teachers outside of seminar sessions is minimized due to the extensive use of asynchronous communication on course forums, bulletin boards, or in email exchanges. Whereas the possibility of traditional, face-to-face meetings is extremely limited or non-existent for distance students, Web-based, asynchronous communication allows for mutually convenient accessibility among students and staff. Students have expressed great satisfaction with the accessibility of their teachers via asynchronous communication.

It is important to consider, however, that although the immediacy and proximity of face-to-face communication can be compromised or even excluded by the distance design, a certain degree of promptness in interaction response is generally expected by students. It is therefore recommended that measures be taken to temper these expectations accordingly, as teachers may find themselves with an unreasonable amount of communication to maintain in the wake of the impression of constant accessibility, emerging as a by-product of the distance program design.

In the case of the distance degree program run by Högskolan Dalarna in cooperation with Vietnam National University, the preference for intense student-teacher contact often resulted in a high amount of teacher-directed communicative efforts among the students. It is not surprising, therefore, that the evaluations have revealed one consistently identified disadvantage to the program design, the small amount of face-to-face, student-teacher contact. While the strategies employed to cultivate a Web-based, interactive learning community among the students have succeeded insofar as they have been acknowledged as benefiting the collective efforts of the group, the students of the program do not feel that the nature of the contact they have with their teachers benefits their professional development as teachers themselves. The general consensus among the Vietnamese students is that it is only the on-site visits at the beginning and end of each term which award them the opportunity to observe Western teaching techniques, which is of particular interest to them in their professional development. In the end, the degree program was delivered as a Web-based program to enable communication and education across a great geographical distance. The importance of face-to-face contact and even the form and quality of ersatz communication modes should be critically evaluated before committing to a distance program.

6. CONCLUSION

When considering distance education, there is a tendency to problematize it. This is mostly due to an equally prevalent tendency to compare distance education to campus-based education, especially from the perspective that sees the latter as the superior form of learning. Some research suggests, however, that in terms of effectiveness, distance education rivals traditional classroom-based programs. Specifically, the use of resources and technologies in distance courses creates a learning environment that is not possible to achieve in the classroom (Turoff et al, in Howard et al, 2003). As for the student experience,

[P]eople usually assume that students in distance education programs are at a disadvantage. On the contrary, it is probably not the distance student who is disadvantaged, but rather many face-to-face students. Learning is enhanced by the physical and social technologies typically used in distance education. Students in distance programs have access to tools that allow them to repeat lectures and interact with their fellow students and faculty. Contrast these students with a student sitting in a 500 student lecture. Which student is most at a distance? (Turoff et al, in Howard et al, 2003:2)

Obviously, not every campus course is designed as a 500-student lecture, just as not every distance course is effectively enhanced by physical and social technologies. For educators and researchers, it is important to resist the futile exercise of comparing the best of one form of education with the worst of the other.

Distance education should instead be acknowledged as another valid form of education, equally subject to scrutiny, with the goal of identifying and developing ways to make it more effective. This case study of Högskolan Dalarna's distance MA program in English Linguistics represents an effort to contribute to the improvement of current distance education programs and encourage the development of future ones. As the number of distance education programs increases, educational systems are evolving from being teacher-centered to technology-centered (Strauss, 2002). The further shift to learner-centered programs is currently being promoted and practiced, particularly in distance programs: "Ultimately, education needs to become learner-centric, using the teachers and technology to unleash students' natural desire for knowledge" (Beck & Schomack, in Howard et al, 2003:121). Högskolan Dalarna's MA degree in English Linguistics in cooperation with Vietnam National University reflects a learner-centered approach to education, in order to acknowledge and mitigate the plethora of challenges the Vietnamese students might face as participants in the program. These challenges include, among others, an unfamiliarity with distance education, the use of English as a foreign language, and, most significantly, cultural differences. The distance format can be effectively exploited to overcome such challenges and ultimately enable successful intercultural education.

REFERENCES

Abrams, Z. I. (2003). The effect of synchronous and asynchronous CMC on oral performance in German. *Modern Language Journal*, *87*(2), 157–167. doi:10.1111/1540-4781.00184.

Apple, M. (2006). Language learning theories and cooperative learning techniques in the EFL classroom. *Doshisha Studies in Language and Culture*, 9(2), 277–301.

Beauvois, M. H. (1992). Computer-assisted classroom discussion in the foreign language classroom: Conversation in slow motion. *Foreign Language Annals*, 25, 455–464. doi:10.1111/j.1944-9720.1992.tb01128.x.

Beck, C., & Schornack, G. R. (2003). Theory and practice for distance education: A heuristic model for the virtual classroom. In Howard, C., Schenk, K., & Discenza, R. (Eds.), *Distance Learning and University Effectiveness: Changing Education Paradigms for Online Learning* (pp. 119–143). Hershey, PA: Information Science Pub. doi:10.4018/978-1-59140-178-0.ch006.

Beers Fägersten, K. (2008). Discourse strategies and power roles in student-led distance learning. *Proceedings of Identity and Power in the Language Classroom*, 15(2), 11–24.

Bhattacharya, M., & Chatterjee, R. (2000). Collaborative innovation as a process for cognitive development. *Journal of Interactive Learning Research*, 11(3), 295–312.

Bonk, C. J., & Cunningham, D. J. (1998). Searching for learner-centered, constructivist, and sociocultural components of collaborative educational learning tools. In Bonk, C. J., & King, K. S. (Eds.), *Electronic Collaborators: Learner-centered Technologies for Literacy, Apprenticeship, and Discourse* (pp. 25–50). Mahwah, NJ: Erlbaum.

Brislin, R. (1993). *Understanding culture's influence on behavior*. Orlando, FL: Harcourt Brace.

Bump, J. (1990). Radical changes in class discussion using networked computers. *Computers and the Humanities*, 24, 49–65. doi:10.1007/BF00115028.

Chun, D. (1994). Using computer networking to facilitate the acquisition of interactive competence. *System*, 22(1), 17–31. doi:10.1016/0346-251X(94)90037-X.

Compeau, D. R., & Higgins, C. A. (1995). Computer self-efficacy: Development of a measure and initial test. *Management Information Systems Quarterly*, 19(2), 189–211. doi:10.2307/249688.

Darhower, M. (2002). Instructional features of synchronous computer-mediated communication in the intermediate L2 class: A sociocultural case study. *CALICO Journal*, 19(2), 249–278.

Davis, F. D., Bagozzi, R. P., & Warshaw, P. R. (1989). User acceptance of computer technology: A comparison of two theoretical models. *Management Science, 35*, 982–1003. doi:10.1287/mnsc.35.8.982.

Deusen-Scholl, N. V., Frei, C., & Dixon, E. (2005). Coconstructing learning: The dynamic nature of foreign language pedagogy in a CMC environment. *CALICO Journal, 22*(3), 657–678.

Donato, R. (1994). Collective scaffolding in second language learning. In Lantolf, J. P., & Appel, G. (Eds.), *Vygotskian Approach to Second Language Research* (pp. 33–56). Norwood, NJ: Ablex Publishing Corporation.

Ene, E., Goertler, S., & McBride, K. (2005). Teacher participation styles in FL chats and their effect on student behavior. *CALICO Journal, 23*(3), 603–634.

Galusha, J. M. (1997). *Barriers to learning in distance education.* Retrieved from http://www.infrastruction.com/barriers.htm

Goertler, S. (2006). *Teacher participation and feedback styles during classroom synchronous computer-mediated communication in intermediate German: A multiple case study.* (Unpublished doctoral dissertation). University of Arizona, Tucson, AZ.

Gumperz, J. (1971). *Language in social groups.* Stanford, CT: Stanford University Press.

Gumperz, J. (1972). The speech community. In Giglioli, P. (Ed.), *Language and Social Context* (pp. 219–231). New York: Penguin.

Harry, K., & Khan, A. (2000). The use of technologies in basic education. In C. Yates & J. Bradley (Eds.), Basic Education at a Distance. Vancouver, Canada: Commonwealth of Learning and Routledge Falmer.

Hiltz, S. R. (1994). *The virtual classroom: Learning without limits via computer networks.* Norwood, NJ: Ablex.

Hiltz, S. R., & Wellman, B. (1997). Asynchronous learning networks as a virtual classroom. *Communications of the ACM, 40*(9), 44–49. doi:10.1145/260750.260764.

Hofstede, G. (1991). *Cultures and organizations: Software of the mind.* London: McGraw Hill.

Howard, C., Schenk, K., & Discenza, R. (Eds.). (2003). *Distance learning and university effectiveness: Changing educational paradigms for online learning.* Hershey, PA: Idea Group Inc. doi:10.4018/978-1-59140-178-0.

Huang, H. (2002). Toward constructivism for adult learners in online learning environments. *British Journal of Educational Technology, 33*(1), 27–37. doi:10.1111/1467-8535.00236.

Hudson, J., & Brockman, A. (2002). IRC Francais: The creation of an internet-based SLA community. *Computer Assisted Language Learning, 15*(2), 109–134. doi:10.1076/call.15.2.109.8197.

Hymes, D. (1972). Models of the interaction of language and social life. In Gumperz, J., & Hymes, D. (Eds.), *Directions in sociolinguistics: The ethnography of communication* (pp. 35–71). London: Blackwell.

Jamieson, N. (1993). *Understanding Vietnam.* Berkeley, CA: University of California Press.

Jonassen, D. (1994, March/April). Thinking technology: Toward a constructivist design model. *Educational Technology,* 34–37.

Keegan, D. (1986). *The foundations of distance education.* London: Croom Helm. Retrieved from HTTP://www.csu.edu.au/division/oli/oli-rd/occpap17/design.htm

Kern, R. (1995). Restructuring classroom interaction with networked computers: Effects on quantity and characteristics of language production. *Modern Language Journal, 79*(4), 457–476. doi:10.1111/j.1540-4781.1995.tb05445.x.

Kirkman, B. L., Rosen, B., Gibson, C. B., Tesluk, P. E., & McPherson, S. O. (2002). Five challenges to virtual team success: Lessons from Sabre, Inc. *The Academy of Management Executive, 16*(3), 67–79. doi:10.5465/AME.2002.8540322.

Kitade, K. (2000). L2 learners' discourse and SLA theories in CMC: Collaborative interaction in internet chat. *Computer Assisted Language Learning, 13*(2), 143–166. doi:10.1076/0958-8221(200004)13:2;1-D;FT143.

Knapper, C. (1988). Lifelong learning and distance education. *American Journal of Distance Education, 2*(1), 63–72. doi:10.1080/08923648809526609.

Kramsch, C., & Sullivan, P. (1996). Appropriate pedagogy. *ELT Journal, 50*(3), 199–212. doi:10.1093/elt/50.3.199.

Littlewood, W. (1999). Defining and developing autonomy in East Asian contexts. *Applied Linguistics, 20*(1), 71–94. doi:10.1093/applin/20.1.71.

Long, M., & Porter, P. (1985). Group work, interlanguage talk, and second language learning. *TESOL Quarterly, 19*(2), 207–228. doi:10.2307/3586827.

Markus, H., & Kitayama, S. (1991). Culture and the self: Implications for cognition, emotion and motivation. *Psychological Review, 98*(2), 224–253. doi:10.1037/0033-295X.98.2.224.

McBride, K., & Beers Fägersten. (2008). The students' role in distance learning. In S. Goertler & P. Winke (Eds.), *Opening Doors through Distance Learning Education: Principles, Perspectives and Practices* (pp. 43-66). San Marcos, TX: CALICO.

Meacham, D., & Evans. (1989). *Distance education: The design of study materials.* Wagga Wagga, New Zealand: Open Learning Institute, Charles Sturt University.

Nipper, S. (1989). Third generation distance learning and computer conferencing. In R. Mason & A. Kaye (Eds.), *Mindweave: Communication, Computers and Distance Education.* Oxford, UK: Pergamon Press. Retrieved from HTTP: http://www-icdl.open.ac.uk/mindweave/chap5.html/

Petraglia, J. (1998). The real world on a short leash: The (mis)application of constructivism to the design of educational technology. *Educational Technology Research and Development, 46*(3), 53–65. doi:10.1007/BF02299761.

Roed, J. (2003). Language learner behaviour in a virtual environment. *Computer Assisted Language Learning, 16*(2-3), 155–172. doi:10.1076/call.16.2.155.15880.

Sanders, R. (2006). A comparison of chat room productivity: In-class versus out-of-class. *CALICO Journal, 24*(1), 59–76.

Schamber, L. (1988). *Delivery systems for distance education.* (ERIC Document Reproduction Service No. ED 304 111).

Shaban, S., & Head, C. (2003). E-learning classroom environment: Description, objectives, considerations and example implementation. *International Journal on E-Learning, 2*(3), 29–35.

Sherry, L. (1996). Issues in distance learning. *International Journal of Educational Telecommunications, 1*(4), 337–365.

Shneiderman, B. (1992). *Designing the user interface.* Reading, MA: Addison-Wesley.

Smith, P. B., & Bond, M. H. (1993). *Social psychology across cultures.* Hemel Hempstead, UK: Harvester.

Strauss, H. (2002). New learning spaces: Smart learners, not smart classrooms. *Syllabus, 16*(2), 13.

Suler, J. (2004). The online disinhibition effect. *Cyberpsychology & Behavior, 7,* 321–326. doi:10.1089/1094931041291295 PMID:15257832.

Tallent-Runnels, M.K., Thomas, J. A., Lan, W. Y., & Cooper, S. (2006). Teaching courses online: A review of the research. *Review of Educational Research Spring, 76*(1), 93–135.

Tinto, V. (1975). Dropout from higher education: A theoretical synthesis of recent research. *Review of Educational Research, 45*(1), 89–129. doi:10.3102/00346543045001089.

Triandis, H. C. (1995). *Individualism and collectivism*. Boulder, CO: Westview.

Turoff, M., Discenza, R., & Howard, C. (2004). How distance programs will affect students, courses, faculty, and institutional futures. In Howard, C., Schenk, K., & Discenza, R. (Eds.), *Distance Learning and University Effectiveness: Changing Education Paradigms for Online Learning* (pp. 1–20). Hershey, PA: Information Science Publishing. doi:10.4018/978-1-59140-178-0.ch001.

Vygotsky, L. (1978). *Mind in society*. Boston: Harvard University Press.

Warschauer, M. (1996). Comparing face-to-face and electronic discussion in the second language classroom. *CALICO Journal, 13*(2-3), 7–25.

Webster, J., & Hackley, P. (1997). Teaching effectiveness in technology-mediated distance learning. *Academy of Management Journal, 40*(6), 1282–1309. doi:10.2307/257034.

Zoltan, E., & Chapanis, A. (1982). What do professional persons think about computers? *Behaviour & Information Technology, 1*, 55–68. doi:10.1080/01449298208914436.

ENDNOTES

[1]   In this chapter, the term distance education is used in a general sense and includes the concepts of online courses and Web-based instruction. For a discussion of the different methodologies associated with each of these terms, see Tallent-Runnels et al. (2006).

Chapter 10

Implementation of Scholarship of Teaching and Learning through an On-Line Masters Program

Klara Bolander Laksov
Karolinska Institutet, Sweden

Charlotte Silén
Karolinska Institutet, Sweden

Lena Engqvist Boman
Karolinska Institutet, Sweden

EXECUTIVE SUMMARY

In this case, the introductory course in an international masters program in medical education (MMedEd) called "Scholarship of Medical Education" is described. Some of the background to why the MMedEd was started and the underlying ideas and principles of the program are provided. The individual course, which consists of 10 weeks part time study on-line with an introductory face to face meeting, is described in terms of the intentions and pedagogical principles underlying the design, the teaching and learning activities, and how the students were supported to achieve the intended learning activities, as well as the challenges and concerns that arose throughout and after the course. Finally, some solutions to these problems are discussed.

DOI: 10.4018/978-1-4666-4486-1.ch010

ORGANIZATION BACKGROUND

Centre for Medical Education

This course was set in a medical university, Karolinska Institutet, in Sweden, and provided by the Centre for Medical Education there. The university is a research intensive university which is internationally famous and provides undergraduate educational programs as well as postgraduate education. Within the University our centre is organized as a part of a department. Our centre has four main tasks. One task concerns the provision of teacher training courses for lecturers and PhD students involved in undergraduate teaching to create a scholarship of teaching and learning (see explanation in the next paragraph). The second task concerns the strategic work in relation to the university, where we are trying to apply our knowledge of Higher Education literature and research in the support of teachers, committees and boards in the strive to enhance the student learning experience. The third task regards researching the area of medical education in terms of student learning in different medical education contexts, professional development and the use of technology to support teaching and learning. The fourth area is handling issues of evaluation within the university context. The development of a Masters Program in Medical Education was intended as a way to provide an extended competency development for lecturers and health professions staff involved in the teaching and learning of students at different levels as well as patients to develop a scholarship of teaching and learning, which is described below, and to provide a basis for people who would like to engage in research of medical education.

A concept that has become central to the activities of our centre is the pursuit of Scholarship of Teaching and Learning. The concept, that was introduced by Boyer (1990), takes as its point of departure the on-going conflict between research and teaching that has become prevalent during the 20th century at Higher Education institutions all over the world. Whilst research is an activity that receives resources, rewards and recognition, teaching stands at the opposite end, leaving little to strive for in the eyes of academics (D'Andrea & Gosling, 2005). However, the concept of scholarship was introduced to overbridge this diversification so that principles of good research could be applied to the teaching and learning context in a way to make teaching recognized and rewarded, and the allocation of resources aligned with good teaching.

Scholarship of Teaching and Learning has been debated and discussed in numerous articles in higher education journals (e.g. Studies in Higher Education, Journal of Higher Education, International Journal of Academic Development). Kreber (2005) has described four different ways of understanding what a pursuit of scholarship of teaching and learning means, out of which the interpretation made by Trigwell and

Shale (Trigwell & Shale, 2004), is the one we have aligned our thinking to. In their article they suggest that scholarship can be viewed as knowledge, as practice and as learning outcomes both with students and teachers. At Our Centre these ideas have been developed into a model for how teachers and educational leaders can go about the scholarship of their own practice, as teachers and learners respectively. By investigating their own practice as teachers the aim of scholarship of teaching and learning is to create opportunities for student learning as well as learning for the individual teachers, their colleagues and the organization they work within, to enhance and develop teaching and learning practice (Trigwell & Shale, 2004). The process of being scholarly about your own practice also aims to create collaboration between teachers as well as between teachers and students. The model, which describes the scholarship process, and which can be seen in Figure 1, constitutes six different activities which together are intended to aim for the enhancement of the student learning experience. The activities are not intended to be carried out in a linear way. Instead the practitioner (teacher or student) is encouraged to go back and forth between them. For instance, a teacher who is concerned about whether or not students actually understand the metabolism will look into her practice by *investigating* the design of learning activities, how well they work to promote student learning, *document* students' understandings, *explore existing knowledge* of e.g. how students understandings of the metabolism differ, by asking colleagues and perhaps search for articles in relevant journals, *develop* the teaching and learning activities and assessment so that they are aligned according to what was found, *make public and/or share* her work in written or oral form for instance in a course meeting or at a local educational conference and seek *peer review* to elaborate the design even further.

Figure 1. Scholarship-model as developed by the centre for medical education. Grafik: Mattias Karlén.

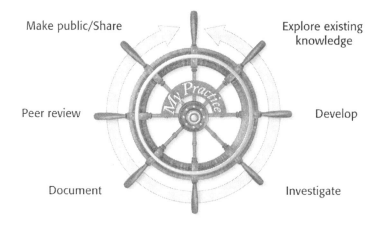

Our Centre for Medical Education has existed for almost ten years in its current form and has grown in terms of staff from four fully employed educational developers and researchers, to twenty individuals whose work commitments range between the three tasks of our centre.

Our Centre is lead by a director and a co-director, who both have academic expertise in the field of medical education, which is described in Box 1. The budget of our centre comes from three different sources, centrally from the University, a) money that is 'top-sliced' from each department in relation to the number of undergraduate students, b) money earned through consultancy in relation to individuals, groups, committees etc. mostly from within the university and c) external funding for (research) projects.

Setting the Stage for a Masters program

Already in 2003, the idea for creating a MMedEd was discussed. It was not, however, until 2006, when the actual work to start it was initiated by one of the authors together with other colleagues within the department. After constructing an idea document, the Dean of Education was invited in 2007 to a discussion of the strategic value for the University of supporting such an initiative. The Dean was very enthusiastic and suggested for us to outline a formal proposal to the Board of Education.

In 2007 a proposal was formulated where our aim was to start the program in the academic year of 2009-2010. We needed to suggest selection criteria for applicants, start negotiating with possible course directors, decide how to market the course, define reference groups and start thinking about delivery. At the first instance we

Box 1. Description of the main field of study : Medical education

Medical education is an interdisciplinary field of knowledge which is based on explanatory bases and perspectives from both care sciences and behavioural sciences, particularly pedagogy but also psychology, sociology and social anthropology.

Within the field of medical education, students study learning processes, conditions for learning and professional development within medical care and health care. This involves students developing knowledge about the conditions, strategies and methods for encouraging, influencing and driving forwards learning processes. This would then lead to positive and appropriate development for students, academics, professional practitioners and patients. Studies within medical education cover individual and system levels, both within academia and within health and medical care

Studies within the main field of study enable students to work to develop a scientific attitude towards individual practice, including investigations, change work and publishing results, which can be summarized as scholarship of medical education. The growing understanding of the conditions for learning within medical care and health care can be used to improve conditions for professional development and to make good use of resources, leading to the overall objective of quality care and improved human health.

Studying medical education can be used to improve the quality of learning, supervision and practice within care, particularly in terms of integration between disciplines, theory and practice, patient interaction, cooperation with management, attitudes, ethics and a scientific approach.

were imagining a mixed delivery program with both on-campus modules and on-line modules, but after some careful consideration of whom the target group was – individuals involved in teaching in health sciences professions world wide – we decided for an on-line approach. We constructed three reference groups, one local, with teacher representatives from the University, one national, with educational developers from all over Sweden, and one international, consisting of international experts from within the field of medical education. During the years of 2007-2009 these groups were consulted mainly by email and in face-to-face meetings. The feedback received strengthened the group in terms of being on the right track.

In the preparation of our proposal, we also looked into International MMedEds that were at the top, from universities like the Universities in Sydney, Dundee, Maastricht, Harvard and McMaster in Canada. Our intention was also to make future participants opt for two different tracks, that of a Diploma and that of a Masters degree. However, in the end it turned out to be against the national regulations to do within the same program.

The Aim and Target Groups

The aim for our MMedEd was initially to support practitioners in health professions to develop scholarship of teaching and learning and hence to over bridge their didactic skill with research. This aim was later developed into *providing advanced education in strategies and methods that can stimulate and guide the learning processes of students, academics, professionals and patients*. Initially, the target group was students with an undergraduate degree who would like to become researchers in medical education, and teachers with an undergraduate degree and a position within the university with responsibilities that can influence the student learning experience. However, after discussion with the reference groups and considering the aim for participants to work scholarly with their own practice, the entering requirements were changed to include work experience in either education or in the health care field, to be admitted to the program. The idea was to introduce the program as an international MMedEd, and therefore recruit participants both from the local, Nordic and international arena.

The aim was also for participants to deepen their knowledge, skills and attitudes in accordance with their individual prospects for the future. As can be seen in Figure 2, five different tracks were outlined, so that participants who wished to pursue a career in any of the areas would be attracted to the program; educational developer, academic leader, teaching and learning expert/didactic expert, and researcher in medical education. A time line was created to make sure all the obligations for putting forward the program were fulfilled.

Figure 2. Different tracks in the masters program in medical education

Virtual Learning Environment

The virtual learning environment (VLE) that was chosen was really not a choice, since the University already had bought into this platform for all their on-line courses and modules. This platform, which is called Ping Pong (www.Ping Pong.se), is a Web-based system for the administration and production of educational activities, with most of the common features:

- Web-pages
- Communication
- Discussion forum
- Link possibilities
- Collaboration in project groups
- Evaluations and tests
- Assessments
- Chat
- Learning portfolio

Some of the individuals in the project group had vast experience of the VLE, whilst others had not. The library is responsible for Internet and Communication Technology (ICT) issues at Karolinska Institutet and teachers who are interested in teaching including distance learning are encouraged to seek their advice. Hence a librarian was invited as a member of the group to give expert advice on design and functionalities. At the start, his advice was aiming at the functionalities of the VLE, but later his competence in information literacy proved very valuable, and he was asked to be in charge of the module on information literacy in the course.

Main Content and Composition of the Program

The following section outlines the content of the MMedEd and how it was divided into different courses. Box 2 illustrates the main content and the composition of the program as it was written in the syllabus.

The Process of the Program: Micro and Macro Perspectives

Figure 3 was produced to provide an overview of how the different courses of the MMedEd function as steps of a staircase, where the student by taking one step at a time, develop their knowledge, competence and attitudes in medical education. We also wanted to envisage how the emphasis moves from the perspective of the learner, via the facilitator to the leader, and that these perspectives investigate teaching and learning at a micro, as well as a macro context, i.e. that of the individual student or local learning community, to that of the full organization and how different systems interact with each other. The metaphor of the door, as pictured in figure 4, is used to describe how the course which provides the case for this chapter, tried to introduce and give an overview to the micro and macro level of the context, as well as the roles of the learner, facilitator and leader.

Case description

Two of the authors (KBL + LEB) were asked to design the introductory course. This is our story of our intentions, the design and how it went.

Framing of the Course

The case presented in this book concerns the first course of the MMedEd, which had the title Scholarship of Medical Education (SoME). The reason for choosing the title had to do with the underlying expectation that course participants would develop a scholarly approach to their practice according to our interpretation of Scholarship of Teaching and Learning as has been described above. However, since our target group included individuals who possibly were not involved in the teaching and learning of university students, but also the teaching and learning of colleagues

Box 2. The program's main content and composition

The majority of the course work is carried out individually or through interaction with fellow participants and teaching staff/supervisors, online via a learning platform. A study period of a few consecutive days each term is spent at Karolinska Institutet. A variety of working methods is used, such as seminars, discussions, presentations, self assessment, peer assessment and supervision work by teaching staff.

Overview lectures are provided, along with links to course literature via a proxy server. Participants' experience and theoretical knowledge are put into practice within the individual's work place. Participation in the programme requires active work on development projects to be performed in the learning environment of each individual's work place.

The study programme is arranged around four themes with the education being based on students' own experiences of – and questions relating to – these themes:

1. Learning processes within medical and health care from a system perspective

   The medical university and health and medical care are explored as contexts and cultures in relation to education, learning and research. There is a particular focus on interprofessional education. System factors such as objectives, frameworks, regulations and conditions for change are analysed. Attention is paid to learning processes at micro to macro levels, in relation to students, teachers, managers, professionals and patients, and the relationships between these levels.

2. Learning processes from an individual perspective

   Theories about learning such as motivation, memory, comprehension, construction of understanding, meaningful learning and meta cognitive processes are studied. There is an emphasis on developing independent learning, information skills, a critical approach and the ability to integrate theory with practice. Central to the programme is the way in which learning situations can be planned and assessed within different contexts in order to encourage and facilitate learning based on pedagogical theories, proven experience and the use of technology. Learning processes arise in a variety of contexts, in relationships between teachers and students, between clinicians and patients, and between colleagues with differing levels of experience.

3. Developing a meta perspective of learning

   There is a focus on investigating, reviewing and evaluating education and learning processes within the field of medical education. A range of paradigms, research initiatives and methods are studied, analysed and applied. The ability to communicate, express oneself and reason in terms of medical education issues and problems with different target groups will be practised in writing, orally and using other media. The personal development process is monitored and documented using the portfolio method, and is related to developing scholarship in medical education.

4. Managing development

   Theories relating to development, change and improvement processes are studied. The programme focuses on the content and development of a strategic pedagogical level within medical academic contexts, as well as skills development and learning processes for teachers and educational managers. Conditions and forms for collaboration in relation to learning and development are key elements of this theme. Particular attention is paid to awareness of and learning for a changing future.

These four themes are addressed with different focuses within the programme's various courses. The content is integrated into the courses, and a number of the themes recur during several of the courses. All themes are introduced and dealt with to a certain degree during the first half of the programme. There are opportunities to study certain fields, based on individual interests, within the framework of the courses.

Throughout the programme, participants use the portfolio method, both to reflect on their own progress and as a basis for assessment. During the second half of the programme, students choose a more in-depth specialisation, which is reflected in both the elective courses and the degree project work. There are four main specialisations within the programme: academic management, educational development work, professional development and teaching and learning of specific disciplines. This means that, during the second year, participants carry out a research project within one of the main specialisation areas.

The programme includes elective courses corresponding to 15 higher education credits (ECTS – European Credit Transfer System). This means that students are offered one or more courses within their chosen specialisation. Independent development work is a key working method. Students can choose to carry out two degree projects corresponding to 15 and 30 ECTS each, or one comprehensive degree project for a total of 45 ECTS.

Courses included in the program 1st year:
- Scholarship of Medical Education, 7,5 ECTS
- Learning Processes, 7,5 ECTS
- Integration of theoretical and practical knowledge, 7,5 ECTS
- Design and assessment of learning, 7,5 ECTS
- Interprofessional Learning, 7,5 ECTS
- Leading Change, 7,5 ECTS
- Exam project, 15 ECTS

Courses included in the program 2nd year.
- Elective courses of 15 ECTS
- Methodology courses, 15 ECTS
- Exam project, 30 ECTS

Figure 3. Different tracks in the masters program in medical education. Grafik: Mattias Karlén

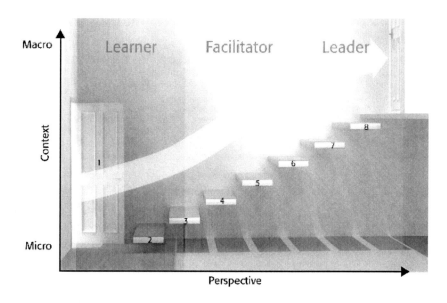

and patients, we wanted to broaden our concept of scholarship in accordance to our description of the main field of study (Box 2) to concern all teaching and learning in Medical Education, hence the term Scholarship of Medical Education.

The course ran over 10 weeks from the 3rd of September to the 8th of November. The days 23-25th of September was organized as 'On-campus days' where the participants were invited to three full days at our University. The reason for this was to get to know each other, make sure everybody got some basic skills in using the learning platform and to introduce the MMedEd as a whole. Also, there was time available for the teaching of content that we anticipated was difficult and we therefore thought would benefit from participants and teachers see each other face-to-face.

The aim of the course was

Figure 4. Time line of the course

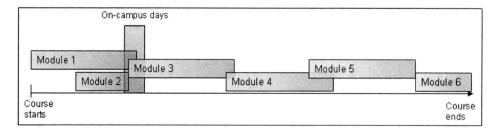

for the participants to develop a reflective approach and an understanding for how the process of scholarship as a model can be a way to support own development. By working scholarly during the terms of the course the participants will gain an understanding for how scholarship of medical education is underlying in the Masters program. By the end of the course participants should be able to:

1. *Show understanding of the concept of Scholarship of Medical Education by identifying and analysing an area of development within a specific context within university or health care practice.*
2. *Analyse teaching and learning at individual and organisational level within a specific context with a scientific approach.*
3. *Create search strategies for relevant medical educational information and be able to compare, evaluate and handle the results of different search strategies.*
4. *Analyse how system factors such as goals, regulations and praxis impact the planning process and development of a practice in university or health organisations.*
5. *Communicate results of an investigation and analysis to a relevant target group and suggest changes (From course syllabus, 2009).*

We wanted to design the course so that after having passed the course, students would have worked their way through our 'Scholarship-model' with focus on the development of an aspect of their own medical education practice. However, after discussions, we realized that 10 weeks half time would not provide enough space for getting both introduced to the full program, the VLE *and* the planning, working on and reporting on a developmental project in their own context. Hence, we concluded on an assessment task that constituted of the presentation of a plan for a project, that we called a 'mini project report'.

In Box 3 you are provided with the information that was provided at the first page for students entering the VLE of the course Scholarship of Medical Education.

In relation to our Scholarship-model, the four themes of the program and our intended learning outcomes, the course was divided into 6 modules. We decided to apply a 2-week cycle for each of the modules described in Box 3. However, as can be seen in Figure 4, when designing the content of the course, and the activities we wanted the students to carry out, some of the modules needed to be overlapping to allow for more time. Also, the overlapping had to do with how we would make good use of the on-campus days.

Box 3. Introduction to the course scholarship of medical education

Hi and welcome to the course Scholarship of Medical Education, 7,5 hp.
The course includes six different modules as you can see in the course outline. In the first module you will get an introduction to the concept of Scholarship of Medical Education and start working according to the scholarship cycle, a process that will continue throughout the course. The second module will focus on the structure, regulations processes and praxis of the organisational context medical education is influenced by. Thereafter you will learn more about how to search for evidence in the available literature to support the development of aspects of your medical education practice. In the fourth module you are introduced to the concepts 'Paradigms' and 'Epistemologies' and finally their relationship to the methodology used in Scholarship of Medical Education. Since the first five modules will support you in developing a mini project, the communication and discussion of the results of your mini project is emphasized in the last module. Assignments will be carried out for each module and will be reviewed by your peers. After revision, each assignment will contribute to the construction of a mini project report, which is presented during module six. All communication is carried out via the learning platform Ping Pong, except from the three days on campus 23-25 September 2009. We hope that you will experience a stimulating course. Please watch the introduction to the course by clicking here.
Welcome!

Intentions and Pedagogical Principles Underlying the Course Design

In the following section we have outlined the principles that informed our course design in terms of the context (on line learning, medical education context and the importance of linking new knowledge to the local context), based in current theory on how we learn in higher education (activating instruction, reflection as a tool for learning and peer learning), and how these impact the role of the teacher. All these principles are underpinned by our educational philosophy, which is outlined in Box 4 and describes the social constructivist view of learning (Vygotsky, 1978).

Box 4. Educational values of the course

Learners construct their knowledge in a context which is situated in a certain time and a certain place. This means that the learning of one individual never can be exactly the same as that of another individual. It requires from the learner to be active and responsible as a learner, not only for their own learning, but also for supporting the learning of their peers. Mutual respect for different perspectives is crucial in the way we communicate with each other. Emotions are always present when learning (Boud, 1995), which means that affects such as curiosity, anger, annoyance and passion, may be present at different times and impact on the learning process. By acknowledging and reflecting on feelings in learning, together we will support and use these feelings as drivers for learning and development. Learning is a challenge that moves us into a more multifaceted understanding of complex phenomena.

Studying Online

We thought that most course participants would be new to studying on-line. This meant that we needed to introduce different features of the VLE step-by-step, but also that this course would have to be stricter in directing participants to different resources and possibilities with the VLE. As teachers on-line we were not very experienced, but we had a lot of theoretical knowledge of how people learn in higher education and in distance based learning and a vast knowledge of teaching and learning processes in general, that we wanted to apply.

Linking New Knowledge to Local Context

We were aware that our participants would provide a wide range of backgrounds and prior knowledge in the field of medical education. Some would have little or no experience of the discipline, and others would be more used to the reading of research from the medical education/higher education field. However, in our criteria for selection of participants, we had required applicants to have work experience of at least 2 years, and were hoping for participants to be involved in teaching and learning processes within an organization, e.g. a university or hospital. The reason for this was for us to be able to design our courses around the principle of linking new knowledge to local context. This principle, which is based on research on student learning, and shows how important it is for learning to link new knowledge to a meaningful context (Entwistle, 1992; Gibbs, 2003; Marton *et al.*, 1996; Ramsden, 1992), was used in the design so that participants would be asked to accomplish a number of assignments where content was linked to their own context.

Activating Instruction

Underlying all courses provided at the Centre for Medical Education is the evidence for how activating instruction positively impacts the quality of learning (Biggs & Tang, 2007; Lonka & Ahola, 1995; Prosser & Trigwell, 1999). It is what students do - not what the teacher does with the subject matter - that has an effect on student learning. Each of the modules in the course was designed in relation to this principle. Also, we wanted to model different ways of activating instruction so that the participants would experience different ways of interacting with content as well as with each other, in accordance to Kolb's theory of experiential learning (1984).

Reflection as a Tool for Learning

Based on the theories of reflection (Boud *et al.*, 2001; Moon, 1999; Schön, 1987) and its importance for learning we wanted to incorporate reflective writing (Moon, 1999). Our idea was for participants to either write a learning journal, or collect samples of their work and discussions on the Web, to reflect over either triggered by us as course organizers, or individually driven. The material produced during the SoME course was thought of as a form of 'data' which the participants would be able to go back to in future courses when investigating a certain aspect of their learning or development.

Peer Learning

In everyday life we continually learn from each other (Boud *et al.*, 2001). During the MMedEd, we wanted the students to experience how their peers in the course could contribute to their learning by the provision of differing perspectives, conceptualizations and contexts. The principle of peer learning affect the role of the teachers (see under the heading 'Group work'), and forces students to make explicit their thinking and understanding. In our design of the assignments of the modules this principle meant that we needed to consider what students would need to make explicit to learn from each other.

The Role of the Teacher

We saw our role as being supervisors and organisers of learning activities as well as keeping track of individuals and their progress to be able to support by asking questions and make visible individuals who did not take so much space in the VLE. We did not intend to steer the content for the students' learning too much, however the ability to search and find relevant literature was something we anticipated the students would develop during the terms of the program. We wanted the students to see us as tutors or facilitators, and as one of many resources for their learning, which meant that we had to make the advantages of other resources viable as early as possible in the program.

Learning Activities of the Course

Different principles of supporting the learning processes of our course participants were described in the previous section. In this section the different learning activities are outlined (Biggs & Tang, 2007). By learning activities are meant such activities that are meant to result in learning and the achievement of the intended learning outcomes of the course. These can be described at different levels, from a larger unit such as studies of literature, down to what students are intended to do with that literature. Learning activities have been described in several taxonomies (e.g. Bloom, 2003; Biggs, 1996) that provide a continuum from activities with less to more cognitive load as well as smaller to higher degree of qualitative differences in learning.

Studies of Literature

The literature consisted of parts of books and articles, where those articles central for all course participants ware listed in the literature list. However, since each participant also would work on an individual mini-project, a large part of the literature was to be searched individually and discussed in smaller groups to be as relevant as possible for each individual's project. In other words the learning activities connected to the literature consisted of reading, discussing, searching, relating and applying to the individual project and reformulating ones understanding of the literature. Since this was a central part of learning to be scholarly, half a day of the on-campus days was devoted to the introduction of how to search for literature in the medical education field.

In the course two books were used as compulsory literature and 2-3 articles for each module. The literature was mainly taken from the higher education field, because of the wide scope looking at organizational as well as individual levels of context, which is to be found linked to learning and teaching, in the field of higher education.

Lectures

The aim with lectures were to introduce a theme or a module, to give a summary or overview of an area of the discipline and facilitate understanding of difficult subjects as well as promote interest in the subject area. Generally the lectures were carried out as PowerPoint presentations with audio using software called Articulate. Articulate makes it possible to produce a film of your PowerPoint slides with your voice recorded over it. Our films were between ten and twenty minutes and were streamed from a server. The learning activity connected to the lectures were listening and watching the lecture. In the lectures the role of the teacher is conventional in the way that it is the lecturer who provides the information and interpretation of the literature, something that we though could be valuable at the introductory stage of the course. However, to keep to our educational philosophy and our educational strategies of peer learning and activating instruction, the lectures were kept at a minimum of two lectures.

Group Work

We wanted the participants to experience the flexibility in time and space that on-line learning provides, but also to let them learn through the process of interaction among peers and see that this can be a very rich and fruitful way of learning. The participants therefore were divided into groups.

During the course, students were divided into groups of 5-6 individuals. Each group was assigned a tutor, whose role was to guide the students through the process of the course. To make the group work progress smoothly, roles were assigned to each group participant. These roles are described in detail in Box 5. During each module one of the group participants was supposed to act a chairperson, one as a secretary and one as something we called 'meta-tracker'. The reason for this was based on the research on Problem-Based Learning (PBL) tutoring groups (Silén & Uhlin, 2008) and also on the research by Prof Carl Bereiter and Marlene Scardamalia in Canada (Bereiter, 2002). They have developed a virtual learning environment called 'Knowledge Forum' with the core idea based on collaborative learning theory (Bereiter & Scardamalia, 2003). In their work they emphasize the participants' responsibility for advancing knowledge within the community of practice. The learning activities for the group work consisted of discussing and comparing their understanding with each other but by outlining the different roles in the group work, participants also had to synthesize the discussions that had been going on, evaluate

Box 5. Roles in group work

The chair person: The role of the chairperson is to make sure everybody in the group is involved in the discussion, by probing individuals to contribute for instance by asking specific questions such as "how does this relate to your experience John/Anne/??" or "it seems that several argue for XX, are there any other opinions?"

The secretary: At the end of each other week the secretary will go through the discussions to provide a 'Rise Above'. A Rise Above is not only a short summary of the discussion, but also a conclusion which points at further topics that can be used in later discussions. The secretary creates a new subject in the group project discussion of each module, called 'Rise Above'. 3-4 days after the module has ended, the secretary uploads the Rise Above. When the Rise Above is written and uploaded, e.g. as attachment in the subject, each group participant is invited by a PIM to comment on it in the discussion forum so that all can agree that the meaning of the discussion was captured.

The concept 'Rise Above' is taken from the theory on knowledge building that has been developed by professor Carl Bereiter and Marlene Scardamalia in Toronto, Canada.

Meta-tracker: At the end of each module each group member evaluates their own contribution to the learning process of the group. Each project group member should answer the questions 'How do you think that you have contributed to the learning of your project group during the module?' This is to be put under a new subject in the discussion forum labled 'contribution for learning' of the project group for each module. The meta- tracker makes an analysis of the development of the learning process of the group. The Meta-tracker is not intended to value the contributions, but to make the group aware of how the discussion is going, and based on own analysis and individual responses to the question (How do you think...above) suggest how the process can be developed. When the Meta-tracker analysis is written, the project group will get a pim and be invited to comment on it so that all can agree on strategies for development of the group work.

their own contributions as well as others', and based on that suggest changes – all activities that can be found at the upper scale of the taxonomies by Biggs and Bloom.

Table 1 provides an example of how the division of roles in the different groups circulated so that each student would experience each of the roles during at least one of the modules of the course.

Unfortunately, because of this course being the first course of the MMedEd, there was a major drop out of participants during the first six weeks. Drop out in on-line courses is not an unusual phenomenon and has been well known since the 1980-s (Kember, 1989).The drop-outs meant that the groups had to be reestablished over and over again, with new members having to get to know each other, and confusion regarding the roles of the individuals. We believe that those who stayed on the course could see how group roles could have worked, but also that too much energy was spent on this aspect – especially in the light of the heavy workload that participants said they were experiencing anyway.

Learning Partnerships

In addition to the project groups we wanted to create closer collaboration among individuals through the creation of 'Learning partnerships' that is described in Box 6. The idea was to be careful about the participants' time schedule, so that they did not have to always respond or give feedback to all the members of their group, but only to one or two. Learning activities involved in learning partnerships were to read and give constructive feedback. Again, since this was the first course, and there was an issue of drop out of the course during the first month, this meant that we constantly had to re-arrange the learning partnerships several times.

Table 1. Example of how the group roles circulated in relation to the modules

Module	Chairperson	Secretary	Meta-tracker
1. Introduction to Scholarship of Medical Education	All, see assignment 2	All, see assignment 2	All, see assignment 2
2. Investigation of structure, regulations, processes and praxis	Student Anna	Student Bertil	Student Cecilia
3. Information literacy	Student David	Student Emma	Student Fiona
4. Paradigm and epistemologies	Student Cecilia	Student Anna	Student Bertil
5. Methodology in Scholarship of Medical Education	Student Fiona	Student David	Student Emma
6. Communication and discussion of results	Student Bertil	Student Cecilia	Student Anna

Box 6. Learning partnerships

> Learning partnership is a way for educators to collaborate to learn and to develop their competence (Boud et al., 2001). One individual who is involved in facilitating learning will work together with somebody from a different context so that they can learn from and with each other. The aim is for the learning partners to develop knowledge and skills that are relevant for all included when it comes to support each other in professional and personal development. During the course you will get assignments where you and your learning partner will exchange and give feedback on each other's work.
>
> Below is a table with the learning partnerships. Sometimes you are made into a triad instead of a dyad. In this case you decide whether you prefer giving feedback to each other all three, or whether the first gives feedback to the second, the second to the third and the third to the first.

Structure and Process of the Course

In the course and its modules a certain structure was strived for, so that the participants would recognize the process in the different modules and for participants to know what to expect, from the course and from their peers. This was facilitated by the spelling out of the process of the course through the provision of study guides and agreed criteria for what it meant to be active in the virtual learning environment.

Study Guides

For each module, a study guide was created. In the study guide - which consisted of a grid - dates, activity and when something was to be completed by, was spelled out. This was a way to make participants get an overview of the different modules and for them to be able to note when each assignment was due. Roughly, we intended for the participants to follow the stages below:

- Individual preparation.
- Upload document to learning partner group.
- Discuss and give feedback during 4 days.
- Secretary makes summary.
- Each participant evaluate their own contribution to the learning process of the group.
- Learning group discuss in forum how to carry the level of discussions forward.
- Meta-tracker makes a summary of the development of the learning process of the group.
- Tutor gives feedback on the two summaries of learning partner groups using examples from the groups.
- Individual revision of documents towards the final assignment, the mini project report.

In this way we hoped that the participants would work continuously on their mini project report, and hence spread out the work during the course instead of getting it cramped up at the last minute before handing in.

Criteria for Activity

During the on-campus days we discussed how we create a learning community on-line, for us to apply as criteria for activity when we discussing and working in Ping Pong. Table 2 shows the suggestions from the groups and the response to these

Table 2. Negotiated criteria for activity in the virtual learning environment

	Group suggestions	Suggestion from tutors
Group A+ D	The tension between promoting activity and be a part of the process and work individually with less deadlines was raised.	Since the course is on-line, and built on principles of learning where the participant is viewed as active and a co-constructer of knowledge as well as emphasising peer learning, participation is necessary. Participation is carried out on-line in Ping Pong, it is hence required from each participant to as far as possible stick to the deadlines. The deadlines are not viewed as 'everything should be put up in Ping Pong at e.g. the 22 September, but that it should be there no later than 22 September, so preferably even earlier, so that a discussion and responses are made possible. The idea behind the course design, with deadlines every third or fourth day, is to enable the participants to discuss and contribute as well as pushing the knowledge forward.
Group B:	• Keep discussion 'flowing' • Not ok to log in on weekend first time without letting others know • Log in (ideally) every second day to contribute in discussion • Create a 'subject' in group for 'café'	If somebody gets ill or cannot contribute regularly (every other day at least) please let your tutor and your project group know, so that they don't start to wonder what is wrong. When it comes to the different roles of the discussions, the secretary's 'summary' of a discussion, as well as the meta tracker's analysis of the development of the learning process of the group is due four days later than the deadline for the discussion. A discussion forum is created for each module, where the group participants can comment on their own contribution to the learning process of the group (for more info on the roles, see in the left margin 'Scholarship in Medical Education --> Introduction --> Group work). A café discussion forum is created for the participants to be social, talk about what ever they like that does not involve course work. It lies under 'Discussion' in the left margin.
Group C:	• Everybody contributes • Formal/less formal language is ok! • Any questions are ok! • Encourage questions! • If you're running late, tell the group! • Give constructive feedback!	Because the course participants come with differing experiences and varying degree of how used they are to reading and writing about medical education issues, each participants contributes at their level with a degree of formality in language that they find comfortable with. Naturally, questions are encouraged to each other as well as to the tutors. It is always better to ask too many questions than too few! Feedback is given in relation to the 'Feedback ladder'.

suggestions from tutors that were made in the light of the discussion that followed at the on campus days. The participants were encouraged to comment on these to refine them into something that everyone in the course could agree on.

Assessment

Two individual assignments were included in the assessment. The writing and handing in of a mini-project report to be reviewed by two other course participants and finally assessed by the teacher. Each of the assignments of the modules 1-5 of the course was designed to contribute to this final individual assignment. During the modules the assignments were not assessed, but the participants got feedback on them from their tutor group and in general terms from the tutor.

As part of the last module, the students also were asked to write a reflection paper on their own scholarship process, and suggest how to develop it.

To pass the course, it was required by each participant to show activity on the learning platform Ping Pong by taking responsibility for following the agreement for level of activity that was made on the campus-based days.

Evaluation

During the terms of the course the tutors and teachers involved in facilitating student learning gathered feedback in many different ways. As a starting point level 1 and level 2 of Kirkpatrick's evaluation pyramid (Kirkpatrick, 1998) was strived for. This involves the collection of students' opinions of the different aspects of the course and their learning, and would give the course director feedback on the success of the course in a way that it would be possible to either a) adjust problems during the course or b) adjust aspects of the following course on Learning Processes.

Concerning level 1, we intended to (at least) every other week put up a survey in Ping Pong, where the students were asked to answer a few questions. The questions may be on different topics that at the moments are of concern for us and by interpreting the feedback we received from the students we hoped to be able to localize problems and be able to adjust the course. In this way it was a formative evaluation. This intention was however not fulfilled, probably due to all the other obligations that popped up during the course, and only two such evaluations were made in week 2 and after the 5th module.

Regarding level 2 of Kirkpatrick's evaluation pyramid; we wanted to constantly look into the learning processes of the participants. This was facilitated by the 'rise aboves' and the 'meta tracking analyses' that we asked the students to produce. Compared to if this course was carried out face to face, this was a lot easier because of the requirement on being explicit with your thoughts when discussing on-line in e.g. the project groups and when handing in assignments.

At the end of the course, when the final assignment was to be handed in, all participants were asked to fill out an evaluation form, which is standard for all the courses given at Karolinska Institutet. However, we added a few questions that were of interest for this specific course design and on the course content.

Teaching and Learning Activities in Relation to the Modules and the Intended Learning Outcomes

In this section, we describe the teaching and learning activities of the different modules and show how we tried to facilitate the achievement of the intended learning outcomes for the students. An overview of how the Intended Learning Outcomes (ILOs) were covered in the modules can be found in Table 3.

Module 1: Introduction to Scholarship of Medical Education

The first module was designed to introduce the concept of Scholarship and specifically aimed to support the students in achieving the intended learning outcome 1: *Show understanding of the concept of Scholarship of Medical Education by identifying and analysing an area of development within a specific context within university or health care practice.*

The concept of Scholarship of teaching and learning, as well as the broadening of the concept to include medical education, was introduced in this module in several ways. Participants were provided with an e-lecture of approximately 10 minutes where the background, the current discussion and our Centre's interpretation of SoTL was presented. As preparation for the on-campus days the students were asked to (as part of module 2) start thinking about an aspect of their educational practice that they would like to develop. The following modules of the course would help

Table 3. Modules in relation to intended learning outcomes

	ILO1	ILO2	ILO3	ILO4	ILO5
Module 1	X				
Module 2	x	X		X	
Module 3	x		X		x
Module 4	x	x		x	
Module 5	x		x		
Module 6	X	X	X	X	X

the students to get through the scholarship process and also analyse how scholarship was carried out in projects relevant to their own area of interest.

In the first learning activity of the course, the students were asked to download an article on the topic of Scholarship of teaching and learning, start reading the main course literature and write a reading log.

A reading log is intended to mirror what happens in the mind of the reader when reading. The reading log should in other words mirror the encounter that takes place between the text and the author of the text and the reader and his/her prior experiences and knowledge. A reading log can be used for further reflections and as a basis for discussions for example in seminars. You can let other comment the quotes chosen and the added thoughts in written or oral format.

During this first module of the course we were also concerned to guide the participants into good practice of being an on-line student. We wanted them to get acquainted with the learning platform Ping Pong and some of its functionalities such as uploading and downloading of documents, discussion forum and sending messages, as well as getting to know each other and the content of the course. Simultaneously we wanted them to see how reading each other's contributions could enhance their learning experience, the course participants were not only other students, but people they could learn from. This obviously stood out as a new way of learning to several students. One participant wrote in her 'contribution for learning'-statement of the module:

I start to realize that this discussion part is really important and nothing you do when you have some time over.

After one week of the course, a survey was sent out electronically by using the survey tool of the learning platform. The aim with the survey was to find out some of the prerequisites of the participants participation of the course such as how used they were to on-line teaching and learning, computer skills, available time for doing the course and how much and how often they expected to work on the course. This survey provided us with valuable information, and I think we had not anticipated that all but two participants had managed to complete the course on top of their full time jobs.

Module 2: Investigation of Structure, Regulations, Processes, and Praxis

In the second module, which only lasted one week, participants were intended to start outlining their mini project and formulate a question or a problem for investigation. The mini project was thought of as a *"core around which you will add and discuss the content of the following modules of the course."* One of the assignments of module 2 was therefore to start outlining a mini project. The mini project outline would provide the participants with a context and a target for their thinking during the on-campus days.

The learning outcome that we intended the students to start their learning process around was *ILO2 and ILO 4:*.

- Analyse teaching and learning at individual and organisational level within a specific context with a scientific approach.
- Analyse how system factors such as goals, regulations and praxis impact the planning process and development of a practice in university or health organisations.

We wanted the participants to start to investigate their own context in order to see how the carrying out of a developmental project is situated and influenced by organizational, political and cultural aspects. One afternoon in the on-campus days was devoted to this topic, and the participants were guided through a workshop, where the theory of teaching and learning regimes (Trowler & Becher, 2002) was applied as a way to analyse different aspects of their culture and the opportunities and obstacles that possibly could affect developmental work.

The main book for the course, *"Improving Teaching and Learning in Higher Education* "by D'Andrea and Gosling (2005), was used as a 'coat' for all the modules of the course. During the second module, a section on learning communities was focused, since the existence of learning communities can be seen as an aspect of the context. Learning communities may be formal and informal (D'Andrea & Gosling, 2005). The course participants were asked to reflect on what learning communities they were involved in, give examples of these, and consider whether they were really learning in, with and from these communities. Box 7 exemplifies the rise aboves created in this module. This was a rather informative and fact-based rise above. But as you can see if you compare it with the rise above in Box 9, the quality of rise above changed into becoming more and more reflective, trying to capture themes and discussions or problems that were common in the contributions into the VLE.

The reactions to the Rise above in Box 7 was spontaneous and confirmed for the author how others agreed with her description of a learning community. One participant expressed it in the following way:

It was, just as XX, with a bit of hesitation about this way of learning I started this course but this learning community really works for me!

Box 7. Rise above of one of the groups

> A learning community is defined as a group of people who share common aims and are actively engaged in learning together and from each other. Such a community could have an interdisciplinary approach. Learning communities can take different formats, such as online learning communities, clinical associations, educational committees, etc. An example of an online learning community is KI's masters program in medical education, with Ping-Pong functioning as an Internet-mediated communication-tool that addresses the learning needs of the members through proactive and collaborative learning-partnership.
>
> The concept of learning communities has become an innovative approach of learning in higher education. However, the inability of institutions to transcend a narrow view of education impacts the successful development of such communities.
>
> Learning communities may have different key focuses- some of which is to identify learning insufficiencies, to promote changes to improve teaching/learning practices, to enhance reflection, and/or to support interventions etc.

This positive expression of satisfaction was confirmed by others in their descriptions of how they thought they had contributed to the learning of the group. Box 8 shows how one of the meta-trackers concluded the work in her group.

Module 3: Information Literacy

Already in the planning of the MMedEd, a librarian was contacted. The expertise provided by the library emphasized the importance of information literacy in the scholarship process. The librarian therefore was made director of the third module. Half a day during the on-campus days was assigned to information literacy. A computer lab was booked for the students to get acquainted with other databases than PubMed, such as Eric and PsychInfo, where the searching for educational literature is commonly carried out.

During the module the course participants were asked to hand in an assignment where a search for literature relevant for their mini project was made, and to write down their search strategies. The module was designed to support the students in achieving *ILO3: Create search strategies for relevant medical educational information and be able to compare, evaluate and handle the results of different search strategies.*

Box 8. Meta-tracker analysis

> *An Analysis of the Development of the Learning Process of the Group*
> Summarizing the contributions for learning it's obvious that those participating actively have first read the reference literature. In addition, most of us have prepared discussion topics, shared own ideas as well as the problems we have encountered, asked questions and commented others. Overall, it has been a positive experience to be a part of this transfer process.
> *Suggestion how the Process can be Developed*
> Collaborative learning is based on interaction – meaning it is in our discussions in Ping Pong much of the learning occurs. I think we can create an even better working climate by increasing the interaction; to become better in motivating and encouraging each other to openness and creativity.
> Please write down your comments here, so that all can agree on strategies for development of the group work.

The search strategies were uploaded as documents to the discussion forum in Ping Pong, and students were asked to critique each others' documents. Three librarians tutored the students in this process, and each student got individual feedback on their assignments.

Box 9 exemplifies one of the rise aboves produced at the end of this module, and shows what was found difficult as well as some reflection over the process of searching literature in the medical education area.

Module 4: Paradigm and Epistemologies

During this module the intention was for participants to learn more about the different perspectives that impact our ideas of what knowledge is and how we can go about investigating the world to find out more about it. Discussions of different perspectives on teaching and learning and how this relates to different organizations were promoted in the discussion forum, and during the on-campus days. A workshop was carried out face-to-face, where participants got a lecture on the meaning of paradigms, epistemologies and methodology, and how these relate to each other according to Guba & Lincoln (Guba & Lincoln, 1994). The students were then provided with a case that should be solved in groups from the three perspectives of; post-positivism, critical theory and constructivism. In the workshop we intended for the students to experience the differences of the paradigms, and what the perspective means for the approach we take when thinking of not only research but also the carrying out of scholarship of our practice.

Box 9. Rise above on searching process

After looking at the different subjects started under the discussion "Information Literacy" I have noticed a few themes of discussion that are more frequent:

- **The Problem of Defining Your Query:** The field of information is new to most of us. The ones of us that have searched for information previously are accustomed to Pubmed and most of us know what to search for in our field
- **Finding the Right Terminology for Your Query:** The terminology of this field is also new to most of us. Instead of organ or disease related/specific terminology you have to search for more wide concepts.
- **Evaluating the Information That You Have Found without Reading All of It:** In our usual fields we know which sources/authors are "reliable". When we read an article in medicine we can quickly browse through the abstract (summary) and know the methods, results and conclusions right away. From there you can go deeper in to the article by looking at the very clear structure of the subjects listed above. You can easily compare different articles and their value to you. In this field most of the articles are more qualitative in their approach and this demands a "recalibration" of your mind. This can be frustrating.

In this attempt to rise above I conclude that in order to find relevant information most of us have used the old method of "trial and error" and let our errors guide to more appropriate search for information. When we continue to work with our mini-projects we will probably learn how to decide which articles are valuable in a quicker way.

The assignment of the module was designed to help students to develop their understanding of the concepts and required them to analyse aspects of their own organisational knowledge culture. To facilitate the understanding of the concepts 'paradigm, ontology and epistemology' the students were asked to read two articles on the subject, and book a meeting with a colleague, to whom they would try to explain what these terms meant and how they related to their mini project. The students found this exercise rewarding and more or less difficult depending on whom they had chosen as their discussion partner, and how much experience this partner had of discussing issues of teaching, learning, and knowledge.

After the exercise, which we called 'sharing with a colleague'; each individual reflected on what was difficult in the discussion with the colleague and posted that as a document in the project group discussion forum. Then the groups discussed and concluded on how the task contributed to their understanding of the concepts, which was written as a 'Rise above' and finally the group product was shared in the common discussion forum with the other groups. In this way the participants would have a dialogue using the concepts at many instances through the process of the exercise that is described in Figure 5, with a colleague; with her/himself; with their project group; and with the class. They would also perform several learning activities with the content: reading; explaining; reflecting; synthesizing; and discussing.

During module 4, a number of issues cramped up concerning the design, the constitution of groups with individuals dropping out, on top of the difficult topic for the module. Box 10 illustrates how this was expressed by two students in the 'contributions for learning'-section of their group.

As you can see the contributions for learning became very personal and therefore also gave the tutors important formative information for us to take into account continuously during the course, as well as in the design of future courses.

Figure 5. Sharing with a colleague exercise

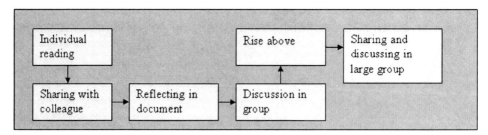

Box 10. Contributions for learning of module 4

This module was very special in many ways (stress, confusion, new members, not present members etc). I tried to fulfill what we agreed on regarding the participation and the assignment. I read the others posts in the discussion forum and I commented. When things did'nt go as planned I tried to solve the problem. However, I think that other factors than I mostly contributed the learning in this module (at least mine). Sometimes it's not so bad when things go wrong because frustration causes a need to engage and change which in turn leads to learning and when you make mistakes and you talk about them you learn from that. But too much confusion can make you feel wanting to give up. I think I could probably have been more active in the common discussion but it was hard to follow all the discussion threads plus at the same time my attention was directed towards our group's organizational problem. I learned the importance of re-organisation when a new member enters the group. I learned to an even greater extent to appreciate the work done by those of you in the group who are active./xa

Good evening!,

It's been really hard work for me to grasp what this module about paradigms and epistemology had to do with my kind of work. Thanks to my colleagues in group X I now realize that I use it nearly every day in [my work] without realizing it. It's just that I and my colleagues at work don't talk in those terms.

As XX pointed out I also had some problem with following all the discussion treads. I think there are too many things going on at the same time, which I think is very stressful.

I had a really tough time trying to understand the content in the article by Guba and Lincoln. I also miss time for reflection and think the timetable is too tight.

I wish I had been more active in the discussions, but for the moment I am happy that I could follow your thoughts about the theory in this module. I have learnt a lot from you and I hope that I could be more active in the future./xb

Module 5: Methodology in Scholarship of Medical Education

During module 5 the participants were asked to start considering the methodology of their mini-project. This module somewhat overlapped with module 4 because of the close link between methodology and that of paradigm and epistemologies. In higher educational research it is of utmost importance that these three aspects of research are properly discussed and aligned to gain credibility (Patton, 2001). Even though the carrying out of educational research was not the purpose of the course, readings of publications from that field is essential to the learning. By gaining a first overview and starting to understand how the different methodologies respond to different paradigms and research questions we wanted to support the students in achieving the learning outcomes formulated for Masters studies in the Swedish Higher Education Ordinance (SFS, 1993:100):

- Ability to independently identify and formulate issues and to plan and, using appropriate methods.
- Skill required to participate in research and development work, carry out advanced tasks.
- Ability to make assessments in the main field of study, taking into account relevant scientific aspects.
- Demonstrate insight into the potential and limitations of science.

The assignment of the module asked the participants to consider the alignment of the paradigm, epistemology and methodology inherent in their mini-project. They were asked to pick and investigate one out of seven methodologies suggested in one of the course books and suggest a design for investigating their question or problem, which had previously been spelled out as the starting point for their mini project during module 2.

The documents for module 4 and 5 on paradigm, epistemology and methodology of their mini project, was to be uploaded and feedback was requested in the learning partner groups in the discussion forum.

Module 6: Communication and Discussion of Results

One important part of the Scholarship process is to share and communicate with others about the development of your own practice. In this module the aim was for students to develop the ability to clearly present and discuss their work to achieve the intended learning outcome on ability to: *ILO5. Communicate results of an investigation and analysis to a relevant target group and suggest changes.*

This was done in two ways, in the form of a Mini project report and as a PowerPoint presentation supported by a word document. The presentation which was targeted to the peers in the course, was subject to a peer assessment procedure, where the students were asked to apply beforehand provided criteria for assessing each others' presentations. The mini project report was reviewed by two other students, and revised in relation to negotiated criteria before it was finally handed in for assessment.

Additionally each student was asked to complete a reflective statement, which was to be handed in individually, and added to their personal learning portfolio. This reflective statement concerned the reflection on their own scholarship in medical education, and provided, together with the mini project report, a basis for which to assess students' achievement of ILO1: *Show understanding of the concept of Scholarship of Medical Education by identifying and analysing an area of development within a specific context within university or health care practice.*

CURRENT CHALLENGES, CONCERNS, AND POSSIBLE SOLUTIONS

In this section, we explore some of the issues that have come up as a result of the evaluations and as comments and contributions for learning written at the end of each module by the participants. Overall the participants were very satisfied with the course and rated it as pretty good (46%) or very good (54%). The course participants thought they had achieved the learning outcomes. Most of them reported that they had developed their knowledge and competences in regard to these and the course design was appreciated as supporting the achievement of the learning outcomes. As regard to the development of critical thinking the evaluation showed differing views on this, which was also confirmed in the assessment where we as examiners could see that the writing was sometimes uncritical in relation to the literature. This is something we need to consider. Reasons could be the limited time that many participants experienced, but also in that we have not modeled in a good way how to critically discuss the literature. We need to be more explicit in what we mean by critical thinking in this course, and at what level we think the students should show it in their assignments. An idea would be to create an assignment where an article is critiqued and to give more feedback in an early stage.

Literature

The literature was appreciated as supporting the learning, and specifically the main book and some of the central articles were rated highly. Some of the literature was rated less useful by some, but very useful by others, which probably has to do with the differing levels and acquaintance with the research process of the group.

The searching of literature was not given enough space in the course, or perhaps we need to design assignments where the students are not only carrying out the search individually, but collaborating around the same search, and for instance comparing what they found, so that they can see how different strategies get different results, and hence learn from that.

Modules

All modules were rated highly. The later modules were assessed as more useful than the earlier modules of the course. We believe this had to do with the link to the final assessment as well as with the group processes and problems with individual dropping out during the first weeks of the course. This caused frustration and insecurity in regards to who was a member of which group as well as lack of activity on the learning platform and feedback from peers. Next time we believe that the assignments should probably not be so dependent on the group work, and perhaps that the groups should be larger at first, up to 8 participants in each, so that no group suddenly only consist of 3-4 individuals.

Local Learning Context

We asked about when the participants studied, and found out that most studied every now and then, in breaks, at the bus or train etc. Those few that have assigned time for the course are those who are not working full time. Most participants worked in Ping Pong a little every day, in evenings and during night. It is remarkable that only a little more than half of the participants (8/13) feel that they are supported by their boss to take the course. This is a problem that is difficult for us to do anything about other than inform and discuss with different employers, possible mainly in the Stockholm area, the prerequisites of the participants to fulfill the program. Hopefully this situation will change during the terms of the full MMedEd. The problem could be seen as a result of the culture of health and higher education organizations in relation to different organizational ideals (Stensaker, 2006). If we see our university as heavily influenced by the professional organisational ideal, the assumption that it is the responsibility of the individual to keep a certain level of professionalism in this context seems to result in a lack of competency development for teachers, since teaching is not considered part of the professionalism as i.e. a nurse or a doctor. We believe this attitude goes back to a master-apprenticeship view on learning, where it is in the aspect of being a good professional nurse/doctor, that good teaching is carried out. The ability to teach comes with the profession so to speak.

Work Load

From the survey after module 5 we got many good ideas for how to develop the course. We realized that we had overloaded the course with work. The group roles with secretary, rise above and meta-tracker worked out, but was stressful for the participants. Next time we believe we should start these roles later in the course, and perhaps only at one or two of the modules. The activity to talk to a colleague about paradigm and epistemology worked out really well, and we should consider the time assigned for module 4, which is really important. One idea could be to merge module 4 and 5.

Generally it is important to be explicit regarding instructions, since some students took on too much work, and read too much into each assignment, which in the end made them very stressed and de-motivated.

It is interesting that several of the students say that they have not had time to reflect. Our idea was that reflection is built into the course through the assignments where the students are asked to discuss and give feedback on each other's contributions. Perhaps we need to bring the issue of reflection up on the on- campus days next time so that we can conclude also on what we mean by reflection.

A problem during the course has been a lack of advance planning. Even though the students got a the study guides for when assignments should be handed in, it was difficult for them - and us - to anticipate the amount of time required for preparation of the assignments. Next time, we will have a better understanding of this, which mean we can be better at distributing the work load. We believe that even though some participants felt stressed by all the assignments that should be fulfilled each week, we have created a culture where the participants respond quickly to each other's comments and are supportive of each other's learning.

An overall reflection is that this course is an introductory course which aims to give an overview. It seemed that when the participants got engaged with the content of the course and started to develop understanding, they got frustrated by not having the time to get deeper into the different areas. It is a difficult issue, but hopefully by being more explicit and reducing some of the content (which also includes a re-writing of the learning outcomes) we can get to terms with it.

Assessment

Regarding the assessment, we had decided to have three different grades; fail, pass and pass with distinction. This was new to us, but we wanted to force ourselves into the situation of having to construct criteria for assessment at three levels instead of two, which is common at Karolinska Institutet. It turned out causing us a lot of thinking and we learned how difficult it is to be explicit in the criteria in a way that is transparent and understandable to the participants. We also believe that the so called 'high achievers' that exist in every class in every course, perhaps were forced into a more stressful studying approach because of this than would have been the case if we did not apply the three graded system. Our plan was also to let the participants create the assessment criteria together with us accordingly to a constructivist approach as this has been recommended for facilitation of the students' understanding of the assessment procedure (Rust, 2002), However, no one of the participants took part in this procedure probably due to lack of time, information and guidance.

The assessment as such was more difficult than we thought it would be. It turned out to be difficult for the students to show ability of transferring knowledge between the specific and the general, something that we need to consider for the next time; how much opportunity for practicing that process did we really provide the students with? This could also be the result of many of the participants' backgrounds, which were from a (post-positivist) paradigm where specificity is strived for, rather than the constant iterative process of transferring between the specific and the general, which is required within a constructivist paradigm.

When the final examination was handed in, a sample of three examinations were anonymized and assessed by the three tutors of the course. The assessment criteria were revised and discussed so that all three of us would assess the same thing and what and how it was meant to be assessed (validity and reliability). The three groups of the course were then divided between us so that each tutor assessed a group they had not tutored. Even though we had agreed upon the criteria after the "pilot" assessment our final assessments still showed discrepancies. We had to discuss it more in detail and justify our thinking and interpretations of the criteria to reach a consensus about the requested levels of performances. This shows the importance of constructing the criteria together in the tutor group as we also create our understanding in different ways just like the students do (Rust, 2002). When any difficulty in assessing work was confronted, the work was assessed by one other examiner.

The idea behind the mini project report, which originated from the scholarship process, had to be limited to a plan instead of the carrying out of a full project. This was misleading to some of the participants so that their understanding was that they would really carry out the project within the time frame of the course. Possibly this accounted for some of the stress that course participants expressed. Next time we will be more cautious with how we label the different assignments/activities – for instance by calling this aspect a mini-project plan instead.

Technology Concerns

The technology worked well for this course. It took longer or shorter time for students and teachers to get to know the VLE and where to find different tools such as discussion forum, where to look for changes and updates, etc.

SOLUTIONS AND RECOMMENDATIONS

There are no single solutions when it comes to education and teaching. However, based on the previous section we need to take into account a number of issues and be creative in how to approach them:

1. There is a need to model how to critically discuss the literature. This could be done in several ways. We have discussed the construction of a number of questions to guide the process, and a document consisting of different examples of writing, where the participants can judge the different levels of quality regarding a critical discussion. In this way the issue is raised, and based on such a discussion we will be able to create criteria for the assessment of the final examination task. Criteria that can be linked to other areas or aspects that will

be assessed, and provide opportunity for co-construction of the assessment criteria in a more systematic fashion.

2. The literature searches need to be made more transparent so that students can learn from each other and see how different strategies generate differing results. The recommendation is to let students compare their searches on a similar topic before getting into the process of searching literature for their own mini project.

3. The examination task needs to be somewhat reduced so that students are not put into a situation with work overload and steered into a reproductive approach to learning (Entwistle, 1992). One solution would be to more clearly let each assignment of the course contribute to the final product, i.e. a project plan. Another approach would be to let students, based on what they have learned during the course, make an analysis of a plan. A third possibility is to integrate the two, let the different assignments contribute to a project plan, and let the final assessment be based on peer assessment, where students assess somebody else's project plan.

4. The drop out issue was not properly taken into consideration in the design of the course. A way forward could be to start off with larger groups as well as scaffolding students who need more support by providing a mentor from the 2009 cohort to let them get in closer contact with somebody more experienced,

Table 4. Previous and suggested intended learning outcomes

Previous Intended Learning Outcome (ILO)	Suggested Changes to ILO
1. Show understanding of the concept of Scholarship of Medical Education by identifying and analysing an area of development within a specific context within university or health care practice.	1. Be able to write a project plan according to the principles of Scholarship of Medical Education
2. Analyse teaching and learning at individual and organisational level within a specific context with a scientific approach.	2. Identify issues of impact on teaching and learning from an individual and organizational perspective.
3. Create search strategies for relevant medical educational information and be able to compare, evaluate and handle the results of different search strategies.	3. Analyse and create search strategies for relevant medical education information.
4. Analyse how system factors such as goals, regulations and praxis impact the planning process and development of a practice in university or health organisations.	4. Identify and discuss how teaching and learning is embedded in a disciplinary and professional context, and how underlying assumptions impacts teaching and learning practice in university and health organisations
5. Communicate results of an investigation and analysis to a relevant target group and suggest changes.	5. Evaluate one's own contribution to the creation of an on-line learning community.

but also for the students of the 2009 cohort to find out what they have learned since they started the program themselves. When conducting the program the second time we believe that the program itself is better known. We will therefore make an effort to inform stakeholders and employers of the existence of the program better, not only possible future students. However a mentor system should not stand in the way for the creation of a strong learning community among the students of the new cohort. This is an issue for further thinking.

5.   The issue of reflection needs to be elaborated possibly already at the very beginning of the program, or at the on-campus days. We will then discuss how it is integrated into the course and its role for learning.

6.   The intended learning outcomes should be rewritten to better show the constructive alignment (Biggs & Tang, 2007) in the course. The first learning outcome is currently written so that the way students can show their understanding of the concept of Scholarship is defined in the learning outcome. Preferably it is the competence or level of understanding that should be outlined instead. The second intended learning outcome is at a too high cognitive level considering this is the first course of the program. The level of analysis is revisited in a later course (Leading change and learning). The third intended learning outcome is presently too explicit. We believe that the analysis and creation of a strategy is more reasonable as learning outcome at this stage. The fourth intended learning outcome aimed at including too much content, and hence system theory and issues in relation to these are suggested to be in a closer link to the everyday lives of the students. The fifth and last intended learning outcome is requiring rather a lot of extra preparation, an issue that made the work load uneven in the course. By emphasizing the ability to contribute to the learning community instead, the communication issue is emphasized, but in the context of the course. A suggestion is shown in Table 4.

REFERENCES

Bereiter, C. (2002). *Education and mind in the knowledge age*. Mahwah, NJ: Laurence Erlbaum Associates.

Bereiter, C., & Scardamalia, M. (2003). Learning to work creatively with knowledge. In De Corte, E., Verschaffel, L., Entwistle, N., & van Merrienboer, J. (Eds.), *Unravelling basic components and dimensions of powerful learning environments*. EARLI.

Biggs, J., & Tang, C. (2007). *Teaching for quality learning at university*. Buckingham, UK: SRHE & Open University Press.

Boud, D., Cohen, R., & Sampson, J. (2001). *Peer learning in higher education: Learning from & with each other.* London: Kogan Page.

Boyer, E. L. (1990). *Scholarship reconsidered: Priorities of the professoriate.* Princeton, NJ: The Carnegie Foundation for the Advancement of Teaching.

D'Andrea, V., & Gosling, D. (2005). *Improving teaching and learning in higher education: A whole institution approach.* Oxford, UK: Open University Press.

Entwistle, N. (1992). *Styles of learning and teaching.* London: David Fulton Publishers.

Gibbs, G. (2003). *Implementing learning and teaching strategies - A guide to good practice.* Milton Keynes, UK: The Open University.

Guba, E. G., & Lincoln, Y. S. (1994). Competing paradigms in qualitative research. In Denzin, N. K., & Lincoln, Y. S. (Eds.), *Handbook of Qualitative Research.* London: Sage.

Kember, D. (1989). A longitudinal-process model of dropout from distance education. *The Journal of Higher Education, 60*(3), 278–301. doi:10.2307/1982251.

Kirkpatrick, D. (1998). *Evaluating training programs: The four levels.* San Francisco, CA: Berrett-Koehler Publishers, Inc..

Kreber, C. (2005). Charting a critical course on the scholarship of university teaching movement. *Studies in Higher Education, 30*(4), 389–405. doi:10.1080/03075070500160095.

Lonka, K., & Ahola, K. (1995). Activating instruction: How to foster study and thinking skills in higher education. *European Journal of Psychology of Education, 10*, 351–368. doi:10.1007/BF03172926.

Marton, F., Hounsell, D., & Entwistle, N. (Eds.). (1996). *The experience of learning: Implications for teaching and studying in higher education.* Edinburgh, UK: Scottish Academic Press.

Moon, J. A. (1999). *Reflection in learning and professional development: Theory and practice.* London: Kogan Page.

Patton, M. Q. (2001). *Qualitative research & evaluation methods.* London: Sage.

Prosser, M., & Trigwell, K. (1999). *Understanding learning and teaching: The experience in higher education.* Buckingham, UK: Open University Press.

Ramsden, P. (1992). *Learning to teach in higher education.* London: Routledge. doi:10.4324/9780203413937.

Rust, C. (2002). The impact of assessment on student learning: How can the research literature practically help to inform the development of departmental assessment strategies and learner-centred assessment practices. *Active Learning in Higher Education, 3*(2), 145–158. doi:10.1177/1469787402003002004.

Schön, D. A. (1987). *Educating the reflective practitioner.* San Francisco, CA: Jossey-Bass Publishers.

SFS. (1993)... *Högskoleförordningen, 1993,* 100.

Silén, C., & Uhlin, L. (2008). Self-directed learning - A learning issue for students and faculty. *Teaching in Higher Education, 13*(4), 461–475. doi:10.1080/13562510802169756.

Stensaker, B. (2006). Governmental policy, organisational ideals and institutional adaptation in Norweigian higher education. *Studies in Higher Education, 31*(1), 43–56. doi:10.1080/03075070500392276.

Trigwell, K., & Shale, S. (2004). Student learning and the scholarship of university teaching. *Studies in Higher Education, 29*(4), 523–536. doi:10.1080/0307507042 000236407.

Vygotsky. (1978). *Mind in society: The development of higher psychological processes.* Cambridge, MA: Harvard University Press.

APPENDIX: COMMENTS FROM SURVEY AFTER MODULE 5

Comment, Good Things about the Course

Interesting! (which creates motivation) Many other participants are very commited and take a lot of responsibility for the group work. Ping pong works fine (I think, with some more time and experience...).

Peer-interaction, support, flexibility clarity of course structure (opps that is four things).

1. It is unique. 2. It has supporting tutors. 3. It is interesting subject.

*Different approaches like reading, reflecting, discussing...all makes you reflect on things from different perspectives. *In distans learning, you can choose when it suits you to study. For me it would not have been possible to study full time/day time at the moment *As we make assignments we deepen our knowledge and by peer reviewing we practice and improve our skills, see things in new perspectives.

1. The Group C offers a good learning community. 2. Multidisciplinary background of the group. 3. Interesting course literature, especially D'Andrea & Gosling and Glynis Cousin.

I like the way the learning processes are planned. I feel like I learn a lot and that the different modules are built up in a logical manner which make learning easy and fun!The things we are supposed to learn "matures" throughout the course of the modules, and it's a new and very intersting way for me to learn!

The discussions and the study guide and the quick answer from the tutor when i have questions.

The assignments are not too difficult or the workload too big I appreciated the campus day I really enjoy the practical contents of this course and its' appicability!

Discussion forum provides motivation and new angles! regular assignments gets you going! Content is relevant! Good that there is a tutor who steps in when needed! I appreciate the study guide!

Rapid feedback from both colleagues taking the course and teachers. Rewarding discussions about how to get on with your project. The discussions! Sometimes you believe or experience things in your work environment that might not be poilitically correct but still it effects you working situation. Its very interesting to hear that some of us have the same experience! The platform gives you freedom to work in the middle of the night if that is what you want.

Without priority: 1. Excellent study guides that have helped planning and to get work done in time + information in Ping Pong 2. Good support from teachers in Ping Pong. 3. The structure of this first course: how beautifully all the modules are linked together and constitute a meningful entirety.

Great participants at least in my group interesting topics, hoped to have more time to really go through them.

Comments on How the Course Could be Improved

Keep track of group members, if some are inactive do something rather soon... If someone starts the course late (like me) it could be good to meet in real life for a short meeting (would have worked for me since I work and live in Sthlm) and discuss things like information about the course and a plan to catch up (did not think of this before, if did I would have suggested it:-) I thougth of it just now). Same numbers for assigments as the module they belong to.

As I missed the campus days I find it would be inappropriate to come with suggestions. Considering how my situation has been I am more than pleased with the course! I find it difficult to say how much I work with the course, as it varies depending upon my work and home life.

1. Change the Time line for assignments. 2. Be more a head with the program descriptions. 3. Literature material would be available to the learners.

For most of the course participants, like for myselt I believe it has been a lot of work, however inspiring. For being a 7,5 hp course I believe it had many assignments. Perhaps I would see if it was possible to put assignments together in order to get moore time for discussion and reflection. I found the content in Ping-Pong most informative, perhaps participants that are not familiar with it found it to be to much information at the same time?

1. More time to each assignment in order to read, reflect and write. 2. Clarify whether we should write portfolio and give time for that, perhaps also elicit the writing process. 3. Clarify the idea of mini-project and its' report.

I think the discussion forums are rather difficult to get an overview of, as there are so many discussions going on at the same time. I tried the "what's new", but didn't feel very helped by that. I don't know if there's any solutions other than staying sharp... When to upload assignments in "documents" and when i "discussions"? I guess there is a purpose behind the choice for the different modules. Some assignments should be discussed by everyone, and some only between learning partners? A bit unclear to me...

TIME and maybe some questions to help penetrating the material, (what you are looking for, what to think off, dont forget... I Also would have made it possible to register for research early in the program.

More campus days?

Important that assignments don't overlap Important to inform when new information is added on the platform! Trying different pedagogical methods is good but sometimes I feel like a test person in an experiment. The deadlines are sometimes too short and too may. Just one set back at work or in your private life and your hopelessly running late in the course.

A common study guide for all the modules would make it easier to keep track of what we are supposed to do. As all students I want the information on upcoming courses as soon as possible. Since this is a "distance" course at 50% everybody has other things in their schedule and it would be easier to plan activity if we know it more in advance.

Chapter 11
The Nature of a Successful Online Professional Doctorate

Gordon Joyes
University of Nottingham, UK

Roger Firth
University of Nottingham, UK

Tony Fisher
University of Nottingham, UK

Do Coyle
University of Nottingham, UK

EXECUTIVE SUMMARY

This chapter provides a case study of a wholly online professional doctorate in Teacher Education that has been running successfully since 2003 within the School of Education at the University of Nottingham, UK. It begins with both the background and context in which the development took place—this covers the team involved and identifies the drivers that led to this innovative course. The main body of the chapter focuses on the course itself, which was constructed collaboratively through written reflections of the team. This illuminates the reasons for its success as measured by healthy recruitment, high student evaluation scores, and high retention and completion rates. The pedagogic rationale for the design of one module involving collaborative knowledge creation is presented with some student reactions to this. Six student voices are then presented, which provide an insight into the value of the course. This leads to a consideration of the current context and the new challenges facing the course.

DOI: 10.4018/978-1-4666-4486-1.ch011

BACKGROUND

This chapter provides a case study of a wholly online professional doctorate in Teacher Education, that has been running successfully since 2003 within the School of Education at the University of Nottingham, UK. It begins with both the background and context in which the development took place—this covers the team involved and identifies the drivers that led to this innovative course. The main body of the chapter focuses on the course itself which was constructed collaboratively through written reflections of the team. This illuminates the reasons for its success as measured by healthy recruitment, high student evaluation scores and high retention and completion rates. The pedagogic rationale for the design of one module involving collaborative knowledge creation is presented together with some student reactions to this. Six student voices are then presented which provide an insight into the value of the course. This leads to a consideration of the current context and the new challenges facing the course.

The University of Nottingham is a traditional campus-based, research-intensive higher education institution, attracting a mix of international, EU and home students. It should be therefore unsurprising that the course was originally intended to be delivered wholly face-to-face and on campus. The drivers for the course in itself relate to the particular context within the School of Education in the 1990s. Initial Teacher Education (ITE) had previously become primarily university based in the UK, but a variety of school based and partnership models were also being piloted. This signalled a period of rapid change in ITE accelerated by Government imposition of competence and then standards frameworks and an emphasis on diversity of provision with a focus on an increased participation in ITE by schools themselves. This called for some radical rethinking in relation to the nature of the ITE curriculum within Schools of Education, as well as the support for student teachers in school and the role of the university tutor and school based mentor. Teacher Education became an important research area in itself. There was a need to explore issues relating to these changes in policy and practice in different contexts and to explore methodologies for this research. ITE providers at the time were recruiting experienced teachers to lead this provision many of whom had little research experience. The expectation within the University of Nottingham and elsewhere was that all academic staff were to be research active and there was an increasing requirement for ITE staff to hold doctoral degrees. The reality was that many teacher educators in the UK and globally did not hold this qualification and many were not research active and this did not fit well within a University culture. This, combined with a pressure to increase international student numbers, led the Head of the School of Education at the time to include an Professional Doctorate in Teacher Education course within a campus-based, part-time professional doctoral programme. This was to be delivered primarily through a one week residential experience and paper-based distance self-study. There were to be four taught modules studied over two years followed by a two year period of research leading to examination by thesis and viva. The Professional Doctorate in Teacher Education was to be designed and delivered by members of the ITE staff, but at the time the course leader was a newly appointed Senior Lecturer with a TESOL background and some experience of developing distance education materials. Because the medium for the course was going to be English it was felt that many of the potential recruits would be likely to be international teacher educators who were training English language teachers and so this appointment seemed appropriate.

As it turned out, the course leader was seconded to another university shortly after course approval was obtained and this left the need to establish the course team and this is discussed in the next section. The face-to-face course initially recruited poorly yet it was clear there was a demand for this qualification. In fact there were large numbers of enquiries about the course, but the high cost coupled with the need to visit the UK for a face-to-face module made it unattractive. A four year part-time distance PhD was a less costly option, though seemingly less attractive from a student experience perspective. The story of how the face-to-face course became an online one unfolds in the next section.

SETTING THE STAGE

The team developing the online course consisted of the four authors, all of whom were experienced secondary school teachers; as ITE tutors they specialised in Modern Languages, Science and Geography. Importantly all were experienced in working internationally and were involved in using new learning technologies to enhance teaching and learning. One of the team had been instrumental in the move by the University to provide the WebCT Virtual Learning Environment (VLE) in his role as the University distance learning advisor. At the time the online course was envisaged in 2003 there was a commonly-held belief within Higher Education that an online educational experience was somehow inferior to face-to-face. The course team were firmly convinced that the experience - although different - could be constructed in a way that could take advantage of the opportunity for an ongoing and sustained learning experience within a learning community. Our experience was that this could not be easily achieved in the face-to-face model in which learners had a few intensive synchronous interactions, being the week-long residential experiences. The online course could offer longer and less intense periods for developing a sense of community and for engaging more fully with the key concepts within the course - a whole semester could be made available for online study. It also could provide a chance for some experiential learning around conducting research within the taught modules themselves. This was a shared belief within the team, but one that is still not shared by most of our colleagues.

The resulting online Professional Doctorate in Teacher Education course can be considered successful on a wide range of measures. It continues to recruit students, has high student retention and completion rates. There are on average four new students per module, resulting in a cohort of around sixteen on the taught modules from around the globe, including Hong Kong, Canada, China, Cyprus, Greece, Cayman Islands, Jamaica, Poland, as well as the UK. There are an equal number who are in the research phase of the module. Participant evaluation of the programme is very positive and aspects of the course have been the subject of research and publication (Joyes, Fisher & Coyle, 2002; Kwame, 2005; Joyes & Fritze, 2006; Joyes, 2006). Additionally the European Centre for Development of Vocational Training has showcased the programme as an exemplar of excellent e-learning practice. This success has not been so easily matched in other institutions and this is still the only fully online research programme at the University of Nottingham. Why is this? What is so different about the Professional Doctorate in Teacher Education? Is it the technologies? Is it the pedagogy? Is it the students? Is it the team of tutors? We would argue it is a combination of all these factors as well as the nature of the professional doctorate itself that makes it ideally suited to online working.

According to the United Kingdom Council for Graduate Education the professional doctorate is defined as follows:

A programme of advanced study and research which, whilst satisfying the University criteria for the award of a Doctorate, is designed to meet the specific needs of a professional group external to the University, and which develops the capability of individuals to work within a professional context. (UKCGE, 2002, p. 62)

Gregory (1995) further captures the focus of the professional doctorate, with use of the term 'scholarly professional' as someone who uses enquiry, learning, and research whilst in professional practice. Such definitions suggest that the professional doctorate is intended for those wishing to positively impact on contemporary professional practice through their programme of doctoral study. Certainly, application to practice is at the philosophical core of the professional doctorate in contrast to the PhD that is not exclusively concerned with professional issues, or explicitly requires application to practice. Similarly, Maxwell (2003) differentiates between the first and second generation of professional doctorates, which identifies a shift in the primary focus of such programmes from one dominated by 'academe' into the professional environment. Central to the Professional Doctorate in Teacher Education is the integration of research for the development and enhancement of professional practice and all this encompasses. The implication here is that the professional doctorate produces knowledge for application 'out there', external to the university, as opposed to academic enquiry, which may or may not be applied to professional practice at a later date. Perhaps unsurprisingly, this emphasis reflects the general trend emerging in the 1990s in how researchers are encouraged to think about knowledge production, the relevance of the research and its application to education. The professional doctorate provides a valuable opportunity for practitioners to make a significant contribution to professional practice and service development through research questions originating from practice and the concomitant development of such expertise.

Our experience is that many applicants are attracted to the professional doctorate after explicitly rejecting the idea of pursuing a conventional PhD as being inappropriate to their needs. They are attracted by the professional doctorate's work-related framework and the opportunity to research their own contexts and have a positive impact on contemporary professional practice through their programme of doctoral study. The reality was that the two year part-time research phase of the course would be conducted within their home country and blocks of study abroad would likely be disruptive to their professional (and personal) lives. An online course seemed an ideal solution. However both distance learning and completing a PhD can potentially be an isolating experience and the course needed to address this. Unlike the PhD the Professional Doctorate in Teacher Education, like many professional doctorates, is cohort based. This affords peer support that includes studying with like-minded individuals facing similar challenges in their places of work.

CASE DESCRIPTION

The background and context to the course has outlined the key drivers for the Professional Doctorate in Teacher Education, and identified a global group of students who would choose to study for this within an online cohort. It has also provided an insight into the ways the course team members were ideally positioned to develop and support innovative online learning with a global cohort or Teacher Educators. The online course team wanted to create a dynamic model for developing bespoke professional education and research which would push out the boundaries beyond traditional and inward looking learning spaces provided by the most popular VLEs of the time. Spaces such as WebCT were not enough for our team- we had a collective vision (not always articulated but understood) built on key ideas such as interactivity for individuals, small group learning, formal and informal communication, a shared sense of professionalism, a sense of purpose and responsibility, whilst responding to individual needs and contexts – all without ever physically meeting the students.

Whilst these drivers may seem ambitious, they motivated the Professional Doctorate team to think creatively, to take risks in terms of what might and might not work, to connect with other colleagues in collaboration on the course design, (e.g. at the university of Melbourne), and to ensure that the modules would satisfy the rigour of doctoral provision whilst operating in very new ways. Put simply we wanted to model good practice in an on-line environment.

The elements in Table 1 represent key features of the pedagogic design, each one having its rationale and each one making a significant contribution to the course. An induction session that only focuses on introducing learners to study at doctorate level, and to studying online without engaging the learner with any of the module content, is not a commonly adopted approach to courses. The use of a common organisational approach and style is also not common and neither is the use of diverse pedagogic approaches. So why did the course team arrive at these approaches?

In reality the starting point for the learning design was the learners themselves - an approach that we would identify as being part of an initial teacher educator culture. This involved a recognition that the nature of the curriculum and the peda-

Table 1. The unique pedagogic features of the professional doctorate in teacher education

Unique features of the course	Function/rationale
An online induction to online working	To familiarise students with what are likely to be new ways of working, i.e. wholly online and working alone as well as collaboratively.
Four taught modules that are quite different pedagogically from one-another.	Learners are experienced teachers and teacher educators and would expect to experience a range of carefully chosen pedagogic approaches to support their learning.
Adoption and adaptation of technologies to meet pedagogic needs to overcome the limitations of a commercial VLE	A pedagogic need was identified to involve students in collaboratively developing an analytic framework.
A uniform organisational and visual style for the learning materials.	A Webquest template is adopted throughout as a study guide. Prepatory activities are included for each module. Key texts are provided as pdfs in a library within each module
Taught modules are commonly supported by 2 tutors.	This provides learners with two different perspectives and approaches - values the diversity of experience within the team.
There is an expectation that learners will work collaboratively as part of an online community in key parts of the course.	This provides learners with an experience of working in a community of co-enquirers on carefully designed authentic learning activities.
The course has been the subject of research and publication by its developers/tutors and one of their Ph.D research students.	The development of the course represented an ongoing inquiry into and dissemination of effective practice.

gogy that would meet learner needs to develop as autonomous inquirers into practice would need to follow from their starting points and where they needed to be by the critical research phase of the course. Table 2 provides a summary of these starting points and the course expectations.

This gap presented a challenge to be able to accommodate variation between students' background, needs and expectations, while harnessing the opportunities provided by such real-life differences as the foundations for an engaging, multi-perspective learning experience involving adult learners. This led to the development of the induction session to make transparent to these learners the course expectations and to provide an opportunity to explore the online learning environment without the added cognitive load of the module activities. It also led to the design of the four taught modules, which are outlined in Table 3.

The course has a 'roll-on, roll-off', twice yearly entry structure and so a learner's journey could start at any of the taught modules which are taught every two years - the free standing induction session supports this approach. The Professional Doc-

Table 2. Course design challenges in terms of student starting position and course expectation

Learner's starting position	Course expectation
Experienced teacher and teacher educator familiar and expert in their own local and possibly national teacher education context.	To share their expertise and experience within a global cohort and develop an understanding of the ways their local practice links with wider teacher education agendas.
Seeking an opportunity to be taught by leading international experts in the field.	Learners to engage with experts within the School of Education and wider using a critical perspective and develop an understading of their own personal expertise.
A personal experience of learning that is predominantly transmission rather than interactive, but this will vary.	The need for constructivist and discursive pedagogies that support engagement with critical thinking and understanding.
A professional interest in pedagogy, curriculum and professional development - receptive of and likely to expect new pedagogic approaches	Work in a variety of ways that will develop knowledge, understanding and skills.
A tendency towards description rather than analysis, but this will vary.	The need to develop analytic and theoretical interpretations of data.
Varying expertise in learning online.	The need to work in a variety of online modes e.g. individual research, collaborative problem solving, etc.
A familiarity with local issues and an interest in pursuing research around a local problem in order to improve local practice.	The need for the doctoral research to be informed by, and to inform, the global agenda in teacher education.
Little understanding of the research process and of teacher education issues beyond local or national contexts.	Research conducted locally which is informed and informs the wider Teacher Education community is to be completed during years 3 and 4.

Table 3. The course structure and pedagogy

The modules	Description	Pedagogic approach
Fundamental Principles in Teacher Education (1 semester)	This module explores both pre-service and in-service education from a wide range of theoretical, political and research perspectives and at a number of different levels – national policy, the higher education institution, the school, the teacher and the classroom.	The module is divided into ten discrete weekly learning activities. School of Education experts in key areas prepared the learning activities using a Webquest template. Seven of the sessions are supported self study and three involve extended discussion forum activities.
The Philosophy of Educational Research (1 semester)	The module provides a theoretical framework for analysing the methodological, ontological and epistemological assumptions underpinning the main research strategies	The module develops criticality through the reading and online discussion of key texts in the area. In this way the influences on research approaches are explored.
Contexts for Teacher Education (1 semester)	The module explores the contexts of national settings and curricular specialism. It draws on participants' own experiences and sets them against an international comparative framework.	Leaners collaboratively develop an analytic framework, and use this to analyse international teacher education programmes including their own -enabling them to set their own local research concerns in a wider international context.
Key Approaches to Educational Research (1 semester)	This module explores how to define a research focus, create a series of research question, design an appropriate methodology, and how to apply research methods critically and appropriately.	Research approaches are explored through the analysis of video researcher narratives and through the collaboration of a small scale enquiry designed and conducted in small groups.
The research phase (2 years)	This involves research in an aspect of Teacher Education chosen and refined during the taught modules that is conducted in the learner's own context.	Learner's work individually under supervision using a variety of online communication modes, i.e. text, audio and video. The community of beginning researchers developed during the taught phase of the course provides an informal support network.

torate initially set about the inculcation of critical reflection, tasks which were built around professional discourse, a common study guide approach to task and activities to provide guidance for busy professionals without being too prescriptive. The programme conceptualised learning from a socio-cultural perspective and therefore we wanted to reflect this in the organisation of the modules, and within the tasks and activities which would encourage criticality and learner autonomy within a collegial environment. Whilst constructs such as these suggest an idealistic view of what was achievable, the team had a range of problems and issues to resolve along the way – some more manageable than others.

The online developments were structured at team meetings and development days, supported by funds from the University Learning and Teaching Development Fund. This allowed the team to reflect upon and analyse what was working well within the face-to-face course, to consider the limitations of the residential face-to-face experience and to consider how a wholly online course could replicate what was of value and also add value to the experience. As can be seen from Table 3 the pedagogic design ranged from a modification of a traditional weekly lecture/seminar format where 'guest' lecturers contributed to the course materials and where the course tutors held several extended discussions at key points in the module to a module involving collaborative knowledge creation where the course tutors, other than designing the module, simply facilitated the learning process. This collaborative knowledge creation module is discussed in the following.

THE CONTEXTS FOR TEACHER EDUCATION MODULE

The ways notions of adult learning (Knowles, 1990) and Grabinger and Dunlap's (2000) Rich Environments for Active Learning (REALs) have informed the design of both face-to-face and the subsequent online learning modes within the course are dealt with in some detail elsewhere (Joyes & Fritze, 2006). A key feature of a REAL is that not only are there opportunities for knowledge creation, but that these are situated within authentic interactions. This focus on authenticity had a strong influence on the Contexts for Teacher Education module that involves an activity that generates 'new' knowledge that is directly relevant to the students' individual studies/interests and utilises appropriate higher order and research relevant thinking skills. It uses the fact that these learners genuinely hold expert knowledge that will be new to the others studying the module. It is the deliberate use of this situation that aims to establish a notion of the need to belong to and participate within the group, and to ensure that students feel part of a professional community (Wenger, 1998). This pedagogic design could not be achieved using the instructionist-influenced online learning environment WebCT alone (Coates et al, 2005). Goodyear (2000) states that "Most of the claimed strengths of networked (online) learning have their roots in both the technology and the ways in which the technology is used. The technology alone won't deliver the desired benefit - except by lucky accident" (p.18). However, the technology needs to be able to be flexible enough to deliver the pedagogy and it is this interplay between strong pedagogic design and careful blending of a range of technologies within the course that makes the course distinct. For example, the Contexts for Teacher Education module uses the institutionally provided WebCT functionality where possible, but where more carefully structured discourse is required, an alternative technology OCCA (Online Courseware Component Architecture) is used as this blends in with, rather than dictates, the pedagogical model. The OCCA Web server/database was developed at the University of Melbourne to support the creation of highly flexible online learning environments based on low-level learning and teaching 'transactions' (Fritze, 2003). A number of curriculum projects developed using OCCA have demonstrated its capacity to support innovative learning environments that incorporate reflection, group work, peer review, learning portfolios and customised tools for teachers, primarily supporting on-campus activities (Fritze, 2003). The Contexts for Teacher Education module was designed for a wholly online modality, whilst maintaining the educational qualities of the previous mixed-mode course model and yielding a sustainable administrative load.

OCCA was essentially used to support a 'Draft Framework Development' activity within the Contexts for Teacher Education module. This activity through which individual understandings and experience are shared and reconciled provides a particular test of an online environment to facilitate a learning experience that would compare with class discussion. Figure 1 indicates the structure of the activity, which occurs over a period of ten weeks, rather than the days over which it was conducted within the classroom setting. Each box represents a specially crafted Web page

*Figure 1. OCCA pages for the online "draft framework development" activity (*via email, phone, or text messaging)*

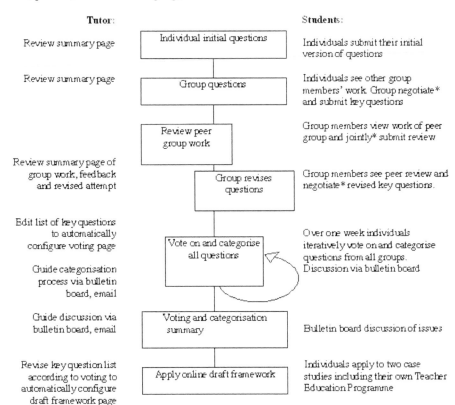

through which each task is undertaken. The OCCA environment makes it possible for the work within each task to be automatically incorporated into later ones, and for unique collaborative activities to be constructed, such as the voting and categorisation tasks. In addition, students have access to an online 'portfolio' progressively summarising their work, and tutors have optimised pages to view students' work, submit individual, group and global comments, and configure exercises.

Interestingly this module involves little support from the tutor as the pedagogic design and the technology work to empower the learners to take centre stage. Student reaction to this has approach has been overwhelmingly positive. For instance:

There was also the concept of the learning community which provided us with a forum to bounce ideas off each other which again was something I had never experienced before. It was my first real student centred learning experience.

I don't have enough adjectives to describe it but it is wonderful. It is the true democratisation of learning. I think that this is a very positive and supportive learning environment. For me, this has always been the main issue – if you care about teaching as a collaborative process how can you make it happen? I think that this module has proved how. (Kwame, 2005).

THE STUDENT EXPERIENCE: SIX STUDENT VOICES

Our original intention when writing this chapter was to provide opportunities for the student voice to emerge and so far within the chapter we have drawn upon the findings of the doctoral study of the Contexts for Teacher Education module by Kwame (2005). What follows provides the authentic perspective of six students who have either completed or are in the final stages of the degree. You will see from these student voices that some began the course by attending modules at residential schools whereas the more recent students studied the course wholly online. The opportunity to include these arose from a request by the book editor to increase the length of the submitted chapter. An email request was sent to past students, six of whom responded within two weeks with a student voice based around the following structure.

- Your context on joining the course.
- Why you decided to do this.
- How your research ideas developed during the whole course.
- The research context and research problem.
- The methodology.

- What you learnt from this.
- How this impacted on your professional life.
- Outputs from the work, conference presentation, papers etc.
- Reflections on the experience

The following are these student voices as submitted and are not anonymised to acknowledge the contributions that each have made to this chapter and to the course.

STUDENT VOICE 1: DR. PAUL SZE – HONG KONG

My Context on Joining the Course

On joining the course, I was a lecturer in a school of education at a university of Hong Kong. The courses I taught were for in-service and pre-service teachers. The programmes included the fulltime B.Ed., the fulltime and part-time PGCE, and a part-time MA in English Language Teaching.

Why I Decided to do This

There was the practical need, and pressure, to upgrade my academic qualification from Master's level to Doctoral level. For me, my choice of this doctoral programme was mainly motivated by my love for teacher education. Although in terms of content, most of the courses I taught were about language and linguistics, and second language methodology, my work at a school of education meant that all my students were either pre-service or in-service teachers. For me, my work was not simply imparting discipline knowledge. My calling, if I may call it, is to nurture competent, reflective, and caring ESL teachers. That was why I did not choose a doctoral programme in linguistics, but rather one in teacher education. Of course, another main reason was the mode of delivery of the Professional Doctorate in Teacher education programme. It began with a short residential course, which was followed by regular online supervisions. I could also come to Nottingham to meet with my supervisor when I could make it, and I did make use of this flexibility by visiting my supervisor throughout the course when I was able to fly to England.

How My Research Ideas Developed during the Whole Course

My research topic started to brew right from the first pre-thesis module, and took shape a year later. The pre-thesis modules enriched my understanding of my research, especially in regard of research methodology.

The Research Context and Research Problem

At the time when the thesis research was carried out, computer-mediated discussion, especially in the form of forum discussion, was a popular activity for the continuing professional development (CPD) of teachers in Hong Kong. This was against the backdrop that Government policy in Hong Kong began to make CPD mandatory for serving teachers. Teachers had to complete a total of 150 CPD hours within a three-year cycle. Yet, the policy was not fully supported by professional development provision, as (a) the government's education department, and teacher education providers, were unable to cope with the sudden huge demand, and (b) schoolteachers were already quite over-taxed. Computer-mediated discussion was then typically employed to complement face to face professional development programmes for teachers. My thesis research aimed to investigate teachers' development of professional development through computer-mediated discussion. Specifically, when teachers engage in computer-mediated discussion, how do they communicate? What do they talk about? Do they challenge each other, or do they simply agree with each other? To what extent are their discussions based on theoretical literature, personal opinion, personal experience, sharing of resources, etc.?

The Methodology

A group of 21 in-service primary school teachers of English taking a professional development course took part in an eight-week online discussion forum on grammar teaching. Grammar teaching was chosen because it was a highly controversial aspect of second language teaching. The discussion was un-mediated. After the eight weeks, all the messages posted were analysed qualitatively for (a) interaction patterns, (b) depth of discussion, and (c) topic content.

What I Learned from This

In terms of research in general that analysis of online discussion is feasible, and will yield significant findings and insights about how participants interact, and the depth of discussion they engage in. In terms of the substantive issue (and I am not exempt from personal bias here, since I am using my personal judgment):

- The teachers' knowledge of the theory of grammar and of grammar teaching was impoverished;
- The teachers tended to agree too much with each other, and seldom challenged each other's beliefs;

- As a result, there was insufficient critical reflection, and insufficient depth in the discussion;
- Hence, it cannot be assumed that as teachers engage in computer-mediated discussion, their professional knowledge will develop
- Some form of moderation by an 'expert' may be necessary.

How This Impacted my Professional Life

Subsequently, when I organized online forum discussion again (for other cohorts), I made sure that that (a) there was sufficient theoretical preparation (lectures, readings, etc.), (b) the discussion was made more focused, by for example, providing participants with guiding questions (i.e., not just a topic), and (c) moderating the discussion to some extent (e.g., by asking follow-up questions, by providing intermediate summaries; by alerting them to the theories concerned; by encouraging them to challenge each other's ideas).

As a teacher educator in TEFL, I could focus my professional interests either on the substantive aspect of second language teaching methodology, or on the teacher education aspect in the sense of nurturing effective and reflective second language teachers. I had always had a stronger interest in the latter, which led me to choose the professional doctorate. This inspired me both theoretically and on practical levels. I was able to critically examine the purpose of teacher education, the attributes of 'good' teachers, as well as my own practice in TEFL teacher training. I was able to further improve my professional practice, which, since doing the Professional Doctorate, led to my obtaining the Faculty Exemplary Teaching Award twice, and the Vice-chancellor's Exemplary Teaching Award in 2006, the year in which I obtained my Professional Doctorate from the University of Nottingham. The professional doctorate has further strengthened my status in my field, and subsequently I was admitted as a Fellow of the Chartered Institute of Linguists, UK, and a Fellow of the Royal Society of Arts, UK. In 2008, I was appointed by the Ministry of Education of the Government of Macau, Special Administrative Region of China, as overseas consultant for their curriculum reform in the area of English Language education.

Outputs from the Research

My outputs were two conference presentations, one article in a refereed journal and one book chapter.

My Reflections on the Experience

I valued the international mix of course participants. All the pre-thesis taught courses were related to teacher education. This greatly prepared us for the thesis stage. I understand that because of budget or manpower constraints, some universities have 'generic' pre-thesis taught modules for a few Professional Doctorate specializations, followed by one or two specialist modules for each specialization. But our Professional Doctorate had its own pre-thesis modules. This was a special 'treat'. I guess most course participants were busy working professionals, who might be tempted to put the thesis writing aside when faced with heavy work duties. Yet, this Professional Doctorate had regular (and actually quite frequent) supervisory meetings (online), and this greatly helped me to stay on track and on schedule. As a result, I was able to submit my thesis for examination five months after the minimum study period (of four years including the pre-thesis modules and thesis writing).

STUDENT VOICE 2: DR. CHRISTINE SAVVIDOU – CYPRUS

My Context on Joining the Course

I am a British born teacher who lives and works in Cyprus. Before starting this course, I had been teaching for fifteen years. Starting off in a primary school in the UK, I had also taught in secondary and higher education in Cyprus. At the point when I decided to apply for the course, I was a lecturer at a college of higher education (HE) in Cyprus where I taught courses in Academic English.

Why I Decided to do This

Two factors influenced my decision to do this course. The first was a direct response to my work context. The college was undergoing a period of rapid change as it went through the process of becoming a university. One consequence of this was increased pressure for lecturers to upgrade professional qualifications and increase research and publication activity. The second factor was my own intrinsic motivation. Over recent years, I had combined teaching with part-time study to achieve a postgraduate degree and this provided me with the confidence and intellectual curiosity to want to pursue my studies further.

How My Research Ideas Developed during the Whole Course

My decision to focus my research on a narrative approach to professional knowledge developed during the first two years of study. I can directly trace my research ideas back to two specific influences. Firstly, exposure to a wide range of literature introduced me to philosophies and theories of learning by cognitive psychologist Jerome Bruner. Secondly, the multimedia aspects of the course, such as opportunity to view video stories by well-known researchers, influenced my own thinking about the nature of research as well as giving me the idea to use video stories in my own research study.

The Research Context and Research Problem

The context of my research was set against a literature review that reflected how relatively little is known about specific patterns of interaction between the stories teachers tell about teaching and teacher learning. While the use of narratives is becoming popular in educational research, relatively few studies have attempted to develop storytelling as an integrated model for teacher learning. Another factor in the research context related to the organisational changes that were taking place in my own teaching context and which were creating new understandings practice and professional knowledge. I was interested to explore the stories that lecturers told about these changes and the effects on their professional development. Against this background, my research addressed two questions: (1) how can storytelling be developed, organized and supported in a community of practice? And (2) in what ways can storytelling be linked to teacher learning?

The Methodology

Narrative methodology is part of an interpretative paradigm and an attempt to explore the relationship between storytelling and learning from the perspective of the storytellers, i.e. the lecturers. In order to do this, my research questions were conceptualized as a digital storytelling tool. Through a process of chain sampling, I collected personal experience stories from lecturers about their own professional development. I then supported participants in transforming their stories of learning into digital representations composed of audio, video and text, which were then published onto a digital storytelling space. These stories were accessible to other colleagues, several of whom responded with their own stories of professional development. A narrative analysis of was then conducted made to look for the types of connections between stories.

What I Learned from This

From my research I learnt more about how storytelling can be organized as a form of conversation through which lecturers interact to create meaning about their professional development. Three key findings emerged from the research about storytelling. Firstly, storytelling provided opportunities for lecturers to define their own concepts of 'professional development', rather than it being ascribed by researchers or teacher educators. While some experiences were more typical of professional development activities such as postgraduate studies and practitioner-research, other activities reflect experiences that relate to lecturers' personal and professional roles and identity, such as being a foreign lecturer, balancing personal and professional lives and conditions of employment. Moreover, storytelling allowed participants to not only give voice to their experiences but also to evaluate them. Stories documented successes and achievements as well as failures, uncertainties and lack of motivation, which although rarely heard, are also part of lecturers' experiences. The second finding related to how digital storytelling facilitates professional dialogue. Firstly, it allowed for asynchronous communication, so that stories were exchanged without constraints of time or place. Moreover, the flexibility of digital storytelling created potential for participants to be both tellers and consumers of stories. Another significant feature of was the type of storytelling interactions that occurred between lecturers with diverse cultural backgrounds, academic experience and professional status that may not typically occur in face-to-face settings. Finally, the third finding looks at how the narrative analysis used in this study, interprets storytelling as a dynamic process of knowledge construction. This analysis revealed several processes used to construct stories. These processes were social, showing the storyteller responding to other stories and storytellers, and cognitive, showing the storyteller in the process of 'thinking' through their story.

How This Impacted my Professional Life

Achieving the doctorate has had an enormous impact on my profession life. Subsequent promotion decreased my teaching hours and increased my research hours. In terms of my collegial relationships, I have been asked to supervise colleagues undertaking postgraduate research and I am regularly asked to give feedback on colleagues' research. In terms of my teaching, I currently teach a new course as part of the Communications degree and I have also submitted proposals for a new course in narrative research methods. In addition, as part of my own research I am exploring narrative pedagogies in teaching. In terms of my teaching, I feel that the research process has made me a better teacher not only in terms of the knowledge I have acquired through the course, but also in terms of my own experience of being a student.

Outputs from the Research

In the two years since I have completed the course, I have made several presentations at conferences in the UK, Europe and the US. I have written conference proceedings, articles for a professional association publication and articles for academic journals, two of which have been accepted for publication.

My Reflections on the Experience

On one hand, the degree gave me a structure that was relevant, motivating and, above all, manageable with work and family life. On the other hand, the content of modules and the variety of student backgrounds provided the flexibility to find and formulate research questions from across a wide educational arena. The use of technology enabled me to become part of a community of learners and during the initial part of the course I felt extremely supported. On a personal level, I felt that the multimedia aspects of the course - videos, audio, text files, and online discussions - really added to the variety and creativity of the learning experience, and ultimately inspired me in my own research and teaching.

STUDENT VOICE 3: DR. MARK MINOT – CAYMAN ISLANDS

My Context on Joining the Course

My name is Mark Minott. During the course I divided my time between working for a local church as Ministry Associate, and a small fledging local university in the Cayman Islands as an adjunct lecturer.

Why I Decided to do This

There are three reasons why I choose a doctoral degree programme in teacher education at Nottingham. One, I wanted to become a teacher educator therefore a doctoral degree in teacher education was not just ideal, but a way to fulfill a dream. Two, a doctoral degree from Nottingham offers prestige and recognition, in that, my peers would now see me as in command of my field of study and can make a worthwhile contribution to it (Phillips and Pugh 1994). Three, I found the hybrid approach, i.e. online and face-to-face, utilised in the delivery of the course attractive. The traditional full time face-to-face method was inappropriate for I had a young family to care for, in particular, a young daughter with a 'special need' who needed my full attention. Taking time away for three to five years of full time face-to-face study was not a viable option for me and would cause undue stress for my family.

How My Research Ideas Developed during the Whole Course

I made a decision to focus my research in the area of reflective teaching, which I found interesting for two reasons. Firstly, while working through the module, 'Fundamental Principles of Teacher Education' I had critically examined and compared reflective teaching with other models of teaching and concluded that both seasoned and novice teachers and, by extension, students could benefit from engaging with it. Secondly, during my second year in the programme, the leadership of the school decided to use the notion of reflection to guide the entire programme of Teacher Education. Initially, reflective teaching was offered as a subject in the course. The shift or policy change, meant that the practice permeated all aspects of teaching and learning in the department/school. Therefore, through this constant bombardment with, and modelling of the practice, I became very interested in learning more about it. Through a series of discussions with my supervisors regarding possible research topics within my area of interest, I decided to examine the degree to which teachers in the Cayman Islands were employing elements of reflective teaching during lesson planning, implementation and evaluation.

The Research Context and Research Problem

The research was motivated by my personal desire to learn more about reflective teaching, and the fact that a number of local researchers in the Cayman Islands highlighted the need to accumulate a body of knowledge addressing local issues in all areas of education, including teaching and learning. The purpose of the investigation was to provide a practically adequate understanding (Sayer, 1992) of lesson planning, implementation, and evaluation--from the perspective of selected seasoned teachers in the Islands--and their use of elements of reflective teaching in these areas.

The Methodology

I employed a qualitative instrumental case study undergirded by a critical-realist philosophic stance. Six broad research questions guided the study. Participants included four seasoned teachers. The field research included interviews and documentary analysis. Interviews focussed on participants' experience and observations, regarding the research areas. Documents, in the form of lesson plans, were used to confirm or make findings more or less plausible. Interview transcripts were analysed to determine similarities and differences in respondents' perspectives, and issues warranting further attention.

What I Learned from This

I ended the study by summarising what I perceived were the respondents' understanding of the areas being researched. In addition, I made two major conclusions, regarding reflective teaching. One, how the respondents carried out their role as lesson planners, implementers, and evaluators, resulted from a dynamic relationship between their teaching philosophy and/or belief, personal choice, mood and the varied contextual constrains such as administratively decreed policies and heavy workload. I then made a case for the relevance and importance of reflection in coping with, understanding, and effectively using this relationship in the teaching/learning dynamics. Two, the respondents employed their practical knowledge or experience of 'what works', and generally, they were found to exercise degrees of reflectivity that is, being 'more or less' reflective about their teaching.

How this Impacted my Professional Life

The course has impacted my professional life in two ways. It enabled me to contribute extensively (as a part of a pioneering team) to the conceptualising, implemenation and development of a fully accredited teacher education programme in the Cayman Islands permeated by the practice of reflective teaching. It also allowed me to expland the body of knowledge in teaching, learning and teacher education locally, by provided me the background knowledge used to publish two books and numerous research articles in reptuable local and international peer reviewed journals.

Outputs from the Research

The thesis was published in 2009 as a monograph. The actual research process and finding appears in the Journal of the University College of the Cayman Islands. Sections of the literature review chapter has been utilised in research published in journals such as the Australian Journal of teacher education, Professional Development in Education, Routledge, Taylor and Francis, the College Quarterly, Seneca College Canada and the Cayman Islands Journal published by Cayman Press. The development of certain ideas emerging from the thesis can be found in Current Issues in Education, Arizona State University, USA. While I have not made conference presentations specifically on my thesis topic, the content and knowledge gained has aided the process of making presentations on aspects of reflective teaching in various countries in the Caribbean.

My Reflections on the Experience

Overall, my experience of participating in a hybrid, i.e. online and face-to-face doctoral course, was mostly positive, although there were negative aspects. On the positive side, I have been able to pursue doctoral studies which, without the online medium would be near impossible. On the negative side I missed the nonverbal cues of face-to-face encounters with tutors and other students. In fact, people I have made long term contacts and relationships with are the ones I met on the university campus during the various face-to-face meetings.

Having successfully pursued and completed the doctoral degree in teacher education I can say without a doubt, that the online environment placed me at the centre of the learning experience allowing me to have total control of my time and the process of learning. I personally found the course beneficial and challenging.

STUDENT VOICE 4: NIKI CHRISTODOULOU – CYPRUS

My Context on Joining the Course

I have been an English as a Foreign Language (EFL) practitioner for twenty-two years. During the first five years of my teaching career I taught English as a Second Language (ESL) in a secondary school in America. In the past seventeen years I have been teaching EFL in a higher education (HE) institution in Cyprus. In both America and Cyprus, I have had the rich experience of teaching English in multicultural and diverse contexts. As an HE EFL practitioner in Cyprus, however, I had also developed an interest in researching the Teaching of English as a Foreign Language (TEFL) field guided by a desire to investigate teacher EFL knowledge through reflection and reflective practice (RP). Aspiring to do so in a more systematic way, I joined the Professional Doctorate in Teacher Education online course in 2006, a year that marked the beginning of my third decade as an EFL teacher, but more importantly the beginning of a journey as a teacher-learner of my practice.

Why I Decided to do This

I decided to do the Professional Doctorate in Teacher Education to fulfil both personal and professional goals, which, I contend, are inextricably intertwined in the life of a caring teacher. In particular:

- I had reached a time in my professional life during which I felt the need to investigate my EFL practice at a 'deeper' level, ultimately aiming at applying

my EFL knowledge into other aspects of the profession, i.e. teacher training. After many years of teaching, I realised that I had become immersed in
my EFL career without dedicating time to consciously and systematically
reflect, analyze and evaluate the many intricate variables that foster or hinder
learning in my professional context. The Professional Doctorate in Teacher
Education online course served as a forum where I could acquire the skills
and methods that would allow me to become a more competent and critical
teacher-researcher of my practice and investigate reflection, my research area
of interest, in a more systematic way.

- Equipping myself with the knowledge and skills offered through the
Professional Doctorate in Teacher Education course offered me the potential to pursue a future career in training other EFL teachers in Cyprus. In
Cyprus, there is always a need for new information and innovative teaching
techniques for novice and in-service teachers who are thirsty for new knowledge and can be trained accordingly.

- Acquiring a doctoral qualification also fulfilled a new requirement set by the
HE institution in which I work that the majority of the teachers should hold or
be pursuing a doctorate degree if the institution was to attain university status
from the government of Cyprus. Moreover, having a doctoral qualification
would allow me to teach others who are holders of Master Degrees.

How my Research Ideas Developed during the Whole Course

A few years before I joined the Professional Doctorate in Teacher Education, my
research interests had been evolving around the role and value of Reflective Practice
(RP) in TEFL. In 2003 I was in the privileged position to be one of the participants
at the annual conference of the UK work-based learning network (WBL) which took
place in Nicosia, Cyprus and was organized jointly between my institution and the
WBL network. The WBL network is part of the UK Universities Association for
Continuing Education (UACE) which aims to promote a HE system that responds
to the needs of lifelong learning for academic, economic and personal development
purposes. My participation at the conference involved presenting a paper on the
value and role of RP in English Language Teaching (ELT) within my dual role as a
work-based learner and HE practitioner. Moreover, the following year I presented
papers both in Cyprus and abroad on the role of reflection and RP in TEFL and in
multicultural teaching.

However, it was not until I began the online Professional Doctorate in Teacher
Education course that I could see my research interests from a different perspective.
It was the first time in my life as a teacher that I participated in an online course.
One new element was the technological aspect of the experience. Although at first,

having to do all the assignments online created feelings of uncertainty and insecurity for a novice user of online technology like myself, the actual structure of the course helped me 'fight' these feelings: I gradually learned to upload my assignments and share them with people in my group and with my supervisors who always provided invaluable insights and guidance throughout the modules and facilitated the 'scaffolding' of the activities.

The structure of the course helped me realize that, in my pursuit of knowledge, I was not alone. On the contrary, I had the opportunity to interact and share knowledge with a large community of learners, i.e., students who were taking the same modules and knowledgeable supervisors who functioned as facilitators of learning. Through the interaction with learners from different parts of the world, I was exposed to numerous other Teacher Education contexts, and I was thus given the opportunity to examine from a critical perspective the educational system of my country identifying its strengths and limitations. In terms of my specific area of research interest in RP I became aware that there is a gap in the educational system of my country as there is an absence of reflective culture. This awareness has heightened my interest to explore the potential of RP in TEFL in HE in Cyprus even further. Learning to adopt a critical perspective through the modules helped me approach my research interest in RP from a critical angle as well. In other words, I no longer hold the view that RP is the 'answer' or the panacea for many problems in Teacher Education or in teaching, but rather I keep an 'open mind' and examine the strengths and weaknesses of RP as an approach in teacher learning and teacher development.

The third year into the Professional Doctorate in Teacher Education program, constituted the data collection phase of my research. During this phase, I discovered that the skills of collaboration that I learned during the four online modules had been very useful as I effortlessly applied them in my interactions with the five HE EFL participating teachers of my research group in my study. Although I was the teacher-researcher, conducting the investigation, I became aware that I was functioning as a facilitator of the whole process, working alongside the five teachers and providing guidance and support on all the activities we engaged together, i.e., the reflective journals, online chats, the reflective inquiry group meetings etc. and learning from them at the same time. In the fall 2009, I began writing my thesis. It has so far been a difficult process which requires concentration, dedication and systematic 'contact' with the literature and the data. Being a full-time HE EFL lecturer and a mother of two, puts constraints and limitations on the time I devote to my thesis writing. I admit that these constraints create feelings of frustration, uncertainty and self-doubt with regard to accomplishing the tasks I set for myself guided by my supervisors. However, the actual writing (when I do get opportunities to write) is a liberating force. Everything I learned in the Professional Doctorate in Teacher Education course somehow falls into place and help me synthesize the information in the literature and the data from the study. During the modules, I had done a lot of writing for the several tasks and activities required in the modules. All that writing, I realise now, had its purpose: it was a form of 'training' of the mind and a way to help us (the students) think, reflect and critically evaluate the material in order to eventually apply the same 'critical reflection' in our own thesis.

I am only at the beginning of the 'thesis journey'; however, despite the difficulties that I encounter, having knowledgeable and supportive supervisors is an inspiration for me as through them, I can receive the best of guidance and advice to continue my work and arrive at the end of the 'thesis journey' successfully.

My Research Context and Research Problem

The purpose of my study was to investigate how an on-going process of guided reflective practice (RP) influences the subsequent teaching decisions and overall practice of five HE EFL lecturers in a private university in Nicosia, Cyprus. In Phase One, the study explored and described the HE EFL lecturers' perceptions on their teaching behaviors and decisions *before* and *after* the implementation of RP in their context evaluating the significance of RP in their teaching. The knowledge acquired in Phase One of the study was then deliberated on during a "meta-reflection" ten-week period between the five participating teachers and the researcher which culminated to a seminar on "Experiencing Reflective Practice in TEFL in HE in Cyprus" organized by the five teachers and the researcher. The idea for the seminar resulted from a belief that the knowledge acquired in Phase One of study could extend beyond the confines of the research group of the five HE EFL lecturers and shared with other HE EFL teachers working in various tertiary institutions in Cyprus. The seminar and its deliberations constituted Phase Two of the study.

The Methodology

The approach used to conduct the study incorporated a multi-method, in-depth investigation into the practices of five HE EFL lecturers in a private university in Nicosia, Cyprus. The methods used consisted of the following: reflective journals kept by the participants and the researcher, reflective inquiry group discussions, observation/dialogue sessions, online chats, and video-recordings of EFL lessons.

How This Impacted my Professional Life

The online Professional Doctorate in Teacher Education experience has had a very positive impact on my professional life and the context in which I work. It has 'opened' a new world for me as it brought me closer to other teacher learner perspectives and showed me that through collaboration with knowledgeable others, our self-knowledge and discipline knowledge can be greatly enhanced and enriched. Co-constructing knowledge with my co-learners on the modules has helped me adopt the same approach with colleagues at work. Such collaboration has led to working together on research projects with other EFL teachers in my department who share the same views.

Outputs from the Research

This has involved several conference presentations, one with fellow Professional Doctorate in Teacher Education research student Christine Savvidou. There are three more planned.

My Reflections on the Experience

I am currently in the fourth year of the Professional Doctorate in Teacher Education course and I am in the process of writing my thesis. Reflecting back on the last four years, I can honestly state that I have seen myself grow as a person and as a professional. Pursuing the online professional doctorate degree and conducting research when one is also heavily engaged in teaching is a very difficult process. It can also be a lonely 'journey'. However, through the online professional doctorate in Teacher Education with the University of Nottingham, I have learned that in this process teacher researchers are not alone. There is much to be gained from collaboration and exchange of ideas through dialogue with others in a reflectively constructive environment.

STUDENT VOICE 5: DR. DESPINA VARNAVA-MAROUCHOU – CYPRUS

My Context on Joining the Course

My name is Despina Varnava Marouchou. I worked and still I am working as a senior lecturer in a university in Cyprus. My main area of teaching is business studies.

Why I Decided to do This

I decided to do the course for three reasons. First my children were now at an age that they did not need me so much and I therefore had time to pursue my career goals. Second, my college where I worked was on its way of becoming a university and I needed a doctorate degree to be considered faculty member. Third, taking time away for three to five years of face-to-face studying was not possible for me. There were only a limited number of universities offering a doctoral degree programme in teacher education in an online format.

How My Research Ideas Developed during the Whole Course

I had no idea what I was letting myself into as I have never before involved in research. The structure of the course helped me developed the ideas for the research. The process of having to take the taught courses that required us to complete four written assignments helped us to form an initial idea of what our research topic should be. For example, the assignment in the subject context for teacher education required the development of a teacher education framework which represents what participants consider an ideal teacher education programme. This initiated possible research ideas during the early stages of the course. The face-to- face encounters during the summer modules also made the online dialogue more meaningful, in that, we now knew who we were communicating and also formed lifelong friendships and collaborations in research.

My Research Context and Research Problem

The overall aim of my research was to offer a more defined understanding of the students' early conceptions of their learning conceptions and lecturers' conceptions of teaching those students. More specifically the research aimed: First, to identify possible opportunities and problems in the development and design of the undergraduate business introductory courses and to provide a forum for lecturers to share teaching experiences; Second, to identify the lecturers' conceptions of teaching and whether there is a difference of perceptions between the different business courses; Third, to develop an understanding of how students in their initial courses conceive their learning and how this affects their studies in the introductory courses. The study was carried out in one of the three- largest private University of Nicosia. Data was gathered through interviews with 7 lecturers and 12 students in one of the three departments of the college - the department of Management and Marketing.

The Methodology

I was initially confronted with the dilemma of choosing a methodological framework when I was developing my research proposal. In my search for straightforward and clear answers, I tried to draw on the 'Qualitative and Quantitative Research Methods' module. Here I was exposed to a range of ontological and epistemological prepositions which underpin various research traditions. After many discussions with my tutors the constructivist – interpretivist approach for exploring students' and lecturers' experience of teaching/learning was adopted. The main methodology approach adopted was the phenomenography.

What I Learned from This

Before I started my interpretive research for a Doctorate in Education, I knew little about interpretive methods, let alone research methods in general. The Research Methods module introduced me to alternatives to positivist approaches which were critiqued here. It took me a long time, however, to digest the meaning of post-modern research, whilst at the same time coming to terms with my positivist background.

How This Impacted my Professional Life

I came to appreciate and understand the importance of carrying out a piece of education research. Through the research process, I came to appreciate the importance of 'what' we do in research, but also of 'how' and 'why' we do it. First, I have learned to be aware of the factors that affect my building of knowledge and how these influences are exposed in organising and writing up the research. More specifically, I believe I became much more aware about the specific ontological, epistemological and other guiding principles informing such research and research in general. This was an extremely valuable tool in undertaking research in the academic environment.

Outputs from the Research

Since I have finished my Professional Doctorate, I have presented papers in many countries including the UK, Sweden, Istanbul, Holland, Poland and Switzerland. I have written three chapters and several papers and have just published my thesis.

My Reflections on the Experience

Before I started this study, what I knew was obvious and 'straight forward'. In my limited understanding, knowledge was in some way universal, and it could be clearly specified. There was little room in my personal view for reflective examination. 'Reality' for me was taken for granted. These issues formed some of the critical ingredients of who and what I was as a lecturer, but most importantly as a person. Through my involvement with the research process and with help from my supervisors, I learnt to change the way I thought about the research methods and approaches I was to use in the study. At the same time, I came to appreciate how useful and rewarding it was to adopt a more personal, active writing style when conducting a piece of research.

STUDENT VOICE 6: TONY DEGAZON – DUBAI

My Context on Joining the Course

I started my career in sales and marketing, working in a publishing company based in Bahrain in the Middle East. I decided to change my career on my return to the UK in 1993 where I trained as a Business Education teacher and taught in a secondary school in County Durham. In 1997 the Higher Colleges of Technology, a federal system of technical colleges across the United Arab Emirate, and worked within Dubai Men's College teaching a number of Business programs in a variety of credentials such as Higher Diploma (equivalent of A levels), Certificate and Diploma and Bachelors. I completed an MBA in 2002 and was promoted to a supervisor or 'chair' position in 2007 taking on administrative responsibility for over 500 students and 17 teachers. Importantly as one of the few teachers in the Business department that had any formal training in teaching, I was keen to promote the continual discovery of effective practice in context of the college environment. I initiated activities that promoted enquiry into practice and conducted workshops that explored constructivism, action research, learning and teaching and assessment. In addition, I worked closely with Zayed University's centre for professional development to coordinate action research into understanding our learners better. In May 2009, and due to a newly appointed director the college management team was restructured and I was appointed the Chair of Learning Innovation and responsible for teacher development in addition to education technology, library services, assessment and pastoral development and quality assurance. My re-assignment was a reflection of the interest and enthusiasm that I have for growing and developing teacher expertise for the benefit of students at the college.

Why I Decided to do This

Before I was promoted to Business Supervisor I enrolled in the Professional Doctorate in Teacher Education course in September 2006. I had a strong interest in deepening my understanding of teacher education that would inform my own practice and ultimately benefit the college and system in which I work and live. I had also some external drivers, my ambition at that time was working for UNESCO in TVET teacher training and consulting, I had also been involved with the World

Bank and considered educational project work in Afghanistan. In addition, I had worked closely with Zayed University and their teacher development department in fostering action research at the college. As soon as I came across the opportunity provided by University of Nottingham I knew immediately that this suited me, the focus on teacher education was appropriate and relevant and that the international and global profile of the students was informative and supportive. The course promoted constructive and collegial co-construction which was facilitated and enhanced by the online nature of the work. I have always appreciated the applied nature of programs that I have completed in the past and felt that the Professional Doctorate, as a professional research credential, would add significant value not just to myself but to my current work.

How my Research Ideas Developed during the Whole Course

The assignments and course work provided the platform needed to develop the area of interest which I wish to explore. The online program supported collegial sharing of thoughts and opinions of teacher educators from across the world. I found people engaged, helpful and supportive focused on a common objective of personal growth and development. The course assignments were ultimately contextual and provided the opportunity to frame real issues. I recall completing one assignment that explored ongoing work with the Ministry of Education and the World Bank in Afghanistan, another allowed the framing of an investigation of in-service professional development through a community of practice, a topic which helped inform my pilot research study. Importantly, the course assignments provided me with the structure to engage with the literature and research already available within the region that was specifically relevant to my context. When I reflect on those assignments I feel that they were substantial building blocks and steppingstones, to inform my area of interest.

My Research Context and Research Problem

My research investigates a complex multicultural environment where newly re-cruited and existing expatriate faculty work, live and engage in practice while being immersed in diverse and challenging learning context within Higher Colleges of Technology (HCT) in United Arab Emirates. In addition, the study is set in a wider context, one where the organisation currently undergoing radical and significant leadership restructuring and development. To understand the context of the inquiry, the research identifies the national, institutional and organisational environment in which the local culture is defined. A number of areas are considered within defining the context, such as my own position as researcher and participant in respects to themes of cultural pluralism, rapid organisational change and development, the expatriate employment context, Emirati students and the way that they view education and learn. This research is of particular significance to the HCT, the United Arab Emirates federal vocational tertiary college system, which prepares local national men and women for the world of work. Teachers are overwhelmingly expatriates coming from a wide variety of foreign countries and consequently have differing cultural and social perspectives and life experiences and need to consider how their students learn in context of their society and culture.

The Methodology

A qualitative research methodology is being used to gather data to inform a multi-layered investigation into the working lives of expatriate teachers. A stratified sample of expatriate teachers, by academic department and ethnicity were invited to explore their personal constructs on teaching and learning. In addition, information was gathered to understand the impact on the broad organisational climate of the college in respect to the significant management restructuring that the college was engaged within at the time. In order to develop the research themes and questions, a pilot study was conducted to identify the core issues and themes related to teaching in a foreign country. A grounded theory approach has been used to develop theories specifically related to the perceptions, motivation and of participants. The themes that came from the pilot study helped shape and determine the final research design which included respondent triangulation and validation.

What I have Learned from This

The research has to date, explored why people have become expatriate teachers in my current context. In addition, the research has investigated and described the background in which they work and live, their educational experiences, their cultural orientation and how it shapes and informs their beliefs and perspectives of teaching and learning. English language teachers chose to become a career expatriate teacher by choice, they actively engage in extensive professional development. They see teaching as a profession with a body of knowledge and need for continual practice. This contrasts by what I would like to call 'accidental educationalists', these are predominately teachers employed as subject specialists, who have secured a job that has allowed them reside in UAE for a variety of reasons. They have no initial teacher training, and their teaching and learning perspectives are shaped from their own educational experiences. In addition, the complexity of the cultural backgrounds within the institution provides significant challenges for those involved in teacher education. I have learned that cultural perspectives can act as a barrier to professional development, where some teachers see this as a necessary growth others see it as unwelcome intrusion and even a matter of honour or pride. My research although unfinished is providing a practical understanding of teacher perspectives within my context.

How this Impacted my Professional Life

The Professional Doctorate has significantly impacted my own professional growth and direction, and ultimately the faculty and the processes and operations of the college. My own research in perspectives of expatriate teachers, has directly informed the development of a teacher success program to support teachers at risk and those on probation and the introduction of evidence based practice through the launch of a teaching portfolio to support development and appraisal as well as the orientation to of in-service professional development to incorporate pedagogy. In addition, planning is currently underway to develop an in-service teacher education program which will be certified and aimed at supporting teachers with no teacher training that enter the college. On a broader level, It has shaped my interest in teacher education within the country, I am now actively engaging with those stakeholders who are concerned with improving teaching and learning in the UAE. These connections have inspired me to create a networking action group to tackle the national gender gap in the UAE with a focus on attracting and retaining Emirati teachers. All, these developments have been tailored to fit the context of the institution to best serve our Emirati students.

My Reflections on the Experience in General

The course allowed me to explore and compare my context in relation to others. I am more aware of the subtle inter-cultural intelligence required to operate in an expatriate environment and appreciate the very different world views and outlooks on teaching and learning. In addition, there has been some very interesting practical global comparisons, I recall collective research of student teacher evaluations and compared and contrasted surveys and feedback from colleagues working in Amsterdam, Antigua. It was through this experience that helped shape and develop my own institution's student evaluation processes. In addition, for me the most important component of the program was the support provided by the tutors and thesis supervisor. I am immensely grateful for the guidance provided, with regular online meetings, insightful comments and observations combined with supporting deadlines and wonderful exemplars has led me to recommend this course to others.

A BRIEF REFLECTION ON THE STUDENT VOICES

We will let these rich perspectives speak for themselves except to say that it is sat-isfying for us as course designers to have confirmation of the impact of the global perspective the course adopted and the value the taught modules have been for supporting the development of research questions and developing understanding and expertise in the research process. In depth video narratives by Paul Sze and Christine Savvidou describing their research journey can be viewed at http:www.v-resort.ac.uk which is a free online resource to support doctoral students to develop an understanding of the research process (Joyes, 2009).

CURRENT CHALLENGES FACING THE ORGANIZATION

In many respects students and the course team were pioneers and in any kind of innovative setting pioneers by definition have to find pathways through uncharted terrain: an unsympathetic university infrastructure which did not necessarily provide the most appropriate support in terms of administrative, technological and peda-gogic innovation. Yet with pioneering comes determination to succeed by building professional learning communities with lasting effects. However, perhaps the most precious symbol of that pioneering era was the discovery that a student of ours in Poland wished to engage in depth with the programme so much that she had to carry out most of her studies in a Cyber Café.

The course represents a significant professional development experience for each of the team. It has greatly influenced our own thinking, set our own ideas on new pathways and allowed us the privilege of being part of an initiative supporting and promoting on-line, distributed, personalised and interactive learning. However there are challenges currently facing the team and these relate to changes in quality assurance procedures, technologies and staff notwithstanding the global financial crisis. The following considers issues arising from these changes.

Improvements in supervisory practice from 2008 have meant that all doctoral students at the University of Nottingham now have two supervisors instead of one, with a minimum entitlement of ten supervision meetings per year. This in effect has reduced the number of students that can be supervised by any individual lecturer. It also means that supervisors have to be sought from outside of the course team. This is problematic as the professional doctorate is not particularly well understood outside of the existing team. The situation is made worse through the practice of recruit-ing teaching-only support for the ITE course as this means there are fewer Teacher Educators within the School able to teach at doctoral level and most of these prefer to work with PhD students around their own research specialisms. The approach that is being adopted from 2009 is for the course leader to be the main supervisor for all of the 'new' students moving onto the research phase with a second subsidiary supervisor from within the team or outside dependent on the particular focus with Teacher Education. Web2.0 technologies are to be used to establish an online community for this cohort; it hoped that this will bring efficiencies and improvements to the supervisory experience. In the past the research phase was typified by informal support communities established during the taught period coupled with the formal supervisory process; a one-to-one supervisor-student experience. This exploration of the use of Web 2.0 to support research communities fits within the e-learning research interests of the course leader - something that has supported course developments by engaging with the latest technologies.

What will be evident from the above is that the course team has a strong shared sense of commitment to the course. Recently a founder member of the tutor team has left the School and this has left a big gap in the team itself. We now face a difficult problem, which is to find a replacement and to induct them into the team. Finding a replacement may be difficult because the teaching commitment does not show up well on the way we calculate workload in the school, so the replacement tutor needs motivation other than to boost their workload return. Online tutoring is a complex process (Joyes & Wang, 2007) and can be very time consuming. Making and sustaining relationships with course participants is a big part of that challenge. They are never just 'this year's group' – they are individuals from the start, and when that works well it is a very powerful relationship, extracting considerable commitment on both sides. Maybe that is because, as a tutor, one does not want students to be disadvantaged by being in a technologically mediated context. Our experience of working with 'new' tutors on the course is that there is a tendency to do 'too much' - it is difficult to manage the increased access to students for those more accustomed to face-to-face working. This increases workload for students and lowers their expectations in relation to being able to contribute effectively to the online community.

Inducting a replacement would also be a problem, because there is a high level of shared understanding among the tutor team, with a fairly high level of tacit knowledge about the course and how it works. This raises an immediate question of sustainability. If the course is to be long-term sustainable, we have to move beyond the team of tutors. We have to find ways to articulate what the course is like, and why it is like it is, in ways that speak to potential colleagues. This is very different from the case of students who have a vested interest in constructing an understanding of a course from which they aim to gain a valuable qualification.

The current team have a strong commitment to move the course forward in spite of the above constraints, and the collective writing of this article has been a useful reflective exercise which has already resulted in the Web2.0 research phase community approach mentioned above. This course has already had significant impact on the course team and on its students most of whom would not have been able to study for a doctorate and progress their careers without it. We hope the chapter may be of use to other practitioners wishing to explore new ways of working with global cohorts of students, using the affordances of new technological tools.

REFERENCES

Coates, H., James, R., & Baldwin, G. (2005). A critical examination of the effects of learning management systems on university teaching and learning. *Tertiary Education and Management, 11*(1), 19–36. doi:10.1080/13583883.2005.9967137.

Fritze, P. (2003). *Innovation in university computer-facilitated learning systems: Product, workplace experience and the organization.* (Unpublished thesis). RMIT, Melbourne, Australia. Retrieved January 28, 2008, from http://eprints.unimelb.edu.au/archive/00000311/

Goodyear, P. (2000). *Effective network learning in higher education: Notes and guidelines.* Retrieved December 14, 2008, from http://csalt.lancs.ac.uk/jisc/advice.htm

Grabinger, R. S., & Dunlap, J. C. (2000). Rich environments for active learning: A definition. In Squires, D., Conole, G., & Jacobs, G. (Eds.), *The changing face of learning technology* (pp. 8–38). Cardiff, UK: University of Wales Press.

Gregory, M. (1995). Implications of the introduction of the doctor of education degree in British universities: Can the EdD reach the parts the PhD cannot? *The Vocational Aspect of Education, 47*(2), 177–188. doi:10.1080/0305787950470206.

Joyes, G. (2006). When pedagogy leads technology. *International Journal of Technology. Knowledge in Society, 1*, 1–13. Retrieved from http://www.Technology-Journal.com.

Joyes, G. (2009). Personalisation and the online video narrative learning tools V-ResORT and the ViP. In O'Donoghue, J. (Ed.), *Technology Supported Environments for Personalised Learning: Methods and Case Studies* (pp. 324–340). Hershey, PA: IGI Global. doi:10.4018/978-1-60566-884-0.ch018.

Joyes, G., Fisher, A., & Coyle, D. (2002). Developments in generative learning using a collaborative learning environment. In S. Banks, P. Goodyear, V. Hodgson, & D. Mcconnell (Eds.), *Proceedings of the Third Networked Learning International Conference 2002* (pp. 398-405). Lancaster, UK: Lancaster and Sheffield University.

Joyes, G., & Fritze, P. (2006). Valuing individual differences within learning: From face-to-face to online experience. *International Journal of Teaching and Learning in Higher Education, 171*, 33–41.

Joyes, G., & Wang, T. (2007). A generic framework for the training of eLearning tutors. In Spencer-Oatey, H. (Ed.), *eLearning in China: eChina Perspectives on Policy, Pedagogy and Innovation* (pp. 109–124). HK Research Press.

Knowles, M. S. (1990). *The adult learner: A neglected species.* Houston, TX: Gulf Publishing.

Kwame, T. (2005). *Researching the online student experience*, Unpublished PhD thesis, University of Nottingham, UK

Maxwell, T. W. (2003). From first to second generation Professional Doctorate. *Studies in Higher Education, 28*(3), 279–291. doi:10.1080/03075070309292.

Phillips, E., & Pugh, D. (1994). *How to get a PhD: A handbook for students and their supervisors.* Philadelphia, PA: Open University Press.

Sayer, A. (1992). *Method in social science: A realist approach* (2nd ed.). London: Routledge.

United Kingdom Central Council for Graduate Education. (2002). *Professional doctorates.* Dudley, UK: UKCGE.

Wenger, E. (1998). *Communities of practice: Learning, meaning and identity.* Cambridge, UK: Cambridge University Press.

Chapter 12

Secure E-Learning and Cryptography

Wasim A. Al-Hamdani
Kentucky State University, USA

EXECUTIVE SUMMARY

This chapter investigates the problem of secure e-learning and the use cryptography algorithms as tools to ensure integrity, confidentiality, non-reputations, authentication, and access control to provide secure knowledge delivery, secure student feedback, and secure assessments. Providing privacy in e-learning focuses on the protection of personal information of a learner in an e-learning system, while secure e-learning focuses on complete, secure environments to provide integrity, confidentiality, authentication, authorization, and proof of origin. The secure e-learning system and the use of cryptography is the main theme of this chapter. In addition, the authors present a new cryptograph e-learning model based on PKI and cryptography access control. The model is based on creating secure shell system based on PKI, and each adding block has to certified itself to be assessable.

INTRODUCTION

This chapter will investigate the problem of creating a secure E-learning environment for distributed mobile E-learning systems, or so-called mobile learning (M-learning). These types of E-learning systems provide service mobility where the learner can access the learning content from anywhere using any suitable device, such as a desktop computer at home or work, laptops, or PDAs with a wireless connection. Privacy in E-learning will focus on the protection of personal information of a learner in an E-learning system, while secure E-learning will focus on complete, secure environments to provide integrity, confidentiality, and availability.

DOI: 10.4018/978-1-4666-4486-1.ch012

E-learning, also known as Distance Learning (DL), refers to learning where teachers and students do not meet face-to-face. E-learning is a special form of e-business. It provides a new set of tools that add value to traditional learning modes. E-learning does not replace the classroom setting experience, but enhances it; taking advantage of incorporated interactivities and multimedia capabilities afforded by new technologies. In an approach to increase user acceptance of E-learning systems, security and privacy are two crucial factors that must be implemented to achieve an increase in user acceptance and the success of E-learning systems. Security is seen as an enabling technology to E-learning, because people often avoid using systems they do not trust to uphold their privacy and usage.

The history of distance education could be tracked back to the early 1700s in the form of correspondence (mail) education, but technology-based distance education might be best linked to the introduction of audiovisual (relating to sound and vision) devices into schools in the early 1900s (Jeffries, 2009).

The first catalog of instruction films appeared in 1910 and, in 1913, Thomas Edison proclaimed that, due to the invention of film, "Our school system will be completely changed in the next ten years" (Saettler, 1968).

This dramatic change did not occur, but instructional media were introduced into many extension programs by 1920 in the form of slides and active pictures just as in the classroom. The introduction of television as an instructional vehicle appears as an important access point for practitioners and theorists outside of correspondence education, and marks support and sometime parallel way for correspondence study, teaching, and training media.

Instructional television was viewed with new hope after instructional radio was unsuccessful in the 1930s. In 1932, seven years before television was introduced at the New York World's Fair, the State University of Iowa began experimenting with transmitting instructional courses.

World War II slowed the introduction of television, but military training efforts had demonstrated the potential for using audio-visual media in teaching. The apparent success of audio-visual generated a renewed interest in using it in the schools, and in the decade following the war, there were intensive research programs. Most of these studies were directed at understanding and generating theory on how instructional media affected classroom learning (Jeffries, 2009).

M-learning is a relatively new development in the E-learning world and it is increasing rapidly because:

- Higher education projects rely on partnerships with many sectors.
- Handheld devices are used to increase interaction in large enrollment classes.
- M-learning may potentially increase the digital divide.

- Content development has been the purview of specialist publishers.
- Readability issues relate to screen size and resolution, mobility, text input, multimedia capability, and other unique challenges.

Advantages of E-learning:

- **Professional Learning:** Professional learning, especially in authentic contexts like hospitals, at engineering sites, and in the courtroom may also be extended with access to online resources, experts in other locations, and participation in distributed group settings.
- **Floating Teachers:** One school district reported an experiment that supported floating teachers, those who moved regularly between classrooms, schools, and even districts. Teachers that were supplied with handheld devices were able to check their e-mail regularly for messages from students and colleagues, could stay in contact with parents, retrieve files stored on a remote server, participate in decision-making through electronic bulletin boards, and download resources from libraries in other schools and in other jurisdictions.

Other advantages of E-learning include (Campbell, 2004):

- Increased efficiency on the work or learning site.
- Just-in-time learning.
- Lower costs.
- Portability.
- Many applications available on one small device.
- Support for Web browsing, e-mail, real-time chat, and access to remote computing resources.

E-learning security is the security that is applied to materials that comprise study notes, references, demonstrations, and similar that together make up one or more courses in education or in training. The goals of security in E-learning are:

- Protect authors' E-learning materials from copyright infringements.
- Protect teachers from students who will undermine their evaluation system through cheating.
- Protect students from being too closely monitored by teachers when using the system.
- In addition to secure authentication and authorization, proof of origin, secure E-assessment.

The goal of privacy is to enable a student (e-learner) to maintain to a certain extent a degree of "personal space," wherein he or she can control the conditions and terms under which personal information is shared with others. From the corporate perspective, employee training is an approach to increase the level and variety of competencies in employees for both hard and soft skills. E-learning has become an important tool to implement corporate learning objectives (Weippl, 2005).

The main issue in the secure E-learning system or M-learning are:

- Holding marital integrity.
- Student confidentiality.
- Student access control.
- Prevent e-cheating.
- Holding authentication and authorization.

In this article, we will look at these cases and at the future of E-learning in terms of security issues and trying to answer the question, "What are the main threats in E-learning 2.0?" especially the next generation of E-learning based on many canons joined together to present the knowledge.

This article combines four elements in one canon to provide and create a secure E-learning system. These are:

- Components of E-learning and the new arena in E-learning through using different resource.
- Components of cryptography to provide secure E-learning environments and provide authentication, authorization, nonrepudiation, integrity, confidentiality.
- The secure E-learning components.
- The suggested model based on PKI and cryptography access control.

And the last part will focus on the Future development in a secure E-learning system as it starts to be building blocks.

E-LEARNING SYSTEM

E-learning is a very broad term. "It is used to describe any type of learning environment that is computer enhanced" (Aranda, 2009). There are multiple technologies that can be engaged in e-learning. It has become one of those types of words that are so general as to have lost some of its meaning. Distance Learning is something that has evolved from E-learning. It is used to describe "a learning environment that takes place away from the actual traditional classroom and campus"

E-learning began at just about the same time that a personal computer was developed that was practical for personal use. In fact, the concept and practice of Distance Learning predates the computer area by almost 100 years. In England in 1840, shorthand classes were being offered by correspondence courses through the mail. The improvements to the postal service made this method of Distance Learning popular in the early part of the last century. This led to a large number of "through the mail" type of educational programs. The computer only made Distance Learning easy and better. Television, video recorders, and even radio have all made a contribution to Distance Learning.

E-learning and Distance Learning are not quite the same thing. The basic thing that distinguishes distance education is the physical separation of the student from the instructor and the class room. E-learning, however, became part of the classroom environment from the beginning. The early use of computers was geared to help the classroom instructor. Gradually, as more and more personal computers became available, the idea of online classes was explored by some pioneering colleges and universities. The early attempts at distance education were hampered by resistance from traditionalists within the education field.

Some invoked what they called the philosophy of education to demonstrate that the teacher was essential to the educational process. This resistance led to the early online degrees being considered inferior to traditionally obtained degrees. This prejudice extended to the personal departments of major employers. When choosing between two otherwise equally qualified applicants, preference was shown to the person holding the traditional degree. In recent years this has changed drastically. The improvements in E-learning technology and the ability to create virtual classrooms and a virtual learning environment (VLE) have gradually broken down the resistance. This process has been helped by the emergence of a new generation that was weaned on the computer. It would not be surprising if within another generation, the pendulum shifts completely and the online degree is the one that is respected and coveted.

Natalie Aranda (Aranda, 2009) wrote about learning and technology. E-learning is a very broad term. It is used to describe any type of learning environment that is computer enhanced. There are multiple technologies that can be employed in E-learning. It has become one of those types of words that are so general as to have lost some of its meaning. Distance Learning in virtual classrooms is something that has evolved from E-learning. It is used to describe a learning environment that takes place away from the actual traditional classroom and campus.

The traditional approach to E-learning has been to employ the use of a virtual learning environment (VLE), software that is often cumbersome and expensive and that tends to be structured around courses, timetables, and testing. That is an approach that is too often driven by the needs of the institution rather than the individual learner. In contrast, E-learning 2.0 takes a "small pieces, loosely joined" approach that combines the use of discrete but complementary tools and Web services - such as blogs, wikis, and other social software - to support the creation of ad-hoc learning communities.

Enter Web 2.0, a vision of the Web in which information is broken up into 'micro-content' units that can be distributed over dozens of domains. The Web of documents has morphed into a Web of data. We are no longer just looking to the same old sources for information. Now we're looking to a new set of tools to aggregate and remix microcontent in new and useful ways. (MacManus & Porter, 2005).

According to Wenger (2009), a community of practice is characterized by "a shared domain of interest" where "members interact and learn together" and "develop a shared repertoire of resources.

E-Learning 2.0 Apps and Web Sites (MacManus, 2007)

Wikispaces.com and Edublogs.org are two examples of blog and wiki resources for E-learning. There are many other examples of edu-blogging, podcasting, media sharing, and social networks. There are some interesting Web applications for students popping up – for example, a collaborative note taking app called stu.dicio.us and the ReadWriteThink Printing Press, which enables users to create a newspaper, brochure, etc.

For an in-depth look at one of the leaders in this space, there's Elgg, a social network for education. This is an excellent example of how Web 2.0 is shaping E-learning. Elgg is social networking software designed especially for education - built from the ground up to support learning. Described by its founders as a "learning landscape," Elgg provides each user with their own Weblog, file repository (with podcasting capabilities), an online profile and an RSS reader. Additionally, all of a user's content can be tagged with keywords so they can connect with other users with similar interests and create their own personal learning network. However, where Elgg differs from a regular Weblog or a commercial social network (such as MySpace) is the degree of control each user is given over who can access their content. Each profile item, blog post, or uploaded file can be assigned its own access restrictions - from fully public, to only readable by a particular group or individual. Click here for an insightful interview with Elgg's founders.

Note that this type of E-learning social network is similar to "smart" social networks, in which you can put access controls around your personal details, so that only people you trust can see them. Facebook, imbee, Vox, and Multiply are all examples of smart social networks.

Another example of an E-learning 2.0 app is ChinesePod, which we profiled in November. ChinesePod teaches Mandarin over the Web. It uses podcasting, RSS, blogging, and other Web 2.0 technologies to teach Mandarin Chinese. The business model is surprisingly simple, featuring mainly subscriptions to language E-learning materials. This complements the free offerings - basically, the Mandarin podcasts - very nicely. For example, if you want to dive into learning Mandarin straight away, select one of the episodes, plus you can participate in the discussions. The first level subscription is called "Basic" and gets you a PDF transcript of the podcast. If you want to get really serious about learning Mandarin, sign up to get the premium subscription service and receive learning resources such as Review Materials and Lesson Plans.

The community aspect of ChinesePod shows what can be done with Web 2.0 technologies in E-learning. Check out the Community page, which has a forum, wiki, blogs, photos, and rss feeds. All the usual pieces are offered, but each has a practical purpose. The wiki has extra links and information, the forum is well-used by users, the photos are lovely (of China), and there are a lot of great rss feeds.

Traditional Learning Management System (LMS) (MacManus, 2007)

These are also known as Virtual Learning Environments (VLE) and examples are Blackboard, Moodle, and Sakai (the latter two are open source). As we hinted at above, the big commercial software like Blackboard is very "old school" and doesn't have much focus on the community aspects of learning. They're expensive and are generally seen as clunky and difficult to use - not unlike traditional content management systems in enterprises. They also have a lot of features that most teachers and students don't want or need. However, there are some newcomers that are interesting, including LMS 2.0, Digication, and Nuvvo.

Trends in E-Learning

- Learners may access courseware using many different computing devices and from different locations, via different networks.
- E-learning technology will overtake classroom training to meet the needs for "know what" and "know how" training.

- E-learning will offer more user personalization; whereas courseware will dynamically change based on learner preferences or needs. In other words, E-learning applications of the future will be intelligent and adaptive.
- Corporate training is becoming knowledge management. This is the general trend in the digital economy. With knowledge management, employee competencies are assets which increase in value through training. This trend has pushed the production of training that is more task specific than generic. Changes in corporate strategic directions are often reflected as changes in e-learning requirements prompted by the need to train staff for those new directions.
- E-learning is moving toward open standards. (Weippl, 2005)

General Elements Required for E-Learning (Barone, 2009)

- **Content:** Learning content comes primarily, the knowledge to deliver is the main focus and it guide the method of delivery (for example mathematic course is not like history course).
- **Collaboration:** Real-time collaboration technology offers many deployment opportunities beyond traditional instructor-lead training.
- **Skills Management:** Skills management consists of a number of components that enable employees and managers to validate on-the-job experience. Together with competency and assessment, this allows organizations to monitor how the learning activity relates and aligns with business objectives.
- **Assessment:** It provides the pieces needed to accurately evaluate an individual's competency of different skills. Assessment solutions include Web-based testing and assessment tools with complete multimedia capabilities.
- **Learning Management:** The management ties all of the solution components together. A learning management system (LMS) can provide the tools needed to integrate the process of scheduling, delivering, and measuring the success of curricula. Whether it's managing Web-based training (WBT) courses, computer-based training (CBT) courses, document-based training, instructor-led training (ILT), or a mixture of training methods, an LMS can provide a centralized location to manage all aspects of training, as well as meeting learner requirements and producing reports. A powerful LMS has the ability to launch, track, and report information from courses produced by a variety of content vendors and can integrate with other business critical systems such as ERP.
- **An Integrated System:** E-learning should not be just about using technology to replace training rooms and purely reduce costs. As learning moves closer to the job, mixed instruction media addresses the need for more just-

in-time and project-based learning, performance support, open and Distance Learning, expert assistance, and a generally greater variety of events and experiences. Moreover, E-learning technologies should be used to link training to business goals in order to achieve the best possible business results.

Instructor-led training will continue to play an important role for several reasons: It is the best delivery approach for certain types of high-level learning, it is the way some people prefer to learn, and it is still the way many trainers prefer to train.

The key success factors for any learning (either "e" or "non-e") initiatives are (and will always be) detailed need analysis, media selection, good design, and people motivation. Learners are amazingly good at adapting to and learning from a wide range of media.

CRYPTOGRAPHY ALGORITHMS

Cryptography (Al-Hamdani, 2010)

The word cryptography means "secret writing". Some define cryptography as the study of mathematical techniques. Cryptography is a function that transfers plaintext (Pt) into ciphertext (Ct,) and decryption is the inverse function that transfers ciphertext into plaintext (Al-Hamdani, 2008).

Cryptographic Goals

The cryptography goals are privacy or confidentiality, data integrity, authentication, and non-repudiation.

Classification

A crypto system could be classified generally as "Unkeyed" (key is not required for encryption and decryption) -based algorithms and "keyed" (key is required for encryption and decryption) based. Unkeyed based are classified further into "hash functions" (a method of turning data into a (relatively) small number that may serve as a digital "fingerprint" of the data) and "pseudorandom generator" (an algorithm generates a sequence of numbers that approximate the properties of random numbers). Keyed based is classified into "symmetric" key ("secret key") (uses identical key for encryption and decryption) and "asymmetric" ("public key") (the key for encryption and decryption are not identical). Symmetric algorithms are classified into "block cipher" (encryption and decryption accomplish on fixed size of plaintext/ciphertext called block of bits),"stream ciphers" (encryption and decryptions are accomplished on sequence of bits one bit at a time), "digital signatures" (an electronic signature that can be used to authenticate the identity of the sender of a message or the signer of a document), hash functions, pseudorandom generator, "identification" (identifying something, map a known entity to unknown entity to make it known), and "authentications" (who or what it claims to be). Asymmetric are classified into digital signatures, identification, and authentications.

The symmetric could be classified as "conventional" or "classical" and "modern" algorithms. The classical are classified into "transposition "and "substitution"; another type of cryptography is called the "hybrid", which combines symmetric and asymmetric to form hybrid ciphers.

Practical Cryptosystems

Symmetric Key Algorithms: DES, AES

- **DES:** Data encryption standard was approved as a federal standard in November 1976, and published on 15 January 1977 as FIPS PUB 46, authorized for use on all unclassified data. It was subsequently reaffirmed as the standard in 1983, 1988 (revised as FIPS-46-1), 1993 (FIPS-46-2), and again in 1999 (FIPS-46-3), the latter prescribing "Triple DES" which still used in some application. DES applies a 56-bit key to each 64-bit block of data. The process involves 16 rounds with major two processes – key and plaintext (Simovits, 1995).
- **Triple-DES (3DES):** is a 64-bit block cipher with 168-bit key and 48 rounds, 256 times stronger than DES, and uses three times the resources to perform the encryption/decryption process compared to DES.
  - **DES-EEE3:** Three different keys.
  - **DES-EDE3:** Three different keys.
  - **ES-EEE2:** Two different keys.
  - **DES-EDE2:** Two different keys.
- **DESX:** is a strengthened variant of DES supported by RSA Security's toolkits. The difference between DES and DESX is that in DESX, the input plaintext is bitwise XORed with 64 bits of additional key material before encryption with DES and the output is also bitwise XORed with another 64 bits of key material (RSA.com, 2007).
- **Advanced Encryption Standard (AES):** "Rijndael" designed to use simple byte operations, the key size and the block size may be chosen from of 128, 192, or 256 with a variable number of rounds. The numbers of rounds are:
  - Nine if both the block and the key are 128 bits long.

○   11 if either the block or the key is 192 bits long, and neither of them is longer than that.

○   13 if either the block or the key is 256 bits long.

The total number of rounds key bits is equal to block length multiplied by the number or rounds plus 1. In the general process of SAE, the first (r-1) rounds are similar and they consists of four transformation called: ByteSub-Substitution Bytes, ShiftRow- Shift Rows, MixColumn- Multiply Columns and AddRoundKey- XORed by the key. The last round only performs the transformations ByteSub and ShiftRow.

The AES standard (NIST FIPS Pub. 197) was published in 2002. The algorithm is adopted for the Internet community through the use of Request for Comments: 3394. The purpose of this document is to make the algorithm conveniently available to the Internet community.

AES is used for other applications and specified with ISO as ISO 26429-6:2008. This defines the syntax of encrypted digital cinema non-interleaved material exchange format (MXF) frame-wrapped track files and specifies a matching reference decryption model. It uses the advanced encryption standard (AES) cipher algorithm for essence encryption and, optionally, the HMAC-SHA1 algorithm for essence integrity. The digital cinema track file format is designed to carry digital cinema essence for distribution to exhibition sites and is specified in the sound and picture track file specification.

- **International Data Encryption Algorithm (IDEA):** IDEA operates on 64-bit blocks using a 128-bit key, and eight rounds and an output transformation (the half-round). It has been used with PGP.
- **Other Block Cipher Algorithms (Al-Hamdani, 2008):** RC2 (block size: 64, key size: 1..128;), RC5 (block size: 32, 64 and 128; key size: 0..2040; number of rounds: 0..255) RC6 (block size: 128; keysize: 0..2040 (128, 192, and 256)).
- **Block Cipher Modes of Operation:** The block cipher works with a message of block size n bits (for example DES n=64), a message M that exceed the size of n bits must be partitioned into m block, then linking these blocks in a certain mechanism. The method of combining all encrypted blocks is called *mode of operations*. There are four basic modes of operations, which are electronic code book (ECB), cipher block chaining (CBC), K-bit cipher feedback (CFB), and K-bit output feedback (OFB).

First Part: Five Confidentiality Mode

In Special Publication 800-38A, five confidentiality modes are specified for use with any approved block cipher, such as the AES algorithm. The modes in SP 800-38A are updated versions of the ECB, CBC, CFB, and OFB modes that are specified in FIPS Pub. 81; in addition, SP 800-38A specifies the CTR mode.

The NIST has developed a proposal to extend the domain of the CBC mode with a version of "ciphertext stealing."1 Eventually, the NIST expects to incorporate into a new edition of SP 800-38A some form ciphertext stealing for CBC mode.

Second Part: An Authentication Mode

The CMAC authentication mode is specified in Special Publication 800-38B for use with any approved block cipher. CMAC stands for cipher-based message authentication code (MAC), analogous to HMAC, the hash-based MAC algorithm.

Third Part: An Authenticated Encryption Mode

Special Publication 800-38C specifies the CCM mode of the AES algorithm. CCM combines the counter mode for confidentiality with the cipher block chaining technique for authentication. The specification is intended to be compatible with the use of CCM within a draft amendment to the IEEE 802.11 standard for wireless local area networks.

Fourth Part: A High-Throughput Authenticated Encryption Mode

Special Publication 800-38D specifies the Galois/Counter Mode (GCM) of the AES algorithm. GCM combines the counter mode for confidentiality with an authentication mechanism that is based on a universal hash function. GCM was designed to facilitate high-throughput hardware implementations; software optimizations are also possible, if certain lookup tables can be precomputed from the key and stored in memory.

In the future, the NIST intends to recommend at least one additional mode: the AES Key Wrap (AESKW). AESKW is intended for the authenticated encryption ("wrapping") of specialized data, such as cryptographic keys, without using a nonce for distribution or storage. AESKW invokes the block cipher about 12 times per block of data. The design provides security properties that may be desired for high assurance applications; the tradeoff is relatively inefficient performance compared to other modes.

Asymmetric Algorithms

There are four general practical cryptography systems. These are:

- **Public Key:** Includes factorization, RSA, and Rabin
    - **RSA (Rivest-Shamir-Adleman):** Is the most commonly used public-key algorithm. It can be used both for encryption and for digital signatures. The security of RSA is generally considered equivalent to factoring, although this has not been proved.
    - **Rabin:** Is an asymmetric cryptographic technique, whose security, like that of RSA, is related to the difficulty of factorization, although it has a quite different decoding process.
- **Discrete Logs:** Diffie-Hellman, ElGamal, and DSS
    - **Diffie-Hellman:** Is a commonly used protocol for key agreement protocol (also called exponential key agreement) was developed by Diffie and Hellman in 1976 and published in the groundbreaking paper "New Directions in Cryptography." The protocol allows two users to exchange a secret key over an insecure medium without any prior secrets.
    - **ElGamal:** Is an extension of Diffie/Hellman's original idea on shared secret generation, it generates a shared secret and uses it as a one-time pad to encrypt one block of data. The ElGamal algorithm provides an alternative to the RSA for public key encryption.
        - Security of the RSA depends on the (presumed) difficulty of factoring large integers.
        - Security of the ElGamal algorithm depends on the (presumed) difficulty of computing discrete logs in a large prime modulus.
        - ElGamal has the disadvantage that the ciphertext is twice as long as the plaintext. It has the advantage the same plaintext gives a different ciphertext (with near certainty) each time it is encrypted.
- **DSS (Digital Signature Standard):** Not to be confused with a digital certificate, DSS is an electronic signature that can be used to authenticate the identity of the sender of a message or the signer of a document, and possibly to ensure that the original content of the message or document that has been sent is unchanged. Digital signatures are easily transportable, cannot be imitated by someone else, and can be automatically time-stamped. The ability to ensure that the original signed message arrived means that the sender cannot easily repudiate it later. A signature-only mechanism endorsed by the United States government. The underlying digital signature algorithm (DSA) is similar to the one used by ElGamal or by the Schnorr signature algorithm. Also it is fairly efficient, although not as efficient as RSA for signature verification.

The standard defines DSS to use the SHA-1 hash function exclusively to compute message digests. The main problem with DSS is the fixed subgroup size (the order of the generator element), which limits the security to around only *80* bits. A digital signature can be used with any kind of message, whether it is encrypted or not, simply so that the receiver can be sure of the sender's identity and that the message arrived intact. A digital certificate contains the digital signature of the certificate-issuing authority so that anyone can verify that the certificate is real.

- **Elliptic Curve:** Elliptic curves are mathematical constructions from number theory and algebraic geometry, which in recent years have found numerous applications in cryptography. An elliptic curve can be defined over any field (e.g., real, rational, complex). Elliptic curves can provide versions of public key methods that, in some cases, are faster and use smaller keys, while providing an equivalent level of security. Their advantage comes from using a different kind of mathematical group for public key arithmetic.

- **Elliptic Curves over Real Numbers:** They are named because they are described by cubic equations. In general, cubic equations for elliptic curves take the form:

$$y^2 + axy + by = x^3 + cx^2 + dx + e$$

where a,b,c,d and e are real numbers and x and y take on values in the real numbers. It is sufficient to be limited to equations of the form $y^2 = x^3 + ax + b$ (Cubic). Also included in the definition is a single element denoted O and called the *point at infinity* or the *zero point,* which to plot such a curve, we need to compute $y = \sqrt{x^3 + ax + b}$ for given values of a and b; thus, the plot consists of positive and negative values of y for each value of x.

Stream Cipher

A onetime pad system (vernam cipher) is defined as

$$C_{li} = P_{li} \oplus K_i \text{ for } i = 1, 2, 3, 4 ... n$$

where $P_{l1}, P_{l2}, P_{l3}, ... P_{ln}$ plaintext bits, key bits, ciphertext bits, and is the XOR function. The decryption is defined by:

$$P_{li} = C_{li} \oplus K_i \text{ for } i = 1, 2, 3, 4$$

- **RC4:** RC4 (RSA.com 2007) is a software type of stream cipher based on tables and internal memory. It is based on the use of a random permutation based on numbers 0... 255 represented as an array of length 256 and two indices in this array. RC4 is most commonly used to protect Internet traffic using the secure sockets layer (SSL) protocol and wired equivalent privacy (WEP).

Integrity and Authentication

The mechanism for ensuring that data is not altered when transmitted from source to destination, or when it is stored, is called integrity; this includes the message authentication code (MAC), hash functions, and the keyed-hash message authentication code (HMAC).

- **MAC:** (RSA.com, 2007): A message authentication code (MAC) is an authentication tag (also called a checksum) derived by applying an authentication scheme, together with a secret key, to a message. Unlike digital signatures, MACs are computed and verified with the same key, so that they can only be verified by the intended recipient. There are four types of MACs: (1) unconditionally secure, (2) hash function based, (3) stream cipher based, or (4) block cipher based.
- **Hash Functions:** (Mogollon, 2007) Are used to prove that transmitted data was not altered. A hash function H takes an input message m and transforms it to produce a hash value h that is a function of the message $h = H(m)$; the input is a variable string and the output is a fixed-size string.
- **The SHA:** (Federal Information, 1993; Eastlake & Motorola, 2001) Hash functions are a set of cryptographic hash functions designed by the National Security Agency (NSA) and published by the NIST as a U.S. Federal Information Processing Standard. SHA stands for secure hash algorithm. The three SHA algorithms are structured differently and are distinguished as SHA-0, SHA-1, and SHA-2. The SHA-2 family uses an identical algorithm with a variable key size which is distinguished as SHA-224, SHA-256, SHA-384, and SHA-512.SHA-1 is the best established of the existing SHA hash functions, and is employed in several widely used security applications and protocols. In 2005, security flaws were identified in SHA-1, namely that a possible mathematical weakness might exist, indicating that a stronger hash function would be desirable. Although no attacks have yet been reported on the SHA-2 variants, they are algorithmically similar to SHA-1 and so efforts are underway to develop improved alternatives. A new hash function, to be known as SHA-3, is currently under development, to be selected via open competition starting in 2008, and to be made official in 2012.

- **A Keyed-Hash Message Authentication Code:** (Bellare, Canetti, & Hugo, 1996a, b; Kim, Biryukov, Prenee, & Hong, 2006) (HMAC or KHMAC) Is a type of message authentication code (MAC) calculated using a specific algorithm involving a cryptographic hash function in combination with a secret key. As with any MAC, it may be used to simultaneously verify both the data integrity and the authenticity of a message. Any iterative cryptographic hash function, such as MD5 or SHA-1, may be used in the calculation of an HMAC; the resulting MAC algorithm is termed HMAC-MD5 or HMAC-SHA-1 accordingly. The cryptographic strength of the HMAC depends upon the cryptographic strength of the underlying hash function, on the size and quality of the key and the size of the hash output length in bits. An iterative hash function breaks up a message into blocks of a fixed size and iterates over them with a compression function. For example, MD5 and SHA-1 operate on 512-bit blocks. The size of the output of HMAC is the same as that of the underlying hash function (128 or 160 bits in the case of MD5 or SHA-1, respectively), although it can be truncated if desired.

Authentication Mechanisms Class

Authentication mechanism fall into two basic categories: password and challenge response.

Password SHA

Password SHA is popular and has some natural limitations. The simplest kind of connection-oriented authentication uses a shared secret in the form of a password, a personal identification number (PIN), or passphrase. The most significant characteristic of password-based systems is that the authentication does not depend on information sent by the side performing the authentication check. HTTP basic authentication is not considered to be a secure method of user authentication, unless used in conjunction with some external secure system such as SSL.

Challenge-Response Authentication

It can be more complex to set up, but it provides a significantly higher level of security the entity performing the authentication check first sends out a challenge. The client system trying to prove the user's identity performs some function on the challenge based on information only available to the user/client and returns the result. If the result is as expected, the user is authenticated.

Kerberos

A computer network authentication protocol, which allows individuals communicating over a non-secure network to prove their identity to one another in a secure manner, is also a client-server model, and it provides mutual authentication — both the user and the server verify each other's identity. Kerberos protocol messages are protected against eavesdropping and replay attacks. Kerberos builds on symmetric key cryptography and requires a trusted third party. Extensions to Kerberos can provide for the use of public-key cryptography during certain phases of authentication.

Other Algorithms

Cryptographic Message Syntax (Housley, 1999, 2004)

The CMS describes encapsulation syntax for data protection. It supports digital signatures and encryption. The syntax allows multiple encapsulations; one encapsulation envelope can be nested inside another. Likewise, one party can digitally sign some previously encapsulated data. It also allows arbitrary attributes, such as signing time, to be signed along with the message content, and provides for other attributes such as countersignatures to be associated with a signature. The CMS can support a variety of architectures for certificate-based key management. The CMS values are generated using ASN.1 [X.208-88], using BER-encoding [X.209-88]. Values are typically represented as octet strings. While many systems are capable of transmitting arbitrary octet strings reliably, it is well known that many electronic mail systems are not. This document does not address mechanisms for encoding octet strings for reliable transmission in such environments.

The CMS is derived from PKCS #7 version 1.5, which is documented in RFC 2315 [PKCS#7]. A PKCS #7 version 1.5 was developed outside of the IETF. It was originally published as an RSA Laboratories technical note in November 1993. Since that time, the IETF has taken responsibility for the development and maintenance of the CMS. Advance encryption standard has been enforced with CMS since 2003 (Schaad, 2003).

NSA Suite B Cryptography (Nsa.gov, 2005)

Suite B is a set of cryptographic algorithms promulgated by the National Security Agency as part of its cryptographic modernization program. It is to serve as an interoperable cryptographic base for both unclassified information and most classified information. Suite B was announced on February 16, 2005. A corresponding set of unpublished algorithms, Suite A, is intended for highly sensitive communication and critical authentication systems. Suite B only specifies the cryptographic algorithms to be used. Many other factors need to be addressed in determining whether a particular device implementing a particular set of cryptographic algorithms should be used to satisfy a particular requirement. These include:

1. The quality of the implementation of the cryptographic algorithm in software, firmware or hardware.
2. Operational requirements associated with U.S. government-approved key and key-management activities.
3. The uniqueness of the information to be protected (e.g. special intelligence, nuclear command and control, U.S.-only data).
4. Requirements for interoperability both domestically and internationally.

The process by which these factors are addressed is outside the scope of Suite B. Suite B focuses only on cryptographic technology, a small piece of an overall information assurance system. Another suite of NSA cryptography, Suite A, contains classified algorithms that will not be released. Suite A will be used for the protection of some categories of especially sensitive information (a small percentage of the overall national security related information assurance market).

SUITE B Includes:

*   **Encryption:** Advanced Encryption Standard (AES) - FIPS 197(with keys sizes of 128 and 256 bits).
*   **Digital Signature:** Elliptic Curve Digital Signature Algorithm - FIPS 186-2 (using the curves with 256 and 384-bit prime moduli).
*   **Key Exchange:** Elliptic Curve Diffie-Hellman Draft NIST Special Publication 800-56 (using the curves with 256 and 384-bit prime moduli).
*   **Hashing:** Secure Hash Algorithm - FIPS 180-2 (using SHA-256 and SHA-384).

The Committee on National Security Systems (CNSS) (Cnss.gov, 2003) stated that AES with either 128- or 256-bit keys are sufficient to protect classified information up to the SECRET level. Protecting top secret information would require the use of 256-bit AES keys1, as well as numerous other controls on manufacture, handling and keying. These same key sizes are suitable for protecting both national security and non-national, security-related information throughout the USG.

Consistent with CNSSP-15, elliptic curve public key cryptography using the 256-bit prime modulus elliptic curve as specified in FIPS-186-2 and SHA-256 are appropriate for protecting classified information up to the SECRET level. Use of the 384-bit prime modulus elliptic curve and SHA-384 are necessary for the protection of TOP SECRET information.

All implementations of Suite B must, at a minimum, include AES with 256-bit keys, the 384-bit prime modulus elliptic curve and SHA-384 as a common mode for widespread interoperability.

Standards

The Suite B Base Certificate and CRL profile is provided as part of the overarching cryptographic interoperability strategy.

Testing, Evaluation, and Certification of "Suite B" Products

Creating secure cryptographic equipment involves much more than simply implementing a specific suite of cryptographic algorithms. Within the USG there are various ways to have cryptographic equipment tested or evaluated and certified. These methods include:

1. The Cryptographic Module Verification Program (CMVP).
2. The Common Criteria Evaluation and Validation Scheme (CCEVS).
3. Evaluation by the National Security Agency.

Access Authentication

Authentication is essential for two parties to be able to trust in each other's identities. Authentication is based on something you know (a password), on something you have (a token card, a digital certificate), or something that is part of you (fingerprints, voiceprint). A strong authentication requires at least two of these factors. The mechanisms of authentication for example are:

- IEEE 802.1X Access Control Protocol.
- Extensible Authentication Protocol (EAP) and EAP methods.
- Traditional passwords.
- Remote Authentication Dial-in Service (RADIUS).
- Kerberos authentication service.
- X.509 authentication.

Cryptography Algorithms Standards

There are three types of standardization organizations.

- **National Standardization Organizations:** National Institute of Standards and Technology (NIST), American National Standards Institute (ANSI), and British Standards Institute (BSI).
- **International Standardization Organizations:** International Organization for Standardization (ISO), International Electrotechnical Commission (IEC), and International Telecommunication Union (ITU).
- **Industrial Standardization Organizations:** Institute of Electrical and Electronics Engineers (IEEE), Public-Key Cryptography Standards (PKCSs), Internet Engineering Task Force (IETF), Standards for Efficient Cryptography Group (SECG), Third Generation Partnership Project (3GPP) and European Telecommunications Standard Institute (ETSI).

Standard is defined as "a level of quality"; "an accepted example of something against which others are judged or measured"; and "a reference point against which other things can be evaluated". A cryptography standard is the "level of algorithm quality in which an algorithm that's been proved theoretically and practically is strong and can stand different attacks for years". Some algorithms need special procedures to satisfy the standard and it should be clarified that certain standardized techniques are known to be weak unless used with care and such guidance is also typically present in the standard itself.

Standards are important because they define common practices, methods, and measures/metrics. Therefore, standards increase the reliability and effectiveness of products and ensure that the products are produced with a degree of quality. Standards provide solutions that have been accepted by a wide community and evaluated by experts in relevant areas. By using standards, organizations can reduce costs and protect their investments in technology.

Standards provide the following benefits:

- Interoperability
- Security
- Quality

Many NIST standards and recommendations contain associated conformance tests and specify the conformance requirements. The conformance tests may be administered by NIST-accredited laboratories and provide validation that the NIST standard or recommendation was correctly implemented in the product.

In sum, standards provide a common form of reference and cost savings. In particular, the NIST Special Publication 800-21 provides a Guideline for Implementing Cryptography in the Federal Government.

The Standards for Efficient Cryptography Group (SECG)

The Standards for Efficient Cryptography Group (SECG), an industry consortium, was founded in 1998 to develop commercial standards that facilitate the adoption of efficient cryptography and interoperability across a wide range of computing platforms. SECG members include leading technology companies and key industry players in the information security industry. The group exists to develop commercial standards for efficient and interoperable cryptography based on elliptic curve cryptography (ECC).

SECURITY COMPONENT IN E-LEARNING

Privacy Current E-Learning Systems

Most E-learning innovations have focused on course development and delivery, with little or no consideration to privacy and security as required elements. However, it is clear from the above trends that there will be a growing need for high levels of confidentiality and privacy in E-learning applications and those security technologies must be put in place to meet these needs. The knowledge of consumers regarding their rights to privacy is increasing, and new privacy legislations have recently been introduced by diverse jurisdictions. It is also clear that confidentiality is vital for information concerning E-learning activities undertaken by corporate staff. While corporations may advertise their learning approaches to skills and knowledge development in order to attract staff, they do not want competitors to learn the details of training provided, which could compromise their strategic directions.

E-learning systems play a primary and/or supportive role in modern education. With E-learning systems E-assessments are an integral part of a course be it to do formative or summative assessments. The reason for security controls in E-learning is that E-assessments are being used more and more to replace paper based tests. The E-assessments need to be in an environment that is at least as secure as conventional, paper-based tests. The urgency to improve E-assessments is due to the fact that electronic corruption is much easier if they are implemented correctly. E-learning security is essential to establish E-learning as a trusted supporting medium or even primary education medium for learners. It is predicted that within five years, education from school to adult education in the workplace will make use of on-screen assessments/e-assessments. Security mechanisms in current E-learning systems and products are lacking, and are not necessarily addressed by applying good Web security principles.

Security Components Required in Secure E-Learning

There are many issues need to be presented to create secure E-learning system, these are:

Authentication

At the core of any E-learning environment is the act of establishing or confirming something (or someone) as authentic – that is, that claims made by or about the subject are true. This might involve confirming the identity of a person, the origins of an artifact, or assuring that a computer program is a trusted one. E-learning system or server required authentication to allow a student access to his/her personal space in the E-learning environment. Authentication is usually integrated into the institution's authentication method for E-learning systems or other portal services; however, some institution provide E-learning system as stand allows without be integrated with other system in which student another access control to access the servers. The student's personal space includes e-mail, a discussion facility, marks, assignments, and assessments. All these services should only be available to the intended student. There are several methods used to authenticate a student to an E-learning system, such as:

- Passwords
- Secure token authentication
- Challenge response protocol
- Smart card authentication
- Biometric authentication (face recognition and fingerprint)

The aim of providing authentication is to ensure that only a correctly authenticated person will be able to hand in an assignment or do an assessment. The mostly used authentication protocol is the password as it is the cheapest comparing to other authentication techniques although being more cumbersome to use and/or more expensive to implement, provide higher security. The last option is where a biometric system is used and this is the ultimate authentication technique for E-learning. Sadly this requires a capital investment to be made by an institution but when done will go a long way to provide E-learning systems with better integrity of its results.

Confidentiality and Privacy

Confidentiality refers to limiting information access and disclosure to authorized users (the right people) and preventing access by or disclosure to unauthorized ones (the wrong people).

The aim is to ensuring that information is accessible only to those authorized to have access, and in E-learning is to ensure that the actual information can be accesses by the authorized student. Confidentiality of information, enforced in an adaptation of the military's classic "need-to-know" principle, forms the cornerstone of information security in today's corporate. The so-called "confidentiality bubble" restricts information flows, with both positive and negative consequences. In any E-learning system, the confidentiality enforced by group policy build in the system, such as to instructor, co-instructor, and student. This is very useful but it is not quit secure – for example, instructor and co-instructor have the same access right, and undergraduate, graduate and non-degree students have the same access right.

A student reserves the right to keep his/her marks and information private and confidential. This is determined by the quality of the password used by the student and is enhanced by any of the other authentication techniques mentioned previously. The integrity of any assessment and any course materials also needs to be protected by whatever authentication technique.

The goal of confidentiality are authentication methods like user IDs and passwords, that uniquely identify a data system's users, and supporting control methods that limit each identified user's access to the data system's resources.

Integrity

This means that data cannot be modified without authorization. Integrity could be violated when a student, malicious person, or program changes information on the server, makes use of resources not specified in the course materials, or helps another student.

Integrity refers to the trustworthiness of information resources. It includes the concept of "data integrity", which means that data have not been changed inappropriately, whether by accident or deliberately through harmful activity. It also includes "origin" or "source integrity", which means the data actually came from the person or entity you think it did. Integrity can even include the concept that the person or entity in question entered the right information means that the information reflected the actual conditions and that under the same circumstances would generate identical data. On a more restrictive view, however, integrity of an information system includes only preservation without corruption of whatever was transmitted or entered into the system, right or wrong.

A normal solution to hold integrity is using a crypto hash function and, more precisely, focusing on a large solution to insure integrity to use the public key infrastructure (PKI). The PKI is a set of hardware, software, people, policies, and procedures needed to create, manage, store, distribute, and revoke digital certificates.

In cryptography, a PKI is an arrangement that binds public keys with respective user identities by means of a certificate authority (CA). The user identity must be unique for each CA. The binding is established through the registration and issuance process, which, depending on the level of assurance the binding has, may be carried out by software at a CA, or under human supervision. The PKI role that assures this binding is called the Registration Authority (RA). For each user, the user identity, the public key, their binding, validity conditions, and other attributes are made unforgettable in public key certificates issued by the CA (Kelm, 2009).

The term "trusted third party" (TTP) may also be used for certificate authority (CA). The term PKI is sometimes erroneously used to denote public key algorithms, which do not require the use of a CA.

- **Access Control:** Ensuring that users access only those resources and services that they are entitled to access and that qualified users are not denied access to services that they legitimately expect to receive.

Access control is one aspect of a wide-ranging computer security solution (e.g., physical, technical, administration, business continuity plans), but it is one of the most visible aspects. Every time a user logs on to a multiuser environment, access control is enforced. To gain a better understanding of the purpose of access control, this discussion will review the risks to information systems, which can be largely classified as confidentiality, integrity, or availability. Confidentiality is the need to keep information secure and private. Integrity refers to the concept of protecting information from being improperly altered or modified by unauthorized users. Finally, availability refers to the notion that information is available for use when needed.

Access control is critical to preserving the confidentiality and integrity of information. Confidentiality requires that only authorized users can read, while integrity requires that only authorized users can modify information in authorized manner. Access control does not clearly preserve availability, but it plays an important role (in an indirect way). For example, an attacker who has unauthorized access to a system can use a little problem to bring the system down.

The elements of access control are (Hansche, 2006):

- **Identification and Authentication:** Establishing the identities of entities with some level of assurance.

- **Authorization:** Determining the access rights of an entity, also with some level of assurance.
- **Decision:** Comparing the rights (authorization) of an authenticated identity with the characteristics of a requested action to determine whether the request should be granted.
- **Enforcement:** May involve a single decision to grant or deny, or may entail periodic or continuous enforcement functions.

Access Control Entities (Al-Hamdani, 2010)

Many entities exist in any access control model. Ferraiolo, Kuhn and Chandramouli specified these entities as users, subjects, objects, operations, and permissions (authorization). These entities share relationships between them. Authentication mechanisms make it possible to match the multiple IDs to a single user. A session is an instance of a user's negotiation with a system. A subject is process acting on behalf of a user; a user may have multiple subjects in operation. An object can be any resource accessible on a computer system, including files, peripherals, databases, and fine-grained entities such as individual fields in database records. Objects are traditionally viewed as passive entities that contain or receive information, although even early access control models included the possibility of treating programs, printers, or other active entities as objects. Meanwhile, an operation is an active process invoked by a subject. Early access control models concerned strictly with information flow (i.e., read-and-write access) applied the term subject to all active processes, but some models (e.g., Role-Based Access Control [RBAC]) require a distinction between subject and operation. Permissions are authorizations to perform some action on the system. In most computer security literature, the term permission refers to some combination of object and operation.

Authorization vs. Authentication

Authentication is the process of determining that a user's claimed identity is genuine. The most common form of authentication is passwords. Authentication is based on one or more of the following factors: something the user knows, something the user has, or something the user is. Authentication is normally stronger if two or more factors are used.

Least Privilege

It is an administrative practice of selectively assigning permission to users so that the user is given no more permission than is necessary to perform his or her job function.

Need-to-Know Access

Subjects are granted access when they can justify their work task-related reason for access or their need to know.

Traditional Access Control Model

Traditionally, access control is used for single-user privilege and implemented using non-cryptographic techniques. These techniques are typically classified into three categories:

- Discretionary Access Control (DAC)
- Mandatory Access Control (MAC)
- Role-Based Access Control (RBAC)

Additional access control models include access control matrix, access control list, task-based access control, team-based access control, and spatial access control. Zou (2006) specified two access control models in shared environments: differential access control (DAC) and hierarchical access control (HAC).

Access Control in Current E-learning System

The current system mostly using RBAC, where there are three entities: administrator, instructors, and students. Instructor and student are associated in certain course. The limitation is very strong; there is no space beyond the existing in (for example) black board capabilities, as student can not create their own space for discussion, or online topic chatting.

- **Nonrepudiation:** Ensuring that the originators of messages cannot deny that they in fact sent the messages. Regarding digital security, the cryptography meaning and application of non-repudiation shifts to mean (wikipedia.org, 2009): A service that provides proof of the integrity; the second is origin of data and an authentication that with high assurance can be asserted to be genuine. Proof of data integrity is typically the easiest of these requirements to accomplish. A data hash, such as SHA1, is usually sufficient to establish that the likelihood of data being undetectably changed is extremely low. Even with this safeguard, it is still possible to tamper with data in transit, either through a man-in-the-middle attack or phishing. Due to this flaw, data integrity is best asserted when the recipient already possesses the necessary verification information.

The most common method of asserting the digital origin of data is through digital certificates, a form of public key infrastructure to which digital signatures. They can also be used for encryption. The digital origin only means that the certified/signed data can be, with reasonable certainty, trusted to be from somebody who possesses the private key corresponding to the signing certificate. If the key is not properly safeguarded by the original owner, digital forgery can become a major concern. The current E-learning system does not offer a meaning or proof of origin.

- **Network Security:** Protecting network and telecommunications equipment, protecting network servers and transmissions, combating eavesdropping, controlling access from untrusted networks, firewalls, and detecting intrusion. The current E-learning system has no control on network security and depends on very simple authentication procedure with campuses SSL if there is any. Basically the secure communication is left to the buyer network security (as the case with black board).
- **Physical Security:** Controlling the comings and goings of people and materials; protection against the elements and natural disasters. The current system left the physical security to the buyer physical security.
- **E-Assessments:** E-Assessments are summative and formative electronic assessments that are a replacement for a written test that is taken in a controlled environment by a correctly authenticated student. The controlled environment ensures that all assessment candidates have an equal playing field to take the assessment, meaning that no student has an unfair advantage over another.

E-assessment has two categories of security:

- Web security
- E-assessment security

Web security is a well-researched area that deals with the securing of the server/s running Web applications as well as the application itself. Unfortunately this is not sufficient to guarantee that anE-assessment will be secure. WithE-assessments it is necessary to ensure that the measures outlined below are applied to E-learning systems to ensure a fair test is taken (Marais, Argles, & von Solms, 2008):

- Authenticity of the person taking the test.
- E-assessment integrity (to deter electronic corruption).
- The E-assessment is taken in the correct/supervised location.
- Test visibility that prevents copying (as first step in e-cheating).

- Confidentiality and privacy.
- Secure client and server software.
- Non-deniability of E-assessment submissions.

Most likely as best solution is to clean the client computer from any documentation and isolate Internet connection outside the e-exam server.

It is important to be sure that a test is taken at the correct location. E-learning systems rely on a communication medium that connects all the computers to give them access to the intranet and Internet. This, unfortunately, implies that the Web-based clients can also access other services, not just the E-learning server as shown in Figure 1.

As seen in Figure 1, only students in the controlled environment are allowed access while a student trying to take the E-assessment from an uncontrolled location is denied access. The reason for blocking such a student is that the student in the uncontrolled environment could be helped by another person or use material not available to students taking the test. Even worse, a student can write the test and leave the venue where after he/she can log into the server again at another location and complete another students test or correct his own (Marais, Argles, & von Solms, 2008).

While this solution is very useful, it needs to enforce another environment access, such as no Internet access, off the copy or/and copying process, and not accessing external input devices.

WebCT currently provides a subnet mask to allow traffic only from a specific subnet to the assessment server. This is similar to using a firewall to distinguish dif-

Figure 1. Controlled and uncontrolled environments

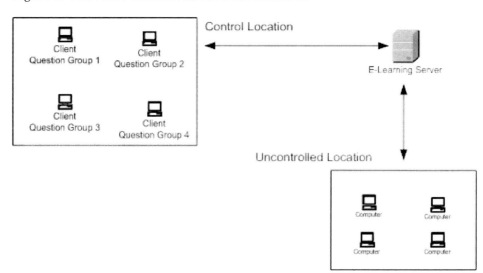

ferent users. This is not full proof, as IP (Internet protocol) addresses can be spoofed and remote administration tools can be used to control a machine in a legal location from an uncontrolled environment. The next level of security that is also supported by WebCT and BlackBoard is to password protect the assessment. This is where a password is set that needs to be entered before the assessment can be retrieved. The password has to be verbally given to the students or physically entered by the instructor(s). Using this method of security is easily compromised.

The solution is to use several of the following techniques:

- Having a tracking console to monitor connections online.
- **Using IP range:** This has limitations due to IP address spoofing.
- Monitoring the network traffic for anomalies.

Other Issues

Other topics concerning secure E-learning should be satisfied, such as:

- **Risk Management:** Identification, assessment, and prioritization of risks followed by coordinated and economical application of resources to minimize, monitor, and control the probability and/or impact of unfortunate events.
- **Incident Response Plans:** What makes up a security incident and outlines the incident response phases. This includes an incident response plan, assessment of the incident, minimizing damage and response strategy, documentation, and preservation of evidence. The incident response plan will define areas of responsibility and establish procedures for handing various security incidents. This document discusses the considerations required to build an incident response plan (comptechdoc.org).
- **Availability:** Is the timely, reliable access to network resources, data, and information services for authorized users. It includes the ability to access network resources, such as hardware and software, but also the user's ability to obtain a desired network bandwidth with reasonable throughput (quality of service). To provide availability, network traffic must be able to traverse local area networks (LANs) and wide area networks (WANs) to reach its intended destination (Hansche, 2006).
- **Digital Signature and Non-Repudiation:** (techtarget.com) A digital signature can be used with any kind of message, whether it is encrypted or not, so that the receiver can be sure of the sender's identity and that the message arrived unbroken. A digital certificate contains the digital signature of the certificate-issuing authority so that anyone can verify that the certificate is real. Digital signatures are easily transportable, cannot be imitated by some-

one else, and can be automatically time-stamped. The ability to ensure that the original signed message arrived means that the sender cannot easily repudiate it later.

More issues as:

- Business Continuity.
- Portability Secure Devises.
- Change Management.
- Disaster Recovery Planning and Data Availability.
- Laws and Regulations.

SECURE E-LEARNING MODEL

The model is based on PKI; an entity in this model is instructor, student, administrator, and course or any software. Group G_i is a collection of entities (one or more). The PKI offers functionality in registration, initialization, certification, key–pair recovery, key generation, key updating, key expiry, key compromise, cross certification, revocation, certification, and revocation notice distribution and publication. The certification authorities (CAs) issue and revoke PKCs. Organizational registration authorities (GORSs) vouch for the binding between public keys and certificate holder identities and other attributes. Meanwhile, G_i certificate holders sign and encrypt digital documents. Clients validate digital signatures, as well as their certification path from a known public key of a trusted CA. Finally, repositories store and make available certificates and certificate revocation lists (CRLs) (see Figure 2).

A more advanced approach is to use public key infrastructure for X.509 certificates (PKIX).

PKIX works on the following five areas:

- Profiles of X.509 v3 Public Key Certificates and X.509 v2 Certificate Revocation Lists (CRLs) (see RFC 2459),
- Management protocols (see RFC 2510),
- Operational protocols (currently describe how LDAPv2, FTP and HTTP can be used as operational protocols) (see RFC 2559, RFC 2585, RFC 2560),
- Certificate policies and Certificate Practice Statements (see RFC 2527), and
- Time-stamping and data-certification/validation services (only Internet drafts available).

Figure 2. PKI entities

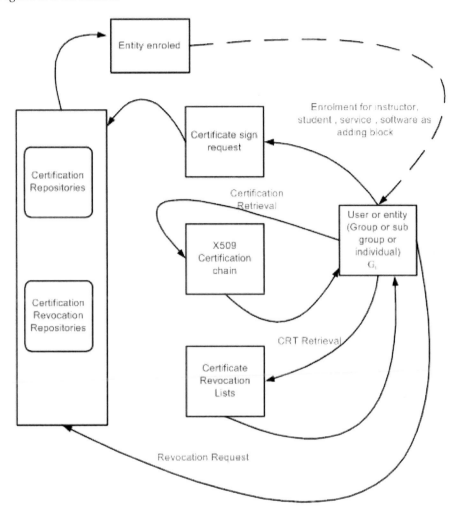

Management protocols require supporting online interactions between PKI users and management entities. The possible set of functions that can be supported by management protocols includes:

- Registration of entities that takes place prior to issuing the certificate
- Initialization (e.g., generation of key–pair)
- **Certification:** The issuance of the certificate
- **Key–Pair Recovery:** The ability to recover lost keys
- **Key–Pair Update:** When the certificate expires and a new key–pair and certificate have to be generated

- **Revocation Request:** When an authorized person advises the CA to include a specific certificate in the revocation list
- **Cross-Certification:** When two CAs exchange information in order to generate a cross-certificate

The operational protocols are those protocols required to deliver certificates and CRLs (or status information) to certificate-using client systems. There is an emphasis to have a variety of distribution mechanisms for the certificates and the CRLs using, for example, LDAP, HTTP, and FTP. For example, the retrieval of the CRL by a merchant to check whether a certificate is valid constitutes an operational protocol.

A basic scenario would be an instructor enrolled for teaching a course and how he/she uses his public key to be added to the course and authenticate himself through biometric (phase recognition). The same scenario goes for a student to be in the course (possibly when a student registers for a course, then the registration office adds his public key to the course). All the communication between the instructor and student(s) or student to studies are:

- **Secure Message Format:** Encrypted by the receiver's public key
- **Open Message Format:** Encrypted by the sender's private key
- **Secure and Signed Format:** Encrypted by the sender's private key and then encrypted with the receiver's public key

Now the other issue is to add a new component (chatting, video conference, biometric device) to an instructor that should have the same as an enrolling student or instructor. To call for a public course video conference will use open message format for two elements: Encrypted by the instructor private key and application private key.

Privilege Management Infrastructure (PMI) (Al-Hamdani, 2010)

PMI is the set of hardware, software, people, policies, and procedures needed to create, manage, store, distribute, and revoke attribute certificates. A PMI consists of five types of components:

- **Attribute Authorities:** To issue and revoke ACs (also called attribute certificate issuer)
- **Attribute Certificate Users:** To parse or process an AC
- **Attribute Certificate Verifier:** To check the validity of an AC and then make use of the result

- **Clients:** To request an action for which authorization checks are to be made
- **Repositories:** To store and make available certificates and certificate revocation lists (CRLs)

Two types of attribute certificate distributions exist: push and pull (see Figure 3).

In some environments, it is suitable for a client to push an AC to a server. This means that no new connections between the client and server are required. It also means that no search burden is imposed on servers, which improves performance. In other cases, it is more suitable for a client to simply authenticate the server and for the server to request or pull the client's AC from an AC issuer or repository.

The second case is very useful for our model since the benefit of the pull model is that it can be implemented without changes to the client or to the client–server protocol. It is also more suitable for some inter-domain cases where the client's rights should be assigned within the server's domain rather than within the client's domain.

Access Control

Designing access control for E-learning is tricky because of the dynamic nature of the organizations and the tasks performed. Most existing implementations solve this need through the use of access control exception mechanisms: if the normal access control mechanism will not grant a user legitimate access, it is possible to use some exception mechanism to gain access to required information, as in the case of an emergency. RBAC is the common principle for designing access control mechanisms.

Figure 3. Different loops

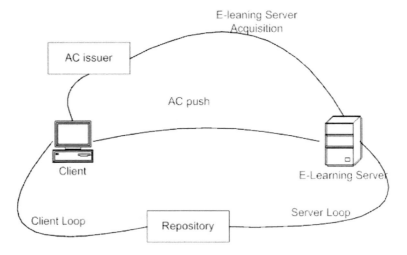

The cryptography access control for an E-learning Web system should be implemented using a distributed approach and hierarchy (within an entity) for all entities (e.g., local hospital, local clinic). Meanwhile, for each entity, the access control should have hierarchical access control. The new access control is based on well-known principles that have proven their efficiency. Group is an entity that has its own facets, including medical records, accounting, personnel, and billing system. This could be a regional hospital, medical center, and local pediatric center. Each group has a flat relationship with another group or sub-group (e.g., a lab in a hospital).

G_i is the group (course) and G_{ij} is any sub-group within G_i; for example, G_1 is project 1 group, G_2 is a project 2 group. G_1 has a flat relationship with G_{21}. A flat relationship is defined as many-to-many relationships, as G_1 could have many relationships with other G_i or sub-groups of G_i. Many-to-many mappings (many-to-one mapping is a mapping in which two or more particular objects may be mapped to the same image) represent the relationships between a collection of source objects and a collection of target objects. The relationships among different entities are shown in Figure 4.

Each entity G_i has the following access control:

- RBAC on the role in the group
  - Administrator, accounting, registration.
  - Instructor, instructor assistants.

Figure 4. Relationships among different entities (groups)

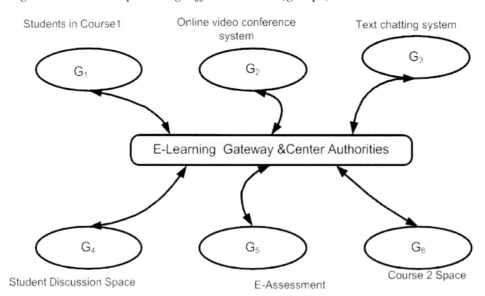

- ○ Each role can access part of the patient record – for example, instructor "has access" to student grading system, registration system, student advisor system. Instructor "can add" software, student, to course group. Instructor can add component (say) software, Web access as his/her course required.
  - ○ "Has access" means the capability to read, write, change, delete, modify, and create.
  - ○ "Can add" means adding an entity to canon of his/her course.
  - ○ Each course canon is completely different from instructor to instructor as the nature of his/her course required.
- Since the element of a group has RBAC, this could be transferred into the hierarchical RBAC relationship (Ferraiolo & Kuhn, 1992) with all privileges inherited.
- Since each G_i has a hierarchy base, it very easy to implement cryptography access control using advanced encryption standard (AES)-FIPS 197 (with key sizes of 128 and 256 bits) with a hierarchy key management system.

The second level secures G_i elements and provides integrity as well as key exchange and non-repudiation:

- **Digital Signature:** Elliptic Curve Digital Signature Algorithm-FIPS 186-2 (using the curves with 256 and 384-bit prime moduli).
- **Key Exchange:** Elliptic Curve Diffie-Hellman Draft NIST Special Publication 800-56 (using the curves with 256 and 384-bit prime moduli).
- **Secure Hash Algorithm:-**FIPS 180-2 (using SHA-256 and SHA-384).

For instance, providing insurance support to a patient should be supported by non-repudiation, while changing/updating a patient's record must be supported by a digital signature and hashing.

To support high-level security between different medical centers and hospitals (G_i)—namely, to support transferred medical reports, billing information, and other issues—the concern has now focused on the national level rather than local hospitals. One recommended solution is to use Public Key Infrastructures (PKIs), which can speed up and simplify delivery of products and services by providing electronic approaches to processes that have historically been paper based. These electronic solutions depend on data integrity and authenticity. Both can be accomplished by binding a unique digital signature to an individual and ensuring that the digital signature cannot be forged. The individual can then digitally sign data and the recipient can verify the originator of the data and that the data has not been modified without the originator's knowledge. In addition, the PKI can provide encryption capabilities to ensure privacy.

As with all aspects of information technology, introducing a PKI into an organization requires careful planning and a thorough understanding of its relationship to other automated systems. This solution can provide data integrity, confidentiality, identification and authentication, and non-repudiation (see Figure 5).

Each G_i and it sub-group G_{ij} can be organized as a hierarchy structure, and cross-certification can be implemented. The other relation is between different G_i, which can be distributed and hierarchy for cross-certification.

FUTURE RESEARCH DIRECTIONS

The future of E-learning is very bright. This concept has been expanding at a very fast rate as more and more uses for the computer in education have been attempted. On the traditional college campus, there is a trend toward the development of a

Figure 5. Detailed relationships among different entities (groups)

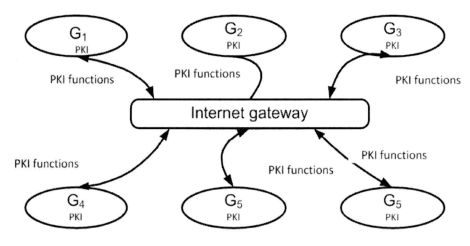

Virtual Learning Environment (VLE). The VLE concept integrates the full range of electronic enhancements into the classroom setting. Under the VLE idea, the instructor is not replaced by the computer but rather uses the computer to reach more students and to reach them more effectively (Aranda, 2009).

Distance education is becoming more accepted as more and more households obtain personal computers. Many schools have developed the idea of the virtual classroom to a high degree. One instructor located at a central location and using video equipment can teach simultaneous classes in several satellite locations. There is no limit to the distance these satellite locations can be from the instructor. Computer based training can be done in much the same way. Such things as e-mails and chat rooms are being used as part of the E-learning arsenal.

The main issue in secure E-learning is the new development in using "building blocks", the philosophy behind building to add a block when it is needed. And since all learners are not in the same level to accept knowledge, some would accept knowledge through sound, while others use graphic modelling.

A block is a group of learner, software, package, mobile devices, and others; since most of these elements could have little security control, then using "add in" security would be most acceptable and is believed to be the next generation of E-learning systems. We believe that the next e-learning system will be a "shell" system with add in security.

We believe that the major components for the security issue for E-learning are:

- Shift toward secure shell system based on PKI.
- The security of a course is instructor responsibilities.
- Moving toward phase recognition and video recognition in addition to online recognizing and authentications.
- More software for copy write checker will be used to figure learner way of writing.
- Progress to cryptography solution for access control and authentication.
- Move toward standardization in encryption as faster and well tested as in Suite B.
- Move to word elliptic curve.
- Progress to depend on open resources.
- The use of new media as iPod and iPhone on compact cell phones to store video, lecture, and building communication will be more in use in the future.
- We believe the new devices in book reader will be more in combination with other devices to be used for the benefit of learners.

CONCLUSION

The secure E-learning system and the use of cryptography is the main theme of this article. In addition, we present a new cryptograph E-learning model based on PKI and cryptography access control. The model is based on creating a secure shell system based on PKI and each adding block has to certified itself to be assessable.

There are four elements in this paper: E-learning components and a new arena in E-learning, the cryptography components to provide authentication, authorization, nonrepudiation, integrity, and confidentiality. And the last part is presenting a new model for a secure E-learning system based on public key infrastructure and cryptography access control. And the last part will focus on the future development in a secure E-learning system as it starts to be building blocks.

REFERENCES

Al-Hamdani, W. (2010aUnder Review). Cryptography-based access control in healthcare web systems. In Ioannis Apostolakis, A. C. (Ed.), *Certification and Security in Health-Related Web Applications*. Academic Press. doi:10.1145/1940941.1940960.

Al-Hamdani, W. (2010b). E-mail, web service and cryptography. In *Applied Cryptography for Cyber Security and Defense: Information Encryption and Cyphering*. Hershey, PA: IGI Global.

Aranda, N. (2009a). *A brief history of e-learning and distance education*. Retrieved from http://www.ezinearticles.com/

Aranda, N. (2009b). *Ezinearticles.com*. Retrieved from http://www.ezinearticles.com/?Future-Trends-of-E-learning&id=496477

Barone, P. (2009). *The key elements of e-learning*. Retrieved from http://www.afe-online.de/elearning.htm

Campbell, K. (2004). *E-ffective writing for e-learning environments*. Hershey, PA: Idea Group Publishing.

Comptechdoc.org. (n.d.). *Incident response plan*. Retrived from http://www.comptechdoc.org/independent/security/policies/incident-response-plan.html

Ferraiolo, D. F., & Kuhn, D. R. (1992). Role-based access controls. In *Proceedings of the 15th National Computer Security Conference*, (pp. 554-563). IEEE.

Hansche, S. (2006). *Official (ISC)2 guide to the CISSP-ISSEP CBK*. New York: Auerbach Publications.

Jeffries, M. (2009). *Research in distance education: The history of distance education*. Retrieved from http://www./edu/DL_history_mJeffries.html

Kelm, S. (2009). *The PKI page*. Retrieved from http://www.pki-page.org/

MacManus, R. (2007). *E-learning 2.0: All you need to know*. Retrieved from http://www.readwriteWeb.com/archives/E-learning_20_all_you_need_to_know.php

MacManus, R., & Porter, J. (2005). *Web 2.0 design: Bootstrapping the social web*. Retrieved from http://www.digital-Web.com/articles/Web_2_for_designers

Marais, E., Argles, D., & von Solms, B. (2008). *Security issues specific to e-assessments*. Retrieved from http://eprints.ecs.soton.ac.uk/11433/1/E-learning_ArticleNewFin.doc

RSA.com. (2007). *What is DESX?* Retrieved from http://www.rsasecurity.com

Saettler, P. (1968). *A history of instructional technology*. New York: McGraw-Hill.

Simovits, M. (1995). *The DES: An extensive document and evaluation*. New York: Agent Park Press.

Techtarget.com. (n.d.). *Techtarget.com*. Retrieved from http://searchsecurity.techtarget.com/sDefinition/0,sid14_gci211953,00.html# Weippl, E. R. (2005). *Security in e-learning*. Berlin: Springer.

Wenger, E. (2009). *Communities of practice a brief introduction*. Retrieved from http://www.ewenger.com/theory/

Wikipedia. org. (2009). *Non-repudiation*. Retrieved from http://en.wikipedia.org/wiki/Non-repudiation

ENDNOTES

[1.] In cryptography Ciphertext Stealing (CTS) is a general method of using a block cipher mode of operation that allows for processing of messages that are not evenly divisible into blocks without resulting in any expansion of the ciphertext, at the cost of slightly increased complexity.

Compilation of References

Abrams, Z. I. (2003). The effect of synchronous and asynchronous CMC on oral performance in German. *Modern Language Journal*, *87*(2), 157–167. doi:10.1111/1540-4781.00184.

Agbayani-Siewert, & Revilla, L. (1995). Filipino Americans. In *Asian Americans: Contemporary Trends and Issues*. Thousand Oaks, CA: Sage Publications.

Agbayani-Siewert, P. (1994). Filipino American culture and family: Guidelines for practitioners: Families in society. *Families in Society*.

Agbayani-Siewert, P. (1997). The dual world of Filipino Americans. *Journal of Multicultural Social Work*, *6*(1/2), 59–76. doi:10.1300/J285v06n01_05.

Alavi, M. (1994). Computer-mediated collaborative learning: An empirical evaluation. *Management Information Systems Quarterly*, *18*(2), 159–174. doi:10.2307/249763.

Al-Hamdani, W. (2010aUnder Review). Cryptography-based access control in healthcare web systems. In Ioannis Apostolakis, A. C. (Ed.), *Certification and Security in Health-Related Web Applications*. Academic Press. doi:10.1145/1940941.1940960.

Al-Hamdani, W. (2010). E-mail, web service and cryptography. In *Applied Cryptography for Cyber Security and Defense: Information Encryption and Cyphering*. Hershey, PA: IGI Global.

Aljaafreh, A., & Lantolf. (1994). Negative feedback as regulation and second language learning in the zone of proximal development. *Modern Language Journal*, *78*(4), 465–483. doi:10.1111/j.1540-4781.1994.tb02064.x.

Allen, I. E., & Seaman, J. (2008). *Staying the course: Online education in the United States.* The Sloan-C Report. Retrieved January 1, 2010, from http://www.aln.org/publications/survey/pdf/staying_the_course.pdf

Alpert, J., & Hajaj, N. (2008, July 25). *We knew the web was big.* Retrieved from http://googleblog.blogspot.com/2008/07/we-knew-Web-was-big.html

Altbach, P. G., & Peterson, P. M. (1998). Internationalize American higher education? Not exactly. *Change*, *30*(4), 36–40. doi:10.1080/00091389809602630.

Altbach, P., & Knight, J. (2006). The internationalization of higher education: Motivations and realities. In *The National Education Association Almanac of Higher Education* (pp. 27–37). Washington, DC: NAE.

Compilation of References

Anderson, T., & Kanuka, H. (2003). e-Research: Methods, strategies and issues. Boston: Pearson Education, Inc.

Anyanwu, R. (2004). Lessons on plagiarism: Issues for teachers and learners. *International Education Journal*, *4*(4), 178–187.

Apple, M. (2006). Language learning theories and cooperative learning techniques in the EFL classroom. *Doshisha Studies in Language and Culture*, *9*(2), 277–301.

Aranda, N. (2009). *A brief history of e-learning and distance education*. Retrieved from http://www.ezinearticles.com/

Aranda, N. (2009). *Ezinearticles.com*. Retrieved from http://www.ezinearticles.com/?Future-Trends-of-E-learning&id=496477

Arbaugh, J. B. (2002). Virtual classroom characteristics and student satisfaction with Internet-based MBA courses. *Journal of Management Education*, *24*(1), 32–54. doi:10.1177/105256290002400104.

Ashworth, P., Bannister, P., & Thorne, P. (1997). Guilty in whose eyes? University students' perceptions of cheating and plagiarism in academic work and assessment. *Studies in Higher Education*, *22*(2), 187–203. doi:10.1080/0307507971233 1381034.

Ashworth, P., Freewood, M., & MacDonald, R. (2003). The student lifeworld and the meaning of plagiarism. *Journal of Phenomenological Psychology*, *34*(2), 257–278. doi:10.1163/156916203322847164.

Atkinson, D., & Ramanathan, V. (1995). Cultures of writing: An ethnographic comparison of L1 and L2 university writing/language programs. *Teachers of English to Speakers of Other Languages Quarterly*, *29*(3), 539–568. doi:10.2307/3588074.

Au, K. H. (2001, July/August). Culturally responsive instruction as a dimension of new literacies. *Reading Online*, *5*(1). Retrieved January 12, 2009, from http://www.readingonline.org/newliteracies/lit_index.asp?HREF=/newliteracies/au/index.html

Au, K. H. (1980). Participation structures in a reading lesson with Hawaiian children: Analysis of a culturally appropriate instructional event. *Anthropology & Education Quarterly*, *11*(2), 91–115. doi:10.1525/aeq.1980.11.2.05x1874b.

Au, K. H. (1993). *Literacy instruction in multicultural settings*. Orlando, FL: Harcourt Brace College Publishers.

Au, K. H., & Jordan, C. (1981). Teaching reading to Hawaiian children: Finding a culturally appropriate solution. In Trueba, H., Guthrie, G., & Au, K. (Eds.), *Culture and the bilingual classroom: Studies in classroom ethnography* (pp. 69–86). Rowley, MA: Newbury House.

Au, K. H., & Kawakami, A. J. (1985). Research currents: Talk story and learning to read. *Language Arts*, *62*(4), 406–411.

Au, K. H., & Mason, J. (1983). Cultural congruence in classroom participation structures: Achieving a balance of rights. *Discourse Processes*, *6*(2), 145–167. doi:10.1080/01638538309544560.

Australian Flexible Learning Framework. (2004). *Cross-cultural issues in content development and teaching online*. Retrieved August 23, 2007, from http://www.flexiblelearning.net.au/flx/Webdav/site/flxsite/users/kedgar/public/quick_guides/crosscultural.pdf

Baker, T., Lee, S., & Hewitt, J. (2007, June). *The development and testing of a video system for online authentication of assessment*. Paper presented at the Second International Blended Learning Conference. Hatfield, UK. Retrieved from https://uhra.herts.ac.uk/dspace/bitstream/2299/1727/1/901869.pdf

Bamford, J., & Sergiou, K. (2005). International students and plagiarism: An analysis of the reasons for plagiarism among international foundation students. *Investigation in University Teaching and Learning, 2*(2), 17–22.

Banks, J. A. (1999). *An introduction to multicultural education*. Boston: Allyn & Bacon.

Barone, P. (2009). *The key elements of e-learning*. Retrieved from http://www.afe-online.de/elearning.htm

Baron, J., & Crooks, S. M. (2005). Academic integrity in web based distance education. *TechTrends, 49*(2), 40–45. doi:10.1007/BF02773970.

Beardlsey, C. (1964). *Guam past and present*. Tokyo: Charles E. Tuttle Company, Inc..

Beauvois, M. H. (1992). Computer-assisted classroom discussion in the foreign language classroom: Conversation in slow motion. *Foreign Language Annals, 25*(5), 455–464. doi:10.1111/j.1944-9720.1992.tb01128.x.

Beauvois, M. H. (1994). E-talk: Attitudes and motivation in computer-assisted classroom discussion. *Computers and the Humanities, 28*(3), 177–190. doi:10.1007/BF01830738.

Beauvois, M. H. (1997). High-tech, high-touch: From discussion to composition in the networked classroom. *Computer Assisted Language Learning, 10*(1), 57–69. doi:10.1080/0958822970100104.

Beauvois, M. H. (1998). Conversations in slow motion: Computer-mediated communication in the foreign language classroom. *Canadian Modern Language Review, 54*(2), 198. doi:10.3138/cmlr.54.2.198.

Beck, C., & Schornack, G. R. (2003). Theory and practice for distance education: A heuristic model for the virtual classroom. In Howard, C., Schenk, K., & Discenza, R. (Eds.), *Distance Learning and University Effectiveness: Changing Education Paradigms for Online Learning* (pp. 119–143). Hershey, PA: Information Science Pub. doi:10.4018/978-1-59140-178-0.ch006.

Beers Fägersten, K. (2008). Discourse strategies and power roles in student-led distance learning. *Proceedings of Identity and Power in the Language Classroom, 15*(2), 11–24.

Beetham, E., & Sharpe. (2007). *Rethinking pedagogy for a digital age – Designing and delivering e-learning*. London: Routledge.

Benbunan-Fich, R., & Hiltz, S. R. (1999). Education applications of CMCS: Solving case studies through asynchronous learning networks. *Journal of Computer-Mediated Communication, 4*(3). Retrieved on Jan 2nd, 2010 from http://jcmc.indiana.edu/vol4/issue3/benbunan-fich.html

Compilation of References

Bereiter, C. (2002). *Education and mind in the knowledge age.* Mahwah, NJ: Laurence Erlbaum Associates.

Bereiter, C., & Scardamalia, M. (2003). Learning to work creatively with knowledge. In De Corte, E., Verschaffel, L., Entwistle, N., & van Merrienboer, J. (Eds.), *Unravelling basic components and dimensions of powerful learning environments.* EARLI.

Berge, Z. L. (1995). *Facilitating computer conferencing: Recommendations from the field. educational technology.* Retrieved on Feb 11, 2009, from http://www.emoderators.com/moderators/teach_online.html

Berg, E. C. (1999). The effects of trained peer response on ESL students' revision types and writing quality. *Journal of Second Language Writing, 8*(3), 215–241. doi:10.1016/S1060-3743(99)80115-5.

Bergen Communiqué. (2005). *The European higher education area – Achieving the goals.* Bergen: Bergen Communiqué.

Bergman, M. M. (2001). The deep web: Surfacing hidden value. *Journal of Electronic Publishing, 7*(1). doi:10.3998/3336451.0007.104.

Besser, H., & Bonn, M. (1996). Impact of distance independent education. *Journal of the American Society for Information Science American Society for Information Science, 47*(11), 880–883. doi:10.1002/(SICI)1097-4571(199611)47:11<880::AID-ASI14>3.0.CO;2-Z.

Bhattacharya, M., & Chatterjee, R. (2000). Collaborative innovation as a process for cognitive development. *Journal of Interactive Learning Research, 11*(3), 295–312.

Biber, D. (1988). *Variation across speech and writing.* Cambridge, UK: Cambridge University Press. doi:10.1017/CBO9780511621024.

Biesenbach-Lucas, S. (2004). Asynchronous web discussions in teacher training courses: promoting collaboration learning - Or not? *AACE Journal, 12*(2), 155–170.

Biggs, J. (1999). *Teaching for quality learning at university.* Buckingham, UK: SRHE and Open University Press.

Biggs, J., & Tang, C. (2007). *Teaching for quality learning at university.* Buckingham, UK: SRHE & Open University Press.

Böhm, A., Davis, T., Meares, D., & Pearce, D. (2000). *Global student mobility 2025: Forecasts of the global demand for higher education.* Paper presented at the 16th Australian International Education Conference. Hobart, Tasmania. Retrieved from www.aiec.idp.com/PDF/Bohm_2025Media_p.pdf

Bolander Lakov, K., Silén, C., & Engqvist Boman, C. (2013). Implementation of scholarship of teaching and learning through and on-line masters program. In *Cases on Professional Distance Education Degree Programs and Practices: Successes, Challenges and Issues.* Hershey, PA: IGI Global.

Bologna Declaration. (1999). *Joint declaration of the European ministers of higher education.* Bologna: Bologna Declaration.

Bonk, C. J. (2000). My hat's on to the online instructor. *e-Education Advisor. Education Ed., 1*(1), 10–13.

Bonk, C. J., & Cunningham, D. J. (1998). Searching for learner-centered, constructivist, and sociocultural components of collaborative educational learning tools. In Bonk, C. J., & King, K. S. (Eds.), *Electronic collaborators: Learner-centered technologies for literacy, apprenticeship, and discourse* (pp. 25–50). Mahwah, NJ: Erlbaum.

Bonk, C. J., Hara, N., Dennen, V., Malikowski, S., & Supplee, L. (2000). We're in TITLE to dream: Envisioning a community of practice: The intraplanetary teacher learning exchange. *Cyberpsychology & Behavior, 3*(1), 25–39. doi:10.1089/109493100316201.

Bonk, C. J., & King, K. S. (1998). *Electronic collaborators: Learner-centred technologies for literacy, apprenticeship, and discourse.* Mahwah, NJ: Erlbaum Associates.

Boud, D., Cohen, R., & Sampson, J. (2001). *Peer learning in higher education: Learning from & with each other.* London: Kogan Page.

Bowers, C. (1988). *The cultural dimension of educational computing.* New York: Teachers College Press.

Boyer, E. L. (1990). *Scholarship reconsidered: Priorities of the professoriate.* Princeton, NJ: The Carnegie Foundation for the Advancement of Teaching.

Braine, G. (1997). Beyond word processing: Networked computers in ESL writing classes. *Computers and Composition, 14*(1), 45–58. doi:10.1016/S8755-4615(97)90037-2.

Branch, R. M. (1997). Educational technology frameworks that facilitate culturally pluralistic instruction. *Educational Technology, 37*(2), 38–41.

Brandt, D. S. (2002). Copyright's (not so) little cousin, plagiarism. *Computers in Libraries, 22*(5), 39–41.

Breuch, L.-A. M. K., & Racine. (2000). Developing sound tutor training for online writing centers: Creating productive peer reviewers. *Computers and Composition, 17*(3), 245–263. doi:10.1016/S8755-4615(00)00034-7.

Brislin, R. (1993). *Understanding culture's influence on behavior.* Orlando, FL: Harcourt Brace.

Brown, P., & Levinson. (1987). *Politeness: Some universals in language use.* Cambridge, UK: Cambridge University Press

Brown, L. F. (1992). The daedalus integrated writing environment. *Computers and Composition, 10*(1), 77–88. doi:10.1016/S8755-4615(06)80021-6.

Bullen, M. (1998). Participation and critical thinking in online university distance education. *Journal of Distance Education, 13*(2). Retrieved on 24 April 2003 from http://cade.icaap.org/vol2013.2002/bullen.html

Bump, J. (1990). Radical changes in class discussion using networked computers. *Computers and the Humanities, 24*(1-2), 49–65. doi:10.1007/BF00115028.

Burley, H. (1998). Does the medium make the magic? The effects of cooperative learning and conferencing software. *Computers and Composition, 15*(1), 83–95. doi:10.1016/S8755-4615(98)90026-3.

Buscall, J. (2009, September 21). *Annual report shows influx of international.* Retrieved from http://www.su.se/english/about/news-and-events/annual-report-shows-influx-of-international-students-1.1674

Butler, W. M. (1999). *Writing and collaborative learning with the Daedalus integrated writing environment.* Retrieved May 29, 2009, from www.greek-language.gr/greekLang/files/document/conference-1999/01_Butler.pdf

Compilation of References

Butterfield, F. (1991, July 3). For a dean at Boston U., a question of plagiarism. *The New York Times.* Retrieved from http://www.nytimes.com

Caine, R. N., & Caine, G. (1997). *Education on the edge of possibility.* Alexandria, VA: ASCD.

Callan, H. (2000). Higher education internationalization strategies: Of marginal significance or all-pervasive? The international vision in practice: A decade of evolution. *Higher Education in Europe, 25*(1), 15–23. doi:10.1080/03797720050002161.

Campbell, K. (2004). *E-ffective writing for e-learning environments.* Hershey, PA: Idea Group Publishing.

Carnevale, D. (1999, November 12). How to proctor from a distance. *The Chronicle of Higher Education, 46*(12). Retrieved from http://chronicle.com PMID:14598855.

Carroll, J. (2004, November). *Deterring, detecting and dealing with plagiarism.* Retrieved from http://www.brookes.ac.uk/services/ocsd/2_learntch/plagiarism.html

Carroll, J., & Appleton, J. (2001). *Plagiarism: A good practice guide.* Oxford, UK: Oxford Brookes University.

Carr, S. (2000). As distance education comes of age, the challenge is keeping the students. *The Chronicle of Higher Education, 23,* A39.

Carson, J. G., & Nelson. (1994). Writing groups: Cross-cultural issues. *Journal of Second Language Writing, 3*(1), 17–30. doi:10.1016/1060-3743(94)90003-5.

Carson, J. G., & Nelson. (1996). Chinese students' perceptions of ESL peer response group interaction. *Journal of Second Language Writing, 5*(1), 1–19. doi:10.1016/S1060-3743(96)90012-0.

Caulk, N. (1994). Comparing teacher and student responses to written work. *TESOL Quarterly, 28*(1), 181–188. doi:10.2307/3587209.

Cazden, C., & Leggett, E. (1981). Culturally responsive education: Recommendations for achieving Lau remedies II. In Trueba, H., Guthrie, G., & Au, K. (Eds.), *Culture and the bilingual classroom: Studies in classroom ethnography* (pp. 69–86). Rowley, MA: Newbury House.

Celentin, P. (2007). Online training: Analysis of interaction and knowledge building patterns among foreign language teachers. *Journal of Distance Education, 21*(3), 39–58.

Charlton, T. (1996). Listening to pupils in classrooms and schools. In Davie, R., & Galloway, D. (Eds.), *Listening to children in education* (pp. 49–63). London: David Fulton Publishers.

Chase, M., Macfadyen, L., Reeder, K., & Roche, J. (2002). Intercultural challenges in networked learning: Hard technologies meet soft skills. *First Monday, 7*(8-5). Retrieved April 10, 2009, from http://firstmonday.org/htbin/cgiwrap/bin/ojs/index.php/fm/article/view/975/896

Chester, G. (2001). *Pilot of free-text electronic plagiarism detection software in five UK institutions.* Retrieved from http://www.jisc.ac.uk/media/documents/programmes/plagiarism/pilot.pdf

Chester, G. (2001). *Plagiarism detection and prevention*. Retrieved from http://www.jisc.ac.uk/uploaded_documents/plagiarism_final.pdf

Christudason, A. (2003). A case for case-based learning. *Ideas of Teaching, 1*, 18–19.

Chun, D. M. (1994). Using computer networking to facilitate the acquisition of interactive competence. *System, 22*(1), 17–31. doi:10.1016/0346-251X(94)90037-X.

Ciekanski, M., & Chanier, T. (2008). Developing online multimodal verbal communication to enhance the writing process in an audio-graphic conferencing environment. *ReCALL, 20*(2), 162–182. doi:10.1017/S0958344008000426.

Coates, H., James, R., & Baldwin, G. (2005). A critical examination of the effects of learning management systems on university teaching and learning. *Tertiary Education and Management, 11*(1), 19–36. doi:10.1080/13583883.2005.9967137.

Collis, C. (1999). Designing for differences: Cultural issues in the design of WWW-based course support sites. *British Journal of Educational Technology, 30*(3), 201–217. doi:10.1111/1467-8535.00110.

Commission of the European Communities (CEC). (2001). *Communication from the commission: Making a European area of lifelong learning a reality (COM 678, final of 21.11.01)*. Luxembourg: Office for Official Publications of the European Communities.

Compeau, D. R., & Higgins, C. A. (1995). Computer self-efficacy: Development of a measure and initial test. *Management Information Systems Quarterly, 19*(2), 189–211. doi:10.2307/249688.

Comptechdoc.org. (n.d.). *Incident response plan*. Retrieved from http://www.comptechdoc.org/independent/security/policies/incident-response-plan.html

Connor, U., & Asenavage. (1994). Peer response groups in ESL writing classes: How much impact on revision. *Journal of Second Language Writing, 3*(3), 256–276. doi:10.1016/1060-3743(94)90019-1.

Cortazzi, M., & Jin, L. (1997). Communication for learning across cultures. In McNamara, D., & Harris, R. (Eds.), *Overseas Students in Higher Education: Issues in Teaching and Learning* (pp. 76–90). London: Routledge.

Crawford, A. (2002). The myth of the unmarked net speaker. In Elmer, G. (Ed.), *Critical perspectives on the Internet* (pp. 89–104). Oxford, UK: Rowman & Littlefield Publishers, Inc..

Culwin, F., MacLeod, A., & Lancaster, T. (2001). *Source code plagiarism in UK HE computing schools: Issues, attitudes and tools (SCISM Technical Report)*. London: South Bank University.

Cummings, R., Maddux, C. D., Harlow, S., & Dyas, L. (2002). Academic misconduct in undergraduate teacher education students and its relationship to their principled moral reasoning. *Journal of Instructional Psychology, 29*(4), 286–296.

Cunningham, L. (1992). *Ancient chamorro society*. Honolulu, HI: The Bess Press, Inc..

Cunningham, L. (1997). The ancient Chamorros of Guam. In Carter, L., Wuerch, W., & Carter, R. (Eds.), *Guam history: Perspectives volume one* (pp. 11–36). Mangilao, Guam: Richard Flores Taitano Micronesia Area Research Center.

Compilation of References

Curtis, D. D., & Lawson, M. J. (2001). Exploring collaborative online learning. *Journal of Asynchronous Learning Networks, 5*(1), 21–34.

D'Andrea, V., & Gosling, D. (2005). *Improving teaching and learning in higher education: A whole institution approach.* Oxford, UK: Open University Press.

Darhower, M. (2002). Instructional features of synchronous computer-mediated communication in the intermediate L2 class: A sociocultural case study. *CALICO Journal, 19*(2), 249–278.

Davis, F. D., Bagozzi, R. P., & Warshaw, P. R. (1989). User acceptance of computer technology: A comparison of two theoretical models. *Management Science, 35*, 982–1003. doi:10.1287/mnsc.35.8.982.

Dehmel, A. (2006). Making a European area of lifelong learning a reality? Some reflections on the European Union's lifelong learning policies. *Comparative Education, 42*(1), 49–62. doi:10.1080/03050060500515744.

DeLacey, B. J., & Leonard, D. A. (2002). Case study on technology and distance in education at the Harvard Business School. *Education Technology and Society, 5*(2), 13–28.

Delta State University Libraries. (n.d.). *Plagiarism detection & prevention: A guide for faculty.* Retrieved from http://www.deltastate.edu/pages/1270.asp

Deusen-Scholl, N. V., Frei, C., & Dixon, E. (2005). Coconstructing learning: The dynamic nature of foreign language pedagogy in a CMC environment. *CALICO Journal, 22*(3), 657–678.

Deutschmann, M. Dyrvold, Gregersdotter, McIntyre, & Sheppard. (2006). Kollaborativ inlärning som startpunkt för utveckling av Internetkurser inom ämnet engelska. In P. Svensson (Ed.), Från vision till praktik: Språkutbildning och informationsteknik. Nätuniversitetet.

Deutschmann, M., & Lundmark. (2008). Let's keep it informal guys – A study of the effects of teacher communicative strategies on student activity and collaborative learning in Internet-based English courses. *Tidskrift för Lärarutbildning och Forskning, 2.*

Deutschmann, M., Ädel, Garretson, & Walker. (2009). Introducing mini-McCALL: A pilot version of the Mid-Sweden corpus of computer-assisted language learning. *ICAME Journal, 33*, 21-44.

Deutschmann, M. (2013). Creating online community — Challenges and solutions. In *Cases on Professional Distance Education Degree Programs and Practices: Successes, Challenges and Issues.* Hershey, PA: IGI Global.

Deutschmann, M., & Panichi. (2009). Talking into empty space? Signalling involvement in a virtual language classroom in Second Life. *Language Awareness, 18*(3-4), 310–328. doi:10.1080/09658410903197306.

Deutschmann, M., Panichi, & Molka-Danielsson. (2009). Designing oral participation in second life – A comparative study of two language proficiency courses. *ReCALL, 21*(2), 206–226. doi:10.1017/S0958344009000196.

Diaz, D. P. (2002). Online drop rates revisited. *The Technology Source.* Retrieved from http://technologysource.org/article/online_drop_rates_revisited/

DiBiase, D. (2000). Is distance education a Faustian bargain? *Journal of Geography in Higher Education, 1*, 130–136. doi:10.1080/03098260085216.

DiGiovanni, E., & Nagaswami. (2001). Online peer review: An alternative to face-to-face? *ELT Journal, 55*(3), 263–272. doi:10.1093/elt/55.3.263.

Dionne, E. J., Jr. (1987, September 17). Biden was accused of plagiarism in law school. *The New York Times*. Retrieved from http://www.nytimes.com

Dockrell, J., Lewis, A., & Lindsay, G. (2000). Researching children's perspectives: A psychological dimension. In Lewis, A., & Lindsay, G. (Eds.), *Researching children's perspectives* (pp. 46–58). Buckingham, UK: Open University Press.

Donato, R. (1994). Collective scaffolding in second language learning. In Lantolf, J. P., & Appel, G. (Eds.), *Vygotskian Approach to Second Language Research* (pp. 33–56). Norwood, NJ: Ablex Publishing Corporation.

Drewery, W. (2004). *Why we should watch what we say: Everyday speech and the production of relational subjectivity*. Unpublished manuscript.

Duarte, D., & Snyder, N. (1999). *Mastering virtual teams: Strategies, tools and techniques that succeed*. San Francisco, CA: Jossey-Bass Inc..

DuBois, D. L., & Karcher. (2005). *Handbook of youth mentoring*. Thousand Oaks, CA: SAGE Publications Ltd.

Dunn, M. (2001). Aboriginal literacy: Reading the tracks. *The Reading Teacher, 54*(7), 678–686.

Dziuban, C. D., Hartman, J. L., & Moskal, P. D. (2004). Blended learning. *Educause Center for Applied Research, Research Bulletin, 7*, 1-12. Retrieved December 10, 2008, from http://www.educause.edu/ir/library/pdf/ERB0407.pdf

Ene, E., Goertler, S., & McBride, K. (2005). Teacher participation styles in FL chats and their effect on student behavior. *CALICO Journal, 23*(3), 603–634.

English Online. (2004). *Listening strategies*. Retrieved on 28 August 2004 from http://english.unitecnology.ac.nz/resources/units/listening/strategies.html

Engström, Y. (2001). Expansive learning at work: Toward an activity theoretical reconceptualization. *Journal of Education and Work, 14*(1), 133–156.

Entwistle, N. (1992). *Styles of learning and teaching*. London: David Fulton Publishers.

Erickson, F., & Mohatt, G. (1981). Cultural differences in teaching styles in an Odawa school: A sociolinguistic approach. In Trueba, H., Guthrie, G., & Au, K. (Eds.), *Culture and the bilingual classroom: Studies in classroom ethnography* (pp. 105–119). Rowley, MA: Newbury House.

Ess, C. (1996). Introduction: Thoughts along the i-way: Philosophy and the emergence of CMC. In Ess, C. (Ed.), *Philosophical perspectives on computer-mediated communication* (pp. 1–12). Albany, NY: State University of New York Press.

Evans, J. (2000). The new plagiarism in higher education: From selection to reflection. *Interactions Journal, 4*(2). Retrieved from http://www2.warwick.ac.uk/services/ldc/resource/interactions/archive/issue11/evans

Compilation of References

Faigley, L. (1992). *Fragments of rationality: Postmodernity and the subject of composition.* Pittsburgh, PA: University of Pittsburgh Press.

Feenberg, A. (1998). *Distance learning: Promise or threat?* Retrieved December 2008 from http://wwwrohan.sdsu.edu/faculty/feenberg/TELE3.HTM

Ferguson, J. (2007, July 27). *Faculty plagiarism resources: Prevention and detection.* Retrieved from http://bullpup.lib.unca.edu/library/lr/plagiarism.html

Ferraiolo, D. F., & Kuhn, D. R. (1992). Role-based access controls. In *Proceedings of the 15th National Computer Security Conference,* (pp. 554-563). IEEE.

Ferris, D. (2003). Responding to writing. In Kroll, B. (Ed.), *Exploring the dynamics of second language writing.* Cambridge, UK: Cambridge University Press. doi:10.1017/CBO9781139524810.010.

Ferris, D. (2003). *Response to student writing: Implications for second language students.* Mahwah, NJ: Lawrence Erlbaum Associates.

Flood, J. (2002). Read all about it: Online learning facing 80% attrition rates. *TOJDE, 3*(2).

Flower, L. (1989). Cognition, context and theory building. *College Composition and Communication, 40*(3), 282–311. doi:10.2307/357775.

Flower, L., & Hayes. (1981). A cognitive process theory of writing. *College Composition and Communication, 32*(4), 365–387. doi:10.2307/356600.

Foster, P., & Ohta. (2005). Negotiation for meaning and peer assistance in second language classroom. *Applied Linguistics, 26*(3), 402–430. doi:10.1093/applin/ami014.

Franklin & Marshall College Library. (2009, August). *Plagiarism: A resource for faculty.* Retrieved from http://library.fandm.edu/plagiarism.html

Fritze, P. (2003). *Innovation in university computer-facilitated learning systems: Product, workplace experience and the organization.* (Unpublished thesis). RMIT, Melbourne, Australia. Retrieved January 28, 2008, from http://eprints.unimelb.edu.au/archive/00000311/

Fulford, C. P., & Zhang, S. (1993). Perceptions of interaction: The critical predictor in distance education. *American Journal of Distance Education, 7*(3), 8–21. doi:10.1080/08923649309526830.

Gabriel, M. A., & MacDonald, C. J. (2002). Working together: The context of teams in an online MBA program. *Canadian Journal of Learning and Technology, 28*(2), 49–65.

Galloway, D., & Davie, R. (1996). A way forward? In Davie, R., & Galloway, D. (Eds.), *Listening to children in education* (pp. 137–142). London: David Fulton Publishers.

Galusha, J. M. (1997). *Barriers to learning in distance education.* Retrieved from http://www.infrastruction.com/barriers.htm

Gamet, J. (2006, May 7). Samsung caught plagiarizing apple icons. *The Mac Observer.* Retrieved from http://www.macobserver.com/tmo/article/Samsung_Caught_Plagiarizing_Apple_Icons

Garrison, D. R., Anderson, T., & Archer, W. (2000). Critical inquiry in a text-based environment: Computer conferencing in higher education. *The Internet and Higher Education, 2*(2-3), 87–105. doi:10.1016/S1096-7516(00)00016-6.

Garrison, D. R., Anderson, T., & Archer, W. (2003). A theory of critical inquiry in online distance education. In Moore, M. G., & Anderson, W. G. (Eds.), *Handbook of distance education* (pp. 113–125). Mahwah, NJ: Erlbaum.

Garrison, R. D., & Arbaugh, J. B. (2007). Researching the community of inquiry framework: Review, issues, and future directions. *The Internet and Higher Education, 10*(3), 157–172. doi:10.1016/j.iheduc.2007.04.001.

Garvey, M. T., O'Sullivan, M., & Blake, M. (2000). Multidisciplinary case-based learning for undergraduate students. *European Journal of Dental Education, 4*(4), 165–168. doi:10.1034/j.1600-0579.2000.040404.x PMID:11168482.

Gay, G. (1988). Designing relevant curricula for diverse learners. *Education and Urban Society, 2*(4), 327–340. doi:10.1177/0013124588020004003.

Gibbs, D. (2000). Cyberlanguage: What it is and what it does. In Gibbs, D., & Krause, K. L. (Eds.), *Cyberlines: Languages and cultures of the Internet* (pp. 11–29). Australia: James Nicholas Publishers Pty Ltd..

Gibbs, G. (2003). *Implementing learning and teaching strategies - A guide to good practice.* Milton Keynes, UK: The Open University.

Gilbert, S., & Gay, G. (1985). Improving the success in school of poor black children. *Phi Delta Kappan, 67*(2), 133–137.

Giminez, M. E. (1997). The dialectics between the real and the virtual: The case of the progressive sociology network. In Behar, J. E. (Ed.), *Mapping cyberspace: Social research on the electronic frontier* (pp. 79–104). New York: Dowling College Press.

Gochenour, T. (1990). *Considering Filipinos.* Yarmoth, ME: Intercultural Press, Inc..

Goertler, S. (2006). *Teacher participation and feedback styles during classroom synchronous computer-mediated communication in intermediate German: A multiple case study.* (Unpublished doctoral dissertation). University of Arizona, Tucson, AZ.

Goodyear, P. (2000). *Effective network learning in higher education: Notes and guidelines.* Retrieved December 14, 2008, from http://csalt.lancs.ac.uk/jisc/advice.htm

Grabinger, R. S., & Dunlap, J. C. (2000). Rich environments for active learning: A definition. In Squires, D., Conole, G., & Jacobs, G. (Eds.), *The changing face of learning technology* (pp. 8–38). Cardiff, UK: University of Wales Press.

Greene, D. (2000). A design model for beginner-level computer-mediated EFL writing. *Computer Assisted Language Learning, 13*(3), 239–252. doi:10.1076/0958-8221(200007)13:3;1-3;FT239.

Gregory, M. (1995). Implications of the introduction of the doctor of education degree in British universities: Can the EdD reach the parts the PhD cannot? *The Vocational Aspect of Education, 47*(2), 177–188. doi:10.1080/0305787950470206.

Grijalva, T. C., Nowell, C., & Kerkvliet, J. (2006). Academic honesty and online courses. *College Student Journal, 40*(1), 180–185.

Guardado, M., & Shi. (2007). ESL students' experiences of online peer feedback. *Computers and Composition, 24*(4), 443–461. doi:10.1016/j.compcom.2007.03.002.

Guba, E. G., & Lincoln, Y. S. (1994). Competing paradigms in qualitative research. In Denzin, N. K., & Lincoln, Y. S. (Eds.), *Handbook of Qualitative Research*. London: Sage.

Compilation of References

Guerrero, M., & Villamil. (1994). Social-cognitive dimensions of interaction in L2 peer revision. *Modern Language Journal, 78*(4), 484–496.

Guerrero, M., & Villamil. (2000). Activating the ZPD: Mutual scaffolding in L2 peer revision. *Modern Language Journal, 84*(1), 51–68. doi:10.1111/0026-7902.00052.

Gumperz, J. (1971). *Language in social groups*. Stanford, CT: Stanford University Press.

Gumperz, J. (1972). The speech community. In Giglioli, P. (Ed.), *Language and Social Context* (pp. 219–231). New York: Penguin.

Hampel, R. (2003). Theoretical perspectives and new practices in audio-graphic conferencing for language learning. *ReCALL, 15*(1), 21–36. doi:10.1017/S0958344003000314.

Hansche, S. (2006). *Official (ISC)2 guide to the CISSP-ISSEP CBK*. New York: Auerbach Publications.

Hara, N., & Kling, R. (2000). Student distress in a web-based distance education course. *Information Communication and Society, 3*(4), 557–579. doi:10.1080/13691180010002297.

Harasim, L., Hiltz, S., Teles, L., & Turroff, M. (1995). *Learning networks: A field guide to teaching and learning online*. Cambridge, MA: MIT Press.

Harris, D. (2001, July 9). Be nice: David Harris's guide to good manners online. *Computerworld New Zealand*, 18-19.

Harry Potter Publisher Denies Plagiarism. (2009, June 16). *The Telegraph*. Retrieved from http://www.telegraph.co.uk

Harry, K., & Khan, A. (2000). The use of technologies in basic education. In C. Yates & J. Bradley (Eds.), Basic Education at a Distance. Vancouver, Canada: Commonwealth of Learning and Routledge Falmer.

Hart, M., & Friesner, T. (2004). Plagiarism and poor academic practice - A threat to the extension of e-learning in higher education? *Electronic Journal on e-Learning, 2*(1), 89-96. Retrieved from www.ejel.org/volume-2/vol2-issue1/issue1-art25-hart-friesner.pdf

Hathorn, L. G., & Ingram, A. L. (2002). Online collaboration: Making it work. *Educational Technology, 42*(1), 33–40.

Hay, A. M., & Hodgkinson, J. W., Peltier, & Drago W. A. (2004). Interaction and virtual learning. *Strategic Change, 13*(4), 193–204. doi:10.1002/jsc.679.

Hay, A., Peltier, J. W., & Drago, W. A. (2004). Reflective learning and on-line management education: A comparison of traditional and online MBA students. *Strategic Change, 13*(4), 169–182. doi:10.1002/jsc.680.

Hayes, B., & Ringwood, J. V. (2008). Student authentication for oral assessment in distance learning programs. *IEEE Transactions on Learning Technologies, 1*(3), 165–175. doi:10.1109/TLT.2009.2.

Hayes, J. R. (1996). A new framework for understanding cognition and affect in writing. In Levy, C. M., & Ransdell, S. (Eds.), *The Science of writing* (pp. 1–28). Hoboken, NJ: Lawrence Erlbaum Associates.

Hayes, N., & Introna, L. D. (2005). Cultural values, plagiarism, and fairness: When plagiarism gets in the way of learning. *Ethics & Behavior, 15*(3), 213–231. doi:10.1207/s15327019eb1503_2.

Haynes, D. (2002, April). *The social dimensions of on-line learning: Perceptions, theories and practical responses.* Paper presented at the Distance Education Association of New Zealand Conference. Wellington, New Zealand.

Heffern, L. (2003). *Improving student dropout rates through student observations and peer contacts.* Retrieved from http://www.pde.state.pa.us/able/lib/able/lfp/lfp03heffern.pdf

Helms, M. M. (2006). Case method of analysis. In M. M. Helms (Ed.), *Encyclopedia of management.* Detroit, MI: Thomson Gale Group, Inc. Retrieved June 3, 2007 from http://www.enotes.com/management-encyclopedia/case-method-analysis

Henderson, L. (1996). Instructional design of interactive multimedia. *Educational Technology Research and Development, 44*(4), 85–104. doi:10.1007/BF02299823.

Hergert, M. (2003). Lessons from launching an online MBA program. *Online Journal of Distance Learning Administration, 6*(4).

Herring, S. C. (2004). Computer-mediated discourse analysis: An approach to researching online behavior. In Barab, S. A., Kling, R., & Gray, J. H. (Eds.), *Designing for virtual communities in the service of learning* (pp. 338–376). New York: Cambridge University Press. doi:10.1017/CBO9780511805080.016.

Herring, S. C. (Ed.). (1996). *Computer-mediated communication: Linguistic, social and cross-cultural perspective.* Amsterdam: John Bejamins Publishing Company.

Heylighen, F., & Dewaele, J.-M. (1999). *Formality of language: Definition, measurement and behavioral determinants.* Brussels, Belgium: Free University of Brussels.

Higgens, D. (2011). Why reflect? Recognising the link between learning and reflection. *Reflective Practice, 12*(5), 583–584. doi:10.1080/14623943.2011.606693.

Hill, J. R., Raven, R., & Han, S. (2002). Connections in web-based learning environments: A research based model for community building. *The Quarterly Review of Distance Education, 3*(4), 383–393.

Hiltz, S. R. (1994). *The virtual classroom: Learning without limits via computer networks.* Norwood, NJ: Ablex.

Hiltz, S. R., & Wellman, B. (1997). Asynchronous learning networks as a virtual classroom. *Communications of the ACM, 40*(9), 44–49. doi:10.1145/260750.260764.

Hine, C. (2000). Internet as culture and cultural artifact. In *Virtual Ethnography* (pp. 14–40). London: Sage Publications.

Hofstede, G. (1991). *Cultures and organizations: Software of the mind.* London: McGraw Hill.

Högskoleförordning. (1993). Retrieved from http://www.notisum.se/rnp/SLS/LAG/19930100.HTM

Holmes, J. (1995). *Women, men and politeness.* New York: Longman.

Howard, C., Schenk, K., & Discenza, R. (Eds.). (2003). *Distance learning and university effectiveness: Changing educational paradigms for online learning.* Hershey, PA: Idea Group Inc. doi:10.4018/978-1-59140-178-0.

Howard, R. M. (1995). Plagiarisms, authorships, and the academic death penalty. *College English, 57*(7), 788–806. doi:10.2307/378403.

Compilation of References

Howard, R. M. (2002). Don't police plagiarism: Just TEACH! *Education Digest, 67*(5), 46–49.

Huang, S.-Y. (1998). *Differences in the nature of discussion between peer response sessions conducted on networked computers and those conducted in the traditional face-to-face situation.* Paper presented at the Annual Meeting of the International Writing 98 Conference. New York, NY.

Huang, H. (2002). Toward constructivism for adult learners in online learning environments. *British Journal of Educational Technology, 33*(1), 27–37. doi:10.1111/1467-8535.00236.

Huang, W., Luce, T., & Lu, Y. (2005). Virtual team learning in online MBA education: An empirical investigation. *Issues in Information Systems, 4*(1), 258–264.

Hudson, B., Owen, D., & van Veen, K. (2006). Working on educational research methods with masters students in an international online learning community. *British Journal of Educational Technology, 37*(4), 577–603. doi:10.1111/j.1467-8535.2005.00553.x.

Hudson, J., & Brockman, A. (2002). IRC Francais: The creation of an internet-based SLA community. *Computer Assisted Language Learning, 15*(2), 109–134. doi:10.1076/call.15.2.109.8197.

Hu, G. (2005). Using peer review with Chinese ESL student writers. *Language Teaching Research, 9*(3), 321–342. doi:10.1191/1362168805lr169oa.

Hyland, F. (2000). ESL writers and feedback: Giving more autonomy to students. *Language Teaching Research, 4*(1), 33–54.

Hymes, D. (1972). Models of the interaction of language and social life. In Gumperz, J., & Hymes, D. (Eds.), *Directions in sociolinguistics: The ethnography of communication* (pp. 35–71). London: Blackwell.

IDP Education Pty Ltd. (n.d.). *The value of international education to Australia.* Retrieved from http://www.idp.com/research/statistics/education_export_statistics.aspx

Information Technology Services. Penn State. (2009, March 3). *Plagiarism prevention resources.* Retrieved from http://tlt.its.psu.edu/plagiarism

Irving, L. (1999). Falling through the net: Defining the digital divide. *US Department of Commerce, National Telecommunications Information Administration.* Retrieved December, 2008, from http://www.ntia.doc.gov/reports.html

Ivey, A. E., Bradford-Ivey, M., & Simek-Downing, L. (1987). *Counseling and pyschotherapy* (2nd ed.). Boston: Allyn and Bacon.

Jacobs, G. M., Curtis, Braine, & Huang. (1998). Feedback on student writing: Taking the middle path. *Journal of Second Language Writing, 7*(3), 307–317. doi:10.1016/S1060-3743(98)90019-4.

Jakobi, A. P., & Rusconi, A. (2009). Lifelong learning in the Bologna process: European developments in higher education. *Compare: A Journal of Comparative and International Education, 39*(1), 51-65.

Jamieson, N. (1993). *Understanding Vietnam.* Berkeley, CA: University of California Press.

Jarvis, J. (2010, January 31). Professors are beating cheating with turnitin.com. *The Cowl.* Retrieved from http://www.thecowl.com/2.7830/professors-are-beating-cheating-with-turnitin-com-1.1103149

Jeffries, M. (2009). *Research in distance education: The history of distance education.* Retrieved from http://www./edu/DL_history_mJeffries.html

Johnson, D. W., Johnson, R. T., Stanne, M. B., & Garibaldi, A. (1990). Impact of group processing on achievement in cooperative groups. *The Journal of Social Psychology.* doi:10.1080/00224545.1990.9924613.

Johnson, D. W., Johnsson, R. T., Stanne, M., & Garibaldi, A. (1990). The impact of leader and member group processing on achievement in cooperative groups. *The Journal of Social Psychology, 130,* 507–516. doi:10.1080/00224545.1990.9924613.

Johnson, H. (2001). The PhD student as an adult learner: Using reflective practice to find and speak in her own voice. *Reflective Practice, 2*(1), 53–63. doi:10.1080/14623940120035523.

Joint Information Systems Committee. (2005). *Deterring, detecting and dealing with student plagiarism.* Retrieved from http://www.jisc.ac.uk/publications/briefing-papers/2005/pub_plagiarism.aspx

Jonassen, D. (1994, March/April). Thinking technology: Toward a constructivist design model. *Educational Technology,* 34–37.

Joo, J. (1999). Cultural issues of the internet in classrooms. *British Journal of Educational Technology, 30*(3), 245–250. doi:10.1111/1467-8535.00113.

Jordan, C. (1985). Translating culture: From ethnographic information to educational program. *Anthropology & Education Quarterly, 16*(2), 105–123. doi:10.1525/aeq.1985.16.2.04x0631g.

Joyes, G., Fisher, A., & Coyle, D. (2002). Developments in generative learning using a collaborative learning environment. In S. Banks, P. Goodyear, V. Hodgson, & D. Mcconnell (Eds.), *Proceedings of the Third Networked Learning International Conference 2002* (pp. 398-405). Lancaster, UK: Lancaster and Sheffield University.

Joyes, G. (2006). When pedagogy leads technology. *International Journal of Technology. Knowledge in Society, 1,* 1–13. Retrieved from http://www.Technology-Journal.com.

Joyes, G. (2009). Personalisation and the online video narrative learning tools V-ResORT and the ViP. In O'Donoghue, J. (Ed.), *Technology Supported Environments for Personalised Learning: Methods and Case Studies* (pp. 324–340). Hershey, PA: IGI Global. doi:10.4018/978-1-60566-884-0.ch018.

Joyes, G. (2013). The nature of a successful online professional doctorate. In *Cases on Professional Distance Education Degree Programs and Practices: Successes, Challenges and Issues.* Hershey, PA: IGI Global.

Joyes, G., & Fritze, P. (2006). Valuing individual differences within learning: From face-to-face to online experience. *International Journal of Teaching and Learning in Higher Education, 171*, 33–41.

Joyes, G., & Wang, T. (2007). A generic framework for the training of eLearning tutors. In Spencer-Oatey, H. (Ed.), *eLearning in China: eChina Perspectives on Policy, Pedagogy and Innovation* (pp. 109–124). HK Research Press.

Keegan, D. (1986). *The foundations of distance education*. London: Croom Helm. Retrieved from HTTP://www.csu.edu.au/division/oli/oli-rd/occpap17/design.htm

Kelm, S. (2009). *The PKI page*. Retrieved from http://www.pki-page.org/

Kember, D. (1989). A longitudinal-process model of dropout from distance education. *The Journal of Higher Education, 60*(3), 278–301. doi:10.2307/1982251.

Kenny, S. S. (1998). *The Boyer commission on educating undergraduates in the research university: Reinventing undergraduate education: A blueprint for America's research universities*. Stony Brook, NY: The Carnegie Foundation for the Advancement of Teaching. Retrieved from http://naples.cc.sunysb.edu/Pres/boyer.nsf

Kenny, A. (2002). Online learning: Enhancing nurse education? *Journal of Advanced Nursing, 38*(2), 127–135. doi:10.1046/j.1365-2648.2002.02156.x PMID:11940125.

Kern, R., & Warschauer. (2000). Theory and practice of networkbased language teaching. In M. Warschauer & R. Kern (Eds.), *Networkbased language teaching: Concepts and practice*, (pp. 1–19). Port Chester, NY: Cambridge University Press.

Kern, R. (1995). Restructuring classroom interaction with networked computers: Effects on quantity and characteristics of language production. *Modern Language Journal, 79*(4), 457–476. doi:10.1111/j.1540-4781.1995.tb05445.x.

Kern, R. G. (1995). Restructuring classroom interaction with networked computers: effects on quantity and characteristics of language production. *Modern Language Journal, 79*(4), 457–476. doi:10.1111/j.1540-4781.1995.tb05445.x.

Kirkman, B. L., Rosen, B., Gibson, C. B., Tesluk, P. E., & McPherson, S. O. (2002). Five challenges to virtual team success: Lessons from Sabre, Inc. *The Academy of Management Executive, 16*(3), 67–79. doi:10.5465/AME.2002.8540322.

Kirkpatrick, D. (1998). *Evaluating training programs: The four levels*. San Francisco, CA: Berrett-Koehler Publishers, Inc..

Kitade, K. (2000). L2 learners' discourse and SLA theories in CMC: Collaborative interaction in internet chat. *Computer Assisted Language Learning, 13*(2), 143–166. doi:10.1076/0958-8221(200004)13:2;1-D;FT143.

Kitchen, D., & McDougall, D. (1999). Collaborative learning on the internet. *Journal of Educational Technology Systems, 27*(3), 245–258.

Klemm, W. R. (1998). *Eight ways to get students more engaged in online conferences*. Retrieved December, 2009 http://168.144.129.112/Articles/Eight%20Ways%20to%20Get%20Students%20More%20Engaged%20in%20Online%20Conferences.rtf

Knapper, C. (1988). Lifelong learning and distance education. *American Journal of Distance Education, 2*(1), 63–72. doi:10.1080/08923648809526609.

Knight, J. (1999). Internationalisation of higher education. In *Quality and Internationalisation in Higher Education* (pp. 13–28). Paris: OECD.

Knight, J., & de Wit, H. (1995). Strategies for internationalization of higher education: Historical and conceptual perspectives. In de Wit, H. (Ed.), *Strategies for internationalization of higher education: A comparative study of Australia, Canada, Europe, and the United States of America* (pp. 5–32). Amsterdam: European Association for International Education.

Knowles, M. (1990). *The adult learner: A neglected species* (4th ed.). Houston, TX: Gulf.

Knowles, M. S. (1990). *The adult learner: A neglected species*. Houston, TX: Gulf Publishing.

Koloto, A., Katoanga, A., & Tatila, L. (2006). *Critical success factors for effective use of e-learning by Pacific learners*. Retrieved December 15, 2008, from elearning.itpnz.ac.nz/files/Koloto_Critical_Success_Factors.pdf

Kottkamp, R. (1990). Means for reflection. *Education and Urban Society, 22*(2), 82–203. doi:10.1177/0013124590022002005.

Kowal, D. M. (2002). Digitizing and globalizing indigenous voices: The Zapatista movement. In Elmer, G. (Ed.), *Critical perspectives on the Internet* (pp. 105–126). Oxford, UK: Rowman & Littlefield Publishers, Inc..

Kramsch, C., & Sullivan, P. (1996). Appropriate pedagogy. *ELT Journal, 50*(3), 199–212. doi:10.1093/elt/50.3.199.

Kreber, C. (2005). Charting a critical course on the scholarship of university teaching movement. *Studies in Higher Education, 30*(4), 389–405. doi:10.1080/03075070500160095.

Kretovics, M., & McCambridge, J. (2002). Measuring MBA student learning: Does distance make a difference? *International Review of Research in Open and Distance Learning, 3*(2), 1–18.

Kwame, T. (2005). *Researching the online student experience*, Unpublished PhD thesis, University of Nottingham, UK

Ladson-Billings, G. (1992). Reading between the lines and beyond the pages: A culturally relevant approach to literacy teaching. *Theory into Practice, 31*(4), 312–320. doi:10.1080/00405849209543558.

Ladson-Billings, G. (1995). But that's just good teaching! The case for culturally relevant pedagogy. *Theory into Practice, 31*(3), 159–165. doi:10.1080/00405849509543675.

Lancaster, R. C. (2006). *Eliminating the successor to plagiarism? Identifying the usage of contract cheating sites*. Retrieved from http://www.plagiarismadvice.org/documents/papers/2006Papers05.pdf

Lantolf, J. P. (2000). *Sociocultural theory and second language learning*. Oxford, UK: Oxford University Press.

Lantolf, J. P. (2003). Intrapersonal communication and internalization in the second language classroom. In Kozulin, A. (Ed.), *Vygotsky's educational theory in cultural context* (pp. 349–370). Cambridge, UK: Cambridge University Press. doi:10.1017/CBO9780511840975.018.

Compilation of References

Lave, J., & Wenger, E. (1991). *Situated learning - Legitimate peripheral participation*. Cambridge, UK: Cambridge University Press. doi:10.1017/CBO9780511815355.

Lawhead, P. B., Alpert, E., Bland, C. G., Carswell, L., Cizmar, D., & DeWeill, J. et al. (1997). The web and distance learning: What is appropriate and what is not: report of the ITiCSE '97 working group on the web and distance learning. *ACM SIGCUE Outlook*, *25*(4), 27–37. doi:10.1145/274382.274383.

Lee, C. D., & Smagorinsky. (2000). Introduction: Constructing meaning through collaborative inquiry. In C. D. Lee & P. Smagorinsky (Eds.), *Vygotskian perspectives on literacy research: Constructing meaning through collaborative inquiry* (pp. 1-18). Cambridge, UK: Cambridge University Press.

Lee, S.-H., Lee, J., Liu, X., Bonk, C. J., & Magjuka, R. J. (2009). A review of case-based learning practices in an online MBA program: A program-level case study. *Journal of Educational Technology & Society*, *12*(3), 178–190.

Leidner, D., & Jarvenpaa, S. (1995). The use of information technology to enhance management school education: A theoretical view. *Management Information Systems Quarterly*, *19*(3), 265–291. doi:10.2307/249596.

Lewis, A., & Lindsay, G. (2000). Emerging issues. In Lewis, A., & Lindsay, G. (Eds.), *Researching children's perspectives* (pp. 189–197). Buckingham, UK: Open University Press.

Lindgren, E., Sullivan, K. P. H., Zhao, H., Deutschmann, M., & Steinvall, A. (2011). Developing peer-to-peer supported reflection as a life-long learning skill: An example from the translation classroom. In Chang, M. (Ed.), *Human Development and Global Advancements through Information Communciation Technologies: New Initiatives* (pp. 188–210). Hershey, PA: IGI Global. doi:10.4018/978-1-60960-497-4.ch011.

Littlewood, W. (1999). Defining and developing autonomy in East Asian contexts. *Applied Linguistics*, *20*(1), 71–94. doi:10.1093/applin/20.1.71.

Liu, J., & Sadler. (2003). The effect and affect of peer review in electronic versus traditional modes of L2 writing. *Journal of English for Academic Purposes*, *2*(3), 193–227. doi:10.1016/S1475-1585(03)00025-0.

Liu, M., Moore, Graham, & Lee. (2003). A look at the research on computer-based technology use in second language learning: Review of literature from 1990-2000. *Journal of Research on Technology in Education*, *24*, 250–273.

Lloyd-Smith, M., & Tarr, J. (2000). Researching children's perspectives: A sociological dimension. In Lewis, A., & Lindsay, G. (Eds.), *Researching children's perspectives* (pp. 59–70). Buckingham, UK: Open University Press.

Lockhart, C., & Ng. (1995). Analysing talk in ESL peer response groups: Stances, functions and content. *Language Learning*, *45*(4), 605–655. doi:10.1111/j.1467-1770.1995.tb00456.x.

Lofland, J., & Lofland, H. (1995). *Analyzing social settings*. Belmont, CA: Wadsworth Publishing Company.

Long, M., & Porter, P. (1985). Group work, interlanguage talk, and second language learning. *TESOL Quarterly, 19*(2), 207–228. doi:10.2307/3586827.

Long, P., Tricker, T., Rangecroft, M., & Gilroy, P. (1999). Measuring the satisfaction gap: Education in the market-place. *Total Quality Management, 10*(4/5), 772–779. doi:10.1080/0954412997794.

Lonka, K., & Ahola, K. (1995). Activating instruction: How to foster study and thinking skills in higher education. *European Journal of Psychology of Education, 10*, 351–368. doi:10.1007/BF03172926.

MacDonald, R. (2000, November 24). Talking shop: Why don't we turn the tide of plagiarism to the learners' advantage? *The Times Higher Education*. Retrieved from http://www.timeshighereducation.co.uk

MacDonald, R., & Carroll, J. (2006). Plagiarism-A complex issue requiring a holistic institutional approach. *Assessment & Evaluation in Higher Education, 31*(2), 233–245. doi:10.1080/02602930500262536.

MacKinnon, D., & Manathunga, C. (2003). Going global with assessment: What to do when the dominant cultures literacy drives assessment. *Higher Education Research & Development, 22*(2), 131–144. doi:10.1080/07294360304110.

MacManus, R. (2007). *E-learning 2.0: All you need to know*. Retrieved from http://www.readwriteWeb.com/archives/E-learning_20_all_you_need_to_know.php

MacManus, R., & Porter, J. (2005). *Web 2.0 design: Bootstrapping the social web*. Retrieved from http://www.digital-Web.com/articles/Web_2_for_designers

Magjuka, R. J., Min, S., & Bonk, C. (2005). Critical design and administrative issues in online education. *Online Journal of Distance Learning Administration, 8*(4). Retrieved January 4, 2006, from http://www.westga.edu/~distance/ojdla/articles/winter2005/magjuka84.htm

Malinowski, C. I., & Smith, C. P. (1985). Moral reasoning and moral conduct: An investigation prompted by Kohlberg's theory. *Journal of Personality and Social Psychology, 49*, 1016–1027. doi:10.1037/0022-3514.49.4.1016.

Mangelsdorf, K. (1992). Peer reviews in the ESL composition classroom: What do the students think? *ELT Journal, 46*(3), 274–284. doi:10.1093/elt/46.3.274.

Mann, C., & Stewart, F. (2000). *Internet communication and qualitative research: A handbook for researching online*. London: Sage Publications Ltd..

Mann, C., & Stewart, F. (2004). Introducing online methods. In Hesse-Biber, S. N., & Leavy, P. (Eds.), *Approaches to qualitative research: A reader on theory and practice* (pp. 367–401). Oxford, UK: Oxford University Press.

Marais, E., Argles, D., & von Solms, B. (2008). *Security issues specific to e-assessments*. Retrieved from http://eprints.ecs.soton.ac.uk/11433/1/E-learning_ArticleNewFin.doc

Compilation of References

Marcus, G., Taylor, R., & Ellis, R. A. (2004). Implications for the design of online case based learning activities based on the student blended learning experience. In R. Atkinson, C. McBeath, D. Jonas-Dwyer, & R. Phillips (Eds.), *Beyond the comfort zone: Proceedings of the 21st ASCILITE Conference* (pp. 557-586). Perth, Australia. Retrieved online on December 1st from http://www.ascilite.org.au/conferences/perth04/procs/marcus.html

Marcus, A., & Gould, E. (2000). Crosscurrents: Cultural dimensions and global web user interface design. *Interaction, 7*(4), 32–46. doi:10.1145/345190.345238.

Markus, H., & Kitayama, S. (1991). Culture and the self: Implications for cognition, emotion and motivation. *Psychological Review, 98*(2), 224–253. doi:10.1037/0033-295X.98.2.224.

Marland, M. (1996). Personal development, pastoral care and listening. In Davie, R., & Galloway, D. (Eds.), *Listening to children in education* (pp. 64–76). London: David Fulton Publishers.

Marsh, B. (1997). Plagiarism thread on ACW-L. *Kairos, 3*(1). Retrieved from http://english.ttu.edu/kairos/3.1/binder.html?reviews/marsh/plagintro.html

Marshall, S., & Garry, M. (2005). How well do students really understand plagiarism? In H. Goss (Ed.), *Proceedings of the 22nd Annual Conference of the Australasian Society for Computers in Learning in Tertiary Education (ASCILITE)* (pp. 457-467). Brisbane, Australia: ASCILITE.

Martinez, M., Bunderson, C. V., Nelson, L. M., & Ruttan, J. P. (1999). *Successful learning in the new millennium: A new web learning paradigm*. Paper presented at the annual meeting of WebNet, International Conference. Honolulu, HI.

Martins, L. L., Gilson, L. L., & Maynard, M. T. (2004). Virtual teams: What do we know and where do we go from here? *Journal of Management, 30*(6), 805–835. doi:10.1016/j.jm.2004.05.002.

Marton, F., Hounsell, D., & Entwistle, N. (Eds.). (1996). *The experience of learning: Implications for teaching and studying in higher education*. Edinburgh, UK: Scottish Academic Press.

Maruca, L. (2004, June). *The plagiarism panic: Digital policing in the new intellectual property regime*. Paper presented at the Conference on new Directions in Copyright. London, UK. Retrieved from http://www.copyright.bbk.ac.uk/contents/publications/conferences/2004/lmaruca.pdf

Matalene, C. (1985). Contrastive rhetoric: An American writing teacher in China. *National Council of Teachers of English. College English, 47*(8), 789–808. doi:10.2307/376613.

Mathur, R., & Oliver, L. (2007). Developing an international distance education program: A blended learning approach. *Online Journal of Distance Learning Administration, 10*(4), 1-10. Retrieved August 10, 2008, from http://www.westga.edu/~distance/ojdla/winter104/mathur104.html

Maxwell, T. W. (2003). From first to second generation Professional Doctorate. *Studies in Higher Education, 28*(3), 279–291. doi:10.1080/03075070309292.

Maznevski, M., & Chudoba, K. (2001). Bridging space over time: Global virtual team dynamics and effectiveness. *Organization Science, 11*(5), 473–492. doi:10.1287/orsc.11.5.473.15200.

Mazzarol, T., Soutar, G. N., & Seng, M. S. Y. (2003). The third wave: Future trends in international education. *International Journal of Educational Management, 17*(3), 90–99. doi:10.1108/09513540310467778.

McBride, K., & Beers Fägersten. (2008). The students' role in distance learning. In S. Goertler & P. Winke (Eds.), *Opening Doors through Distance Learning Education: Principles, Perspectives and Practices* (pp. 43-66). San Marcos, TX: CALICO.

McCabe, D. L. (1993). Faculty responses to academic dishonesty: The influence of student honor codes. *Research in Higher Education, 34*(5), 647–658. doi:10.1007/BF00991924.

McCabe, D. L. (2001). Why students do it and how we can help them stop. *American Educator, 25*(4), 38–43.

McCabe, D. L., Butterfield, K. D., & Trevino, L. K. (2006). Academic dishonesty in graduate business programs: Prevalence, causes, and proposed action. *Academy of Management Learning & Education, 5*(3), 294–305. doi:10.5465/AMLE.2006.22697018.

McCabe, D. L., & Trevino, L. K. (1993). Honor codes and other contextual influences. *The Journal of Higher Education, 64,* 522–538. doi:10.2307/2959991.

McCarthy, T. L., Lynch, R. H., Wallace, S., & Benalla, A. (1991). Classroom inquiry and Navajo learning styles: A call for reassessment. *Anthropology & Education Quarterly, 22*(1), 42–59. doi:10.1525/aeq.1991.22.1.05x1172b.

McDonald, H. (1993). Aboriginal and Torres Strait islander creativity and the affirmation of identity: Educational potentials. In Loos & Osanai (Eds.), Indigenous Minorities and Education. Tokyo: Sanusha Publishing Co Ltd.

McGee, C. (2001). Classroom interaction. In McGee, C., & Fraser, D. (Eds.), *The professional practice of teaching* (2nd ed., pp. 106–133). Palmerston North, Australia: Dunmore Press Ltd..

McGorry, S. Y. (2002). Online, but on target? Internet-based MBA courses: A case study. *The Internet and Higher Education, 5*(2), 167–175. doi:10.1016/S1096-7516(02)00089-1.

McGowan, U. (2005). Plagiarism detection and prevention: Are we putting the cart before the horse? In Brew, A., & Asmar, C. (Eds.), *Higher education in a changing world* (pp. 287–293). Adelaide, Australia: Higher Education Research and Development Society of Australasia.

McGroarty, M. E., & Zhu. (1997). Triangulation in classroom research: A study of peer revision. *Language Learning, 47*(1), 1–43. doi:10.1111/0023-8333.11997001.

Compilation of References

McInnis, C., James, R., & Hartley, R. (2000). *Trends in the first year experience in Australian Universities.* Canberra, Australia: AGPS..

McLaughlin, C., Carnell, M., & Blount, L. (1999). Children as teachers: Listening to children in education. In Carolin, B., & Milner, P. (Eds.), *Time to listen to children: Personal and professional communication* (pp. 97–111). London: Routledge.

McLoughlin, C., & Oliver, R. (2000). Designing learning environments for cultural inclusivity: A case study of indigenous online learning at a tertiary level. *Australian Journal of Educational Technology, 16*(1), 58–72. Retrieved August 22, 2008, from http://www.ascilite.org.au/ajet/ajet16/mcloughlin.html

McLoughlin, C. (1999). Culturally responsive technology use: Developing an online community of learners. *British Journal of Educational Technology, 30*(3), 231–245. doi:10.1111/1467-8535.00112.

McLoughlin, C. (2000). Cultural maintenance, ownership, and multiple perspectives: Features of web-based delivery to promote equity. *Journal of Educational Media, 25*(3), 229–241.

McLoughlin, C. (2001). Inclusivity and alignment: Principles of pedagogy, task and assessment design for effective cross-cultural online learning. *Distance Education, 22*(1), 7–29. doi:10.1080/0158791010220102.

McLoughlin, C., & Luca, J. (2002). A learner-centred approach to developing team skills through web-based learning and assessment. *British Journal of Educational Technology, 33*(5), 571–582. doi:10.1111/1467-8535.00292.

McMurtrie, B. (2009, April 2). Australian universities see increase in foreign enrolments. *The Chronicle of Higher Education.* Retrieved from http://chronicle.com

Meacham, D., & Evans. (1989). *Distance education: The design of study materials.* Wagga Wagga, New Zealand: Open Learning Institute, Charles Sturt University.

Menchaca, M., & Hoffman, E. (2008). *Qualitative analysis of student experiences with distance education in the Pacific Rim*. Paper presented at University of Hawaii Manoa Campus. Honolulu: HI.

Menchaca, M., Yong, L., & Hoffman, E. (2008). Understanding barriers to native Hawaiian participation in distance education. In *Proceedings from Distance Learning and the Internet Conference*. Retrieved May 15, 2009, from http://www.waseda.jp/DLI2008/program/proceedings/session7-9.html

Mendonca, C. O., & Johnson. (1994). Peer review negotiations: Revision activities in ESL writing instruction. *TESOL Quarterly, 28*(4), 745–769. doi:10.2307/3587558.

Merriam, S. B. (1998). *Case study research in education: A qualitative approach.* San Francisco, CA: Jossey-Bass Publishers.

Min, H.-T. (2005). Training students to become successful peer reviewers. *System, 33*(2), 293–308. doi:10.1016/j.system.2004.11.003.

Ministry of Education. (1994). *English in the New Zealand curriculum.* Wellington, New Zealand: Learning Media.

Ministry of Education. (1996). *Exploring language: A handbook for teachers.* Wellington, New Zealand: Learning Media Ltd..

Minott, M., & Marouchou, D. (2013). Experiences of an online doctoral course in teacher education. In *Cases on Professional Distance Education Degree Programs and Practices: Successes, Challenges and Issues*. Hershey, PA: IGI Global.

Monteith, M. (2002). *Teaching primary literacy with ICT*. Buckingham, UK: Open University Press.

Moon, J. A. (1999). *Reflection in learning and professional development: Theory and practice*. London: Kogan Page.

Morrow, V. (1999). It's cool... 'cos you can't give us detentions and things, can you?!: Reflections on research with children. In Carolin, B., & Milner, P. (Eds.), *Time to listen to children: Personal and professional communication* (pp. 203–215). London: Routledge.

National Center for Education Statistics. (2008). *Postsecondary degrees conferred by sex and race*. Retrieved from http://nces.ed.gov/fastfacts/display.asp?id=72

Nelson, G., & Murphy. (1993). Peer response groups: Do L2 writers use peer comments in revising their drafts? *TESOL Quarterly, 27*(1), 135–142. doi:10.2307/3586965.

Nesbitt, E. (2000). Researching 8 to 13-year-olds' perspectives on their experience of religion. In Lewis, A., & Lindsay, G. (Eds.), *Researching children's perspectives* (pp. 135–149). Buckingham, UK: Open University Press.

Newstead, S. E., Franklyn-Stokes, A., & Armstead, P. (1996). Individual differences in student cheating. *Journal of Educational Psychology, 88*(2), 229–241. doi:10.1037/0022-0663.88.2.229.

Ngeow, K., & Kong, K. Y. S. (2002). *Designing culturally sensitive learning environments*. Retrieved April 20, 2009, from https://secure.ascilite.org.au/conferences/auckland02/proceedings/papers/055.pdf

Nilsson, B. (2003). Internationalisation at home from a Swedish perspective: The case of Malmö. *Journal of Studies in International Education, 7*, 27–40. doi:10.1177/1028315302250178.

Nipper, S. (1989). Third generation distance learning and computer conferencing. In R. Mason & A. Kaye (Eds.), *Mindweave: Communication, Computers and Distance Education*. Oxford, UK: Pergamon Press. Retrieved from HTTP: http://www-icdl.open.ac.uk/mindweave/chap5.html/

Nunamaker, J., Dennis, A., Valacich, J., Vogel, D., & George, J. (1991). Electronic meeting systems to support group work. *Communications of the ACM, 34*(7), 41–61. doi:10.1145/105783.105793.

Palloff, R. M., & Pratt. (1999). *Building learning communities in cyberspace: Effective strategies for the online classroom*. San Francisco, CA: Jossey-Bass.

Palloff, R., & Pratt, K. (1999). *Building learning communities in cyberspace: Effective strategies for the online classroom*. San Francisco, CA: Jossey-Bass Publishers.

Palloff, R., & Pratt, K. (2001). *Transforming courses for the online classroom: Lessons from the cyberspace classroom*. San Francisco, CA: Jossey-Bass Inc..

Park, C. (2003). In other (people's) words: Plagiarism by university students - Literature and lessons. *Assessment & Evaluation in Higher Education, 28*(5), 471–488. doi:10.1080/02602930301677.

Patri, M. (2002). The influence of peer feedback on self- and peer-assessment of oral skills. *Language Testing*, *19*(2), 109–133. doi:10.1191/0265532202lt224oa.

Patton, M. Q. (1990). *Qualitative evaluation and research methods*. Thousand Oaks, CA: Sage.

Patton, M. Q. (2001). *Qualitative research & evaluation methods*. London: Sage.

Pennycook, A. (1996). Borrowing others' words: Text, ownership, memory, and plagiarism. *TESOL Quarterly*, *30*(2), 201–230. doi:10.2307/3588141.

Petraglia, J. (1998). The real world on a short leash: The (mis)application of constructivism to the design of educational technology. *Educational Technology Research and Development*, *46*(3), 53–65. doi:10.1007/BF02299761.

Phillips, E. M., & Pugh, D. S. (2000). *How to get a PhD A handbook for students and their supervisors* (3rd ed.). London: Open University Press.

Phillips, E., & Pugh, D. (1994). *How to get a PhD: A handbook for students and their supervisors*. Philadelphia, PA: Open University Press.

Phillips, V. (1998). Online universities teach knowledge beyond the books. *HRMagazine*, *43*(8), 120–126.

Phipps, R., & Merisotis, J. (2000). *Quality on the line: Benchmarks for success in Internet-based distance education*. Washington, DC: The Institute for Higher Education Policy. Retrieved January 16, 2010, from http://www.ihep.org/assets/files/publications/mr/QualityOnTheLine.pdf

Plagiarism Investigation Ends at Virginia. (2002, November 26). *The New York Times*. Retrieved from http://www.nytimes.com

Plagiarism. (n.d.). *Oxford English Dictionary*. Retrieved from http://dictionary.oed.com

Ponzurick, T. G., France, K. R., & Logar, C. M. (2000). Delivering graduate marketing education: An analysis of face-to-face versus distance education. *Journal of Marketing Education*, *22*(3), 180–187. doi:10.1177/0273475300223002.

Powell, G. C. (1997). On being a culturally sensitive instructional designer and educator. *Educational Technology*, *37*(2), 6–14.

Pratt, M. (2005, April 2). Telegram & Gazette fires sports writer accused of plagiarism. *USA Today*. Retrieved from http://www.usatoday.com

Prensky, M. (2001). Digital natives, digital immigrants. *On the Horizon*, *9*(5), 1-6. Retrieved on 15 January 2005 from www.marcprensky.com/writing/default.asp

Price, M. (2002). Beyond gotcha! Situating plagiarism in policy and pedagogy. *College Composition and Communication*, *54*(1), 88–115. doi:10.2307/1512103.

Prosser, M., & Trigwell, K. (1999). *Understanding learning and teaching: The experience in higher education*. Buckingham, UK: Open University Press.

Ramsden, P. (1992). *Learning to teach in higher education*. London: Routledge. doi:10.4324/9780203413937.

Rao, K. (2007). Distance learning in Micronesia: Participants' experiences in a virtual classroom using synchronous technologies. *Innovate Journal of Online Education*, *4*(1), 1-10. Retrieved January 20, 2009, from http://www.innovateonline.info/index.php?view=article&id=437

Rao, K. R. (2008). Plagiarism - A scourge. *Current Science – Bangalore*, *94*(5), 581-586.

Rao, K., & Giuli, C. (2008). *What works in distance learning: Early indicators from an evaluation of REMOTE, an online master's degree program for Micronesia and American Samoa.* Paper presented at the 13th ANNUAL TCC Worldwide Online Conference. New York, NY.

Reeves, T. C., & Reeves, P. M. (1997). Effective dimensions of interactive learning on the world wide Web. In Kahn, B. (Ed.), *Web Based Instruction* (pp. 5–18). Englewood Cliffs, NJ: Educational Technology Publications.

Renard, L. (1999). Cut and paste 101: Plagiarism and the net. *Educational Leadership, 57*(4), 38–42.

Riel, M., & Fulton, K. (2001). The role of technology in supporting learning communities. *Phi Delta Kappan, 82*(7), 518–523.

Rise in Foreign Students in UK. (2008, January 10). *BBC News*. Retrieved from http://news.bbc.co.uk/2/hi/uk_news/education/7181806.stm

Roed, J. (2003). Language learner behaviour in a virtual environment. *Computer Assisted Language Learning, 16*(2-3), 155–172. doi:10.1076/call.16.2.155.15880.

Rollinson, P. (2005). Using peer feedback in the ESL writing class. *ELT Journal, 59*(1), 23–30. doi:10.1093/elt/cci003.

Rovai, A. P. (2000). Online and traditional assessments: What is the difference? *The Internet and Higher Education, 3*, 141–151. doi:10.1016/S1096-7516(01)00028-8.

RSA.com. (2007). *What is DESX?* Retrieved from http://www.rsasecurity.com

Rust, C. (2002). The impact of assessment on student learning: How can the research literature practically help to inform the development of departmental assessment strategies and learner-centred assessment practices. *Active Learning in Higher Education, 3*(2), 145–158. doi:10.1177/1469787402003002004.

Ryan, J. (1992). Aboriginal learning styles: A critical review. *Language, Culture and Curriculum, 5*(3), 161–183. doi:10.1080/07908319209525124.

Sachuo, S. (1992). Impact of communication technology on traditional discourse in the culture of Micronesia. In D.H. Rubinstein (Ed.), *Pacific History: Papers from the 8th Pacific History Association Conference* (pp. 405-418). Pacific History.

Saettler, P. (1968). *A history of instructional technology.* New York: McGraw-Hill.

Salmon, G. (2002). *E-tivities: The key to active online learning.* London: Kogan Page.

Salmon, G. (2004). *E-moderating: The key to teaching and learning online* (2nd ed.). London: Routledge. doi:10.4324/9780203465424.

Sanders, R. (2006). A comparison of chat room productivity: In-class versus out-of-class. *CALICO Journal, 24*(1), 59–76.

Savage, S. (2004). *Staff and student responses to a trial of turnitin plagiarism detection software.* Retrieved from http://www.indiana.edu/~tltc/technologies/savage.pdf

Savenye, W. C., Olina, & Niemczyk. (2001). So you are going to be an online writing instructor: Issues in designing, developing, and delivering an online course. *Computers and Composition, 18*(4), 371–385. doi:10.1016/S8755-4615(01)00069-X.

Compilation of References

Sayer, A. (1992). *Method in social science: A realist approach* (2nd ed.). London: Routledge.

Schab, F. (1991). Schooling without learning: Thirty years of cheating in high school. *Adolescence, 26*(104), 839–848. PMID:1789171.

Schamber, L. (1988). *Delivery systems for distance education.* (ERIC Document Reproduction Service No. ED 304 111).

Schön, N. D. (1988). *Educating the reflective practitioner: Toward a new design for teaching and learning in the professions.* San Francisco, CA: Jossey-Bass.

Schrum, L., & Benson, A. (2000). Online professional education: A case study of an MBA program through its transition to an online model. *Journal of Asynchronous Learning Networks, 4*(1), 52–61.

Schultz, J. M. (2000). Computers and collaborative writing in the foreign language curriculum. In Warschauer, M., & Kern, R. (Eds.), *Network-Based Language Teaching: Concepts and Practice* (pp. 121–150). Cambridge, UK: Cambridge University Press. doi:10.1017/CBO9781139524735.008.

SFS. (1993)... *Högskoleförordningen, 1993,* 100.

Shaban, S., & Head, C. (2003). E-learning classroom environment: Description, objectives, considerations and example implementation. *International Journal on E-Learning, 2*(3), 29–35.

Shank, G., & Cunningham, D. (1996). Mediated phosphor dots: Toward a post-cartesian model of computer-mediated communication via the semiotic superhighway. In Ess, C. (Ed.), *Philosophical perspectives on computer-mediated communication* (pp. 27–41). New York: State University of New York Press.

Shaw & Polovina. (1999). Practical experiences of, and lesson learnt from, internet technologies in higher education. *Journal of Educational Technology & Society, 2*(3), 16–24.

Sheard, J., Dick, M., Markham, S., Macdonald, I., & Walsh, M. (2002). Cheating and plagiarism: Perceptions and practices of first year IT students. *ACM SIGCSE Bulletin, 34*(3), 183–187. doi:10.1145/637610.544468.

Shepherd, J. (2006, March 17). Polls find elite top cheats list. *The Times Higher Education.* Retrieved from http://www.timeshighereducation.co.uk/story.asp?storyCode=201977

Shepherd, J. (2008, May 6). History essay in the making. *The Guardian.* Retrieved from http://www.guardian.co.uk/education/2008/may/06/highereducation.students

Sherry, L. (1996). Issues in distance learning. *International Journal of Educational Telecommunications, 1*(4), 337–365.

Sherry, L. (2000). The nature and purpose of online discourse: A brief synthesis of current research a related to the web project. *International Journal of Educational Telecommunications, 6*(1), 19–36.

Shneiderman, B. (1992). *Designing the user interface.* Reading, MA: Addison-Wesley.

Silén, C., & Uhlin, L. (2008). Self-directed learning - A learning issue for students and faculty. *Teaching in Higher Education, 13*(4), 461–475. doi:10.1080/13562510802169756.

Silva, T. (1993). Toward an understanding of the distinct nature of L2 writing: The ESL research and its implications. *TESOL Quarterly, 27*(4), 657–677. doi:10.2307/3587400.

Simovits, M. (1995). *The DES: An extensive document and evaluation.* New York: Agent Park Press.

Smith, G. P. (1991). *Toward defining a culturally responsible pedagogy for teacher education: The knowledge base for educating the teachers of minority and culturally diverse students.* Paper presented at the Annual Meeting of the American Association of Colleges for Teacher Education. Atlanta, GA.

Smith, D., & Ayers, D. (2006). Culturally responsive pedagogy and online learning: Implications for the globalized community college. *Community College Journal of Research and Practice, 30,* 401–415. doi:10.1080/10668920500442125.

Smith, L. J. (2001). Content and delivery: A comparison and contrast of electronic and traditional MBA marketing planning courses. *Journal of Marketing Education, 23*(1), 35–44. doi:10.1177/0273475301231005.

Smith, P. B., & Bond, M. H. (1993). *Social psychology across cultures.* Hemel Hempstead, UK: Harvester.

Smith, P. L., & Dillon, C. L. (1999). Comparing distance learning and classroom learning: Conceptual considerations. *American Journal of Distance Education, 13*(2), 6–23. doi:10.1080/08923649909527020.

Sowden, C. (2005). Plagiarism and the culture of multilingual students in higher education abroad. *ELT Journal, 59*(3), 226–233. doi:10.1093/elt/cci042.

Sparrow, L., Sparrow, H., & Swan, P. (2000, February). *Student centred learning: Is it possible?* Paper presented at Teaching and Learning Forum. Perth, Australia. Retrieved from http://lsn.curtin.edu.au/tlf/tlf2000/sparrow.html

Stanley, J. (1992). Coaching student writers to be effective peer evaluators. *Journal of Second Language Writing, 1*(3), 217–233. doi:10.1016/1060-3743(92)90004-9.

Stansfield, M. H., McLellan, E., & Connolly, T. M. (2004). Enhancing student performance in online learning and traditional face-to-face class delivery. *Journal of Information Technology Education, 3.*

Stanton, C. (2006). Diversity challenges in online learning. In Rahman, H. (Ed.), *Empowering marginal communities with information networking* (pp. 1–15). Hershey, PA: Idea Group Publishing. doi:10.4018/978-1-59140-699-0.ch001.

Stefani, L., & Carroll, J. (2001). *A briefing on plagiarism.* Retrieved from http://www.bioscience.heacademy.ac.uk/ftp/Resources/gc/assess10Plagiarism.pdf

Stensaker, B. (2006). Governmental policy, organisational ideals and institutional adaptation in Norweigian higher education. *Studies in Higher Education, 31*(1), 43–56. doi:10.1080/03075070500392276.

Stevenson, D. (2010, February 16). How schools beat the net cheats. *PC Pro.* Retrieved from http://www.pcpro.co.uk/features/355597/how-schools-beat-the-net-cheats

Storch, N. (2001). How collaborative is pair work? ESL tertiary students composing in pairs. *Language Teaching Research, 5*(1), 29–53.

Storch, N. (2002). Patterns of interaction in ESL pair work. *Language Learning, 52*(1), 119–158. doi:10.1111/1467-9922.00179.

Storch, N. (2005). Collaborative writing: Product, process and students' reflections. *Journal of Second Language Writing, 14,* 153–173. doi:10.1016/j.jslw.2005.05.002.

Strauss, A., & Corbin. (1990). *Basics of qualitative research.* Thousand Oaks, CA. *Sage (Atlanta, Ga.).*

Strauss, H. (2002). New learning spaces: Smart learners, not smart classrooms. *Syllabus, 16*(2), 13.

Student Plagiarism. 'On the Rise'. (2005, February 11). *BBC News.* Retrieved from http://news.bbc.co.uk/2/hi/uk_news/education/4257479.stm

Suler, J. (2004). The online disinhibition effect. *Cyberpsychology & Behavior, 7,* 321–326. doi:10.1089/1094931041291295 PMID:15257832.

Sullivan, N., & Pratt. (1996). A comparative study of two ESL writing environments: A computer-assisted classroom and a traditional oral classroom. *System, 24*(4), 491–501. doi:10.1016/S0346-251X(96)00044-9.

Susser, B. (1994). Process approaches in ESL/EFL writing instruction. *Journal of Second Language Writing, 3*(1), 31–47. doi:10.1016/1060-3743(94)90004-3.

Svensson, P. (2003). Virtual worlds as arenas for language learning. In Felix, U. (Ed.), *Language learning online: Towards best practice.* Lisse: Swets & Zeitlinger.

Swain, H. (2005, January 28). Nip double trouble in the bud. *The Times Higher Education.* Retrieved from http://www.timeshighereducation.co.uk

Swan, K. (2001). Virtual interaction: Design factors affecting student satisfaction and perceived learning in asynchronous online courses. *Distance Education, 22*(2), 306–331. doi:10.1080/0158791010220208.

Tait, J. (2002). *H850 postgraduate certificate in teaching and learning in higher education.* Milton Keynes, UK: The Open University.

Tallent-Runnels, M.K., Thomas, J. A., Lan, W. Y., & Cooper, S. (2006). Teaching courses online: A review of the research. *Review of Educational Research Spring, 76*(1), 93–135.

Taylor, A. S. (2000). The UN convention on the rights of the child: Giving children a voice. In Lewis, A., & Lindsay, G. (Eds.), *Researching children's perspectives* (pp. 21–33). Buckingham, UK: Open University Press.

Techtarget.com. (n.d.). *Techtarget.com.* Retrieved from http://searchsecurity.techtarget.com/sDefinition/0,sid14_gci211953,00.html# Weippl, E. R. (2005). *Security in e-learning.* Berlin: Springer.

Thaler, R., & Sunstein, C. (2008). *Nudge: Improving decisions about health, wealth, and happiness.* New Haven, CT: Yale University Press.

Tharp, R., & Gallimore, R. (1988). *Rousing minds to life: Teaching, learning and schooling in social context.* New York: Cambridge University Press.

The Culture of Guam. (n.d.). Retrieved March 15, 2009, from http://ns.gov.gu/culture.html

The Plagiarism Plague. (2003, February 7). *BBC News.* Retrieved from http://news.bbc.co.uk/2/hi/uk_news/2736575.stm

Thomas, M. (2008). Plagiarism detection software. In Bonk et al. (Eds.), *Proceedings of World Conference on E-Learning in Corporate, Government, Healthcare, and Higher Education* (pp. 2390-2397). Las Vegas, Navada: Springer.

Thompson, L. (1969). *Guam and its people.* Westport, CT: Greenwood Press.

Thornburg, D. (n.d.). *Quote.* Retrieved from http://thinkexist.com/quotation/any_teacher_that_can_be_replaced_by_a_computer/203766.html

Tinto, V. (1975). Dropout from higher education: A theoretical synthesis of recent research. *Review of Educational Research, 45*(1), 89–129. doi:10.3102/00346543045001089.

Tomlinson, C. A. (1999). *The differentiated classroom: Responding to the needs of all learners by association for supervision and curriculum development.* Alexandria, VA: US Government.

Topping, D. (1992). Literacy and cultural erosion in the Pacific islands. In Dubin, F., & Kuhlman, N. (Eds.), *Cross-cultural literacy: Global perspectives on reading and writing* (pp. 19–31). Englewood Cliffs, NJ: Prentice Hall.

Triandis, H. C. (1995). *Individualism and collectivism.* Boulder, CO: Westview.

Trigwell, K., & Shale, S. (2004). Student learning and the scholarship of university teaching. *Studies in Higher Education, 29*(4), 523–536. doi:10.1080/0307507042000236407.

Truluck, J. (2007). Establishing a mentoring plan for improving retention in online graduate degree programs. *Online Journal of Distance Learning Administration, 10*(1), 1-7. Retrieved November 20, 2008, from http://www.westga.edu/~distance/ojdla/spring101/truluck101.htm

Tsui, A., & Ng. (2000). Do secondary L2 writers benefit from peer comments? *Journal of Second Language Writing, 9*(2), 147–170. doi:10.1016/S1060-3743(00)00022-9.

Turoff, M., Discenza, R., & Howard, C. (2004). How distance programs will affect students, courses, faculty, and institutional futures. In Howard, C., Schenk, K., & Discenza, R. (Eds.), *Distance Learning and University Effectiveness: Changing Education Paradigms for Online Learning* (pp. 1–20). Hershey, PA: Information Science Publishing. doi:10.4018/978-1-59140-178-0.ch001.

Tuzi, F. (2004). The impact of e-feedback on the revisions of L2 writers in an academic writing course. *Computers and Composition, 21*(2), 217–235. doi:10.1016/j.compcom.2004.02.003.

Underwood, R. (1998). *English and Chamorro on Guam.* Mangilao, Guam: University of Guam, College of Education Book of Readings.

Underwood, R. (1998). *Hispanicization as a socio-historical process on Guam.* Mangilao, Guam: University of Guam, College of Education Book of Readings.

United Kingdom Central Council for Graduate Education. (2002). *Professional doctorates.* Dudley, UK: UKCGE.

University of Cincinnati Libraries. (n.d.). *Plagiarism: Prevention and detection strategies.* Retrieved from http://www.libraries.uc.edu/instruction/faculty/plagiarism.htm

University of Nottingham. (2002). Advance studies handbook, B.Ed, MA/Diploma/MRes, MPhil, PhD, EdD: Doctor of education EdD in teacher education. Nottingham, UK: University of Nottingham School of Education United Kingdom.

Usoof, H., & Lindgren, E. (2008). Who is who and doing what in distance education? Authentication and keystroke dynamics. *Journal of Research in Teacher Education, 3*(4), 173–187.

Uzawa, K. (1996). Second language learners' processes of L1 writing, L2 writing, and translation from L1 into L2. *Journal of Second Language Writing, 5,* 271–294. doi:10.1016/S1060-3743(96)90005-3.

Villamil, O. S., & Guerrero. (2006). Sociocultural theory: a framework for understanding the socio-cognitive dimensions of peer feedback. In K. Hyland & F. Hyland (Eds.), *Feedback in second language writing: Contexts and issues* (pp. 23-41). Cambridge, UK: Cambridge University Press.

Villamil, O. S., & Guerrero. (1996). Peer revision in the L2 classroom: social-cognitive activities, mediating strategies, and aspects of social behaviour. *Journal of Second Language Writing, 5*(1), 51–75. doi:10.1016/S1060-3743(96)90015-6.

Villamil, O. S., & Guerrero. (1998). Assessing the impact of peer revision on L2 writing. *Applied Linguistics, 19*(4), 491–514. doi:10.1093/applin/19.4.491.

Virtual Academic Integrity Laboratory. (2002). *Faculty and administrators guide: Detection tools and method.* Retrieved from http://www.umuc.edu/distance/odell/cip/vail/faculty/detection_tools/detectiontools.pdf

Vogt, L., Jordan, C., & Tharp, R. (1987). Explaining school failure, producing school success: Two cases. *Anthropology & Education Quarterly, 18*(4), 276–286. doi:10.1525/aeq.1987.18.4.04x0019s.

Voiskounsky, A. E. (1998). Telelogue speech. In F. Sudweeks, McLaughlin, & Rafaeli (Eds.), Network and Netplay: Virtual Groups on the Internet (pp. 27-40). Cambridge, MA: The MIT Press.

Vygotsky. (1978). *Mind in society: The development of higher psychological processes.* Cambridge, MA: Harvard University Press.

Wang, A., & Newlin, M. (2000). Characteristics of students who enroll and succeed in psychology web-based classes. *Journal of Educational Psychology, 92*(1), 137–143. doi:10.1037/0022-0663.92.1.137.

Ware, P. D., & Warschauer. (2006). Electronic feedback and second language writing. In K. Hyland & F. Hyland (Eds.), *Feedback in Second Language Writing: Contexts and Issues* (pp. 105-122). Cambridge, UK: Cambridge University Press.

Warschauer, M. (1996). Computer assisted language learning: An introduction. *Multimedia Language Teaching.* Retrieved May 29, 2009, from http://www.ict4lt.org/en/warschauer.htm

Warschauer, M. (1996). Comparing face-to-face and electronic discussion in the second language classroom. *CALICO Journal, 13*(2-3), 7–25.

Warschauer, M. (1996). Motivational aspects of using computers for writing and communication. In Warschauer, M. (Ed.), *Telecollaboration in foreign language learning* (pp. 29–48). Hawaii, HI: University of Hawaii Press.

Warschauer, M. (1997). Computer-mediated collaborative learning: Theory and practice. *Modern Language Journal, 81*(4), 470–481. doi:10.1111/j.1540-4781.1997.tb05514.x.

Warschauer, M. (1999). *Electronic literacies: Language, culture, and power in online education*. Mahwah, NJ: Lawrence Erlbaum Associates.

Warschauer, M. (2007). Technology and writing. In Cummis, J., & Davison, C. (Eds.), *International Handbook of English Language Teaching* (*Vol. 15*, pp. 907–930). New York: Springer US. doi:10.1007/978-0-387-46301-8_60.

Watters, J. J., & Ginns, I. S. (2000). Developing motivation to teach elementary science: Effect of collaborative and authentic learning practices in preservice education. *Journal of Science Teacher Education, 11*(4), 301–321. doi:10.1023/A:1009429131064.

Webster, J., & Hackley, P. (1997). Teaching effectiveness in technology-mediated distance learning. *Academy of Management Journal, 40*(6), 1282–1309. doi:10.2307/257034.

Weeks, S. (2001, May 18). Plagiarism: Think before pointing finger of blame. *The Times Higher Education.* Retrieved from http://www.timeshighereducation.co.uk

Weigle, C. S. (2002). *Assessing writing.* Cambridge, UK: Cambridge University Press. doi:10.1017/CBO9780511732997.

Weissberg, R. (2006). Scaffolded feedback: Tutorial conversations with advanced L2 writers. In Hyland, K., & Hyland, F. (Eds.), *Feedback in second language writing: Contexts and issues* (pp. 246–265). Cambridge, UK: Cambridge University Press. doi:10.1017/CBO9781139524742.015.

Wenger, E. (2009). *Communities of practice a brief introduction.* Retrieved from http://www.ewenger.com/theory/

Wenger, E. (1998). *Communities of practice: Learning, meaning and identity.* Cambridge, UK: Cambridge University Press.

Westera, W., & Sloep, P. B. (2001). The future of education in cyberspace. In *Cybereducation.* Larchmon, NY: Mary Ann Liebert Inc..

Westerberg, P., & Mårald. (2006). *Avbrott på nätutbildningar – En studie av när och varför studenter hoppar av alternativt fullföljer IT-stödda distanskurser* [Interrupted net courses: A study of when and why students drop out or finish IT-supported distance courses]. Umeå, Sweden: Umeå University, Umeå Centre for Evaluation Research.

Weston, C., & Cranton, P. A. (1986). Selecting instructional strategies. *The Journal of Higher Education, 57*(3), 259–288. doi:10.2307/1981553.

Wikipedia. org. (2009). *Non-repudiation.* Retrieved from http://en.wikipedia.org/wiki/Non-repudiation

Wilhoit, S. (1994). Helping students avoid plagiarism. *College Teaching, 42*(4), 161–165. doi:10.1080/87567555.1994.9926849.

Wilkinson, I. (2000). *Building collaborative learning communities in an online course environment for human service education.* Paper presented at the Distance Education Association of New Zealand 2000 Conference. Dunedin, Australia.

Williams, M. (2004). *Exploring the effects of a multimedia case-based learning environment in pre-service science teacher education in Jamaica.* (Unpublished doctoral dissertation). University of Twente, Twente, The Netherlands.

Williams, E. A., Duray, R., & Reddy, V. (2006). Teamwork orientation, group cohesiveness, and student learning: A study of the use of teams in online distance education. *Journal of Management Education, 30*(4), 592–616. doi:10.1177/1052562905276740.

Williams, M., & Robson, K. (2004). Reengineering focus group methodology for the online environment. In Johns, M. D., Chen, S. S., & Hall, G. J. (Eds.), *Online social research: Methods, issues, and ethics* (pp. 25–45). New York: Peter Lang Publishing, Inc..

Willson-Quayle, J. (1997). Cyberspace democracy and social behavior: Reflections and refutations. In Behar, J. E. (Ed.), *Mapping cyberspace: Social research on the electronic frontier* (pp. 229–244). New York: Dowling College Press.

Worthen, K. J. (2004). Discipline: An academic dean's perspective on dealing with plagiarism. *Brigham Young University Education and Law Journal, 2*, 441–448.

Writing Centre, Virginia Commonwealth University. (2009, October 4). *SafeAssign: Interpreting SafeAssign scores - For instructors.* Retrieved from http://www.vcu.edu/uc/writingcenter/safeassign/InterpretingForInstructors.html

Yorke, M., & Thomas, L. (2003). Improving the retention of students from lower socio-economic groups. *Journal of Higher Education Policy and Management, 25*(1). doi:10.1080/13600800305737.

Zamel, V. (1983). The composing processes of advanced ESL students: six case studies. *TESOL Quarterly, 17*(2), 165–187. doi:10.2307/3586647.

Zeleny, J. (2008, February 19). Clinton camp says Obama plagiarized in speech. *The New York Times.* Retrieved from http://www.nytimes.com

Zepke, N., & Leach, L. (2002). Appropriate pedagogy and technology in a cross-cultural distance education context. *Teaching in Higher Education, 7*(3), 309–321. doi:10.1080/13562510220144806.

Zhang, S. (1995). Reexamining the affective advantage of peer feedback in the ESL writing class. *Journal of Second Language Writing, 4*(3), 209–222. doi:10.1016/1060-3743(95)90010-1.

Zhang, S. (1999). Thoughts on some recent evidence concerning the affective advantage of peer feedback. *Journal of Second Language Writing, 8*(3), 321–326. doi:10.1016/S1060-3743(99)80119-2.

Zhu, W. (1995). Effects of training for peer response on students' comments and interaction. *Written Communication, 12*(4), 492–528. doi:10.1177/0741088395012004004.

Zhu, W. (2001). Interaction and feedback in mixed peer response groups. *Journal of Second Language Writing, 10*(4), 251–276. doi:10.1016/S1060-3743(01)00043-1.

Zoltan, E., & Chapanis, A. (1982). What do professional persons think about computers? *Behaviour & Information Technology, 1*, 55–68. doi:10.1080/01449298208914436.

About the Contributors

Kirk P. H. Sullivan is Professor of Linguistics in the Department of Language Studies Umeå University, Sweden. Kirk teaches online and on campus classes in linguistics, cognitive science, and special educational needs. His research interests concern distance education, iPad pedagogy, indigenous language literacies, writing, and forensic linguistics. Kirk has published in Swedish and international journals and books. Kirk enjoys life-long learning and makes the most of the opportunities distance education via the Internet affords the student.

Peter E. Czigler is Senior Lecturer in Hearing Sciences in the Department of Health and Medical Sciences at Örebro University, Sweden. He teaches on campus and online classes in speech and hearing sciences, communication, and health communication. He is the director of the Audiology Program, and as such, he is responsible for the structure and content of the program. He specifically focuses on the progression of student's scientific development during three years of studies. Peter's research interests concern computer supported education, e-learning, e-portfolio, and health communication.

Jenny M. Sullivan Hellgren currently works in the Department of Science and Mathematics Education at Umeå University and researches motivation for learning STEM subjects in high school. She completed her PhD in 2003 at the Department of Forest Genetics and Plant Physiology, Swedish University of Agricultural Sciences. Before taking up her current position, Jenny trained as a high school teacher and taught distance-based courses. Her research interest in distance learning is grounded in her practitioner experience.

* * *

Wasim A. Al-Hamdani plays a leading role at KSU in developing the Information Security program. He was at the University of Technology in Baghdad from 1985 to 1999. He has published six textbooks dealing with Computer Science and

Cryptography. For the past 20 years, he has concentrated his research in cryptographic algorithms and computer security. Currently, he is engaged in information security research and teaching. Dr. Al-Hamdani has contributed many chapters in research textbooks. He attended the *University of East Anglia, UK (Ph.D. in Computer Science, 1985)*, Loughborough University of Technology (M.Sc. in Computer Science, 1981), and University of Basrah (B.Sc. Math, 1976).

Klara Bolander Laksov is associate professor in Medical Education at Karolinska Institutet, Sweden, with a background and training in sociology and medical education. While working with the enhancement of educational quality as an educational developer, she has developed an interest in the Scholarship of Teaching and Learning. Klara is leading a research group on learning environments and educational development and is currently supervising three PhD students and five Masters students. She is involved in the development of educational quality at local and national level in her capacity as member of the educational board at Karolinska Institutet and former chair of the Swedish network for educational development (SwedNet). Her current research project is investigating the meaning of the clinical learning environment for the quality of student learning in medical and health undergraduate programs and the enactment of policy and change in higher education.

Lena Engqvist Boman, licentiate and lecturer at Karolinska Institutet, Sweden, has a background and training in nursing and teaching. She works as an educational developer for teacher training in higher education and educational development at Karolinska Institutet (KI). In 2009, a new master's program in medical education started, and Lena was a part of the organizing committee and acted as director of studies. She currently supervises three master's students. Previously, Lena was a member of the program committee for the nursing program, and she now works with the educational development of the program. She is a part of a research group on learning environments and educational development and is involved in the strategic development of interprofessional learning on all levels at Karolinska Institutet.

Do Coyle is Professor in Learning Innovation at the University of Aberdeen, Scotland. Formerly at Nottingham University, she has been involved with innovative teacher education programmes for many years. She introduced teacher education programmes for bilingual teachers and was in the Nottingham team, which introduced the first global on-line doctoral programme for teacher education and has successfully supervised over twenty doctoral students in this field. Do's particular interests lie in the role of technologies in enhancing student learning especially how networked 'borderless classrooms' linked by video technologies enable teacher education to be constructed across time zones and spaces. Do's work aims to empower teachers to be autonomous professionals, skilled to reflect upon and analyse their own practice with their learners. She has created the LOCIT concept where teachers and learners use digital tools to analyse their 'learning moments' and share these captured scenarios visually with others across professional learning communities.

Mats Deutschmann, PhD, is Associate Professor in Language Didactics at the Department of Language Studies, Umeå University, Sweden. He has over ten years' experience in the field of online language learning, and over the past five years, he has worked extensively in virtual worlds. His research includes didactic design for collaborative language learning in online contexts, the language pragmatics of online education, and the use of innovative technology for raising engagement and active participation. He is currently involved in a number of international telecollaborative projects, some of which involve the use of virtual worlds in language learning, for example "Access to Virtual and Action Learning live Online" (AVALON), an EU-funded project with the aim of developing new methods for language learning in virtual worlds. He has published extensively in the field and is co-editor of the book *Learning and Teaching in the Virtual World of Second Life* (2009) (Molka-Danielsen & Deutschmann, eds., Tapir Academic Press).

Kristy Beers Fägersten is an Associate Professor in English Linguistics at Södertörn University, Sweden. She received her PhD in Linguistics from the University of Florida in 2000, with a dissertation on the social functions of swearing in American English. Since receiving her degree, Beers Fägersten has worked in the United States, Germany, and Sweden, teaching a variety of courses in English linguistics for both undergraduate and graduate students, including teacher candidates. Beers Fägersten's research interests include interactional sociolinguistics as well as discourse and conversational analysis. She has published articles on computer-mediated communication, video-mediated communication, classroom discourse, code-switching, intertextuality in discourse, and comic strip discourse. Beers Fägersten recently published *Who's Swearing Now? The Social Functions of Conversational Swearing* (Cambridge Scholars Publishing, 2012) and is currently researching the use of English swear words by non-native speakers.

Roger Firth is a teacher educator and researcher at the University of Nottingham. He taught geography and environmental education in secondary schools in England before moving into higher education. He completed his PhD in environmental education in 2000 funded by a studentship from a British agrochemicals company. At Nottingham, he teaches on the PGCE and Professional Doctorate (EdD) Teacher Education courses as well as supervising doctoral research students. His current research interests are concerned with the relationship between knowledge and curriculum design and what a curriculum might look like that is designed with young peoples' epistemic and social agency in mind.

Tony Fisher is a teacher educator and researcher at the University of Nottingham School of Education and Learning Sciences Research Institute. His main research interests lie in the field of educational technology in schools, with a particular focus on the implications for the work of teachers from a 'sociology of technology' perspective. He has worked as co-investigator on a number of government-funded national evaluations of aspects of ICT in schools in England. He also teaches on a number of postgraduate courses. Before taking up his current position at The University of Nottingham, he was a school teacher and, for two years, an advisory teacher.

Dianne Forbes is a Senior Lecturer in Professional Studies in Education, working at the School of Education, University of Waikato (New Zealand). Formerly a primary/elementary school teacher, Dianne teaches online and on campus classes in Teacher Education, focusing on learning theory, reflective practice, assessment, and learning through Information and Communication Technologies. Her research interests concern effective pedagogy and elearning, with specific work in the area of asynchronous online discussion. Dianne has published in New Zealand journals, textbooks, and international journals of elearning, leadership, and classroom uses of ICT. She lives in Hamilton, New Zealand.

Brian Hudson is Professor of Education and Head of the School of Education and Social Work at the University of Sussex. Currently he is Chair of the Teacher Education Policy in Europe (TEPE) Network; Chair of the Publications Committee of the College of Teachers; Associate Editor of the Journal of Curriculum Studies and represent the Scottish Educational Research Association (SERA) on the Council of the World Education Research Association (WERA). Prior to joining Sussex in worked as Professor of Education and Associate Dean for Research in the School of Education, Social Work and Community Education at the University of Dundee. Prior to joining Dundee in October 2009, he worked full time as Professor in Educational Work for ICT and Learning at Umeå University where he continues to work in a supervisory capacity. Whilst at Umeå he was leader of the Work Packages on 'New Technologies of e-Learning' and the Action Research framework as part of the e-JUMP 2.0 project and leader of the Internal Evaluation Work Package of the e-Lene TLC project. He is the network co-ordinator of the Teacher Education Policy in Europe (TEPE) Network and main convenor for Network 27 of the European Educational Research Association (EERA) on Didactics – Learning and Teaching.

Gordon Joyes is Associate Professor in e-learning at the University of Nottingham, UK, and holds the Lord Dearing Award for Excellence in Teaching and Learning. He is an experienced online course developer and online tutor and course leader of an online Professional Doctorate in Teacher Education. Gordon is an accomplished director of international e-learning projects involving both research and innovation. Between 2004-9, he was project manager for five HEFCE funded eChina-UK projects and also Director the HEFCE funded V-ResORT project. From 2007-9, he was an e-learning expert consultant for the Joint Information Systems Committee (JISC) advising on policy and practice. He has a major research interest in the use of online tools for mediating learning and uses Activity Theory to underpin this work.

Eva Lindgren, PhD, is a member of the Department of Language Studies at Umeå University, where she is a researcher and PhD-student supervisor. Her research interests include early language learning, writing, writing development and revision. She has published internationally in the areas of foreign language development, self-assessment, peer feedback, keystroke logging, revision and fluency. Together with Kirk Sullivan she has edited the book Computer Keystroke Logging and Writing: Methods and Applications. She is the Swedish country manager of the EU funded research project Early Language Learning in Europe (Project n°. 135632-LLP-2007-UK-KA1SCR), which takes a broad perspective on young learners' foreign language learning processes, including variables such as the teacher, language exposure and digital media.

Xiaojing Liu is a senior research analyst at Kelley Direct Program in the Kelley School of Business at Indiana University, Bloomington. Her research interest focuses on online learning, computer-supported collaborative learning, case-based learning, communities of practices, and knowledge management. She received her Ph.D. in instructional systems technology from Indiana University. Her work has appeared in academic journals such as *British Journal of Education Technology, Quarterly Review of Distance Education, Education Technology and Society*, and *International Journal of E-Learning*.

Richard J. Magjuka is a professor of business administration in the Kelley School of Business. He has been the faculty chair of Kelley Direct since its inception. His primary research interests are the design and delivery of effective online education and in online pedagogy. He received his undergraduate degree from the University of Notre Dame and his Ph.D. from the University of Chicago.

Mark A. Minott is an Assistant Professor at the University College of the Cayman Islands in the Department of Teacher Education. He has published an eclectic array of articles on Reflective Teaching Teacher Education, Church-school relationship, ICT, and the Arts in Christian Worship. Examples of his work are found in journals such as *Professional Development Journal* (UK), *Australian Journal of Teacher Education, McGill Journal of Education* (Canada), *Journal of the University College of the Cayman Islands, International Journal of Music Education* (UK), and *Journal of Interactive Learning and Research* (USA). He has over twenty-four years of teaching experience at the Primary, Secondary, and Higher Educational levels. He has made academic and non-academic presentations in the United Kingdom, Guyana, Antigua and Barbuda, Jamaica, and the Cayman Islands.

Charlotte Silén is an associate professor in medical education at Karolinska Institute, Stockholm, and is currently programme director of the international distance master's degree programme in medical education. She holds a PhD in Education from Linköping University, and has worked for about 35 years within higher education with faculty and educational development, and teaching, designing courses and educational programmes within the healthcare field. For the past five years, Charlotte has been the director of the Centre for Medical Education and has lead the development of the centre to create a solid basis for faculty and educational development, introduced scholarship of teaching and learning, set up a two year international Master's programme in medical education, and overseen an expansion of research in medical education. Charlotte has been project leader for several educational development projects related to Problem-Based Learning (PBL), clinical education, qualitative assessment, e-learning, and visualization. She has also worked with tutor training and consultancy concerning PBL in a wide range of fields within higher education. Charlotte was one of the pioneers who planned and implemented PBL and the first interprofessional student ward at Linköping Hospital, Sweden. Linköping University was the first university in the Nordic countries to implement PBL. She is currently supervising seven PhD students and six Master students, and her research interests include the understanding of learning processes related to students, professionals, and patients in different contexts. Several of these studies are carried out in the clinic, but on the agenda now are also projects involving the role of visualisation, virtual reality, and multimodal media in learning and meaning making.

Catherine E. Stoicovy, PhD, is an associate professor of Language and Literacy at the University of Guam. In addition to university teaching, she has 15 years of classroom teaching experience in the Guam Department of Education. Her research interests include culturally responsive literacy instruction for Pacific islanders, culturally responsive online learning, and English language learners.

Hakim Usoof took his PhD in ICT and Education at Umeå University in Sweden. He received his Bachelors degree in Computer Science from the University of Peradeniya in Sri Lanka and currently holds a lecturer post at the University of Colombo School of Computing. His interest in ICT and Education occurred during his participation in a Teaching/Learning staff development course and in the National eLearning Centre project of Sri Lanka. He has also received accreditation from the Staff and Educational Development Association of UK. He was awarded a scholarship from the NeLC in Sri Lanka and SIDA/SPIDER of Sweden to pursue his PhD studies. The focus of his PhD research is unsupervised summative e-assessment for higher order skills of students in large groups. His research interests also include study of keystroke dynamics for remote authentication, technological and pedagogical solutions for plagiarism, and assessment for learning.

Despina Varnava-Marouchou is a senior lecturer at the European University Cyprus. She has presented many papers at various conferences on issues regarding education and has written several papers regarding teaching in higher education, the most recent is titled "Faculty Conceptions of Teaching: Implications for Teacher Professional Development." In addition, she has written several chapters in books. For example, "Improving Students Outcomes" published last August in the *Anthology*. This is available on Amazon. She has also participated in the running of various workshops on qualitative research methods in education. Dr. Varnava-Marouchou is a member of various committees and the chair of the SSNC Committee (Students with Special Needs Committee) at the European University Cyprus. One of the many responsibilities of the committee is to organise at least one event annually such as training, workshops, or conference for the faculty of the university.

Huahui Zhao obtained her doctoral degree in Applied Linguistics at the University of Bristol, United Kingdom. She is currently working as a postdoctoral researcher in online peer collaboration in the Department of Language Studies, Umeå University, Sweden. Her main research interests lie in computer-enhanced learning and teaching, classroom-based language assessment, collaborative learning, and education research methodology.

Index

CPSIA information can be obtained at www.ICGtesting.com
Printed in the USA
BVOW06*1342130813

328318BV00007B/261/P